SCHOOL FINANCE

A Policy Perspective

SCHOOL FINANCE
A Policy Perspective

ALLAN R. ODDEN

LAWRENCE O. PICUS
University of Southern California

McGraw-Hill, Inc.
New York St. Louis San Francisco Auckland Bogotá
Caracas Lisbon London Madrid Mexico City Milan
Montreal New Delhi San Juan Singapore
Sydney Tokyo Toronto

This book was developed by Lane Akers, Inc.

SCHOOL FINANCE
A Policy Perspective

4 5 6 7 8 9 0   DOC/DOC   9 9 8 7 6 5

ISBN 0-07-047486-9

This book was set in Caledonia by Publication Services.
The editor was Lane Akers;
the production supervisor was Leroy A. Young.
The cover was designed by Elizabeth Harriss.
Project supervision was done by Publication Services.
R. R. Donnelley & Sons Company was printer and binder.

Library of Congress Cataloging-in-Publication Data

Odden, Allan.
    School finance: a policy perspective / Allan R. Odden, Lawrence
 O. Picus.
       p.   cm.
    Includes bibliographical references and index.
    ISBN 0-07-047486-9
    1. Education—United States—Finance.   2. Education—United
States—Finance—Computer simulation.   I. Picus, Larry, (date).
II. Title.
LB2825.0315   1992   91-4166
379.1′21′0973—dc20

ABOUT THE AUTHORS

Allan R. Odden is Professor of Education Policy and Administration at the University of Southern California and Director of Policy Analysis for California Education (PACE), an educational policy studies consortia of USC, Stanford University, and the University of California, Berkeley. He is also the Director of the USC Center for Research in Education Finance. He worked with the Education Commission of the States for a decade, serving as director of policy analysis and research and as director of its educational finance center. A past president of the American Educational Finance Association, he currently is directing a Carnegie Corporation–funded project on the financial aspects of current education reform issues.

Professor Odden has written widely, publishing over 130 journal articles and book chapters. He received Ph.D. and M.A. degrees from Columbia University, a master of divinity from the Union Theological Seminary, and a B.S. from Brown University. Prior to that he was a mathematics teacher and curriculum developer in New York City's East Harlem for five years.

Lawrence O. Picus is an Assistant Professor in the School of Education at the University of Southern California. He also serves as Associate Director of the Center for Research in Education Finance (CREF), a School of Education research center whose purpose is to study issues of school finance and productivity in the wake of the recent school reform movement. From 1977 to 1983, Picus was a principal investigator for the Northwest Regional Educational Laboratory's Center for State Policy Studies.

Professor Picus earned a Ph.D. in public policy analysis from the RAND Graduate School in August 1988. In addition, he holds a master's degree in social science from the University of Chicago and a bachelor's degree in economics from Reed College. He has a strong background in research design, statistics, and econometrics and is an expert in the application of microcomputers to research. He has designed and implemented a number of analysis and database systems on both Macintosh and IBM or compatible computers.

To my wife Eleanor who said,
"Write a school finance book."

To Susan,
who is always there for me.

Contents

Preface   xv

1 INTRODUCTION AND OVERVIEW TO SCHOOL FINANCE   *1*

The Scope of Education Finance in the United States   3
Early Developments in School Finance   8
Examples of School Finance Fiscal Disparities   10

2 LEGAL ISSUES IN SCHOOL FINANCE   20

The Early School Finance Cases   *21*
Equal Protection Litigation   *21*
 The Minimal Scrutiny Test   22
 The Strict Judicial Scrutiny Test   23
School Finance Equal Protection Litigation   *24*
 Serrano v. Priest   26
 Rodriguez v. San Antonio   27
 Robinson v. Cahill   28
School Finance State Education Clause Litigation   *29*
 Historical Meaning of the Education Clause   29
 Education Clauses Requiring More Than Just
  an Education System   30
 Qualitative Demands of the Education Clause   31
 The Education Clause and Absolute Deprivation   31
Special Issues in School Finance Litigation   *32*
 Equal Educational Expenditures   32
 Equal Programs and Services   32
 Municipal Overburden   33
 Achievement of Low-Income and Minority Students
  in Big Cities   34
 School Finance Reform and Education Reform   35

Trends in School Finance Litigation   *36*
   A School Finance Scorecard   *36*
   Recent Litigation Trends   *37*
   New Issues in School Finance Litigation   *46*
Conclusion   *48*

3 A FRAMEWORK FOR ANALYZING SCHOOL FINANCE EQUITY   *49*

The School Finance Equity Framework in Brief   *51*
Children's Equity in School Finance   *53*
Children's Equity Objects   *53*
   Fiscal and Physical Inputs   *54*
   Educational Process Variables   *56*
   Achievement or Outcome Variables   *58*
Children's Equity Principles   *60*
   Horizontal Equity   *60*
   Vertical Equity   *61*
   Fiscal Neutrality   *63*
   Effectiveness   *63*
Measures of School Finance Equity   *64*
   Unit of Analysis   *65*
   Horizontal Equity   *65*
   Fiscal Neutrality   *69*
   Effectiveness   *70*
Studies of School Finance Equity   *71*

4 FISCAL FEDERALISM AND INTERGOVERNMENTAL GRANTS   *76*

Advantages of a Federal Approach to Financing
   Governmental Services   *77*
   Fiscal Capacity Equalization   *77*
   Equity in Service Distribution   *78*
   Efficiency in Service Production   *78*
   Decentralized Decision Making   *79*
Mandates and Their Use in Intergovernmental
   Relations   *79*
   Arguments against Mandates   *80*
   Arguments for Mandates   *80*

Intergovernmental Grants and Their Objectives   *81*
  Unrestricted General Aid   84
  Matching General Grants   86
  Categorical Grants   87
  Final Comments on Grants   89
Alternative Measures of Fiscal Capacity   *90*

**5 SALES, INCOME, AND OTHER TAX REVENUE
    SOURCES**   *93*

Overview of Trends in Federal, State,
    and Local Taxes   *94*
Overview of Changes in Tax Structures   *95*
Public Finance Criteria for Evaluating Taxes   *98*
  Tax Base   98
  Yield   101
  Tax Equity   102
  Economic Effects   107
  Administration and Compliance   107
The Income Tax   *108*
  Basis   108
  Yield   110
  Equity   112
  Economic Effects   113
  Administration and Compliance   116
  Income Tax Trends and Issues at the State Level   117
  Conclusions about the Income Tax   118
The Sales Tax   *118*
  Basis   119
  Yield   119
  Equity   120
  Sales Tax Exemptions   124
  Economic Effects   125
  Administration and Compliance   126
  Expanding the Sales Tax to Services   126
  Conclusions About the Sales Tax   130
Lotteries   *131*
  Basis   132
  Yield   132
  Equity   133

Administration   *133*
Conclusion   *134*
Summary   *134*

**6   THE PROPERTY TAX   *136*

Basis   *136*
Determining Market or True Value   *138*
Determining Assessed Valuation   *140*
Yield   *142*
Property Tax Rates   *143*
Property Tax Elasticity   *143*
Property Tax Stability   *145*
Equity   *145*
Estimating Property Tax Incidence   *146*
Economic and Social Effects   *150*
Administration and Compliance   *151*
Low-Income Property Tax Relief Programs   *151*
Classification of the Property Tax Base   *154*
Circuit Breaker Programs   *154*
Homestead Exemptions and Credits   *155*
Tax Deferrals   *155*
Final Comments   *155*
The California Approach to Property Taxation:
What Not to Do   *156*
Basis and Horizontal Equity   *157*
Yield   *158*
Summary   *158*
Conclusions about the Property Tax   *158*

**7   SCHOOL FINANCE FORMULAS   *160*

School Finance Equity and Policy Goals   *161*
The Simulation: Sample Districts   *162*
School Finance General Aid Programs   *166*
Flat Grant Programs   *167*
Foundation Programs   *173*
Guaranteed Tax Base Programs   *182*
Combination Foundation and Guaranteed Tax Base
Programs   *192*

*Full State Funding and State-Determined Spending
    Programs   202*
Suggested Problems and Other Strategies for Using
    the Simulation   *203*
Problem 7.1   *203*
Problem 7.2   *204*
Problem 7.3   *205*
Problem 7.4   *205*
Problem 7.5   *206*
Problem 7.6   *206*
    Endnote   206

8 ADJUSTMENTS FOR STUDENT NEEDS, EDUCATION LEVEL, SCALE ECONOMIES, AND PRICE   *208*

Adjustments for Different Pupil Needs   *209*
    Development of Special-Needs Student Programs   210
    *Issues in Determining Costs of Special-Needs
        Programs   219*
    *General Approaches to Special-Needs
        Formula Adjustments   221*
    *Costs and Formulas for Financing Compensatory
        Education Programs   224*
    *Costs and Formulas for Financing Bilingual
        Education Programs   226*
    *Costs and Formulas for Financing Special Education
        Programs   229*
    Simulation of Adjustments for Special-Needs Students   231
Adjustments for Different Grade Levels   *234*
Adjustments for Size   *234*
Adjustments for Price Differences   *239*
Conclusions   *241*

9 THE POLITICS AND IMPACTS OF SCHOOL FINANCE CHANGES, 1970–1990   *242*

How Issues Become Part of the Formal Policy
    Agenda   *242*
School Finance Reform During the 1970s   *243*
    The Politics of School Finance Reform   243

The Impacts of the 1970s School Finance Reforms 247

School Finance Changes During the Education Reform
   Era of the 1980s 249
   *The Politics of the 1980s Education and School Finance
   Reforms* 250
   *The Impacts of the 1980s Education and School Finance
   Reforms* 252
Prognosis for the 1990s 255

**10 ALLOCATION AND USE OF FUNDS
AT THE DISTRICT, SCHOOL, AND
CLASSROOM LEVELS** 256

Expenditures by Function And Staffing Patterns 258
   Expenditures by Function 259
   Staffing Patterns 262
Expenditure Patterns Across Districts with Different
   Spending Levels 265
   *Expenditure Patterns across Districts within
   a State* 265
   How Districts Use New Money 268
Expenditures by Program, School, Classroom, Student,
   and Curriculum Content Area 271
   Expenditures by School and Classroom 273
   Expenditures by Student 275
   Expenditures by Curriculum Content Area 277
Knowledge on the Relationship Between Fiscal and
   Physical Resources and Student Achievement 277
Approaching Educational Productivity
   in the 1990s 281

11 FISCAL INCENTIVES FOR SCHOOLS 285

School Finance Formula Incentives 286
   School-Based Fiscal Incentives 290
   South Carolina's School Incentive Reward Program 293
   California's Cash for CAP 294
   Implications for School Finance 295
Budget Incentives 295
Summary 296

12 **SITE-BASED MANAGEMENT AND SCHOOL-BASED DECISION MAKING**   *298*

Site-Based Management—A Definition   *299*
School District Budgeting Procedures   *300*
Authority Changes for Site-Based Management   *302*
  Authority over Utilities and Substitute Teachers   *302*
  Authority over Staff Development, Curriculum Development,
    and Other Central Office Support   *303*
  Authority over the Mix of Professionals   *303*
  Authority over the Source of Supply   *303*
  Authority to Carry Over Resources
    to the Next Fiscal Year   *304*
  Relief from Regulation   *304*
  Establishment of Site Authority   *304*
The Role of School Site Councils   *305*
  Council Membership   *305*
  School Site Council Authority   *306*
  Location of Formal Decision-Making Authority   *307*
Site-Based Management as a Tool for Improving School
    Accountability, Productivity, and Flexibility   *308*
  Accountability   *308*
  Productivity   *308*
  Flexibility   *309*
Implications for State School Finance Systems   *309*
Summary   *310*

Appendix: Using the School Finance Simulation   *312*

Glossary   *330*

References   *337*

Index   *355*

Preface

School finance is one of the most discussed and least understood aspects of public education policy in the United States. Educational administrators, teachers, political leaders, and the public wonder what happens to all the dollars provided for public schools. Although most educators think the country underinvests in public education, the public and policymakers feel that school systems consume vast quantities of money, with no end to their appetite. There is an awareness that the courts play a role in setting education fiscal policy but little understanding of the constitutional issues involved or the substance of the court requirements. While educators and school finance analysts discuss the problems of financing schools with local property taxes, the public thinks that most school funds derive from the federal government (which in fact provides only 6 percent of total school revenues). All educational administrators have taken a school finance course, but few really understand how school finance formulas and structures work, their primary role in state-local intergovernmental fiscal policy, or the politics of education fiscal decision making.

Our intent in writing *School Finance: A Policy Perspective* is to take some of the mystery out of school finance and substantially raise understanding of this important component of education policy. The most distinguishing feature of this book is the school finance simulation that accompanies it. The simulation transforms school finance from a course in the algebra of formulas, which makes it incomprehensible for too many, to a course in the design of education fiscal policy in which nearly anyone can engage.

For the first time ever, this user-friendly computer simulation allows all students of school finance to design alternative school finance systems and analyze their fiscal, political, and equity impacts. The 100-district sample portion of this simulation allows readers to select a random sample of school districts in their state and analyze the equity of that structure. They will be able to simulate alternative finance structures and analyze both costs and overall fiscal impacts. The computer simulation brings the design of school finance policy, long a monopoly of only a few of the country's school finance experts, into the classrooms, offices, studies, and living rooms of everyone who develops an interest in the topic. Our intent in developing this simulation is to open up the world of school finance to a much wider audience; to deepen understanding of how the funding mechanisms for schools work; and, we hope, over the long run to improve school funding and education productivity.

The book has a strong policy focus throughout. The emphasis is on setting education and fiscal goals, and on designing school finance structures that implement those goals in comprehensive, fair, affordable, and politically feasible ways. Although the technicalities of school finance formulas are discussed, the emphasis is on their conceptual properties, their connection to different education and fiscal policy goals, associated costs, and system impacts. Even in Chapters 7 and 8, where we discuss each school finance formula in depth, political feasibility is a major theme. In fact, Chapter 7 describes a two-tiered school finance structure, increasingly being adopted by states, explicitly designed to achieve both political acceptability and school finance equity. In a real sense, the book is policy oriented.

An additional feature of the book is its use of an explicit framework to analyze school finance equity. Drawing upon the pioneering work of Berne and Stiefel (1984), Chapter 2 develops a framework that is used throughout the book to discuss the various problems and policy issues in school finance. The framework was also used to design a portion of the school finance simulation, which provides several equity statistics for each school finance system simulated. This framework suggests that school finance in the 1990s must push beyond the fiscal and dollar input issues that have dominated (and limited) school finance during this century, in order to investigate the resource equity into which those dollars are translated. Specifically, the framework suggests that the actual curriculum and instruction resources provided to students (which are the critical variables related to student learning) should be the resource equity issues of the future. Finally, Chapter 2 suggests that school finance indicators need to be imbedded in the broader educational indicators movement in education policy.

The later chapters of the book address the issues of where education dollars go and of which strategies to improve school productivity are best. The research and knowledge base for addressing these issues is thin. Unfortunately, there are few studies of where education dollars go. That is, in part, why the issue remains a mystery—to the public as well as the education and policy communities. Existing research shows that large sums of money do not end up in the alleged "administrative blob"; changes in the proportion of school district budgets spent on administration during the past 45 years have been small. Moreover, although schools tend to spend new funds on two major items—reducing class size and raising average teacher salaries—research suggests that these are not very productive uses for new money. These spending choices may help explain the gap between the public perception that schools consume large amounts of money with little improvement in performance and educators' perceptions that not enough money is given to schools.

In fact, the nation has provided large increases in education revenues every decade since the mid-twentieth century. Total school revenues per pupil adjusted for inflation rose 30 percent in the 1980s, 35 percent in the 1970s, and 67 percent in the 1960s! The kinds of education programs and services offered have changed dramatically during that time, and the high school graduation rate has increased by over 50 percent, but the public still wants its schools to perform better. Indeed, the education fiscal imperative for the 1990s may not be how to find additional dollars for schools; historical trends indicate that inflation-adjusted resources could "naturally" increase by one-third. The education finance imperative of the 1990s will likely be how to use those dollars productively to boost all students' performance and accomplish our national education goals.

Strategies to improve educational productivity include site-based performance incentives (discussed in Chapter 10) and site-based management and budgeting (Chapter 12). These two approaches to school organization and management are being implemented at an accelerating rate. Other sections in the last five chapters discuss the efficacy of programmatic strategies such as preschool, extended-day kindergarten, one-to-one tutoring, and class size reductions.

The book includes three chapters addressing the traditional public finance and tax components of school finance. Chapter 4 shows how school finance formulas are specific cases of intergovernmental grants and discusses design aspects of these intergovernmental grant mechanisms and their related school finance formulas. Chapter 5 assesses the structure and equity of income and sales taxes, the primary taxes states use to raise school revenues. Since most local school revenues are raised through the property tax, a separate chapter is devoted to this complex and misunderstood tax. Chapter 6 covers the property tax structure, assessment practices and their linkage to school finance structures, alternative views of the burden the property tax places on households with varying levels of income, and the wide variety of property tax relief and reduction programs.

In short, this book has a clear policy focus that places school finance within its broad public finance context. The accompanying computer simulation pushes school finance beyond the technicalities of school finance formulas and allows students to understand more fully the design of school finance systems. The end of the book focuses on the future and emphasizes educational productivity. The long-term fiscal issue is how school finance structures and educational programs can be aligned with ambitious education goals to improve the use of education dollars. We hope this will help the country accomplish its goals of having all students learn to think, solve problems and communicate, graduate from high school, and be first in the world in mathematics and science.

ACKNOWLEDGMENTS

A work of this magnitude would not be possible without the assistance of many people. We would like to thank our colleagues William Sparkman, Texas Tech University; David Thompson, Kansas State University; and Craig Wood, University of Florida; for their thoughtful reviews and insightful comments on earlier drafts of our manuscript. In addition there are a number of people at USC whose dedication, hard work and thoughtful insights have improved the material presented in the text. Nancy Kotowski, Lori Kim, and Jennifer Sevilla spent many hours reviewing drafts of each chapter and pilot-testing our computer simulation. We could not have met our publication deadlines without the strong support that Cindy Stueler and Jean Square provided on a daily basis. Finally, we would like to thank our students in School Finance courses who read early drafts of this book and helped find all the bugs in the simulation.

ALLAN R. ODDEN
LAWRENCE O. PICUS

SCHOOL FINANCE
A Policy Perspective

—Chapter 1———

Introduction and Overview to School Finance

School finance concerns the distribution and use of money for the purpose of providing educational services and producing student achievement. For most of the twentieth century, school finance policy has focused on equity—issues related to widely varying education expenditures per pupil across districts within a state, and the uneven distribution of the property tax base used to raise local education dollars. In the 1990s, new attention will be given to education productivity—the linkages among level of funds, use of funds, and amount of student achievement. As the 1990s evolve, the country's policymakers will increasingly want to know how much money will be needed to accomplish the nation's education goals (White House, 1990); how those dollars should be distributed effectively and fairly among districts, schools, programs, and students; and how both level and use of dollars affect student performance. These policy demands will push school finance beyond its traditional emphasis on fiscal equity.

This book begins to move school finance in these new directions. It emphasizes the traditional equity issues and also raises anew several effectiveness issues, including what is known about the linkages among dollars, educational strategies, and student performance. The decade of the 1980s was remarkable not only for the intensity of the school reform movement, but also for the duration of interest in educational reform. Fuhrman and Elmore (1990) argue that the last decade saw a dramatic increase in the level of state activity in education. Most of this activity focused on regulations to increase standards for students; revisions of teacher licensure requirements, teacher training, and teacher compensation; and information on school performance. In most instances, the implications of these reforms on school finance were not fully considered. During the 1990s, the states and their respective school districts will need to adapt their school finance systems to meet the new accountability requirements and productivity expectations inspired by these reforms.

This book takes a policy approach to school finance analysis. It is important for graduate students in education, as well as educators and education policymakers, to understand both school finance theory and the actual types of school finance policy a state can design. Finance policy includes the actual education finance laws that a state might enact. The text attempts to integrate theory about school finance structures with the politics of getting a school finance bill through the legislature and the constraints of state and local budgets. The resultant policy often is a compromise package (see Brown and Elmore, 1982).

The book begins with a discussion of traditional school finance issues, including the legal issues surrounding school finance, and an analysis of general taxation systems, intergovernmental grants, and traditional school finance formulas. The analysis of school finance formulas is supplemented with a computer simulation designed to allow students to model the effects of different school finance distribution decisions on a sample of 10 school districts. By designing their own school finance formulas and simulating the effects on a sample of school districts, students will attain a more realistic sense of how changes in funding formulas affect school districts across a state. The simulation will help students understand the technical and political complexities that result when one attempts to redesign school funding programs.

The simulation also provides students with the capacity to select a random 100-district sample from any state's school finance structure. Using this sample, students can analyze the distributional equity and simulate the costs and impacts of alternative school finance structures.

The book then moves beyond this traditional approach to school finance and, in a series of chapters, discusses important issues for the 1990s and how they relate to school finance. Included are chapters dealing with allocation and use of funds at the district school and program level, site-based management, educational choice programs, and fiscal incentives. Current research and state activity in each of these areas are summarized, and the implications for school finance programs are discussed.

This introductory chapter has three sections. The first section outlines the scope of school finance within the United States. Funding public schools is big business, and this section outlines the fiscal magnitude of that business. The second section provides a quick history of school finance developments, beginning in the seventeenth century. This section shows how schools evolved from privately funded, parent- and church-run entities to the large publicly and governmentally controlled systems of today. The last section gives several examples of the fiscal inequities on which school finance has focused during the twentieth century and that led to school finance litigation in the late 1960s, the primary subject of Chapter 2.

THE SCOPE OF EDUCATION FINANCE IN THE UNITED STATES

Education is an enormous enterprise in the United States. It constitutes the largest portion of most state and local governmental budgets; engages more than 100,000 local board members in important policymaking activities; employs millions of individuals as teachers, administrators, and support staff; and educates tens of millions of children.

Figure 1.1 provides detail on public school enrollment and the numbers of school districts and schools during most of the twentieth century. Enrollment was relatively constant during the 1930s and 1940s but rose quickly after World War II as the postwar baby boomers became school-aged. After 25 years of rapid enrollment growth, public school enrollment declined during the 1970s and then began to grow again in the mid-1980s as the offspring of the baby boom generation began to enter schools. In 1989–90, public school enrollment was estimated at just over 40 million students, having peaked at slightly above that level during the 1970s.

One of the major stories of this century has been the consolidation of school districts into larger entities. In 1990, there were 15,449 school districts, the lowest number during this century. In 1940, by contrast, there were 117,108 school districts. The number of school districts dropped by almost 40,000 between 1940 and 1950 (i.e., after World War II) and then dropped by another 40,000 between 1950 and 1960. During the 1970 school year, there were only 17,995 local school districts. The number of districts varies across the states, however, with Texas and California each having more than 1,000 districts in 1990 and Hawaii being a single, statewide school district.

Interestingly, although school district consolidation also entails consolidation of the local property tax base, remaining inequities in local school financing after the bulk of district consolidation had occurred still led courts, during the late 1960s and early 1970s, to declare finance structures unconstitutional (see Chapter 2).

Figure 1.1 also shows that the number of public schools has dropped over time while enrollments have risen, indicating that schools too have grown in size during the twentieth century. There were over 238,000 public schools in *elementary* 1930, but that number had dropped to around 60,000 schools by 1990. On the other hand, the number of private schools has almost doubled since 1930, from *high schools* a low of 12,533 then to around 22,470 in 1980–81. *have stayed constant*

FIGURE 1.1 Historical Data on the Size of the Nation's School Systems: 1919–20 to 1989–90

Year	Public Student Enrollment (in 1,000s)	Public School Districts	Public Elementary Schools	Public Secondary Schools	Private Elementary Schools	Private Secondary Schools	Private Schools as Percent of Total
1919–20	21,578	—	—	—	—	—	—
1929–30	25,678	—	238,306	23,930	9,275	3,258	5
1939–40	25,434	117,108	—	—	11,306	3,568	—
1949–50	25,112	83,718	128,225	24,542	10,375	3,331	8
1959–60	36,087	40,520	91,853	25,784	13,574	4,061	13
1969–70	45,619	17,995[a]	65,800[a]	25,352[a]	14,372[a]	3,770[a]	17[a]
1979–80	41,645	15,912[b]	61,069[b]	24,362[b]	16,792[b]	5,678[b]	21[b]
1989–90	40,608	15,449	61,490[c]	22,937[c]	—	—	—

[a] Data for 1970–71.
[b] Data for 1980–81.
[c] Data for 1987–88.

Source: National Center for Educational Statistics, *Digest of Education Statistics, 1989;* National Education Association, *Estimates of School Statistics, 1989–90.*

Funding public schools requires large amounts of dollars. In 1990, public school revenues totaled more than $195 billion, an increase of $98 billion from the 1980 total (Figure 1.2). Indeed, the data show that public school revenues more than doubled during each decade from 1940 to 1990—a remarkable fiscal record.

Figure 1.2 also shows that during this century public education consumed an increasing portion of the country's total economic activity—gross national product—until 1970, then dropped a bit during the enrollment decline of the 1970s, and remained constant during the 1980s. The same pattern is true for total public school revenues as a percent of the country's personal income. In short, the country devotes approximately 4.4 percent of its personal annual income to public schools, a considerable portion considering all the other items that individuals could purchase with their annual income, either themselves or through government tax revenues.

This observation is undergirded by the data in Figure 1.3. Column 2 shows that *real*[1] revenues per pupil have increased each decade at extraordinarily large rates: 100 percent between 1920 and 1930, 67 percent during the 1960s, and 36 percent during the 1970s. Even during the last decade of government tax and expenditure limitations, expenditures per pupil increased by 30 percent, to a total of $4,448 for current operating purposes in 1989–90. It seems that real resources for public school students rise substantially each decade.

These facts certainly are at odds with popular perceptions that schools do not get much more money each year. Although real resources per pupil

---

[1] Real revenues are nominal revenues adjusted for inflation. Real revenues indicate the actual purchasing power over a time period.

FIGURE 1.2   Educational Revenues, GNP, and Personal Income (billions), 1930–1990

Year	Total Educational Revenues	Gross National Product (GNP)	Revenues as Percent of GNP	Personal Income (PI)	Revenues as Percent of PI
1930	$ 2.1	$ 104	2.0	$ 84	2.5
1940	2.3	100	2.3	78	3.0
1950	5.4	288	1.9	228	2.4
1960	14.7	515	2.8	409	3.6
1970	40.3	1,015	4.0	832	4.8
1980	96.9	2,732	3.6	2,259	4.3
1990	195.2	5,471[a]	3.6	4,672	4.2

[a] Estimated

Source: National Center for Educational Statistics, *Digest of Educational Statistics, 1989;* National Center for Educational Statistics, *Key Statistics for Public Elementary and Secondary Education: School Year 1989–90.*

FIGURE 1.3 Educational Expenditures per Pupil and Revenues by Source, 1920–1990

Year	Expenditures per Pupil		Total Revenues (in millions)	Percent Revenues by Source		
	Real	Nominal		Federal	State	Local
1919–20	$ 268	$ 40	$ 970	0.3	16.5	83.2
1929–30	535	72	2,089	0.4	16.9	82.7
1939–40	697	76	2,261	1.8	30.3	68.0
1949–50	1,006	187	5,437	2.9	39.8	57.3
1959–60	1,523	350	14,747	4.4	39.1	56.5
1969–70	2,534	750	40,267	8.0	39.9	52.1
1979–80	3,434	2,089	96,881	9.8	46.8	43.4
1989–90	4,448	4,448	195,166	6.3	49.4	44.3

Source: National Center for Educational Statistics, *Digest of Education Statistics, 1989;* National Center for Educational Statistics, *Key Statistics for Public Elementary and Secondary Education: School Year 1989–90.*

may increase only 1–3 percent each year, over a 10-year period that amounts to nearly a one-third increase in real resources—a substantial increase.

The last columns in Figure 1.3 show that the sources of school revenues have changed over the years. Earlier in the century, local districts provided the bulk of school revenues; the federal role was almost nonexistent. In the 1960s, the federal government began to increase its financial role, which reached its maximum, at 9.8 percent, in 1980. Since then the federal contribution has dropped by almost one-third. Today the states are the primary providers of public school revenues, outdistancing local school districts during the 1970s era of school finance reforms. During the 1989–90 school year, the states provided 49.4 percent of public school revenues, local districts (primarily through the local property tax) 44.3 percent, and the federal government 6.3 percent.

These are national patterns, however, and amounts are very different across the 50 states, as shown by Figure 1.4. Although the national average expenditure per pupil was $4,448 in 1989–90, it ranged from a low of $2,423 in Arkansas to a high of $7,411 in Alaska, a difference of more than 3 to 1.

States also differ in their sources of public school revenues. In Hawaii, for example, 92 percent of revenues are from the state, and in New Hampshire only 7.8 percent of school revenues come from state sources. States provide over 60 percent of school revenues in 11 states, and local districts provide over 60 percent of school revenues in 6 states. This variation reflects differences in local perceptions of appropriate state and local roles, as well as differences in school finance formula structures (Verstegen, 1988). These data document one enduring characteristic of state school finance structures: Although there are some general similarities, the differences are dramatic. Students of school finance need to understand both the generic similarities and the factors causing the specific differences.

FIGURE 1.4 Educational Expenditures per Pupil and Revenues by Source, by State: 1989–90

State	Expenditures per Pupil	Percent of Revenues by Source		
		Federal	State	Local
Alabama	$3,021	13.5	67.1	19.4
Alaska	7,411	9.9	60.5	29.6
Arizona	3,660	4.7	45.1	50.2
Arkansas	2,423	9.7	59.5	30.8
California	4,392	8.0	66.8	25.1
Colorado	5,211	4.8	38.1	57.0
Connecticut	6,705	3.7	44.7	51.6
Delaware	4,895	7.9	66.8	25.3
District of Columbia	6,221	10.1	0	89.9
Florida	4,380	6.0	53.6	40.5
Georgia	3,110	6.5	60.9	32.6
Hawaii	4,160	7.9	92.0	0.1
Idaho	2,611	7.2	59.9	32.9
Illinois	4,330	7.7	37.9	54.4
Indiana	3,994	4.5	59.2	36.2
Iowa	4,448	5.3	51.0	43.7
Kansas	4,089	5.2	43.3	51.5
Kentucky	2,984	9.2	69.7	21.1
Louisiana	3,121	11.3	54.4	34.3
Maine	4,774	6.7	53.2	40.1
Maryland	5,335	4.9	38.7	56.3
Massachusetts	5,493	4.4	42.4	53.2
Michigan	5,099	4.7	36.3	59.0
Minnesota	4,790	4.4	53.2	42.4
Mississippi	2,676	15.5	56.7	27.8
Missouri	3,804	5.6	38.0	56.4
Montana	3,880	8.0	47.7	44.3
Nebraska	4,206	4.8	24.3	70.8
Nevada	3,648	4.1	36.7	59.3
New Hampshire	5,355	2.7	7.8	89.6
New Jersey	7,312	3.8	41.5	54.7
New Mexico	3,339	12.0	76.4	11.6
New York	7,153	5.0	43.4	51.7
North Carolina	3,582	6.3	65.7	27.9
North Dakota	3,305	7.0	49.7	43.3
Ohio	4,107	5.4	47.1	47.5
Oklahoma	3,034	8.7	59.1	32.2
Oregon	4,694	6.3	26.8	66.9
Pennsylvania	5,315	5.3	45.9	48.9
Rhode Island	5,980	4.4	43.8	51.8
South Carolina	3,557	7.7	53.3	39.0
South Dakota	3,659	9.3	27.3	63.4
Tennessee	3,235	9.4	48.3	42.4
Texas	3,717	7.9	43.1	48.9
Utah	2,516	6.3	56.7	37.0
Vermont	5,526	5.3	36.5	58.2
Virginia	4,472	4.7	34.7	60.6
Washington	4,497	5.8	73.4	20.8
West Virginia	3,624	8.2	64.3	27.5
Wisconsin	4,867	4.1	39.1	56.8
Wyoming	5,373	4.5	56.8	38.8
United States	*4,448*	*6.3*	*49.4*	*44.3*

Source: National Center for Educational Statistics, *Key Statistics for Public Elementary and Secondary Education: School Year 1989–90;* National Education Association, *Estimates of School Statistics, 1989–90.*

EARLY DEVELOPMENTS
IN SCHOOL FINANCE

The country has not always had a system of free, tax-supported schools. Free public education was an idea created in the United States during the nineteenth century, and the large network of public school systems was formed in a relatively short time, primarily during the latter part of the nineteenth century and early part of the twentieth century.

American schools began as local entities, largely private and religious, during the seventeenth, eighteenth, and even early nineteenth centuries. As in England, educating children was considered a private rather than a public matter. Providing for education was a mandate for parents and masters, not governments. Eighteenth-century leaders of the new American republic viewed education as a means to enable citizens to participate as equals in affairs of government and, thus, as essential to ensure the liberties guaranteed by the constitution. Even though Thomas Jefferson proposed the creation of free public elementary schools, his proposal was not adopted until the mid-1800s, largely through the efforts of Horace Mann and Henry Barnard, state superintendents of public instruction. Mann spearheaded the development of publicly supported "common schools" in Massachusetts, and Barnard did the same in Connecticut.

In the nineteenth century, education began to assume significance in economic terms, and that also was when compulsory attendance laws were passed. Even when school attendance became compulsory in the mid-1800s, however, government financing of schools was not uniformly required.

In 1647, the General Court of Massachusetts passed the famous Old Deluder Satan Act. The act required every town to set up a school or pay a sum of money to a larger town to support education. It required towns with at least 50 families to appoint a teacher of reading and writing, and it required towns with more than 100 families also to establish a secondary school. The act required that these schools be supported by masters, parents, or the inhabitants in general, thereby establishing one of the first systems of financing schools through local taxation. Pulliam (1987) states that the first tax on property for local schools was levied in Dedham, Massachusetts, in 1648. By 1693, New Hampshire also required towns to support elementary schools.

Initially, one-room elementary common schools were established in local communities, often fully supported through a small local tax. Each town functioned, moreover, as an independent school district—indeed, as an independent school system, since there were no state laws or regulations providing for a statewide public education system. At the same time, several large school systems evolved in the big cities of most states. Even at this early time, these different education systems reflected differences in local ability to support them. Big cities usually were quite wealthy, whereas the smaller, rural school districts usually were quite poor, many having great difficulty financing even a one-room school.

As the number of these small rural and big-city school systems grew, however, and as the importance of education as a unifying force for a developing country became increasingly realized by civic and political leaders, new initiatives were undertaken to create statewide education systems. By 1820, in fact, 13 of the then 23 states had constitutional provisions, and 17 had statutory provisions pertaining to public education.

In the mid-nineteenth century, several states began completely to rewrite their constitutions, not only calling for creation of statewide systems of public education, but also formally establishing government responsibility for financing schools. Today all states have constitutional provisions related to free public education.

Creation of free common schools reflected the importance of education in America. It also shifted control over education from individuals and the church to the state. Control over schools was a problematic aspect in crafting statewide education systems. The resolution of the control issue was creation of local lay boards of education, which, it was argued, would function in the place of parents and the church.

For the first century of common schools, local boards were the dominant source of control of public schools, but the strength of local control has changed substantially in recent years. In the early twentieth century, much school control was given to the new breed of educational professionals, as the progressives sought to take politics out of education (Tyack and Hansot, 1982). Beginning in the 1960s, both the states and the federal government began to exert new initiative and control affecting public schools. States continued this trend by taking the lead for education policy throughout the 1980s education reform period (Doyle and Hartle, 1985). Local boards were largely uninvolved in those reforms (Usdan and Danzberger, 1986). In the early 1990s, the president and the nation's governors established nationwide education goals.

Today some predict—even advocate—elimination of local control (Finn, 1991). With nationwide student testing and student performance goals and emerging national curricula, the key roles for local school boards, they argue, have been eliminated.

The development of the state-controlled and governmentally financed "common school" also raised many fundamental issues about school finance. These issues concerned the level of government (local or state) that would support public education and whether new constitutional terminology such as "general and uniform," "thorough and efficient," "basic," and "adequate" meant that an equal amount of dollars would be spent for every student in the state, or whether it meant just providing a basic education program for every student, with different amounts of total dollars determined at the local level. As discussed in Chapter 2, this controversy persists today and is resolved in different ways by legislatures and courts in the 50 states.

Although major differences exist in the specific approaches taken, most states finance public schools primarily through local property taxes. Indeed, in the mid- to late 1800s, most states required local districts to fully finance

mandated public schools through local property taxation. Just as today, moreover, there was a wide variation in the local property tax base. In some local
school districts, the per-pupil property tax base was large, and a small tax rate
was sufficient to raise monies for the public schools. In other school districts,
especially rural districts, the per-pupil property tax base was small, and districts
had to levy a large tax rate to raise even a small amount of funds to support
the local schools.

As discussed at greater length in Chapter 7, states began to intervene
in school financing first through small "flat grant" programs, in which the state
distributed given amount of money per pupil to each local school district. The
idea was for the state to provide at least some assistance in support of a local
basic education program. Over the years, these flat grants became recognized
as too small.

In the early 1920s, states began to implement "minimum foundation programs," which provided a much higher level of base financial support and were
financed with a combination of state and local revenues. These programs were
the first examples of a state policy explicitly recognizing the wide variation in
the local property tax base. Aid structures were designed to distribute larger
amounts to districts with a small property tax base per pupil and smaller
amounts to districts with a large property tax base per pupil.

These "equalization formulas" were designed to counteract differences in
local fiscal capacity to finance education. Over time, however, the level of the
minimum foundation programs also proved inadequate, and additional revenues
were raised by school districts solely through local taxation. As a result, educational expenditures per pupil varied widely across local districts in most states,
with the differences related primarily to the size of the local per-pupil property
tax base.

Beginning in the late 1960s, these fiscal disparities led to legal challenges
to state school finance systems. Plaintiffs, usually from low-wealth and low-
spending districts, argued that the disparities not only were unfair but also were
unconstitutional (Coons, Clune, and Sugarman, 1970; Berke, 1974). Chapter
2 traces the course of these suits, which spawned a new political channel to
improve the fiscal equity of the ways in which states finance public education.

EXAMPLES OF SCHOOL FINANCE
FISCAL DISPARITIES

There are many illustrations of fiscal disparities among school districts created
by state school finance structures. Figure 1.5 shows 1969 data that were presented in the original *Serrano* v. *Priest* court case in California; at that time,
California had a typical minimum foundation program, and most districts raised
additional funds to spend at a higher level. These data represent property value
per child, the local school tax rate, and resulting expenditures per pupil for a

FIGURE 1.5   Comparison of Selected Tax Rates and Expenditure Levels in Selected California Counties, 1968–69

School District	Pupils	Assessed Value per Pupil	Tax Rate	Expenditure per Pupil
Alameda Co.				
Emery Unified	586	$100,187	$2.57	$2,223
Newark Unified	8,638	6,048	5.65	616
Fresno Co.				
Colinga Unified	2,640	33,244	2.17	963
Clovis Unified	8,144	6,480	4.28	565
Kern Co.				
Rio Bravo Elementary	121	136,271	1.05	1,545
Lamont Elementary	1,847	5,971	3.06	533
Los Angeles Co.				
Beverly Hills Unified	5,542	50,885	2.38	1,232
Baldwin Park Unified	13,108	3,706	5.48	577

Source: California Supreme Court Opinion in *Serrano* v. *Priest*, August 1971.

property-rich district versus a property-poor district in each of four counties. In each county example, the assessed valuation per pupil—the local tax base—varied substantially: by a factor of more than 13 in Los Angeles County and a factor of more than 16 in Alameda County. In each example, moreover, the district with the higher assessed value per child also had the higher expenditure per pupil and the lower tax rate.

These examples were selected to show that the California school finance structure produced a situation—similar to that in other states at that time, and even today—in which districts with a low property tax base usually spent less than the state average, even with above-average tax rates, while districts with a high property tax base usually spent more than the state average, even with below-average tax rates. The wealthy enjoyed the advantages of both high expenditures and low tax rates while the poor were disadvantaged by both low expenditures and high tax rates. The shortcoming of the data in Figure 1.5 is that school finance information is provided for only a few districts. Although these districts reflected the trends in the system, system trends should be analyzed statistically using a random sample of districts or data from all districts, rather than selected pairs of districts from different counties.

Another potentially misleading approach in presenting school finance data is to show the extreme cases. Figure 1.6, for example shows for Colorado the value of assessed valuation per pupil for the richest and poorest districts, districts at the 90th and 10th percentiles, and the district in the middle. These 1977 data show that the ratio of the wealthiest to the poorest was 77.7 to 1; at a 1 mill tax rate, the wealthiest district would raise $326.27 per pupil, and the

FIGURE 1.6   Assessed Valuation per Pupil in Colorado School Districts, 1977

Highest: Rio Blanco–Rangely	$326,269
90th percentile: Eagle-Eagle	57,516
Median: Mesa–Plauteau Valley	20,670
10th percentile: Montezuma-Dolores	10,764
Lowest: El Paso–Fountain	4,197
Ratio: Highest/lowest	77.7:1
Ratio: 90th/10th percentiles	5.3:1

Source: Education Finance Center, Education Commission of the States, from official data of the Colorado Department of Education.

poorest district would raise only $4.20![2] To raise the amount that the wealthiest district produced at 1 mill, the poorest district would have had to levy a 77.7 mill tax rate—prohibitively high. To blunt the criticism that the extreme cases might represent anomalies, the values for districts at the 90th and 10th percentiles also are presented. The figures show that property wealth per child still varied substantially, from a high of $57,516 to a low of $10,764—a ratio of 5.3 to 1. Although this is less of a difference, the data indicate that district ability to raise school funds through the local property tax varied widely.

This figure also shows the emphasis on variation in the local tax base per se in many early school finance analyses. What really matters, or course, is the interaction of the local tax base, state equalization aid, and local tax rates on the final per-pupil spending figure. But even in the first school finance case taken to the U.S. Supreme Court (see Chapter 2), primary emphasis was given to the variation in the local tax base. The data in Figure 1.6 *implied* that the Colorado school finance system would have substantial per-pupil spending disparities, even though only data on the variation in the local tax base were provided.

Figure 1.7 shows the magnitude of the actual spending disparities by displaying statistics calculated from a sample of all Colorado school districts in 1977. At that time, Colorado had a guaranteed tax base program (see Chapter 7) but had "frozen" all local expenditures and allowed only modest increases from year to year, letting lower-spending districts increase at a somewhat faster rate than higher-spending districts. This figure organizes all data into groups— in this case five groups, or quintiles—and presents averages for each quintile.[3] Note that each quintile includes approximately an equal percentage of

[2] See the glossary of School Finance and Tax Terms for an explanation of property tax rates: mills, dollars per hundred, etc.

[3] Other studies categorize districts into 7 groups (septiles) or 10 groups (deciles). The most common practice today is to use deciles, each of which contains districts that enroll about 10 percent of all students.

FIGURE 1.7   ARB and Current Operating Expenditures per Pupil by Quintiles of Assessed Valuation per Pupil, 1977

Assessed Valuation per Pupil	Percent of Pupils	Number of Districts	Authorized Revenue Base	Current Operating Expenditures per Pupil
$ 4,197– 12,800	19	33	1,196	$1,532
12,800– 15,500	20	25	1,312	1,594
15,500– 17,600	14	14	1,299	1,667
17,600– 24,500	27	32	1,476	1,742
24,500–326,269	20	77	1,692	2,342

Source: Education Finance Center, Education Commission of the States, from official data of the Colorado Department of Education.

students—not districts.[4] Interestingly, although property wealth per pupil varied substantially, both the authorized revenue base (ARB)[5] and current operating expenditures per pupil varied by much smaller magnitudes. Indeed, the ratio between the ARB of the top or wealthiest quintile and that for the bottom or poorest quintile is 1.4 to 1, much less than the 5.3 to 1 ratio of wealth at the 90th percentile to wealth at the 10th percentile. The ratio of current operating expenditures per pupil at the top quintile to those at the bottom quintile is slightly higher, at 1.5 to 1. Unfortunately, the local tax rate and state aid figures are not provided, so it is not possible to determine whether the more uniform revenue and expenditure results are produced by fiscal capacity equalizing state aid or by high tax rates in the low-wealth districts.

New Jersey data for two time periods, 1975–76 and 1978–79, are presented by septiles (seven groups) in Figure 1.8. The purpose of these two analyses was to show differences in the New Jersey school finance structure three years after the courts, responding to a 1973 decision overturning the school finance structure, forced the legislature in 1976 finally to enact a major school finance reform (see Chapter 2). These tables are somewhat difficult to read because they do not include any typical univariate or relationship statistics (see Chapter 3). Nevertheless, several characteristics of the data are clear. First, in general, expenditures per pupil increased as property value per pupil increased; it seems that, both before and after reform, expenditures were a function of local property wealth in New Jersey. But expenditures per pupil in 1978–79 were nearly the same for the first four groups, suggesting that some expenditure equality had resulted for the bottom half of all districts from the New Jersey 1976 reform.

---

[4] Several earlier studies grouped data into categories with equal numbers of districts, and that practice still is followed. However, the emerging practice is to have an equal number of students in each category, to assess the impact of the system on students. See Berne and Stiefel (1984) and Chapter 3 for discussion of the unit of analysis.

[5] The ARB is a Colorado-specific, general fund revenue per-pupil limit that varies for each local school district. It includes revenues for the regular education program.

FIGURE 1.8   New Jersey School Finance: Relationship between Property Wealth, Current Expenditures, and Tax Rates

	Equalized Valuation per Pupil	Current Expenditures per Pupil	Current Expenditures per Weighted Pupil	Current School Tax Rate
1975–76				
Group 1	Less than $33,599	$1,504	$1,372	$1.79
Group 2	$33,600–45,499	1,414	1,324	2.12
Group 3	45,450–58,699	1,411	1,347	2.00
Group 4	58,700–67,199	1,460	1,401	1.99
Group 5	67,200–78,499	1,604	1,543	1.89
Group 6	78,500–95,499	1,689	1,628	1.74
Group 7	95,500 and over	1,752	1,681	1.17
State Average		1,550	1,473	1.69
Range		248	309	N.A.
1978–79				
Group 1	Less than $37,000	$1,994	$1,760	$1.67
Group 2	$ 37,000–54,999	1,933	1,763	1.57
Group 3	55,000–73,999	1,978	1,816	1.55
Group 4	74,000–87,999	1,994	1,882	1.58
Group 5	88,000–102,999	2,200	2,061	1.69
Group 6	103,000–125,199	2,268	2,154	1.67
Group 7	125,000 and over	2,390	2,262	1.11
State Average		2,113	1,959	1.47
Range		396	502	N.A.

Second, the range[6] increased for both expenditures per pupil and expenditures per weighted pupil between 1976 and 1979; even the range divided by the statewide average increased, suggesting that overall spending disparities increased over those three years.

Third, there seem to be wider expenditure disparities on a weighted pupil basis, where the weights indicate special pupil needs (see Chapter 8). Indeed, using the weighted pupil count substantially reduces the per-pupil expenditure figure for the lowest-wealth districts, indicating—correctly it turns out, for New Jersey—that these districts have large numbers of special-need students.[7]

[6] The range is the difference between the highest and lowest value; see Chapter 3.

[7] Many of these districts are large urban districts with large numbers and percentages of poor students, physically and mentally handicapped students, and low-achieving students.

Finally, and quite interestingly, school property tax rates dropped in New Jersey over these three years, and these rates were almost equal across all but the wealthiest group of districts in 1979.

It seems, therefore, that the major impact of the 1976 New Jersey reform was to equalize school tax rates for most districts and to increase unweighted expenditures per pupil in the bottom half to about the same level. On a weighted pupil basis, however, spending was not uniform in the bottom half, and overall spending disparities seemed to increase. The New Jersey system was overturned through litigation in 1990, in a case filed in the mid-1980s (see Chapter 2).

New York school finance presents a different set of problems—at least as of 1978, as the data in Figure 1.9 show. The data are from a study conducted for a New York task force formed after a 1978 lower court found the state's school finance system unconstitutional (Odden, Palaich and Augenblick, 1979). At that time, New York had a school finance system that functioned like a minimum foundation program but was actually a spending level percentage equalizing formula (see Chapter 7). The data in Figure 1.9 are presented for all districts divided, except for New York City, into 10 equal groups, or deciles. Each decile has approximately the same number of students. New York City, with an enrollment of nearly 1 million in a state with a total of 3 million, is shown separately, since it alone would include over three of the deciles if it were included.

Several elements of the data should be discussed. To begin, they are grouped by deciles of *spending* per pupil; the idea in New York was that per-pupil expenditure disparities constituted the most important variable, and analysis of correlates of that variable should be the focus of the study. Column 8 shows that revenues per pupil from local and state sources varied widely in New York during the 1977–78 school year, from a low of $1,759 in the lowest-spending decile to a high of $3,443 in the highest-spending decile, a ratio of about 2 to 1. Note that this is a much smaller disparity than the 5.8 to 1 ratio in spending between the very highest ($5,752) and the very lowest ($988) spending districts.

Second, both spending per pupil and revenues per pupil from local and state sources increase with property wealth, the traditional school finance pattern. But note also that the school property tax rate also increases; in fact, the tax rates for the top few deciles are 50 to almost 100 percent higher than the tax rates in the lowest-spending districts. This anomaly set New York school finance apart from most other states. Indeed, one of the reasons the wealthier districts spent more per pupil was that they taxed local property at a higher rate. They had a larger property tax base, and they also taxed it more.

It also was true that household income, as measured by gross income stated on New York state income tax returns, increased with property wealth, and thus with spending and school tax rates. It turns out that higher-income families, not only in New York but generally, choose to levy higher tax rates for schools. Thus, although higher spending in New York was caused in part

FIGURE 1.9 Selected New York School Finance Variables, 1977–78

Deciles of Approved Operating Expenditures per Pupil	Assessed Value per Pupil	Gross Income per Return (1977)	Property Tax Rate (mills)	Local Property Tax Revenue per Pupil	Other Local Revenue per Pupil	Total State Aid per Pupil	Total Local and State Revenue per Pupil	Total Federal Aid per Pupil
First decile ($988–$1,389)	$ 37,957	$12,225	13.01	$ 485	$ 54	$1,120	$1,759	$ 35
Second decile ($1,390–1,471)	41,924	12,446	15.34	634	56	1,176	1,866	37
Third decile ($1,473–$1,542)	46,902	12,422	17.11	770	62	1,107	1,939	58
Fourth decile ($1,544–$1,640)	50,968	13,527	17.61	862	67	1,081	2,010	40
Fifth decile ($1,642–$1,789)	57,916	14,190	19.63	1,086	68	1,006	2,160	63
Sixth decile ($1,790–$1,899)	58,986	13,311	21.68	1,178	72	998	2,248	117
Seventh decile ($1,903–$2,017)	64,323	15,274	23.48	1,430	81	953	2,464	44
Eighth decile ($2,021–$2,255)	66,469	16,157	23.69	1,526	178	896	2,600	74
Ninth decile ($2,250–2,474)	78,069	16,778	25.26	1,896	102	866	2,864	57
Tenth decile ($2,475–5,752)	115,535	21,639	23.84	2,583	154	706	3,443	36
New York	81,506	13,607	22.52	1,760	41	864	2,665	217
Rest of state	61,732	14,762	20.05	1,240	89	1,002	2,331	57
Statewide average	67,715	14,412	20.79	1,397	75	960	2,432	105

Source: Allan Odden, Robert Palaich, and John Augenblick, Analysis of the New York State School Finance System, 1977–78, Denver Colo., Education Commission of the States, 1979.

by higher local tax effort, that higher tax effort in part was aided by higher household income. Further, household income and property wealth per pupil were highly and positively correlated in New York at that time. Unlike the Texas data of the early 1970s, which were not correlated but were taken to the U.S. Supreme Court, the New York data might have made a better case for using the equal protection clause of the U.S. Constitution to find the fiscal disparities shown in this table to be unconstitutional (see Chapter 2, on litigation).

In short, the New York data showed that higher spending occurred in districts with higher property wealth, higher household income, and higher school tax rates, and that lower spending occurred in property-poor and income-poor districts with low tax rates. These variations from the traditional pattern complicated the formulation of a school finance reform that could pass muster for both the courts and the legislature. When the state's highest court ruled that the system, although unfair, was not unconstitutional, the push for reform abated, and school finance was changed incrementally over time; it still displays these general characteristics.

As Chapter 2 discusses, the U.S. Supreme Court in 1973 ruled the Texas school finance system inequitable and unfair but not unconstitutional, and the state enacted a major school finance reform as part of a comprehensive education reform during 1984 (Odden and Dougherty, 1984); however, that system was challenged in state court a few years later. The 1984 law provided for a minimum foundation program with a higher per-pupil expenditure level, a small guaranteed-yield program on top of the foundation program, weights for several different categories of pupil need, and a price adjustment to account for the varying prices Texas districts faced in purchasing education commodities. In the fall of 1987, the court ruled the school finance system unconstitutional, and the state created the Education Finance Reform Commission in early 1988.

The data in Figure 1.10 were presented to that commission. The data are organized according to groups of approximately equal numbers of children; this time, 20 different groupings are provided, showing the impact of the finance structure on each 5 percent of students. The numbers show that, indeed, property wealth per pupil varied substantially in Texas, from $56,150 to over $440,987, a ratio of 7.9 to 1. In fact, the difference was greater, since several districts had assessed valuation per pupil in the range of $800,000 to over $1 million; these districts, moreover, were not anomalies but included several of the state's largest cities and some very wealthy suburban districts. The bottom line in Texas was that the local property tax base per pupil clearly was distributed unequally among local school districts.

The column for state and local revenues per pupil shows, however, that although there is a trend for per-pupil revenues to increase with wealth, this trend exists primarily for the top 20 percent and the bottom 5 percent of districts. For the districts in between, revenues per pupil seem to be within about 10 percent of $3,300 per pupil. This is not a dramatic variation. In fact, it could be argued that such data indicate that, for the bulk of students in the middle, revenues per pupil were fairly equal, that the problem with the system

FIGURE 1.10 Selected Texas School Finance Variables, 1986–87

Number of Districts	Range of Property Wealth per Pupil	Average Property Wealth per Pupil	Local Revenue per Pupil	State Revenue per Pupil	State and Local Revenues per Pupil	Federal Revenue per Pupil
26	Under $56,150	$ 46,217	$ 508	$2,528	$3,036	$564
57	$ 56,150–79,652	68,793	647	2,309	2,956	426
73	79,653–96,562	87,980	801	2,204	3,005	277
123	96,563–117,462	107,516	1,006	2,092	3,096	269
68	117,463–128,425	120,325	1,050	2,109	3,159	309
73	128,426–144,213	136,285	1,192	2,074	3,266	283
52	144,214–156,931	152,061	1,355	1,864	3,215	227
34	156,932–167,090	161,971	1,610	1,711	3,321	145
46	167,091–177,108	169,925	1,658	1,711	3,369	203
84	177,109–202,136	190,514	1,727	1,643	3,370	171
37	202,137–218,238	208,862	1,904	1,499	3,403	126
44	218,239–239,117	224,173	1,963	1,473	3,436	139
26	239,118–253,338	244,493	2,055	1,403	3,458	130
42	253,339–276,674	260,613	2,281	1,342	3,623	181
36	276,675–308,780	294,373	2,942	1,123	4,065	113
1	308,781–308,862	308,862	2,006	1,125	3,131	312
45	308,863–356,189	330,130	2,494	1,039	3,533	128
45	356,190–436,960	399,954	3,459	830	4,285	89
3	436,961–440,987	440,607	2,862	960	3,822	294
146	Over $440,987	799,896	4,764	418	5,182	143

Source: Texas Department of Education.

was the low spending of the districts at the very bottom and the very high spending of the districts at the top. This problem definition requires a different policy response than if disparities were spread more evenly across the entire system. Nevertheless, the Texas lower court overturned the system, and that decision was upheld on appeal by a unanimous state supreme court in the fall of 1989. Thus, even modest variations in spending per pupil that are linked to local property wealth are likely to be overturned if taken to court.

These examples present different aspects of school finance disparities and conditions across a number of different states. Although the specific school funding structures in these states differed, each state had some type of fiscal capacity equalization program designed to provide more school finance equity. Yet all states fell short of providing equal spending per pupil. Spending differences in all cases were strongly related to the local property tax base. These fiscal realities were the central concern of school finance policy from 1900 to the 1960s. Policy tended to diminish but not eliminate the disparities. In the late 1960s, these fiscal disparities were subject to legal challenge through the courts, the subject of the next chapter.

Chapter 2

Legal Issues
in School Finance

Differences in educational expenditures per pupil across school districts in a state—the basic school finance problem recognized as early as 1905 (Cubberly, 1905) and discussed at length in Chapter 1, became the subject of court litigation in the late 1960s. The impetus for legal action was increasing use of the federal equal protection clause to ensure rights for individuals who had been the subject of discrimination. Lawyers and education finance policy analysts began to think that equal protection arguments could also apply to school finance inequities, and they filed several suits to have traditional school finance disparities—long considered unfair—declared unconstitutional and illegal as well.

This chapter reviews the past 25 years of school finance litigation. It begins with the unsuccessful *McInnis* and *Burruss* cases in Illinois and Virginia, respectively, and then discusses the issues involved in equal protection litigation generally. It follows with an analysis of the course of school finance equal protection litigation. The next section discusses litigation based on state education clauses, a second channel for legal action that began in the wake of the 1973 U.S. Supreme Court's ruling in the *Rodriguez* case that school finance inequities did not violate the Constitution. Next the chapter discusses several special issues that have emerged in school finance litigation, including municipal overburden. The last section discusses overall trends in school finance litigation, focusing on the 1989 and 1990 decisions in Kentucky, Texas, and New Jersey overturning those states' school finance structures, and suggests possible courses for litigation during the 1990s—an era with new national education goals (White House, 1990) and new interdistrict, open enrollment programs (Odden, 1991).

THE EARLY SCHOOL FINANCE CASES

In the late 1960s, two court cases were filed—*McInnis* v. *Shapiro*[1] in Illinois and *Burruss* v. *Wilkerson*[2] in Virginia—challenging the legality and constitutionality of differences in educational expenditures across each state's school districts. Although brought on equal protection grounds, these early cases argued that the systems were unconstitutional because education was a fundamental right, and the wide differences in expenditures or revenues per pupil across school districts were not related to "educational needs." Both suits held that there was no educational justification for wide disparities in per-pupil revenues and that differences in expenditures per pupil had to be related to "educational need," not to educationally irrelevant variables such as the local tax base.

In trial, however, the court reasonably asked how educational need should be identified and measured. To rule whether or not differences in educational expenditures were or were not related to educational need, the court needed a standard by which to assess such need. Plaintiffs did not have a strong response or a measure of educational need; in fact, at that time, educational need was a diffuse term on which there was no agreement as to definition or measurement. The wide variation in expenditures per pupil in itself was not sufficient to move the court to find the system unconstitutional, largely because the court could not develop an "educational need" standard. In both cases, therefore, the court ruled that the suits were nonjusticiable because the court did not have a standard with which to assess plaintiffs' claims.

Thus, these first attempts to use the courts as a route to resolve school finance inequities were unsuccessful. In nearly all subsequent school finance cases, moreover, one of the defendants' first motions has been to declare the case nonjusticiable, citing *McInnis* and *Burruss* as precedents. School finance litigants, however, have continued to use equal protection as the legal route to challenge state school finance structures. The next section outlines the key issues involved generally in equal protection litigation (see also Levin, 1977).

EQUAL PROTECTION LITIGATION

The U.S. Constitution was written by people who were strong proponents of individual rights, especially in the light of possible governmental action that might constrain individual actions. The founding fathers believed that everyone was entitled equally to "life, liberty, and the pursuit of happiness." To give this broad phrase substantive meaning and to protect individuals from various governmental actions that might limit these rights, the Constitution's authors added the Bill of Rights as the first 10 amendments. These amendments

[1] *McInnis* v. *Shapiro*, 293 F. Supp. 327 (N.D. Ill. 1968) affd.
[2] *Burruss* v. *Wilkerson*, 310 F. Supp. 572 (W. D. Va. 1969) affd., 397 U.S. 44 (1970).

identified several key rights of U.S. citizens, including the right to free speech, freedom of religion, a free press, the right to bear arms, and the right of assembly. Other amendments to the U.S. Constitution also identified citizen rights, including the Thirteenth (prohibition of slavery), the Fourteenth (due process and equal protection), the Fifteenth (barring denial of the right to vote on the basis of race), the Nineteenth (female suffrage), and the Twenty-sixth (18-year-old voting rights). Article 1, Sections 9 and 10 of the Constitution create the rights of habeus corpus and prohibit ex post facto laws. The president also can designate fundamental rights through executive orders.

The U.S. Supreme Court has the responsibility and authority for defining the meanings of the rights identified in the Constitution, the Bill of Rights, and other amendments, and also for determining whether the president, Congress, and state governors and legislatures exercise their power properly, especially as their actions might impact a right specified in the Constitution.

The equal protection clause of the Fourteenth Amendment provides that no state shall "deny to any person within its jurisdiction the equal protection of the laws." This amendment was enacted in the mid-nineteenth century, during the time of slavery in the southern states, and was designed to prohibit states from treating blacks differently than whites. But as events evolved, new governmental actions were taken, and suits were filed claiming that governmental actions violated the equal protection clause. Over time, the U.S. Supreme Court created mechanisms for determining whether—and if so, how—governmental actions violated the equal protection clause.

The equal protection clause could be read to mean that governments—local, state, and federal—could not treat individuals differently for any reason. But that is clearly not the case. Laws specify that some individuals can drive a car (those with a license) and others cannot, that some can practice medicine (again, those with a license) and some cannot, and that some can teach in public schools (those with a certificate or license) and some cannot. In each of these cases, governments have determined that individuals need certain skills or expertise to engage in the action; the state provides a license to engage in such action only to those individuals who demonstrate that they have the expertise. There are several other examples of differential treatment of individuals by government, all of which have been found by the courts to be constitutionally permissible, i.e., not to violate the equal protection clause.

The Minimal Scrutiny Test

How, then, does a court determine whether a governmental action that treats individuals differently is constitutional? When equal protection suits are brought, the court uses either of two tests to determine whether the equal protection clause has been violated. The first is the minimal scrutiny test. This test simply asks whether the government has a rationale, or reason, for the differential treatment. In the preceding examples, the reason is that governments feel individuals need to demonstrate certain expertise to drive a car, practice medicine, or teach in the public schools. Thus, there is a "rational relationship" between the laws and the differential treatment. Courts have accepted these rational relationships as acceptable bases for treating individuals differently. Indeed, states usually can cite some rationale for any action they take. Thus, if the court invokes the minimal scrutiny test, the state action usually is upheld because the state can identify some rationale for its law.

The Strict Judicial Scrutiny Test

The second test[3] is strict judicial scrutiny. When the court invokes this test, the government has to show that there is a "compelling state interest" for its particular action and that there is "no less discriminatory" policy the state can use to satisfy that compelling interest. This is an onerous test; both conditions must be met. When the court invokes this test, states commonly have difficulty identifying the compelling state interest, and other state policies can be identified that have less discriminatory impact. Indeed, when strict judicial scrutiny is invoked, the state usually loses and plaintiffs win. The strict judicial scrutiny test usually overturns the governmental action that is the basis of the suit.

Fundamental rights.   The key, then, is to identify the circumstances under which the court can invoke strict judicial scrutiny. Courts invoke strict judicial scrutiny in only two circumstances: when governmental action affects a "fundamental right" or when governmental action creates a "suspect classification" of individuals. Fundamental rights are those identified in the Constitution or, as a consequence of equal protection litigation, are the subject of a U.S. Supreme Court ruling. Fundamental rights today include, the right to practice any religion, the right of free speech, the right of a free press, the right of assembly, and the right to due process.

Through equal protection litigation during the 1950s and 1960s, the right to vote and the right to appeal a court case also were designated as fundamental rights. Many states had required individuals to pay a poll tax in order to register to vote. Poor individuals were unable to pay the tax and thus lost the opportunity to vote. Cases challenging this governmental requirement were brought on two grounds: that voting was a fundamental right of U.S. citizens and that the poll tax created a suspect classification (to be discussed) of poor and nonpoor individuals. The court ruled that voting was indeed a fundamental right and that there were less discriminatory ways for the state to collect the small amount of revenues than through the poll tax. The poll tax was ruled unconstitutional.

During those same times, some states required individuals who lost a lower court case to pay for a reproduction of the court transcript if they wanted to appeal the court decision. Individuals without the economic means to do so thus lost their opportunity to appeal. Cases challenging this governmental

---

[3] Equal protection litigation is not quite as simple as the two-tiered analysis suggested here, but the issues presented are the key issues that have arisen in school finance litigation (Sparkman, 1990).

requirement were again brought on two grounds: that the right to appeal was a fundamental right of U.S. citizens and that the requirement to pay for a reproduction of the lower court transcript as a condition of appeal created a suspect classification of poor and nonpoor individuals. The court ruled that the right to appeal was indeed a fundamental right and that there were less discriminatory ways for the state to cover the small cost for reproducing the transcript (the cost could be borne by the government); it ruled unconstitutional the practice of requiring individuals to pay the cost of the transcript as a condition to appeal. In both of these cases, the U.S. Supreme court identified new fundamental rights and overturned state actions that differentiated individuals in their exercising these fundamental rights.[4]

Suspect classifications.   The second basis for invoking strict judicial scrutiny is government action that creates a "suspect classification" of individuals. The Constitution directly prohibits government actions that affect individuals differently because of their religion or national origin, but it is silent on race. It was the 1954 U.S. Supreme Court decision on desegregation in the *Brown* v. *Board of Education* case[5] that identified race as a suspect classification. In this decision, the court ruled that the "separate but equal" schools created in many southern states violated the equal protection clause of the U.S. Constitution because it classified individuals according to race. In overturning these segregative school practices, the court created a new suspect classification—race—and effectively overturned all state laws that treated individuals differently solely on the basis of race.

Income, although identified as a potential suspect classification in both the poll tax and right-to-appeal cases, has not been recognized by the U.S. Supreme Court as such. Although the decisions in both of these instances showed sympathy toward recognizing income as a suspect class, the cases turned on the fundamentality of the rights affected, not on the classification of poor and nonpoor. Thus, today individual income is not recognized as a suspect classification.

SCHOOL FINANCE EQUAL PROTECTION LITIGATION

In the wake of *McInnis* and *Burruss*, school finance litigation has had two general challenges: to determine a strategy that would place challenges to interdistrict expenditure disparities directly in the mainstream of equal protection

---

[4] In both of these cases, the issue involved absolute deprivation of a right—to vote or appeal a lower court decision. In school finance cases, courts note that education is not absolutely denied to any student. Thus, the issue becomes one of relative deprivation, i.e., a lower-quality education in one district compared to another. Courts have been reluctant to overrule school finance structures on the basis of relative deprivation.
[5] *Brown* v. *Board of Education of Topeka*, 347 U.S. 483 (1954).

litigation, and to identify a standard that could be used by the court to decide how school finance realities met equal protection requirements.

Arthur Wise (1969), then a doctoral student at the University of Chicago, argued that education was a fundamental right and that the equal protection clause required education to be provided equally across all school districts. He further argued that the variations in educational expenditures across districts in most states did not reflect uniformity of educational offerings, because the variations were not related to educational need. But, as discussed earlier, the educational need argument was not accepted by the court.

At about the same time, John Coons, then a law professor at Northwestern University, and two law students, William Clune and Stephan Sugarman, began to frame another argument, namely, that education funding created a suspect classification defined by district property wealth per pupil (Coons, Clune, and Sugarman, 1970). They argued that local school districts were creations of state governments and that by making school financing heavily dependent on local financing, the states gave school districts unequal opportunities to raise educational revenues because the property value per child varied widely across school districts. Coons, Clune, and Sugarman argued that school financing systems needed to be "fiscally neutral," i.e., that expenditures per pupil could not be related to local district property wealth per pupil. Put differently, they argued that education could not be dependent on local wealth, only the wealth of the state as a whole.

This argument created two new major "hooks" for school finance litigation. First, it gave the litigation a "suspect classification" argument, namely, district property wealth per pupil. Second, and as important, it created a new standard—the fiscal neutrality standard, which established that the quality of education could be a function only of the wealth of the state as a whole, not local wealth. More concretely, the fiscal neutrality standard required that there be no relationship between educational spending per pupil and local district property wealth per pupil. Both of these variables were easily measured—and both used in nearly all state school finance systems—and standard statistical measures could be used to identify the degree of relationship between the two. Thus, Coons, Clune, and Sugarman gave school finance litigation a standard that the court could use, and they added the "suspect class" legal hook to the litigation arsenal. In addition, their strategy simply identified aspects of a school finance system that could not continue and left wide legislative discretion in the design of a structure that could pass constitutional muster.[6]

School finance litigants make two equal protection arguments before the court. The first is that education is a fundamental right and must be provided equally to all individuals. The second is that state school finance structures create a suspect classification based on property wealth per pupil, which makes the quality of education higher for students in districts high in such wealth and lower for students in districts low in wealth.

---

[6] Chapter 7 details several different school finance systems and discusses the degree to which they will create constitutional structures.

From a legal perspective, however, this strategy, although admittedly creative, faced several challenges. First, litigants were asking the court both to recognize a new fundamental right—education—and to recognize a new suspect classification—property wealth per pupil. Second, the suspect class not only was a new one, but a different kind. District property wealth per pupil related to governmental entities—school districts—and not individuals, to which all previous suspect classifications had pertained; it was an economic measure that had not yet been recognized as a suspect class. Again, even though the court had appeared sympathetic to treating individual income as a suspect class, it had not recognized it as one. But even if it had, district property wealth per pupil was different, both because it related to a government entity rather than an individual and because it related to wealth—property valuation—and not income. Even though this equal protection strategy was devised during a time when the U.S. Supreme Court was expanding its list of fundamental rights and suspect classifications, the Court naturally takes a conservative stance, and school finance litigants knew they would need to develop a litigation strategy carefully, on a case-by-case basis, to "help" the Court make these two new additions to equal protection litigation.

Serrano v. Priest

The first case filed using the Coons, Clune, and Sugarman strategy was *Serrano v. Priest*[7] in California. The case was filed in 1969, and there was an immediate motion to dismiss on the grounds that school finance cases were nonjusticiable, citing *McInnis* and *Burruss* as precedents. The trial court dismissed the case on that basis. The dismissal was appealed all the way to the California Supreme Court, which rendered an opinion in August 1971. In that opinion, based on both the 14th Amendment to the U.S. Constitution and the equal protection clause of the California constitution, the court ruled that: (1) the case was justiciable, using the fiscal neutrality standard; (2) education was a fundamental right, and property wealth per pupil was a suspect class; and (3) if the facts were as alleged, the California school finance system was unconstitutional. This was a precedent-setting opinion that received nationwide media, policy, and legal attention and spawned a series of similar court cases in other states.[8]

It is important to understand that neither the *Serrano* opinion nor those of subsequent school finance court cases found use of the property tax per se in financing schools unconstitutional. Unfortunately, this policy implication was incorrectly suggested in several media reports on the *Serrano* opinion. As

---

[7] *Serrano v. Priest*, 96 Cal. Rptr. 601, 487 P. 2d 1241, 5 Cal. 3d 584 (1971).

[8] Other states include Arizona (*Shofstall* v. *Hollins*, 1973), Connecticut (*Horton* v. *Meskill*, 1977), Idaho (*Thompson* v. *Engleking*, 1975), Illinois (*Blase* v. *Illinois*, 1973), Kansas (*Knowles* v. *Kansas*, 1981), Minnesota (*Van Dusartz* v. *Hatfield*, 1971), New Jersey (*Robinson* v. *Cahill*, 1973), Oregon (*Olsen* v. *State*, 1976), Texas (*Rodriquez* v. *San Antonio*), Washington (*Northshore* v. *Kinnerar*, 1974), and Wisconsin (*Buse* v. *Smith*, 1976).

Chapter 7 indicates, there are several ways states can use the local property tax to help finance schools and still create a fiscally neutral, constitutionally acceptable system. It is only when there is heavy reliance on local property taxes and there is no state aid program to offset the differences in what districts can raise with a given tax rate that a system can become unconstitutional, i.e., when a strong relationship evolves between expenditures or revenues per pupil and local property wealth per pupil.

Rodriguez v. *San Antonio* ✱

One case filed after the *Serrano* opinion was *Rodriguez* v. *San Antonio School District* in Texas. This case was taken directly to a three-judge federal district court panel, which meant that the next stage was a direct appeal to the U.S. Supreme Court.[9] The district court ruled for the plaintiffs, finding education to be a fundamental right and property wealth per pupil to be a suspect classification. The decision held that the Texas school finance system violated the equal protection clause of the Constitution and ordered the legislature to devise a constitutional system.

The case was immediately appealed to the U.S. Supreme Court, literally before any other school finance case had been appealed to a state supreme court for a decision on the facts and the constitutional issue. In March 1973, in a split 5–4 decision, the Supreme Court held that the Texas system did not violate the Constitution. The majority opinion held that, important as education was for U.S. citizens and for discharging citizen responsibilities, it was not mentioned in the Constitution. Further, all public school students in Texas were provided some type of education program. Thus, the Court was unwilling, on its own, to recognize education as a fundamental right. Further, the decision held that property wealth per pupil was not a suspect class, in large part because it related to governmental entities (school districts) and not individuals, and because property wealth was so different from individual income.[10]

Thus, the Court did not invoke "strict judicial scrutiny." Instead, it invoked "minimal scrutiny." As was the practice then (and now) for states being sued, Texas responded that the extant system, which relied on local property taxing to support schools, reflected the principle of local control. And this response, as for most responses to the rationale test, was accepted as reasonable by the courts.

[9] Some have argued that the *Rodriguez* case should not have been filed so as to force an appeal to the U.S. Supreme Court so early in the process of school finance litigation. They claim it would have been better to win several cases at the district and state levels, to show that states could respond to a decision overturning the school finance system and that such a decision would not simply put a state's education system into disarray.
[10] In addition, the state of Texas showed that low-income children did not generally attend schools in low-wealth districts. Indeed, many low-income children attended school in districts—the big-city districts—that had quite high property value per pupil. Thus, if the court had been inclined to recognize income as a suspect class, the data did not allow plaintiffs to argue that low income and low property wealth were correlated.

The *Rodriguez* decision dealt a blow to hopes that had been raised by the *Serrano* opinion about the efficacy of reforming school finance inequities through the courts. Just a year and a half after *Serrano's* precedent-setting opinion, *Rodriguez* had eliminated the U.S. Constitution as a legal route to school finance reform. The decision threw all school finance cases out of the federal courts and back to state courts, to be argued state by state on the basis of state equal protection clauses,[11] as well as state education clauses.[12]

Indeed, the *Rodriguez* decision somewhat encouraged litigation at the state level. One part of the decision suggested quite directly that states could find education to be a fundamental right because, unlike the federal government, most state constitutions not only mention education but have constitutional clauses explicitly creating student access to a free, public education.

Robinson v. Cahill

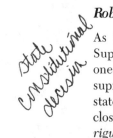

state constitutional decision

As if responding to the U.S. Supreme Court's nudgings, the New Jersey Supreme Court rendered a decision in *Robinson* v. *Cahill* in April 1973, just one month after the *Rodriguez* decision. This was the first case to reach a state supreme court.[13] A loss in *Robinson*, although not cutting off litigation in other states, would have been a further blow to school finance litigation, following so closely in the wake of *Rodriguez*. The New Jersey court acknowledged the *Rodriguez* test for finding education to be a fundamental right and acknowledged that education was mentioned in the New Jersey constitution. Nevertheless, the court held that education was not a fundamental right. Further, the court held that property wealth per pupil, although it created rich and poor school districts that had, respectively, above- and below-average spending per pupil, nevertheless was not a suspect class. Thus, the *Robinson* court found that the New Jersey school finance system did not violate the New Jersey equal protection clause.

But the court overturned the New Jersey finance system on the basis of New Jersey's constitutional education clause, which required the state to create a "thorough and efficient" public education system. The court held that a school finance structure that allowed for wide disparities in per-pupil spending that were strongly linked to local property wealth per pupil was not a "thorough and efficient" system, and it sent the issue to the state legislature so they could design a new system.

This case was important for two reasons. First, it kept school finance litigation alive just after *Rodriguez* seemed to toll its death knell. Second, it paved the way for challenging school finance systems on the basis of state

---

[11] All state constitutions have the functional equivalent of an equal protection clause.
[12] All states have some sort of education clause requiring them to create a system of public schools.
[13] Remember that the *Serrano* ruling simply overturned a motion to dismiss the case. The California Supreme Court remanded the case back to a lower court for trial.

education clauses, a substantively separate and different strategy from equal protection.

Interestingly, the New Jersey legislature procrastinated in its response to *Robinson*. The state did not have an income tax, and each year the state budget was short of the level of funds needed to finance a constitutionally permissible school finance structure. In July 1976, therefore, the New Jersey Supreme Court, in a symbolic but dramatic action, enjoined the expenditure of state funds for schools, which had the effect of shutting down the entire New Jersey school system.[14] In response, the legislature designed a new school finance structure and enacted a new tax system to fund it, as well as provide local property tax relief.

SCHOOL FINANCE STATE EDUCATION CLAUSE LITIGATION

Challenging state school finance structures under the state education clause entails a different legal strategy from that used for equal protection litigation. The strategy is to inject substantive meaning into a state education clause. Although the wording of such clauses varies substantially across the states— some calling only for creation of an education system and some calling for "thorough and efficient," "thorough and uniform," or "general and uniform" school systems, for example—all states have some requirement for the creation of a system of public schools. There are four aspects to challenging the school finance system on the basis of the state education clause.

Historical Meaning of the Education Clause

The first step is to use the history of the constitutional convention to determine how the constitutional framers viewed education, and to analyze the debates at the convention as they related to the phrasing of the education clause. In some states, the "general and uniform" clause appears to have been merely an attempt to create one statewide system of public schools, albeit with numerous districts. Prior to most states' nineteenth-century constitutional conventions, there was no *state* education system. Education systems were local entities that differed from district to district. Sometimes there were city and noncity school districts or regional groupings of districts. But there was no statewide system. States then began to consolidate these diverse systems into one statewide system, defined primarily by state regulations, especially as they pertained to school accreditation and teacher licensure. In these states, the "general and uniform" type of clause simply meant one, statewide education system, i.e., one set

---

[14] Since this occurred during the summer break, only summer schools were affected. The action, however, indicated the serious posture of the supreme court and was highly symbolic.

of laws that applied to all local school districts. The phrase had no particular implications for school finance or differences in per-pupil education spending; indeed, in these states, the financing systems usually continued to rely heavily on local property taxes, with flat grants playing a small role (see Chapter 7).

In other states, such clauses meant much more than simply creating one statewide system. Records from the debates surrounding the creation of the constitution in some cases indicated that the framers envisaged a statewide uniform system, with equal spending per pupil across local districts, often fully financed with state funds. Especially in western states, there was hope that proceeds from the Northwest section lands and other land grants could provide all the funds needed for the public school system. In these states, "thorough and uniform" and "general and uniform" could reasonably be taken to mean something close to equal spending or equal access to educational opportunities across all school districts.

Unfortunately for school finance litigation, there is no single answer to the type of education and education finance system that framers meant to create when they wrote the state constitutions, including the education clauses. Nevertheless, one avenue that is explored in litigation based on state education clauses—by both plaintiffs and defendants—is to review the constitutional history and determine whether the framers had specific ideas in mind about the nature of the state education system and the type of school finance structure that would support it, and whether those notions are relevant to current school finance legal issues.

Education Clauses Requiring More than Just an Education System

The other three routes to school finance litigation based on state education clauses seek to inject qualitative meaning into clauses. State constitutional framers might or might not have implied specific school finance structures, but today state supreme courts decide what education clauses require in terms of finance structures. Thus, the task for litigants is to convince the court to interpret the education clause as addressing school finance.[15]

One strategy is to argue that the education clause places an "affirmative duty" on the legislature to create more than just an education system, which all states have created. This argument was used in the 1973 *Robinson* case, in which the court argued that the "thorough and efficient" clause required an education system that allowed all students equal opportunity to compete in the labor market. The argument was used again by the New Jersey court in the 1990 *Abbot v. Burke* case[16] (to be discussed) to ensure higher educational

---

[15] The next few paragraphs are based on Odden, McGuire, and Belsches-Simmons (1983), pp. 38-39.

[16] *Abbott* v. *Burke*, 100 N.J. 269, 495 A. 2d 376 (1985) administrative law opinion rendered, EDU 5581-85 (Aug. 24, 1988), slip opinion decided by the Commissioner of Education (Feb. 22, 1989).

attainment for low-income and minority students in the state's property-poor, low-income, central-city school districts. In both instances, the court overturned the state's education finance structure. But the Georgia Supreme Court, in a 1981 case, concluded that the state education clause requiring state provision of an "adequate education" placed no affirmative duty on the state to equalize educational opportunities, upholding the state's school finance system.

Qualitative Demands of the Education Clause

Another strategy is to focus explicitly on the qualitative demands of the education clause. In the West Virginia *Pauley* v. *Kelley* case,[17] the state supreme court—in response to an initial motion to dismiss (again based on *McInnis* and *Burruss*)—ruled that the case was justiciable but required the trial court first to determine what a "thorough and efficient" (T&E) education system was, and to assess the degree to which the extant system met the T&E test. The resulting trial concluded that T&E required equal programs and services (this case is discussed more in a later section) across all school districts.[18] Other courts have concluded that the education clause simply requires the state to provide a basic education program. The Colorado court in *Lujan* v. *Colorado*[19] found the state's "thorough and uniform" clause was met by provision of an education program in each school district, even though the quality of the programs varied substantially.

The Education Clause and Absolute Deprivation

Finally, courts are asked to determine whether a school finance system, even though it allows fiscal and programmatic disparities across districts, functions to deprive plaintiffs of an education program. Such courts usually find that state education clauses require only provision of a basic education program, and that anything above that is conditioned on local control of schools. The 1982 Court of Appeals in New York[20] (which is New York's highest state court) held that "if what is made available by this system . . . may properly be said to constitute an education, the constitutional mandate [for a system of free common schools] is met."

In short, using the education clause in school finance litigation is different from using the equal protection strategy, and it generally raises issues about the substance and quality of the education program required for all school districts in the state (see also Wise, 1983). Unfortunately for school finance litigants, there has been little uniformity in decisions about the substantive requirements

---

[17] *Pauley* v. *Kelly,* 162 W. Va. 672, 255 S.E. 2d 859 (1979).
[18] Even though the lower court's decision overturned the school finance system, the state did not appeal, so the lower court ruling holds.
[19] *Lujan* v. *Colorado State Board of Education,* 649 P. 2d 1005 (Colo. 1982).
[20] *Board of Education, Levittown Union Free School District* v. *Nyquist,* 94 Misc. 2d 466, 408 N.Y.S. 2d 606 (1978), affd., 83 A.D. 2d 217, 443 N.Y.S. 2d 843 (1981), revd., 57 N.Y. 20 27, 439 N.E. 2d 359, 453 N.Y.S. 2d 643 (1982), appeal dismissed, 459 U.S. 1139 (1983).

of state education clauses, as to either the nature of the program or the type of school finance structure and interdistrict disparities allowed. Moreover, there has not even been uniform treatment of the same or similar education clauses across states. In other words, litigation based on state education clauses is a state-by-state strategy that is heavily dependent on the state's history and the individuals who happen to be the supreme court justices at the time the case is heard and decided.

SPECIAL ISSUES
IN SCHOOL FINANCE LITIGATION

As school finance litigation has evolved, several special issues have been incorporated into different cases. Five of these issues are discussed here.

Equal Educational Expenditures

Although most school finance litigation uses the fiscal neutrality argument devised by Coons, Clune, and Sugarman (1970) and challenges the linkage between expenditure disparities and district property wealth, most cases also argue that education is a fundamental right. The fundamental right argument, though, challenges wide disparities in educational expenditures per se, whether or not they are related to property value per pupil. The argument, somewhat similar to the educational need argument, is that if education is a state interest and is recognized by the courts as a fundamental right, then it must be provided on an equal basis to all students in all districts within a state.

Courts that find education to be a fundamental right and that limit spending disparities still allow states to distribute varying dollar amounts for special student needs, for handicapped or low-achieving students, and for different district circumstances, such as price variations and transportation needs. Thus, some courts have ruled that base education spending per pupil must be equal across all districts, and they use their finding that education is a fundamental right as the rationale for such a requirement. The Wyoming court in *Washakie* v. *Herschler*[21] held that education was a fundamental right and required the state to provide equal expenditures per pupil for the base educational program.

Equal Programs and Services

If the requirement of equal expenditures per pupil seems like an implicit return to an educational needs standard, the West Virginia court in *Pauley* v. *Bailey* made explicit reference to the standard, and the resultant litigation required the state to provide equal programs and services across all school districts. The

---

[21] *Washakie County School District No. 1* v. *Herschler,* 606 P. 2d 310 (Wyo. 1980), rehg. denied, 606 P. 2d 340 (1980), cert. denied sub. nom.

court held that the state had a "legal duty to provide equal educational opportunities by allocating resources ... according to criteria substantially related to educational needs and costs."

During the court trial, experts from different programmatic areas testified about standards that reflected high quality in their areas of expertise. Thus, the court was presented a set of high standards in all content areas — mathematics, science, language arts, history/social science, art, music, physical education, vocational education, etc. These standards became the definition of a "thorough and efficient" education and represented educational needs standards. The court found that the state's education system fell short of these standards, and the system was ruled unconstitutional.

In a subsequent report, the state issued a document identifying the standards that should be implemented to provide a "thorough and efficient" education. Although clearly characterizing a high-quality program, the standards would have required nearly a doubling of state funding for schools, which the state could not and to this day has not been able to afford.

Even though the ultimate proposal was probably too costly, the importance of the court decision was a return to the educational needs standard and development of both an approach and a set of measures the court could use to assess educational need.

Municipal Overburden

Another issue that crept into school finance litigation in the late 1970s and early 1980s was "municipal overburden." This is a concept relating generally to central-city school districts whose students not only have expensive education needs but also live in jurisdictions with enormous demands for non-education-related services, such as welfare, health, and immigration. The argument is that cities experience municipal overburden, that is, have above-average demands for noneducational services, which decreases their ability to fund and provide educational services. This disadvantage, it is argued, should be recognized in school aid formulas; city districts should provide an adjustment to state aid or a separate categorical program to compensate for their noneducation municipal overburden (Berke and Callahan, 1972; Sacks, 1974).

A group of large-city interveners in the 1978 New York *Levittown* v. *Nyquist* case were the first to inject the notion of municipal overburden into school finance litigation. The district judge accepted the argument and ruled that the New York school finance system was unconstitutional not only because differences in expenditures per pupil were related to property value per pupil, but also because the system did not explicitly recognize municipal overburden through a special adjustment.

Shortly thereafter, a lower court in Maryland[22] also ruled that municipal overburden needed to be explicitly recognized in constitutionally permissible

---

[22] *Hornbeck* v. *Somerset County Board of Education*, 295 Md. 597, 458 A. 2d 758 (1983).

school finance structures. But on appeal, both of these decisions were over-turned, including the findings on municipal overburden.

Municipal overburden has been a controversial issue in the public finance community, where there still is no consensus on what it is or whether it exists. Miner and Sacks (1980) have used the municipal overburden argument and showed the nature of its impact on city districts in New York state. Netzer (1974) argued, after quite sophisticated attempts to determine actual tax burdens, that some cities actually benefit from municipal "underburden"! Brazer and McCarty (1987) showed for Connecticut, New Jersey, and Virginia that there is little interaction between education and noneducation services and that demand for both is a function of income, price, and preferences. Others have argued that big cities generally are under fiscal stress (Ladd and Yinger, 1990; Ladd and Yinger, 1989; Bahl, 1990) and that big-city districts face special needs (Knickman and Reschovsky, 1981) and high costs (Levin, Muller, and Sandoval, 1973) that ought to be recognized in school aid formulas (Sjogren, 1981; Berke, Goertz, and Coley, 1984). Nevertheless, the argument of municipal overburden had a short life in school finance litigation and has not been included in recent cases, although New Jersey approached the special case of cities in a new way, as discussed next.

Achievement of Low-Income and Minority Students in Big Cities

Over the years, New Jersey Supreme Court school finance decisions have raised some of the most interesting and challenging issues. As mentioned earlier, in the original *Robinson* decision, the court held that the education system had to produce educational outcomes sufficient to allow students to compete in the labor market. This not only gave substantive meaning to the "thorough and efficient" requirement, but it also shifted part of the school finance argument from educational inputs such as dollars per pupil to educational outcomes. Unfortunately, this focus was not maintained in subsequent school finance action in New Jersey.

However, the 1990 decision in the *Abbot* school finance case made specific reference to the poor achievement of low-income and minority students concentrated in New Jersey's property-poor, low-income big-city school districts. The city districts also had the lowest expenditures per pupil. The court indicated that on moral grounds, the state could not allow these phenomena. It wrote that the current economy and state labor market needed students who were well schooled and had the skills necessary to compete in the new information and service economies. Further, the court noted that poor and minority students constitute a large portion of new entrants into the labor market.

Thus, the court ruled that the New Jersey school finance system was unconstitutional, but only for the poorest 28 school districts. The decision mandated that the state increase education spending in these 28 districts up to the spending level in the wealthiest suburban school districts, and that the state provide additional funds for the low-achieving students in city districts. In short, this decision not only implied an equal spending criterion, but it also gave specific attention to the achievement—outcomes—of students in large city school districts. It was the first school finance decision specifically to mention low achievement for poor and minority students in certain districts—the poorest and lowest-spending districts—and to use that finding as a key rationale for overturning the system.

Unlike the legislature's delay in responding to the 1973 *Robinson* decision, New Jersey responded quickly to the 1990 *Abbot* court decision, redesigning and funding a new structure within two months. The degree to which this new finance system is implemented and its impact on achievement of low-income and minority students in the large city districts will need to be assessed during the 1990s. But the decision has set new directions for school finance issues and school finance court mandates.

School Finance Reform and Education Reform

Another element associated with school finance litigation in the 1980s was the increased linkage of school finance to education reform and substantive, programmatic issues in education. A good example is the 1982 Arkansas *Alma School District No. 30 v. Dupree* case. This decision held that the school finance system lacked a rational relationship to any state goal, thus using minimal scrutiny to overturn the Arkansas school finance structure.

But the state did not respond immediately. The governor first empaneled a blue-ribbon commission to create a set of new educational standards and an Arkansas education reform plan. The governor argued that it was unwise simply to revise the funding system and inject new dollars into the system without an accompanying education reform program. This school finance case was decided at about the same time that the *Nation at Risk* (National Commission, 1983) report spawned a decade of education reform efforts in the country. Thus, linking school finance and education reform seemed logical at the time.

Nevertheless, the explicit connection and the statements that fiscal reform alone (i.e., reduction of fiscal inequities per se) was an insufficient rationale for spending new money, that finance reform needed to proceed hand in glove with substantive education program reform generally, created another new dimension to school finance litigation and subsequent legislative response. Indeed, in 1984 Arkansas enacted both school finance and education reforms, programs designed in tandem.

Texas, without a court case, also enacted a major education reform and school finance reform package in 1984. This time the connection was reversed. The argument was that a major and expensive education reform program could not be implemented using the old school finance structure. Thus, the state changed the school finance structure as an integral component of the overall education reform package (Odden and Dougherty, 1984).

TRENDS IN SCHOOL FINANCE LITIGATION

School finance litigation did not stop after *Rodriguez*. There was a great deal of litigation in the late 1970s, and, following a somewhat dormant period in the 1980s, four states overturned school finance systems in 1989 and 1990. In 1990, new cases were filed in more than 20 states, many raising a host of new issues. This section summarizes the school finance decisions that have been rendered since 1968, outlines recent trends in school finance litigation, and reviews two new issues likely to affect school finance legal arguments during the 1990s.

A School Finance Scorecard

Figure 2.1 summarizes the key school finance court cases since 1968 and indicates whether the system was overturned or upheld and the constitutional basis for court action. The figure shows that school finance cases were decided in 27 states. This number is likely to increase during the 1990s. In late 1990, for example, cases were pending in 16 states[23] and being developed in five additional states,[24] suggesting that the 1990s will be an active period for new school finance litigation.

For the 27 states included in Figure 2.1, existing school finance systems were upheld in about half the cases and overturned in the other half. Thus, school finance litigants are batting about .500 in their attempts to overturn finance structures that allow wide variations in educational expenditures linked to local property wealth per pupil. In several states, moreover, second and third rounds of litigation were filed, and these next-generation cases have generally been more successful in making their claims. Washington and Texas are two states in which the finance structure was initially upheld but subsequently overturned. In New Jersey and Connecticut the finance system was initially overturned, and later cases found that legislative action had been insufficient and required more fundamental changes.

In terms of the particular constitutional route used to overturn school finance structures, the score again is about even. About half the courts (Arkansas, Connecticut, Kansas, Kentucky, New Jersey, Washington, and West Virginia) used the state education clause as the basis for their decisions, and half (Arkansas, California, Connecticut, Texas, Wyoming, and Wisconsin) used equal protection. Those using equal protection have held both that education is a fundamental right and that property wealth per pupil is a suspect classification. Yet only Wyoming has created a standard of equal expenditure per pupil that the school finance system must meet. Although many assume that *Serrano* requires substantially equal per-pupil expenditures, the actual court decree requires only that "wealth-related" per-pupil spending vary by no more than

---

[23] Alaska, Alabama, Connecticut, Idaho, Illinois, Indiana, Kansas, Massachusetts, Michigan, Minnesota, Missouri, Nebraska, North Dakota, Oklahoma, Oregon, and Tennessee.
[24] North Carolina, Ohio, Pennsylvania, Virginia, and Wyoming.

$100,[25] which suggests that spending could differ according to local tax effort if the yield were "power-equalized" by the state (see Chapter 7).[26] LaMorte (1989) and Sparkman (1990) provide another overview of school finance litigation up to the late 1980s.

Recent Litigation Trends

The Kentucky, Texas, and New Jersey cases of 1989 and 1990 portend not only a new round of school finance litigation, but also some new trends as well. The Kentucky case, which began as a school finance case, ended as a case overturning the entire Kentucky public education system. The court decided that not only the funding but also the governance, structure, and programmatic aspects of the overall system were unconstitutional. This decision took the Arkansas political linkage of school finance reform (in response to a court case) to education program reform and incorporated it legally into the school finance case. The decision required the Kentucky legislature to create an entirely new education structure—governance, finance, and program—not just a new school finance formula.

Response to this decision, moreover, occurred during the 1989–90 setting of nationwide education goals by the nation's governors and President George Bush (White House, 1990), a time when most states began to set clear and specific student outcome (i.e., achievement) goals for their education systems. In that spirit, Kentucky created an outcome-based, reward- and sanction-oriented, site-managed education program and finance system.

At least five aspects of the Kentucky policy response are significant. First, the system is focused on student performance, not just dollar and education inputs. The key goal is to identify and produce high student achievement in a variety of academic areas. The concern is more with what students know and are able to do than with disparities in educational inputs.

Second, school sites are to be given substantial discretion in allocating and using dollars. The state anticipates implementing a school-based management and budgeting system. Thus, finance decisions will be decentralized from the district to the school.   *site-based management*

Third, schools will be rewarded financially for meeting educational outcome goals and sanctioned—including the prospect of being taken over by the state—for consistently not meeting goals. Teachers at specific school sites will be eligible for a salary bonus of up to 40 percent. These incentives are new education finance components that several states began to implement during the 1990s; they are formally a part of the Kentucky response.

Fourth, preschool—a new grade, if you will—will be provided for all students, which represents a substantial new cost.

---

[25] Later court rulings have allowed this $100 "band" to be adjusted for inflation. In 1990, this inflation-adjusted band was $268.

[26] Such a system would also require a change in California's Proposition 13, which currently prohibits increases in the local tax rate.

FIGURE 2.1

State	State Education Clause	Case Name	Status						Overturned	
			Filed	Lower Court	Appeal	State Court	U.S. Supreme Court	Upheld	Education Clause	Equal Protection
Arizona	"The Legislature shall provide for a system of common schools by which a free school shall be established and maintained in every school district for at least six months in each year" (Ariz. Const. Art II, Sec. 6)	*Shofstall v. Hollins*, 515 P. 2d 590 (1973)	1971	1972		1973		Yes		
Arkansas	"(T)he State shall ever maintain a general, suitable and efficient system of free schools whereby all persons in the State between the ages of six and twenty-one years may receive gratuitous instruction" (Ark. Const. Art. 14, Sec. 1)	*Alma School Dist. No. 30 of Crawford County et al. v. Dupree et al.*, No. 77-406 (Ch. Ct. of Pulaski Cty., Ark., Oct. 26, 1981)	1977	1981		1983			Yes	Yes
California	"The Legislature shall provide for a system of common schools by which a free school shall be kept up and supported in each district at least six months every year"	*Serrano v. Priest*, 487 P. 2d 1241 (1971) (*Serrano I*)	1968			1971				Yes
		Serrano v. Priest, 557 P. 2d 929 (1976) (*Serrano II*), reh. denied, Jan. 27, 1977; as modified Feb. 1, 1977 cert. denied, 432 U.S. 907 (1977)		1974		1976				
Connecticut	"There shall always be free public elementary and secondary schools in the state" (Conn. Const. Art. B., Sec. 1)	*Horton v. Meskill*, 172 Conn. 615, 376 A. 2d 359 (1976)	1973	1974		1977			Yes	Yes

State	Constitutional Provision	Case			
Florida	"Adequate provision shall be made by law for a uniform system of free public schools" (Fla. Const. Art. IX, Sec. 1)	*School Bd. of Palm Beach City v. Board of Educ.*, No. 82-888-CA-(L)-01-E (2d Jud. Cir., Tallahassee, Fla.)	1982			
Georgia	"The provision of an adequate education for the citizens shall be a primary obligation of the State of Georgia, the expense of which shall be provided for by taxation" (Ga. Const. Art. VIII, Sec. I; Ga. Code Sec. 2-4901)	*Thomas v. Stewart*, No. 8375 (Sup. Ct. of Polk Cty.), revd. in part and affd. in part sub. nom. *McDaniel v. Thomas*, 243 Ga. 632, 285 S.E. 2d 156 (1981)	1974	1981	1981	Yes
Idaho	"(I)t shall be the duty of the legislature of Idaho to establish and maintain a general, uniform and thorough system of public, free common schools" (Idaho Const. Art. IX, Sec. 1)	*Thompson v. Engleking*, 537 P. 2d 635 (id. 1975)	1972	1973	1975	Yes
Illinios	"A fundamental goal of the People of the State is the educational development of all persons to the limits of their capacities. The State shall provide for an efficient system of high quality public education institutions and services....The State has primary responsibility for financing the system of public education" (Ill. Const. Art. X, Sec. 1)	*McInnis v. Shapiro*, 293 F. Supp. 327 (N.D. Ill.) (1968), affd. sub. nom. *McInnis v. Ogelvie*, 394 U.S. 322, (1969)	1968	Fed 1968	1969	Yes
		People v. Adams, 350 N.E. 2d 376 (1976)		1976	1976	Yes
		Blase v. Illinois, 302 N.E. 2d 46 (1973)		1973	1973	Yes

(Continued)

Figure 2.1 (Continued)

State	State Education Clause	Case Name	Status					Upheld	Overturned	
			Filed	Lower Court	Appeal	State Court	U.S. Supreme Court		Education Clause	Equal Protection
Kansas	"The legislature shall provide for intellectual, educational, vocational and scientific improvement by establishing and maintaining public schools" (Kan. Const. Art. 4, Sec 1)	Knowles v. State Board of Educ., 547 P. 2d 699 (1976)		1975		1976			Yes	
		Knowles v. Kansas, No. 77CV251 (Shawnee Dist. CL. 1981)	1977	1981				Yes		
Kentucky	"to provide an efficient system of common schools throughout the Commonwealth" (Kent. Const., Sec. 183)	Council for Better Education, Inc. v. Wilkinson, No. 85-CI-1759 (Franklin Circuit Court, Div. I)	1986		1988				Yes	
		Rose v. Council for Better Education, Inc., Ky., No. 88-SC-804-TG.				1989			Yes	
Maryland	"The General Assembly...shall, by law, establish throughout the state a thorough and efficient system of free public schools" (Md. Const. Art. VIII, Sec. 1)	Hornbeck v. Somerset County Board of Educ. et al. v. Hornbeck et al., No. A-58438 (Cir. Ct. Baltimore, Md., May 19, 1981)	1979	1981				Yes		

State	Constitutional Provision	Case				
Massachusetts	"(I)t shall be the duty of legislatures and magistrates, in all future periods of this commonwealth, to cherish the interests of literature and the sciences, and all seminaries of them;...public schools and grammar schools in the towns" (Mass. Const. Ch. 5, Sec. 2)	*Webby v. King*, No. 78–179 (Civil Sup. Jud. Ct.)	1978			
Michigan	"The legislature shall maintain and support a system of free public elementary and secondary schools as defined by law" (Mich. Const. Art. VIII, Sec. 2)	*East Jackson Public Schools v. State of Michigan*, File No. 82-27983-CZ (Jackson Cty. Cir. Court)	1982			
		Milliken v. Green, 203 N.W. 2d 457 (Mich. 1972), vacated mem., 212 N.W. 2d 711 (Mich. 1973)				Yes
Montana	"The Legislature shall provide a basic system of free quality public elementary and secondary schools" (Mont. Const. Art. X, Sec. 1)	*Helena School District #1 et al. v. State of Montana et al.*, 46 St. Rep. 169 (1989)	1985	1988	1989	Yes
New Hampshire	"(I)t shall be the duty of the legislatures and magistrates, in all future periods of this government, to cherish the interest of literature and the sciences, and all seminaries and public schools" (N.H. Const. Art. 33)	*Jesseman v. New Hampshire*, Eq. No. 89-E-088 (Merrimac Cty. Sup. Ct. 1982)	1982			

(Continued)

Figure 2.1 (Continued)

State	State Education Clause	Case Name	Filed	Lower Court	Appeal	Status		Upheld	Overturned	
						State Court	U.S. Supreme Court		Education Clause	Equal Protection
New Jersey	"The legislature shall provide for the maintenance and support of a thorough and efficient system of free public schools" (N.J. Const. Art. 8, Sec. 4)	Robinson v. Cahill, 62 N.J. 473, 303 A. 2d 273, cert. denied sub. nom. Dickey v. Robinson, 414 U.S. 976, (1973)	1970	1972		1973			Yes	
		(Robinson I); after remand, 355 A. 2d 129 (1976) (Robinson II)		1975		1976			Yes	
		Abbott v. Burke, No. C-1983-80 (Sup. Ct. N.J., Chancery Div. Mercer Cty. 1982)	1981			1990			Yes	
New York	"The legislature shall provide for the maintenance and support of a system of free common schools, wherein all the children of the state may be educated" (N.Y. Const. Art. 11, Sec. 1)	Board of Education, Levittown v. Nyquist, 408 N.Y.S. 2d 606 (Nassau Cty. Sup. Ct. 1978); affd. 443 N.Y.S. 2d 843 (1982); revd. 453 N.Y.S. 2d 643 (N.Y. 1982) petition for cert. filed sub. nom. Board of Education, City School District, Rochester v. Nyquist	1974	1978	1981	1982		Yes		

State	Provision					
Ohio	"The general assembly shall make such provisions, by taxation, or otherwise, as, with the income arising from the school trust fund, will secure a thorough and efficient system of common schools throughout the state" (Ohio Const. Art. XI, Sec. 2)	*Board of Education of the City School Dist. of Cincinnati v. Walter,* 390 N.E. 2d 813 (1979), cert. denied, 444 U.S. 1015 (1980)	1976	1977	1979	Cert. den. 1980	Yes
Oklahoma	"The Legislature shall establish and maintain a system of free public schools wherein all children of the state may be educated" (Okla. Const. Art. 13, Sec. 1)	*Fair School Finance Council of Okla. v. Oklahoma* (Dist. Ct. Ok. City, No. C.J. 80-3294 1981)	1980	1982	On appeal		Yes
Oregon	"The Legislative Assembly shall provide by law for the establishment of a uniform, and general system of common schools" (Or. Const. Art. VIII, Sec. 3)	*Olsen v. State,* 554 P. 2d 139 (Or. 1976)	1972	1975	1976		Yes
Pennsylvania	"The General Assembly shall provide for the maintenance of a thorough and efficient system of public education to serve the needs of the Commonwealth" (Pa. Const. Art. 3, Sec. 14)	*Dansen v. Casey,* 484 A. 2d 415 (Pa. 1979)	1977	1978	1979		Yes
South Dakota	"(I)t shall be the duty of the legislature to establish and maintain a general and uniform system of public schools wherein tuition shall be without charge, and equally open to all; and to adopt all suitable means to secure to the people the advantages and opportunities of education" (S.D. Const. Art. VIII, Sec. 1)	*Oster v. Kneip* (S.D. Hughes Cty. Cir. Court)	1977				

(Continued)

Figure 2.1 (Continued)

State	State Education Clause	Case Name	Status						Overturned	
			Filed	Lower Court	Appeal	State Court	U.S. Supreme Court	Upheld	Education Clause	Equal Protection
Texas	"(I)t shall be the duty of the legislature of the state to establish and make suitable provision for the support and maintenance of an efficient system of public free schools" (Tex. Const. Art. VIII, Sec. 1)	San Antonio Independent School District v. Rodriguez, 411 U.S. 1, 93 S. Ct. 1278, 36 L. Ed. 2d 16 (1973)	Fed 1968	Fed 1969			1973	Yes		
Washington	"The legislature shall provide for a general and uniform system of public schools" (Wash. Const. Art. IX, Sec. 2)	Northshore v. Kinnear, 530 P. 2d 178 (Wash. 1974)	1972			1974		Yes		
		Seattle Sch. Dist. No. 1 of King County v. State, No. 81-2-1713-1 (Thurston Cty. Superior Ct. 1981)	1977 1981	1977		1978			Yes	
West Virginia	"The legislature shall provide, by general law, for a thorough and efficient system of free schools" (W. Va. Const. Art. XII, Sec. 1)	Pauley v. Kelly, 255 S. E. 2d 859 (W. Va. 1979), on remand sub. nom. Pauley v. Bailey, C.A. No. 75-126; (Cir. Ct. Kanawha Cty., W. Va., May 11, 1982)	1977	1982		1979			Yes	Yes

State	Constitutional Provision	Case							
Wisconsin	"The legislature shall provide by law for the establishment of district schools, which shall be as nearly uniform as practicable; and such schools shall be free and without charge for tuition to all children between the ages of 4 and 20 years" (Wis. Const. Art. 10, Sec. 3)	*Buse v. Smith*, 74 Wisc. 2d 650, 247 N.W. 2d 141 (1976)			1976				Yes	Yes
		Kukor v. Thompson, No. 79-CV-5252 (Dane Cty. Cir. Ct. 1982)	1979	1982						
Wyoming	"The legislature shall provide for the establishment and maintenance of a complete and uniform system of public instruction, embracing free elementary schools of every kind and grade" (Wyo. Const. Art. 7, Sec. 1)	*Washakie Co. Sch. Dist. No. One v. Herschler*, 606 P. 2d 310 (Wyo. 1980) cert. denied, 449 U.S. 824, 101 S. Ct. 86, 66 L. Ed. 2d 28 (1980)	1978	1979	1980	Cert. den. 1980			Yes	Yes

Finally, the finance system will include a greatly increased foundation program for base expenditures across all districts. And the state will limit local add-ons to an extra 30 percent, of which the first 15 percent will be "equalized" by the state through a guaranteed tax base.

If this response portends the future, school finance will shift to a standard of equal expenditure per pupil (or a standard that severely limits the degree of expenditure disparity). Indeed, the Kentucky court, in defining "efficient," stated that "each child . . . must be provided with an equal opportunity to have an adequate education. *Equality* is the key word here" (emphasis added). Further, the comprehensiveness of the overall response is a clear indication that school finance litigation and response to it will entail more than just designing a new finance formula.

The New Jersey decision in *Abbot* also suggests an evolution toward a new equal expenditure standard. Although the court decree requires only that the state raise the spending level of the poorest 28 districts, many of which are big-city districts, to the level of the wealthiest suburban districts, it will be difficult for the state to ignore the districts in the middle. Thus, if the court decree is followed, it is likely that New Jersey could—over time—implement a system focused on creating much more uniform per-pupil spending across all districts.

Finally, although the Texas decision did not explicitly focus on equal spending, the legislative response moved in this direction by raising the base spending level supported by the foundation program and adding an enhanced guaranteed tax-base second tier to ensure equal extra spending for equal extra tax efforts. These two formula adjustments should help produce more uniform per-pupil spending across Texas school districts, which was quite uniform for most districts even at the time the *Edgewood* v. *Kirby*[27] case was filed.

In short, it could be argued that recent court actions and legislative responses are beginning to move states, and perhaps the country, to a stronger focus on disparities in educational expenditures per pupil per se, i.e., to more equality of expenditures per pupil across all districts. This would represent a new reality in school finance. Both late-1970s and mid-1980s studies of school finance equity (Berne, 1988) found that per-pupil expenditure disparities had improved little, if at all.

New Issues in School Finance Litigation

An additional factor that might push the states toward more expenditure equality is the creation of national education goals. These goals set an ambitious educational agenda for the country. They suggest that preschool be made available for all three- and four-year-olds, hike expectations for student performance and shift achievement basic goals to thinking and problem solving skills, seek to make the United States first in the world in mathematics and science, and propose increasing the high school graduation rate from 75 to 90 percent.

---

[27] *Edgewood Independent School District* v. *Kirby*, No. 362516 (Travis County Dist. Ct. June 1, 1987).

States are likely to adopt these as state goals as well (National Governors Association, 1990). They will place new burdens on nearly all school districts, and most districts probably will have to increase effort as well as spending to accomplish them. Indeed, some districts may have to increase spending considerably to meet these goals. In this new era of high nationwide education objectives, moreover, states might not be willing to let local districts decide on a lesser-quality education program, as many states now do in the name of "local control." Although states could set much higher foundation or minimum expenditure levels, somehow designed to let each district meet these new education goals, the level might have to be so high that spending above it will be unaffordable. The result could be evolution toward more equal spending, albeit at a much higher level than exists on average today.

Whether this comes about is an empirical question. The point simply is that nascent trends in recent court cases, combined with a new, bold, nationwide push for students in all states to meet rigorous, high-level achievement goals, could interact with current school finance mechanisms and litigation to move states toward more equal educational expenditures per pupil.[28] Indeed, as the nation and each state agrees to conform to these high-level student performance goals, accomplishing them could become the substantive definition for what education as a fundamental right means. And the only affordable response might be a high level of uniform per-pupil expenditures.

A last issue that might influence the course of school finance litigation, as well as school finance structures themselves (Odden, 1991), is the rising popularity of interdistrict open enrollment programs. As of mid-1990, 15 states had enacted laws that let students choose to attend schools in districts outside *vouchers ?* their district of residence. Minnesota has one of the most comprehensive interdistrict choice programs. In that state, students literally can choose to attend any school in the state (as long as there are enough seats). The state moves funds around to adjust for the shifts in enrollment, but a district cannot refuse to accept a student (unless there are no seats available) and cannot charge the student any additional tuition.

This policy changes the basic school finance argument, which assumes that students can only attend the school of the district in which they live. In Minnesota, which has a high base spending level across all districts, if students are unhappy with the quality of education in their local school or any school in their district, they can choose to attend a school in another district. And money follows the child.

Although the state only partially funds transportation to the new school, and although some school districts still spend more than others, the interdistrict open enrollment policy at the minimum adds a new twist to school finance litigation. One state defense to a school finance suit filed in Minnesota is that Minnesota school districts provide choices of education philosophy, levels of funding, and school quality, and that all districts provide a uniform base of quality education. The state could argue that is all that is required. Even if

---

[28] Of course, variations for special pupil and district needs would continue.

education is a fundamental right, all students have access to a sound base education and can select from a variety of options, for practical purposes, in and around the area where their parents happen to reside. If the court rules that this choice policy obviates the standard school finance case, other states might enact similar interdistrict open enrollment programs combined with increased foundation programs that even allow districts to spend above the foundation level. Such a combined program could respond to rising political interest in educational choice and school organization, and continued political resistance to dramatically changing school finance structures.

CONCLUSION

School finance litigation is alive and well. Some predicted its slow demise in the early 1980s; however, it only went dormant and bounced back at the end of the decade. As the 1990s began, a flurry of new and far-reaching decisions were rendered, and over 20 cases were pending or planned. Standard equal protection and state education clause arguments continue as the base of most school finance challenges, but the specific issues are evolving, and new education policy agendas may continue to reshape litigation. New, ambitious nationwide and state education goals could become the substantive requirement for state education clauses, as well as the definition of education as a fundamental right under equal protection clauses. There might be movement toward (or backward to) equal expenditures per pupil and an educational needs test for school finance and state education systems. Interdistrict open enrollment programs could become a nonfiscal policy response to make traditional school finance systems constitutional. The seemingly simple days of school finance in the 1970s, when only a new school finance formula was required, seem to have passed. In the 1990s, school finance and education governance have become intertwined, in both policy debates and court cases.

—Chapter 3———————————————————

A Framework for Analyzing School Finance Equity

Chapter 1 provided several examples of fiscal inequities that have plagued state school finance systems during the twentieth century and that have been the primary focus of school finance litigation since the late 1960s. These inequities are caused in large part by local financing of public schools. Because the property tax base is distributed unevenly across school districts, districts with a low per-pupil tax base typically raise below-average revenues per pupil, even with above-average tax rates, whereas districts with a high per-pupil property tax base typically raise above-average revenues per pupil, even with below-average tax rates. But this is not the only inequity that can exist in state school finance systems.

Wise (1969) argued that the basic school finance inequity is unequal per-pupil spending per se, or, more broadly, unequal access to a uniform level of education services. Since education is a state constitutional responsibility, he argued that the state should not let education quality vary across local school districts for any reason. Education for the child should not vary because of the accident of a child's living in a rich or poor school district, or the accident of taxpayer willingness to support through local taxation either a high-, medium-, or low-quality education program. The quality of the education program, Wise argued, should be decided statewide and provided to all students on an equal basis.

There are many ways to conceptualize and define school finance equity. During the late 1970s and early 1980s, Berne and Stiefel (1984) helped bring conceptual, intellectual, and technical clarity to school finance equity discussions. Over a series of years, they produced a major contribution to the field of school finance by developing an equity framework that helped sort out the issues, and they provided the technology for calculating the degree of equity in any state's school finance structure. Although Berne and Stiefel were not the only scholars to outline a school finance equity framework (see also, for example, Wise, 1969 and 1983; Garms, 1979; Alexander, 1982), theirs is the most comprehensive and has been increasingly used by analysts to conceptualize empirical studies of the equity of state school finance structures (see, for example, Odden, 1978; Goertz, 1983; Hickrod, Chaudhari, and Hubbard, 1981; and Kearney, Chen, and Checkoway 1988).[1]

This chapter uses Berne and Stiefel's work as the basis for outlining a school finance equity framework for the 1990s. Three major additions to their work are provided. First, the school finance framework outlined in this chapter links indicators of finance equity to the developing work in educational indicators more generally (Odden, 1990a; Shavelson, McDonnell, and Oakes, 1989; Smith, 1988; Council of Chief State School Officers, 1990). There is renewed interest in improving national data bases in school finance (Forgione, 1990), enhancing interstate measures of the status of state school finance systems, and including finance and related data in broader attempts to provide indicators of the condition of the U.S. education system.[2] These efforts place the earlier attempts to define and measure school finance equity into a broader policy context in which finance indicators are part of a set of more comprehensive educational indicators.

Second, this chapter's equity framework moves beyond the use of expenditures and revenues as indicators of educational resources, examining the curriculum and instructional resources into which dollars are transformed. Although fiscal inequities have dominated the analysis of school finance for decades, dollars are used by school districts to purchase educational resources. Further, the curriculum and teaching to which students are exposed are key determinants of what they learn (McKnight et al., 1987; Schwille et al., 1982; Borg, 1980).

---

[1] Admittedly, equity has different meanings for different people depending on philosophical orientation, substantive perspective, and even political stance. The equity orientation used in this chapter is gaining prominence within school finance circles but is not the only way to approach fairness in school finance (see also Strike, 1988).

[2] In late 1989, for example, the U.S. Secretary of Education created the Educational Indicators Panel; their mission was to propose a design for a U.S. education indicator system, which would include indicators of finance and productivity.

Since a primary goal of the education system is student learning, knowledge of the equity of the distribution of the key resources most directly linked to student learning—curriculum and instruction—ought to be an express part of a comprehensive school finance equity framework. Thus, the school finance or educational resource equity framework outlined in this chapter includes key educational processes as resource variables.

Third, this chapter attempts to link school finance equity to the educational goals agreed to by the president and the 50 state governors in early 1990. Since many of the goals pertain to student achievement in key academic subjects—mathematics, science, history, geography, language arts, and writing—this chapter shows one way in which school finance equity can be reconstructed to relate to variations in student achievement. This linkage has been a long-time objective of education policy. This chapter does not resolve all of the difficult issues and questions about the causal relationship between dollars and achievement, but it does attempt to use the unequal distribution of student performance as a starting point for reconceptualizing school finance equity.

In short, this chapter provides a framework for conceptualizing and measuring school finance equity not only in dollar terms, but also in terms of curriculum, instruction, and student output. Thus, the chapter expressly attempts to link the finance side of providing education more directly to the program, or curriculum and instruction, side. Although such connections always seem to be discussed as goals, the chapter takes concrete steps to turn these elusive goals into reality.

THE SCHOOL FINANCE EQUITY FRAMEWORK IN BRIEF

Determining the equity of a state's school finance structure requires answers to four key questions:

1. For *whom* should school finance be equitable? There are two major groups to consider: children who attend the public schools, and taxpayers who pay the costs of public education. The equity issues for the respective groups are quite different. This chapter outlines the equity issues for children. Chapter 5 begins with a discussion of equity for taxpayers. [3]
2. *What* resource objects or educational services should be distributed equitably among the group of concern? The traditional answer to

---

[3] This book defines taxpayer equity solely in terms of tax equity. Berne and Stiefel (1979, 1984) discuss other, more "school finance"–related taxpayer equity issues, but these concepts have not really taken hold. Thus, this book discusses taxpayer equity in the more general public finance context of the equity of different taxes.

this question for children is dollars or revenues. But processes such as curriculum and instruction are also key educational resources. Outcomes such as student achievement also are possible objects to analyze. Deciding on the specific object is important to assessing the degree of school finance equity. Some objects could be distributed equitably, others inequitably.

3. *How* is equity to be defined? What are the specific principles used to determine whether a distribution is equitable? This chapter, following Odden, Berne, and Stiefel (1979) and Berne and Stiefel (1984), first describes three equity principles: (1) *horizontal equity,* in which all members of the group are considered equal; (2) *vertical equity,* in which legitimate differences in resource distributions among members of the group are recognized; and (3) *equal opportunity,* which identifies variables (such as property value per pupil) that should not be related to resource distribution. Because equal educational opportunity has been used in several non–school finance contexts and has several meanings, this book uses the term *fiscal neutrality.* The chapter adds an additional equity principle, *effectiveness,* which assesses the degree to which resources are used in ways that research has shown to be effective. Although the common approach to equity is to analyze whether one student or district has more or fewer resources than another, the effectiveness principle shifts the perspective to whether or not resources are deployed in research-proven effective ways. The effectiveness principle suggests that a resource inequity exists not only when insufficient resources are available, but when resources are not used in ways that produce desired impacts on student performance.

4. *How much* equity is in the system, or the specific status of equity. This component includes the statistics used to measure the degree of equity in the system.

In short, assessing school finance equity entails answering, in specific terms, four questions: who is the group, what is the object, what is the principle, and what is the statistic used to measure the degree of equity. As Berne and Stiefel (1984) demonstrate, different answers to these questions can produce different conclusions about the equity of a system. One major objective in developing and using a school finance equity framework is to help clarify why one analyst might declare a system equitable while another says it is inequitable; the reason may simply be different answers to these four key questions. In other words, there may not be a definitive answer as to whether any state's school finance system is equitable. For some groups and some objects, and under some principles and some statistics, it might be equitable; for others it might be inequitable. Using the equity framework helps to sort out the issues behind these complex conclusions.

CHILDREN'S EQUITY IN SCHOOL FINANCE

Children are just one, although probably the most important, group for whom the equity of a state's school finance system is an important policy issue. Children are a key group of concern because they are the primary "clients" of the education system: the system is designed to educate children. Further, the ability of children to compete as adults in the labor market and, ultimately, their incomes are determined significantly by what happens to them—by what they learn—in schools and classrooms. Thus, school finance equity emphasizes equity for children.

Taxpayers—both those who have children in public schools and those who do not—pay for public education services and clearly are another group for whom school finance equity is an important policy issue. The beginning sections of Chapter 5 discuss in detail taxpayer equity, in terms of the burdens various taxes place on different taxpayers.

In addition, teachers are a group for whom the equity of a state's school finance system is increasingly important. The distribution of teacher salaries, the state role in supporting minimum teacher salaries, other policies designed to promote teacher and education system productivity, and the state fiscal role in supporting teacher professionalism initiatives all are key 1990s education policy issues, and possible issues with which to assess the equity of the overall state school finance structure (Odden, 1986). Unfortunately, these issues have not received much attention and will not be discussed in this book. But as the 1990s unfold, it is likely that the equity of the school finance system as it relates to evolving teacher policy (Darling-Hammond and Berry, 1988) will become a more salient issue.

Parents are another group for whom school finance equity might be a policy issue. Especially as states enact interdistrict open enrollment policies, the impact of the overall school finance system on parents may become more important. Indeed, current school finance structures may be at odds with possible new finance structures when families can choose any school in the state for their children to attend (Odden, 1990b).

The list could expand. Nevertheless, children are the dominant group and have received the most attention in school finance. The remainder of this chapter discusses issues related to school finance equity for children.

CHILDREN'S EQUITY OBJECTS

Berne and Stiefel (1984) used three categories of children's equity objects: fiscal or physical inputs, outputs such as student achievement, and outcomes such as lifetime incomes. This chapter uses these three categories but combines the last two and adds an additional category: educational processes such as curriculum and instruction. In this way, children's school finance equity objects can easily be added to a state's overall education indicator system, for which analysts suggest measures on inputs, processes, and outcomes (Shavelson, McDonnell, and Oakes, 1989; Porter, forthcoming).

Fiscal and Physical Inputs

A wide variety of fiscal and physical inputs could be targeted for analysis as school finance equity objects. The traditional object of analysis has been some measure of educational dollars. Dollars, however, can be categorized in several ways, each of which can lead to different conclusions about the equity of the system.

First, dollars can be divided into current operating dollars and dollars for capital outlay or debt service. Analysis of current dollars and capital dollars is usually done separately. Current dollars are analyzed on an annual basis since education services need to be provided each year. Capital and debt service dollars are usually (or should be) analyzed on a multiple-year basis because schools are built only periodically, last for decades, and are paid for incrementally over several years. Other capital items, such as buses and computers, are purchased periodically and also can be used for several years.

Second, dollars can be divided into revenues and expenditures, which are quite different. Revenues are usually identified by source and type. Sources include funds from local, state, and federal governments. Types include general aid and restricted aid. General aid can be used for any educational purpose, whereas categorical or restricted aid can only be used for specific purposes, such as special education for the handicapped or special services such as transportation. Many studies analyze current unrestricted revenues from local, state, and federal sources and leave categorical or special-purpose dollars out of the analysis. Other studies just use state and local general revenues. These general revenues, it is argued, are the revenues that support the regular or base education program, which is the key issue of concern across districts. Further, the focus is on the equity of the state school finance system; thus, some claim that federal dollars should be excluded from the analysis. Others analyze total current revenues from all sources, arguing that dollars are partially fungible and that total dollars are what districts have to run the entire education program. Different revenue figures can yield different conclusions about the equity of the system.

Expenditures, which usually include dollars from all three government sources, can by analyzed on a total basis (total current operating expenditures per pupil), by function (expenditures on administration, instruction, operation and maintenance, transportation, etc.), or by program (regular, special education, compensatory education, bilingual education, etc.). Although it also would be desirable to analyze expenditures by level of education (elementary, middle high school, and high school) or by curriculum content area (mathematics, science, social studies, etc.), few states have an accounting code that allows expenditures to be tabulated across these categories.

In the medium term, however, getting data by program area is important for nationwide education policy. If the country wants to be first in the world in mathematics and science, it would be helpful to know how much is spent for these content areas, relative to other expenditures, and how spending changes over time. Second, many argue that if the education system can be successful in teaching all students at the elementary and middle school levels, high school and college education will be much easier. Most states, however, traditionally spend between 25 and 33 percent more for high school students than for elementary school students (see Chapter 8), and insufficient public money supports preschool services for poor children. Perhaps a shift of dollars already available could improve student achievement. Thus, knowing educational expenditures by level and curriculum content area likely will become a salient focus for school finance in the 1990s as the country seeks to accomplish its ambitious student performance goals.

Most school finance equity studies that use an expenditure figure rely on total current operating expenditures per pupil or instructional expenditures per pupil, largely because these figures commonly are available. But other, more detailed figures are preferred, especially expenditures by program, level, and content area. The latter are the key substantive policy issues. At any rate, different choices of dollar input variables can lead to different conclusions about the equity of the system. For example, Carroll and Park (1983), in their study of school finance equity in six school finance reform states, found a much higher degree of equity for instructional expenditures per pupil than they did for either total revenues per pupil or total current operating expenditures per pupil.

Physical objects traditionally include teacher/pupil ratios, administrative/teacher ratios, support staff/pupil ratios, numbers of books in the library, and square footage of total space or of just instructional space. The most common figures used are teacher/pupil ratios. But care should be given to defining the ratio used. The ratio of total professional staff per pupil includes professionals who do not teach in the classroom, thus implying a much smaller class size than actually exists. A classroom teacher/student ratio, i.e., the average or median number of students actually in a teacher's classroom, is the most accurate class size indicator.

Key fiscal and physical input variables to analyze. Any fiscal and physical input variable could be analyzed, but the following key variables, in per-pupil terms, are suggested. These variables have been suggested for inclusion in many educational indicator systems as well (Forgione, 1990; Catterall, 1989).

- Total revenues from local, state, and federal sources
- Total revenues from local and state sources
- Total general revenues from local and state sources, i.e., total state and local revenues minus restricted revenues (categorical aids)
- Total current operating expenditures

- Total instructional expenditures
- Total expenditures for the regular program, if available
- Average student/classroom teacher ratio

Educational Process Variables [4]

School finance has generally ignored measures of the resources into which dollars are transformed, except for measures of physical objects. But in an era of national education goals when the policy focus has shifted from inputs to outputs, or to what students know and are able to do, analysis of resources more closely related to student learning than dollars becomes important in order for resource equity analysis to be policy-relevant. Thus, school finance analysis, particularly equity analysis, needs to gather and analyze information on educational process variables as a further step in increasing the substantive depth of educational resource analysis.

Porter (forthcoming) describes how district and school organizational, curriculum, and instructional variables can be conceptualized and collected for an educational indicators system. School finance analysts can draw from Porter's work to identify several education process variables—the educational resources that dollars purchase—that could become part of equity analyses. Three categories of variables could be used.

First would be *district* indicators of school organization, curriculum, and instruction. Specific variables on school organization could include school and class size, grade level organization, and indicators of teacher empowerment (Lieberman, 1988) and site-based management (Clune and White, 1988)—all current policy issues, many of which are related to school effectiveness. Variables taken from the effective school literature also could be included. Variables for curriculum would emphasize the *intended* curriculum,[5] such as time allocated, topics to be covered by content areas, specific areas within different topics, and course-specific resources (such as laboratory space and equipment for science, or degree of manipulative materials for new mathematics). Variables for instructional quality could include measures of teacher quality, such as number of college credits in subject area taught, number of hours in staff development to improve pedagogy, district-funded opportunities to engage in professional development, and, in the future, number of teachers with national board certification (Baratz-Snowden, 1990).

Given the importance to student learning of exposure to curriculum, measures of the *enacted* curriculum in schools and classrooms might even be more important than district measures of the intended curriculum. Porter (forthcom-

---

[4] This section draws heavily from Porter (forthcoming).

[5] The "intended" curriculum is the curriculum—subject areas, topics, and pedagogical strategies—that is in district/school formal policy, including curriculum guidelines. It is the curriculum that "should" be implemented. The "enacted" curriculum consists of the subjects, topics, and instruction actually delivered in classrooms.

ing) suggests that measures of the enacted curriculum would be, by content area, topics actually taught and areas within topics actually taught, including length of time devoted to that instruction.

Finally, Porter suggests gathering data on actual instructional practices, arguing that there is a growing research base on good teaching (Porter and Brophy, 1988; Rosenshine and Stevens, 1986). He also suggests gathering data on more general dimensions of teaching, such as the types of knowledge teachers expect students to learn, for example, skills vs. application, understanding concepts vs. following rules or doing algorithms, solving routine vs. novel problems, and interpreting data. McDonnell et al. (1990) provide even more detailed suggestions for gathering coursework indicators for the enacted curriculum.

In short, a school finance equity framework for the 1990s should include a variety of district, school, and classroom measures of curriculum and instruction, i.e., measures of school processes that are most directly linked to student learning. Porter (forthcoming) and McDonnell et al. (1990) argue that, although observation of teachers is the most accurate way to gather such data, for purposes of developing educational indicator systems, surveys and questionnaires could be used to gather key data. They further argue that such data can be gathered on a sample basis, with the sampling size large enough to allow, just as school finance analysis has traditionally allowed, analysis by geographic location (city, suburb, and rural) as well as by academic track (regular, general, special education, compensatory education, etc.), sex, race, level of schooling (K–5, 6–8, 9–12), and subject matter, i.e., mathematics, science, language arts (including reading at the elementary levels), and history/social science.

Most of these variables have not been isolated, but many have, and data for several others might be readily available in some states. Further, as states and the country create more comprehensive educational indicator systems, more of these curriculum and instructional variables will be identified, and it will be easier to include them in analyses of the equity of the distribution of educational resources.

Key educational processes to analyze. Porter argues that the most important curriculum and instruction indicators are those that measure the enacted curriculum, i.e., the curriculum actually taught to students. He suggests that states with limited resources should begin to collect those data and to focus such collection on mathematics and English, subjects key to student performance in all other content areas. But states might want to collect such data for *all* key content areas. For each of the education levels of grades K–5, 6–8, and 9–12, he suggests gathering data on

- The general nature of instruction
- Types of knowledge emphasized (skills vs. application, concepts vs. algorithms, routine vs. novel problems)

- Subject topics taught, including length of time for each topic, which in mathematics would include algebra, geometry, probability, statistics, and trigonometry, and which in English would include writing
- Areas within each of the subject topics, including length of time for each subtopic

In many states, similar content measures of the intended curriculum would be determined through district questionnaires, and measures of school organization and school and classroom size would be available through state computerized data bases.

Achievement or Outcome Variables

The category of outputs includes the results of the education process—student achievement or performance in the short run, and participation in the labor market, family, and civic affairs in the long run. Berne and Stiefel (1984) discuss longer-term outcomes, such as an individual's income, job, occupational status, and ability to compete in the labor market, but the connections between these outcomes and K–12 schooling are somewhat tenuous, since numerous other factors intervene, which will not be discussed in this book. Showing connections between K–12 schooling and longer-term outcomes should be a research topic. As the connections are developed, analysis of the outcomes and their linkage to the distribution of school resources could be included in school finance equity analyses.

Shorter-term education system outcome variables include student performance, or, more specifically, student achievement. Such variables could include student achievement in different content areas—mathematics, science, etc.—or more global achievement measures such as the overall score from an achievement test. High school graduation rates are also an important output measure. Number of academic courses taken is another outcome indicator that is being collected in several states. Finally, postsecondary attendance rates are outcome measures that indicate behavior in the year immediately following high school graduation.

Several issues arise in deciding how to measure these variables. The most debated are those related to student achievement. Traditionally, norm-referenced measures of student achievement were used. These measures can be developed at different grade levels and in different content areas, but they indicate only how an individual compares to other individuals at the same age or grade; they do not indicate the degree to which a student knows a certain content area. Further, they tend to focus more on basic skills than on thinking and problem solving skills.

Norm-referenced measures of student achievement are gradually being replaced by criterion-referenced measures, which indicate what a student knows in a certain content area. California, Minnesota, Connecticut, and Michigan are examples of states with such achievement measures. In California and Connecticut, moreover, these measures are available at the school level. Further, as tests move from multiple-choice to actual student performance assessments, they will be able to indicate not only what students know but also what they can do, e.g., whether they can conduct a laboratory experience, solve multiple-step mathematics problems, or write a persuasive paragraph. Trends indicate that performance or "authentic" assessments are likely to replace norm-referenced testing during the 1990s in many schools, districts, and states. As these sophisticated measures of student achievement become available, they should be the measures used in a school finance equity analysis.

[handwritten margin note: Edison slowly making the switch to authentic assessment]

Once the specific measures of student achievement have been selected, there are additional issues of how to use those measures. Traditionally, the debate has been whether to compare the actual measures and argue that resources should be allocated to produce equal achievement, or to compare gains in student achievement and argue that student ability varies, so resources should be used to produce equal gains in achievement.

A new way to present achievement data has been suggested for monitoring nationwide and state progress in achieving the country's educational goals. This is to identify the percent of students who should be performing at different levels on criterion-referenced assessments, such as basic, proficient, and advanced levels. The argument is that the country needs a workforce with a certain level of absolute skills, and measures of student performance should indicate the degree to which the educational system produces students, on average, with that skill level. If states adopt this strategy, and several seem to be moving in that direction, wide variations in such achievement could reveal economic, sex, or other factors related to variations in student performance, which could lead either to additional adjustments in resource allocation to compensate for different needs (see Chapter 8) or to reallocation to ensure that all schools, districts, and states meet the target levels.

Key student achievement measures to analyze. There are short-term and medium-term measures of student performance that should be included in school finance analyses. In general, the preference in the short term is for criterion-referenced measures of achievement and, in the medium term, measures of actual student performance. The following measures are suggested:

- High school graduation rate
- Postsecondary attendance rate
- In the short term, percent correct on criterion-referenced tests of student achievement in mathematics, science, language arts (including reading in elementary grades), history, and geography at the elementary, middle, and high school levels
- In the medium term, percent scoring at basic, proficient, and advanced levels in mathematics, science, language arts (including reading in elementary grades), history, and geography at grades 4, 8, and 12, the

grades tested by the National Assessment of Education Progress,[6] which is very likely to be the student achievement assessment used to measure progress on national education goals

CHILDREN'S EQUITY PRINCIPLES

Once an object has been selected for measurement, an approach to assessing equity needs to be determined. This entails selection of an equity principle. There are four different but related children's equity principles:

- Horizontal equity
- Vertical equity
- Fiscal neutrality
- Effectiveness.

This section discusses several issues surrounding each of these principles.

Horizontal Equity

The horizontal equity principle is similar to the horizontal principle in public finance; indeed, Berne and Stiefel (1984) used traditional public finance principles and concepts initially in the design of their school finance equity framework. Horizontal equity provides that students who are alike should be treated equally. "Equal treatment of equals" reflects the horizontal equity principle. Horizontal equity requires that all students receive equal shares of an object, such as total local and state general revenues, total current operating expenditures, instructional expenditures, instruction in the intended curriculum, focus on thinking and problem solving, and scores on student criterion-referenced assessments.

When horizontal equity is used, one assumes that all students are alike. Although this is a crude assumption at best, it is implicit in the argument that spending should be equal across school districts or schools. Thus, horizontal equity has been widely used in school finance.

The principle of horizontal equity is best used for subgroups of students— all elementary students in the regular program, all high school students in an academic program, or all students performing below the first quartile on a student achievement measure. For carefully selected subgroups of students, it is reasonable to require equal distribution of resources, or some other object selected for equity analysis. Of course, care must be taken to create a legitimate subgroup of students, for which homogeneity claims are accurate.

[6] The National Assessment of Educational Progress (NAEP) is a federally funded project that obtains indicators of student performance in various subject areas for grades 4, 8, and 12. See Mullis, Owen, and Phillips (1990).

Assessing the degree of horizontal equity entails measuring inequality or dispersion. Such statistics are univariate, i.e., they measure aspects of the distribution of one variable, specifically, the object chosen for analysis. Various statistics and their properties are discussed later in this chapter.

Vertical Equity

Vertical equity specifically recognizes differences among children and addresses the education imperative that some students deserve or need more services than others.[7] "Unequal treatment of unequals" is the traditional way to express the vertical equity principle in public finance. This phrase means that in some circumstances or for some reasons it is acceptable to treat students differently, or to provide more dollars and services to some students (or districts) than to others. A key step in vertical equity is to identify the characteristics that legitimately can be used as the base for distributing more of the specific object selected. Three categories can be identified: characteristics of children, characteristics of districts, and characteristics of programs.

Characteristics of children that could lead to the provision of more resources include physical or mental handicaps, low achievement, and limited English proficiency. It is generally accepted in this country, and around the world, that students with these characteristics need additional educational services to perform adequately in school. More controversy surrounds the characteristic of gifted and talented. Some argue that such students learn more from regular instruction and do not need additional resources; others argue that the best and brightest should be given some measure of extra services.

District characteristics that could lead to provision of more resources include prices, scale economies, transportation, energy costs, and enrollment growth. As Chapter 8 shows, some districts face higher prices than others; they need more money simply to purchase the same level of resources as other districts. Some districts face higher costs because of features related to their very small size, such as a one-room school in a sparsely populated rural area, or factors related to a large size, as in most large-city school districts. Although size adjustments can be controversial—some argue that small districts should be consolidated and large districts "broken up"—differential size can be a legitimate basis for allocating some districts more resources than others. Finally, transportation costs vary widely across districts. Geographically sparse districts must transport students long distances and thus face higher per-pupil transportation costs. Many big-city districts must bus for racial desegregation. States recognize these different district circumstances by allocating additional funds, generally to be used only for a specified service.

Some programs also cost more than others. For example, vocational education, laboratory science, bilingual education, and small classes in specialized,

---

[7] Chapter 8 discusses how adjustments can be made in school finance formulas to recognize vertical equity issues.

advanced topics, tend to cost more than regular programs. State and district decisions to provide these programs can be a legitimate reason for allocating additional resources for some students than for others.

Although there is general agreement that additional funds should be provided in most of these circumstances, controversy surrounds other school and student distinctions. For example, differential treatment on the basis of race or sex is generally viewed as illegitimate. More controversy exists over whether, in the short to medium term, additional funds should be provided on the basis of race to foster desegregation or on the basis of sex to foster greater female participation in school athletics and in mathematics and science. Also controversial are issues about whether cost differences due to grade level (see Chapter 8), urbaness, or municipal overburden (see Chapter 2) should be considered.

In school finance, it is generally agreed that additional availability of resources should not be based on factors related to fiscal capacity, such as property value per pupil or household income. More controversy surrounds tax rates as a legitimate reason for resource variation. Those who support "local control" argue that higher local tax rates are a legitimate reason for having more resources; others argue that, from a child perspective, educational resources should not vary because of local taxpayer preference for education.

In short, vertical equity, although simple on the surface, is controversial in its implementation. There is substantial agreement on some rationales for providing more resources to some students or districts and substantial disagreement on others. Thus, implementation of vertical equity entails making significant value and political judgments, many of which have no bottom-line consensus.

Assessing vertical equity.   There are two major ways to assess vertical equity. The first is to weight all students who need extra services and then conduct a horizontal equity analysis using the number of "weighted pupils" as the pupil measure. This approach combines vertical and horizontal equity into a joint analysis. Vertical equity is reflected in the weights; with the factors that can lead to different resource levels recognized and appropriate adjustments made in resource distribution, equality of resources per weighted child indicates the degree of resource equity.

This approach can be used only when good data are available to quantify the degree to which students with different needs require different levels of resources. This approach is strengthened if some independent analysis is made of the weights themselves, to assess whether they accurately represent the degree of extra services needed. It is more valid when the different weights have been calculated relative to the statewide average expenditure per pupil.

Alternatively, categorical revenues for extra services can be eliminated and analysis conducted just for general revenues. This approach assesses the degree of equality of the base program for all students but essentially skirts analysis of vertical equity.

If price differences are part of the state aid formula, the equity analysis should be conducted with price-adjusted dollars, not with nominal dollars, which is the usual approach taken (Barro, 1989). Further, all dollars should be price-adjusted, not just those that might be affected by a state formula price factor.

Fiscal Neutrality

The fiscal neutrality principle addresses traditional school finance issues stating that resources or other educational objects should not vary with local fiscal capacity as measured by property wealth per pupil, property value per pupil, household income, or other measure. This equity principle derives from the standard fiscal disparities that have plagued state school finance structures throughout the twentieth century and directly relates to the legal standard of fiscal neutrality used in most school finance court cases.

Assessing the degree of fiscal neutrality entails analyzing the relationship between two variables: the object chosen and the measure chosen to analyze resource differences. Traditionally, fiscal neutrality assesses the relationship between current operating expenditures per pupil and property wealth per pupil, or local and state general revenues per pupil and property wealth per pupil. But analysis of the relationship between any object discussed here and any measure of fiscal capacity reflects analysis according to the fiscal neutrality principle. Analyzing fiscal neutrality is different from analyzing horizontal or vertical equity, because fiscal neutrality requires at least two variables and uses bivariate or multivariate analysis, whereas the others require only one variable and use univariate analysis.

Effectiveness

Effectiveness was not included in Berne and Stiefel's (1984) equity framework and thus is an additional principle with which to judge the fairness, or equity, of a state's school finance system. Indeed, this principle could constitute a way to assess the equity (and effectiveness) of the state's overall education system, but discussion here will focus only on its school finance implications.

One rationale for an effectiveness principle is that current comparisons assume that more resources reflect greater quality, and greater quality reflects greater effectiveness. Challenges to both of these assumptions can be made. The purpose here is not to resolve the issues about the linkages among resources, education quality, and school effectiveness. The goal is to identify conceptually how the equity of the distribution of educational resources can be analyzed within an effectiveness framework, and to identify the types of new knowledge needed to engage in this analysis.

Indeed, this approach ultimately is what policymakers want. They want to know how much money is needed and how it should be used to accomplish specified educational goals. Quantifying the degree to which resources are or are not equally distributed, the focus of school finance equity analysis in the past, is interesting but does not address this more substantive and complex policy concern.

How would an effectiveness principle work in assessing the equity of the finance or resource structure? Assume, for a group of students with certain characteristics, that one could specify a level and use of dollars (across programs, curriculum, and instruction resources) that would produce a certain degree of student performance or a desired percentage distribution of achievement at basic, proficient, and advanced levels. Equity would then be defined as the degree to which other schools with similar students had that level of resources *and* used them to provide the same types of programs, curriculum, and instructional resources. Divergence from this level and use of dollars would constitute an inequity. This approach incorporates the more complex issues of how resources are used, in addition to the level of resources needed.

Obviously, this equity principle cannot be implemented with current knowledge. As Chapter 10 shows, not much is known about how dollars are used. There is some information on use across educational functions, but very little about use across educational programs. Further, even less is known about use across curriculum and instructional variables, as discussed earlier in this chapter, especially at the school and classroom levels. Finally, even if there were information on these use patterns, it needs to be analyzed with respect to impact on student performance in order to produce data on the level and use of educational resources needed to produce a desired range of student achievement.

In short, an effectiveness criterion for school finance equity analysis is conceptually desirable but cannot be implemented currently. Nevertheless, as the nation moves toward education goals that stress desired levels of student achievement and seeks to raise and use funds to produce that range of achievement, the effectiveness issue should become part of school finance analysis since the policy community will want answers to these questions. Perhaps the newly funded federal Education Finance and Productivity Center will help fill the information gaps in these important areas during the first half of the 1990s.

MEASURES OF SCHOOL FINANCE EQUITY

Selecting measures, or statistics, to determine quantitatively the degree of equity—once an object and a principle have been selected—involves several additional decisions, many of which also have value judgments associated with them. This section first discusses the unit of analysis and then discusses horizontal and fiscal neutrality statistical measures.[8]

---

[8] For additional and technical definitions and more detailed analyses of the various statistics, see Berne and Stiefel (1984).

Unit of Analysis

The unit of analysis is a conundrum in school finance equity analysis, especially if the group of concern is children. Ideally, what is needed is a measure of the object for each individual child. Unfortunately, most fiscal data are not collected on individual children. In the medium term, however, educational process and achievement data are likely to be collected on an individual student basis. Thus, we will not need to use such data from other levels—classroom, school, or district—and we will assume it pertains equally to individuals within a given level.

However, nearly all dollar and fiscal resource data are available only on a district or, at best, school basis. The challenge is to "convert" these data to the individual child. Of course, there is no perfect way to make this conversion. But if the analysis is conducted on a district basis, each district, regardless of size, is treated as one observation. Thus, in New York, for example, New York City, with a million students, would affect the statistical findings exactly as much as a small, rural district with only 100 students. That simply does not make sense, although for years analyses of school finance systems have used the district as the unit.

The usual and recommended approach is to "weight" the figure for each district or school by the number of students in it.[9] This procedure would give New York City more impact on the analysis than the district with only a few students. This approach also indicates more accurately how the overall resource distribution system affects students. It makes the assumption that all students within a district or school receive the level of resources indicated by the district or school measure. This assumption is somewhat bold, but more than 25 years of experience with federal Title I and Chapter 1 regulations requiring districts to distribute resources equally among all schools and students make it palatable.[10]

This should not be confused with the "weight" discussed earlier and in Chapter 8 that reflects differences in student need. Both weights should be considered and addressed separately in equity analyses.

Horizontal Equity

Numerous statistical measures can be used to assess the degree of equality for a single variable, such as expenditures per pupil in school finance. Berne and Stiefel (1984) identify several and analyze their various properties. Six statistical measures will be discussed here, although many more are discussed by Berne and Stiefel.

Range. The range is the difference between the values of the largest and smallest observations. The larger the range, the greater the inequality. This

[9] This is simple to do in most statistical packages.
[10] In analyses that group districts or students into categories such as deciles, this approach requires that each category have about the same number of students. This approach is taken in Chapter 7.

statistic indicates the maximum difference in the distribution of a variable among students in a state. This is a disadvantage in that it indicates the difference between only two observations, the top and the bottom. The fact is that there are a few outlier districts in every state—some very poor, low-property-wealth, low-income rural districts, and some very wealthy districts that might have a nuclear power plant or oil wells and few students. These districts are anomalies; they usually do not reflect common circumstances.

The range does not indicate the degree of equality or inequality for any of the other observations and thus is a poor indicator for assessing the degree of equity of the *system*. Furthermore, the range increases with inflation. As inflation occurs and all other structural variables remain the same, the range increases. Indeed, a possible reason for the use of this statistic in some school finance court cases is that each year the range generally increases, and an increasing range indicates a system with increasing inequality. Nevertheless, although it is used extensively and routinely and shows the maximum degree of inequality in a distribution, the range has several detracting features and is not a preferred univariate statistic.

Restricted range.   The restricted range is the difference between an observation close to the top and an observation close to the bottom, such as the difference between the 5th and 95th percentiles or the 10th and 90th percentiles. The restricted range generally avoids the problem of outliers, but it still measures the degree of inequality between just two observations, not in the overall system. Further, like the range, the restricted range increases (i.e., worsens) with inflation, even if all other characteristics of the finance system remain the same. If a range statistic is to be used, the restricted range is preferred to the unrestricted range, but neither is a good indicator of the equality of the distribution of the object for the entire education system.

Federal range ratio.   The federal range ratio is the difference between the values of the observations at the 95th percentile and the 5th percentile, divided by the value at the 5th percentile. In percentage terms, it indicates how much larger the observation at the 95th percentile is than the observation at the 5th percentile. Its shortcomings as well as strengths are nearly the same as those for the restricted range, but since it is expressed in ratio terms, the federal range ratio does not change with inflation. As such, it probably is an acceptable range statistic. It is currently used in federal education finance policy as part of the federal government's Impact Aid Program.

Coefficient of variation.   The coefficient of variation is the standard deviation divided by the mean (i.e., the average of the data sample); it can be expressed in decimal or percent form. Its value ranges from 0 to 1 or, in percentage terms, from 0 to 100. A coefficient of variation of 0 indicates that the object is distributed uniformly among all children.

The coefficient of variation indicates the percent of variation about the mean. For example, a coefficient of 10 percent (or .1) indicates that two-thirds of the observations have a value within one standard deviation of the mean, i.e., 10 percent above or below the value of the average, and that 95 percent of the observations have a value within two standard deviations of the average, i.e., 20 percent above or below the mean.[11]

The coefficient of variation is a statistic that includes all values of a data set, unlike range statistics, which include only selected values. Further, the coefficient of variation does not change with inflation—an attractive characteristic. Thus, if the structural properties of a school finance system remain constant but all economic and dollar variables rise with inflation, the coefficient of variation would remain the same, indicating—correctly—that the equity of the system had not changed. The coefficient of variation is also easy to understand. Because of these features, the coefficient of variation is used increasingly by analysts.

Another issue, however, is determining the value that indicates an equitable or fair distribution of school funds. Determining a standard for the coefficient of variation is a value judgment. Berne and Stiefel (1984) suggest a variety of ways to determine such a standard. The key distinction is whether to use a relative standard, which would compare districts in the top, middle, and bottom quartiles, or an absolute standard, which would establish a cutoff point for determining equity. The problem with a relative standard is that some observations are always at the bottom, no matter how small the degree of inequality. An absolute standard provides a cutoff point, which separates equitable from inequitable resource distribution patterns. It is difficult to determine an absolute standard. Nevertheless, an absolute standard of about 10 percent for the coefficient of variation is generally used in this text. This is a tough standard; few states have a coefficient of variation for per-pupil revenue below 10 percent.

Standard setting is a value and political issue; different states and different analysts might reasonably determine different levels for an acceptable coefficient of variation.

Gini coefficient.   The Gini coefficient is a statistic taken from economists' measures of income inequality. To determine the Gini coefficient, a graph is made by plotting the cumulative measure of the object as a percent of the total value on the vertical axis, and the number of observations, as a percentage, on the horizontal axis. The resulting graph indicates the degree to which the object is distributed equally to children at various percentiles; put differently, the graph indicates the degree to which children at different percentiles have the same amount of the object. If the object is perfectly distributed, the Gini graph will be a straight 45° line. If the object is not perfectly distributed, the Gini graph will be a concave curve below that line. In school finance, the measure on the

---

[11] These comments assume a normal distribution.

vertical axis is typically the cumulative percentage of school district expenditures, and the measure on the horizontal axis is typically percent of students enrolled in the state, as shown in Figure 3.1.

The Gini coefficient is the area between the curve and the 45° line, divided by the area under the 45° line. Its value ranges from 0 to 1, with a completely equitable distribution occuring when the index equals 0. Most values in school finance are in the .1 to .2 range. The Gini coefficient includes all observations and is insensitive to inflation.

The Gini coefficient is hard to understand. What does it mean when the area between the Gini curve and the 45° line—even in a system with what most would call large differences in expenditures or revenues per pupil—is .1 or very close to 0? A value close to 0 suggests equality, but the system may, in school finance terms, be quite unequal. Nevertheless, the Gini coefficient is a popular horizontal equity statistic in school finance. A standard for it has not been set, although a value below .1 is desirable. But the smaller the Gini coefficient, the more equal the distribution of the object.

McLoone index.   The McLoone index is a statistic unique to school finance, created by and named after an economics professor at the University of Maryland, Eugene McLoone. The McLoone index was created to provide an equity measure for the bottom part of a distribution, i.e., to indicate the degree of equality only for observations below the 50th percentile. Since the American political culture often shows more interest in the condition of those at the bottom, the McLoone index is a statistic that reflects that perspective.

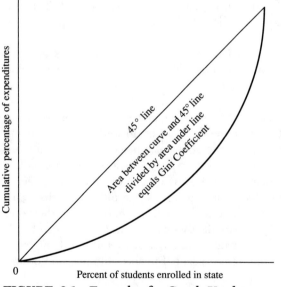

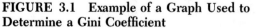

FIGURE 3.1   Example of a Graph Used to Determine a Gini Coefficient

Technically, the McLoone index is the ratio of the sum of the values of all observations below the 50th percentile (or median) to the corresponding sum if all observations had the value of the median. It ranges in value from 0 to 1, with 1 indicating perfect equality.[12] The value of the McLoone index for most school finance data sets is in the .7 to .95 range. Again, a standard has not been set for a "good" McLoone index, but one higher than .9 is desirable.

Berne and Stiefel (1984) analyze other standard statistics that are sensitive to changes in the bottom half of the distribution, but they are complex and difficult to understand by policymakers. Because the McLoone index is a measure of the equity of the distribution for the bottom half and is more straightforward, it has become popular in school finance and is included in many school finance equity analyses.

Fiscal Neutrality

To measure the degree of fiscal neutrality, statistics that indicate the relationship between two variables are needed. Two have been increasingly used in school finance:

- The correlation coefficient
- The elasticity calculated from a simple one-variable regression

For both statistics, measures of two variables are needed: (1) the measure of fiscal capacity, such as property value per pupil; and (2) the measure for the object of concern, such as current operating expenditures per pupil. Both fiscal neutrality statistics indicate whether the educational object is a function of some variable to which it should not be related, such as the local tax base.

The simple correlation is a statistic that indicates the degree to which there is a linear relationship between two variables (i.e., as one variable increases, the other increases or decreases). It ranges in value between -1 and 1. A value of 1 or close to 1 indicates a positive relationship—for example, as property wealth increases, so do expenditures per pupil. A negative correlation indicates that as one variable rises, the other falls; it indicates an inverse relationship between the two variables. In school finance, there is usually a negative correlation between state aid per pupil and property wealth per pupil, indicating that state aid flows inversely to wealth, that the poorer the district, the greater the state aid. A correlation coefficient of 0 indicates no linear relationship between the two variables.

---

[12] A value of 1 for the McLoone index indicates that per-pupil expenditures in the lowest-spending districts containing 50% of the state's children is equal. A value of less than 1 implies that, among the low-spending districts with that 50% of schoolchildren, expenditures vary. The smaller the McLoone index, the larger the spending differential among the low-spending districts.

Whereas a correlation coefficient indicates whether or not there is a linear relationship between two variables, the elasticity indicates the magnitude or policy importance of that relationship. For example, expenditures and wealth could be strongly related, but if a tenfold increase in property wealth resulted in only a small increase in revenues, one could argue that the magnitude of the relationship was not of policy significance.

Technically, the elasticity indicates the percent change in one variable, such as expenditures per pupil, relative to a 1 percent change in another variable, such as property value per pupil. It is a statistic that ranges in value from 0 to any positive number. In school finance, an elasticity of 1 indicates that spending increases, in percentage terms, at the same rate as property wealth. Elasticities far below 0.5 indicate that local property wealth does not have a major relationship to spending differences.

The simple elasticity between a dollar object such as expenditures per pupil and property wealth per pupil can be calculated using the slope of the simple linear regression of expenditures on wealth; the elasticity equals the slope (the regression coefficient for wealth) times the ratio of the mean value of property wealth per child to the mean value of expenditures per child.

It often is wise to assess the correlation coefficient and elasticity jointly. If the correlation is high and the elasticity is low, there is a relationship between the two variables—fiscal neutrality does not hold—but the relationship is not of policy importance. On the other hand, if the correlation is low and the elasticity high, even the tenuous link might have policy significance. If both the correlation coefficient and elasticity are high, then fiscal neutrality clearly does not exist: the two variables are linked, and the magnitude of the link is strong.

Berne and Stiefel (1984) discuss other relationship statistics for fiscal neutrality. Further, more complex econometric methods can be used to quantify the relationship between educational objects such as revenues per pupil and (1) property wealth, (2) the composition of the local property tax base (residential, commercial, and industrial property), and (3) household income (see Chapter 4; Ladd, 1975; Adams and Odden, 1981).

Effectiveness

Statistical approaches for quantifying the degree of divergence from effectiveness criteria have not yet been developed. The focus today is to identify effective uses of education dollars at district and school levels, which constitutes a major research agenda. If such information on effective use is known, percentage differences from those use patterns can be used to identify divergence between less effective districts and schools and more effective practices.

Figure 3.2 summarizes the equity framework in chart form, and Figure 3.3 provides a summary of the statistics used to measure the degree of equity. Both charts portray the key aspects of the framework and important statistics, but there is a substantial number of related issues, many of which this chapter has attempted to discuss.

STUDIES OF SCHOOL FINANCE EQUITY

The Berne and Stiefel equity framework has come to dominate empirical analyses of school finance equity (see, for example, Goertz, 1983; Hickrod, Chaudhari, and Hubbard, 1981; and Kearney, Chen, and Checkoway, 1988). Further, during the 1970s and 1980s that framework was used in four different studies of the status of school finance equity across the 50 states (Brown et al., 1977; Odden, Berne, and Stiefel, 1979; Odden and Augenblick, 1981; Schwartz and Moskowitz, 1988). These studies all referred directly to the equity framework and generally used the statistics discussed here.

The findings were interesting. The Brown et al. study, using a 50-state sample, found that expenditure disparities actually increased nationwide during the 1970–75 time period. Further analysis, however, showed that, for the early 1970s school finance reform states, expenditure disparities might have increased more had the states not changed their school finance systems. The Odden, Berne, and Stiefel study, using data from only 35 states, showed that several school finance reform states improved both horizontal equity and fiscal neutrality over a multiple-year period during the mid-1970s. The Odden and Augenblick study used 1977 NCES data for all 50 states and found that state school finance equity ratings changed depending on the equity object selected and the statistic used. Finally, the Schwartz and Moskowitz study compared 50-state data for the years 1976–77 and 1985–85 and concluded that school finance fiscal equity had stayed, on average, about the same for both horizontal and fiscal neutrality principles and for several different statistics (primarily the ones discussed here).

These findings led Berne (1988) to conclude that school finance equity nationwide worsened somewhat during the early 1970s but then stayed about the same from the mid-1970s to mid-1980s. But a study published in the early 1990s (Wycoff, forthcoming) concluded that between 1980 and 1987, horizontal equity had improved in the majority of states—a striking reversal of the findings on horizontal equity during most of the 1970s and 1980s. Whether this trend continues will be an empirical issue that, it is hoped, will be analyzed in sophisticated ways during this decade.

Further, Berne and Stiefel revisited the conceptual framework they developed, and they argued, as this chapter has argued, that it should be broadened to include throughputs, outputs, and outcomes, such as the curriculum, instruction, and student achievement measures outlined in this chapter (Berne and Stiefel, 1990). They also argued that most school finance equity reports had not yet incorporated the broad elements of the equity framework into their analyses, suggesting that school finance equity analyses could continue to improve dramatically during the 1990s.

FIGURE 3.2   School Finance Equity Framework: Summary and Examples of Variables

Factor	Components	Variables and Statistics
Group (who)	Children Taxpayers Teachers Parents	District value weighted by the number of students
Objects (what)	Inputs Fiscal (per pupil)	Total revenues from local, state, and federal sources Total revenues from local and state sources Total general revenues from local and state sources Total current operating expenditures Total instructional expenditures Total expenditures for the regular programs Average student/classroom teacher ratio
	Physical	
	Educational processes	General nature of instruction Types of knowledge emphasized Subject topics taught, including length of time Areas within subject topics, including length of time
	Outcome (student achievement)	High school graduation rate Postsecondary attendance rate Percent correct on criterion-referenced measures Percent scoring at basic, proficient, and advanced levels by content area

Principles (how)	Horizontal equity	Equal treatment of equals: Equal distribution of resources
	Vertical equity	Unequal treatment of unequals: Legitimate needs for: Children (handicaps, low achievement, limited English) Districts (price, size, transportation, enrollment growth) Programs (voc ed, lab science, advanced topics)
	Fiscal neutrality	Linear relationship between object and fiscal capacity variable Magnitude of the relationship
	Effectiveness	Effective use of education dollars at district/school level
Statistics (how much)	Horizontal equity	Range Restricted range Federal range ratio Coefficient of variation Gini coefficient McLoone index
	Vertical equity	Weighted pupils for needs Elimination of categorical revenues in the analysis Price-adjusted dollars
	Fiscal Neutrality	Correlation coefficient Elasticity
	Effectiveness	Not developed

FIGURE 3.3 Assessing Equity Statistics

Statistic	Calculation	Value	Other Attributes	Overall Evaluation
Range	Subtract value of highest observation from that of lowest observation	Maximum difference in observations; the larger the range, the greater the inequity	Based on only two observations, highest and lowest Can reflect anomalies Sensitive to inflation	Poor
Federal range ratio	Difference between observations of 95th and 5th percentiles, divided by value of 5th percentile	Ratio of the range between 95th and 5th percentile observations; ranges from 0 to any positive number	Based on only two observations Not sensitive to inflation	A good range statistic
Coefficient of variation	Standard deviation divided by the mean	Ranges from 0 to 1, or 0% to 100% with 0 indicating equal distribution; equitable if CV less than .1	Includes all values Does not change with inflation	Good
McLoone index	Ratio of sum of all observations below median (50th percentile) to sum if all observations had value of median	Ranges from 0 to 1, 1 indicating perfect equality; most school finance data sets are between .7 and .95; .9 is desirable	Compares bottom half of the districts to the median (50th percentile)	Good; sensitive to bottom half of distribution

Gini coefficient	Area of the graph between Gini curve and 45° line divided by area under 45° line	Ranges from 0 to 1; value close to 0 suggests equality, but in school finance values usually are greater than .6	Indicates degree to which children at different percentiles have same amount of the object Includes all observations Insensitive to inflation	Complicated, but a good statistic
Correlation coefficient	Measure of linear relationship between two variables	Ranges from -1 to $+1$; values close to 0 indicate no relationship; values closer to -1 or $+1$ indicate a strong negative or positive relationship	Includes all observations Insentive to inflation Not good for indicating a nonlinear relationship	Good for indicating existence of relationship, but not magnitude of relationship
Elasticity	Ratio of percent increase in one variable to percent increase in another	Ranges from 0 to any positive number; can exceed 1, with numbers greater than or equal to 1 indicating an elastic relationship	Includes all observations Insensitive to inflation	Good for indicating the magnitude of the relationship. If correlation is low and elasticity is high, there is an important link between the two variables

Chapter 4

Fiscal Federalism and Intergovernmental Grants

Chapter 1 showed that U.S. education financing is achieved through the efforts of all three levels of government: local school districts, each of the 50 states, and the federal government. Indeed, the general pattern for financing public services in this country entails contributions from all three governments. This pattern of multiple levels of government finance is known as fiscal federalism.[1]

This chapter discusses several aspects of the fiscal federalism approach to school financing. The first section discusses general advantages of this approach to financing government services, specifically, school districts. In a federal structure, upper-level governments use two approaches—mandates and intergovernmental grants—to influence local government behavior. Therefore, the second section of this chapter discusses mandates, and the next section analyzes intergovernmental grant theory and its application to school financing. The fourth section discusses alternative fiscal capacity measures. The subject of this chapter is an important component of school finance. Because a school

---

[1] See Musgrave and Musgrave (1989) for a more comprehensive discussion of fiscal federalism within the broader context of public finance.

finance formula is a specific form of intergovernmental grant, this chapter provides valuable background information. A full understanding of how school finance formulas work requires knowledge of the more general theories of public finance and intergovernmental grants.[2]

ADVANTAGES OF A FEDERAL APPROACH TO FINANCING GOVERNMENTAL SERVICES

Financing public services through the operation of multiple—specifically, three—levels of government offers four general advantages: (1) fiscal capacity equalization, (2) equitable service distribution, (3) more economically efficient production of governmental service, and (4) decentralized decision making authority (Musgrave and Musgrave, 1989).

Each of these advantages is discussed here in terms of the state role in financing local school district operations. The discussion emphasizes the state fiscal role but includes other roles as well. The state is the focus because the U.S. Constitution is silent on education, placing responsibility for this important function with the states. Moreover, the intergovernmental grant theory discussed here is applicable to the federal government as well.

Although the state is the focus, the policy issue is the state role in a function that has been primarily financed at the local level. The problem with local financing that suggests a needed state role, as discussed in the preceding chapters, is the variation in local ability to raise education funds, i.e., the variation in local fiscal capacity. Fiscal capacity is generally measured by a jurisdiction's tax base which, as discussed in Chapters 5 and 6, can be income, sales, or property.

This chapter's initial discussion of intergovernmental fiscal issues uses property value per pupil as the measure of local school district fiscal capacity, i.e., its ability to raise local tax revenues. Property value per pupil is the fiscal capacity measure used most in the 50 state school finance systems because, historically, most school districts have raised revenues by taxing property. However, other measures of fiscal capacity—such as personal income, sales, or more complex measures that include the composition of the property tax base—could be used instead of, or in addition to, property wealth per pupil. These alternatives are discussed in the last section of the chapter.

Fiscal Capacity Equalization

The first, and perhaps most important, advantage of a fiscal federalism approach to financing schools is that a state, and only a state, can equalize the fiscal

---

[2] This chapter refers often to various specific school finance formulas. The reader might want to quickly read Chapter 7 to gain some familiarity with these formulas before reading this chapter.

capacity of its local school districts. As Chapter 1 showed, in most states there are substantial disparities among school districts in their ability to raise revenues through local property taxes. Some districts have a large per-pupil property tax base, and others have a much smaller base. Consequently, the same tax rate produces widely varying amounts of revenue per pupil. Local districts cannot compensate for these varying dimensions of fiscal capacity; that is a role for a higher level of government, such as the state.

Indeed, school finance has a long tradition of providing state assistance to offset local disparities through what are called fiscal capacity equalization formulas (see Cubberly; 1906, and Chapter 7). Fiscal capacity equalization mitigates inequalities in the financial ability of school districts by offering larger amounts of aid to districts that are less able to raise funds from their own sources. Fiscal capacity equalization has been the major focus of school finance during the twentieth century, and it is possible only because education is financed through a fiscal federalism system, i.e., by all three governmental levels.

Equity in Service Distribution

A second advantage of a fiscal federalism approach to school financing is that states can create mandates or provide financial assistance to school districts to promote equity in service distribution. As will be shown, fiscal equalization grants do not guarantee that districts will make the same decisions regarding the level of services they offer students. In fact, different approaches to providing quantity and quality of education services (or any local government service, for that matter) is one of the strengths of a fiscal federal system. However, if the state believes a minimum level of service must be provided, a federal structure offers a number of mechanisms to ensure the provision of minimum service levels.

Efficiency in Service Production

A third advantage of a multilevel school system concerns efficiency in the production of educational services. Many schools or school districts can benefit from economies of scale. That is, as the size of the school grows, the unit costs of educating each child decline; a larger school or district organization might be more efficient than a very small one. The state may be able to use its influence to encourage small school districts to consolidate and thus promote efficiency in the local production of educational services. It is possible that if a school or district grows beyond a certain size, it will no longer realize these efficiencies, and that the unit cost of providing educational services may begin to increase. Indeed, statewide school systems may suffer from such diseconomies of large scale. Therefore, a decentralized system of schools helps avoid the diseconomies that would exist if each state were simply one large school system. Monk (1990, Chapter 13) contains an excellent summary of current research on scale economies in education.

Decentralized Decision Making — *local control* *site-based management ↑ new term*

The fourth advantage of a fiscal federal system is that decentralized decision making provides individuals choices in selecting the mix of public services that matches their personal preferences. Tiebout's (1956) classic theory of local expenditures describes this phenomenon as "voting with your feet." He suggests that when there are a number of jurisdictions in close proximity, individuals will choose to live in the area that offers a mix of public services most closely matching their preferences.

The nearly 16,000 school districts in the United States provide an example of Tiebout's theory. For example, realtors report that home buyers frequently ask about the quality of local schools. Clearly, many people make decisions about where to live, at least in part, on the basis of their perception of the quality of local educational services. One would expect young families concerned about the education of their children to move into areas identified as having good schools, even if that required higher property tax payments. By contrast, a retired couple living on a fixed income might be less concerned with the quality of the local schools and more interested in an area with substantial senior citizen services and generally lower property taxes. This is not to imply that people without children in schools are not concerned about the quality of education, nor that the reputation of local schools is the only item that matters to young families with school-age children. This example merely suggests how individuals make decisions about where to live on the basis of a number of factors, with the mix of governmental services—including the quality of the local schools—and resulting tax payments being only two of those factors.

In a fiscal federal system, there are two ways the central government can influence or coordinate the decisions of local governments—specifically, school districts—in order to capitalize on these four advantages. The central government—state or federal—can mandate changes in the way local services are provided, or it can use intergovernmental grants to influence local behavior. Although mandates offer the most direct way of achieving legislative goals, there are political and, in many states, financial problems with their use. Consequently, state and federal legislators frequently use grants to stimulate desired local action. Central government grants provided to local governments can either be general or categorical in nature, and can come with or without the requirement that the recipient provide matching funds to qualify for the grant. These two approaches are discussed in the next two sections. In recent years, states have begun experimenting with incentive grants to achieve educational policy goals. Incentive programs are discussed in Chapter 12.

MANDATES AND THEIR USE
IN INTERGOVERNMENTAL RELATIONS

The Advisory Commission on Intergovernmental Relations (ACIR) defines a mandate as "any constitutional, statutory or administrative action that either limits or places requirements on local governments" (ACIR, 1984). A mandate exists when costs are imposed on a local government or when its decision making authority is restricted in some way.

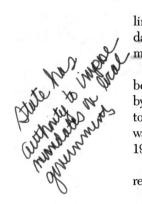

State has authority to impose mandates on local governments

A state's authority to impose mandates on local governments has long been recognized. This authority stems from "Dillon's rule," an 1868 court ruling by Iowa judge John F. Dillon holding that local governments owe their origin to, and derive their powers from, state legislatures (ACIR, 1984). This principle was upheld by the U.S. Supreme Court in *City of Trenton* v. *New Jersey*[3] in 1923, and state courts adhere to it today.

The Advisory Commission on Intergovernmental Relations postulates four reasons for the use of mandates (ACIR, 1984):

1. Mandates are used for an activity deemed by the state to be so important that it does not want to allow local governments to decide whether or not to engage in it. Desegregating schools and serving handicapped children are two education examples.
2. Mandates are used to promote desirable social or economic goals. Many argue that K–12 education has that level of importance.
3. Mandates are used by states to shift financial responsibility for providing certain services to local governments. Local school districts often raise this issue in relation to state and federal mandates to fully serve certain groups of children.
4. Mandates sometimes are merely justified by past practice or tradition.

Arguments against Mandates

Opponents of mandates argue for decentralization of decision making authority; they claim that local government is in the best position to respond in flexible and diverse ways to community problems and issues. They argue that revenue and expenditure mandates constrain the ability of local officials to respond to local circumstances. They further argue that if local and state policies are not aligned, constraints become divisive. In short, the loss of "local control" is the most frequently voiced criticism of mandates.

Another argument against mandates is that they are often enacted with little or no information about the cost burdens they place on local governments. This makes it difficult for mandate sponsors to consider the benefit-cost trade-offs of their proposals. As a result, mandates could fall short on economic efficiency goals.

Arguments for Mandates

Proponents of mandates argue they are legitimate tools to spur governmental activity that may not be fully provided by local governments, such as education

---

[3] 262 U.S. 182.

generally, desegregation, or serving handicapped students. Mandates also make it possible to move in the direction of uniform levels of service across an entire state. For example, many state-mandated programs concern areas affecting more than one local jurisdiction. Highways, education, and welfare are three examples. Proponents of mandates argue that for such programs over which the state has considerable responsibility, the reordering of local priorities through the use of mandates is an appropriate state action, countering the economic efficiency arguments made by mandate opponents.

Another advantage of state mandates is that they make equity in service distribution feasible. By mandating a certain level of service among all school districts, for example, the state can ensure that a minimum level of education is offered to each student across the state. However, without state assistance to mitigate differences in the ability to pay for those services, quality may vary depending on the local district's ability to pay and its willingness to carry out the mandate.

Mandates also fall short of fiscal capacity equalization goals. A state-imposed mandate will require greater effort from low-wealth governments or school districts than from high-wealth governments or school districts, thus intensifying the problem of unequal access to local fiscal capacity.

One way to mitigate the local impact of mandates is for the central government making the mandate to pay the costs associated with its implementation. One of the first states to enact legislation requiring full reimbursement for costs of new state mandates was California. Section 2231 of the California Revenue and Taxation Code requires that:

> the state shall pay to each local agency and each school district an amount to reimburse the local agency or the school district for the full costs, which are mandated by acts enacted after January 1, 1973 of a new state-mandated program or any increased level of service of an existing mandates program.

Figure 4.1 lists all states and their provisions regarding funding of mandates. As a result of these statutes, reliance on mandates to achieve legislative goals could be very costly. Consequently, policymakers frequently turn to the use of grants-in-aid to influence school district spending.

INTERGOVERNMENTAL GRANTS AND THEIR OBJECTIVES

The most common approach taken by the states and the federal government to influence local behavior is through intergovernmental grants. For example, when the federal government decided that more attention needed to be given to low-achieving students in districts with large numbers of students living in poverty, it created a program—the Elementary and Secondary Education Act

FIGURE 4.1 **State Requirements for Funding State Mandates on Local School Districts**

State	Requires: Estimates of Local Cost Burden	Mandate Reimbursement
Alabama	X	
Alaska		
Arizona	X	
Arkansas	X	
California	X	X
Colorado	X	X
Connecticut	X	
Delaware	X	
Florida	X	X
Georgia	X	
Hawaii		X
Idaho	X	
Illinois	X	X
Indiana	X	
Iowa	X	
Kansas	X	
Kentucky	X	
Louisiana	X	
Maine		
Maryland	X	
Massachusetts		X
Michigan	X	X
Minnesota		
Mississippi	X	X
Missouri	X	X
Montana	X	X
Nebraska	X	
Nevada	X	
New Hampshire	X	X
New Jersey	X	
New Mexico	X	X
New York	X	
North Carolina	X	
North Dakota	X	
Ohio	X	
Oklahoma		
Oregon	X	
Pennsylvania	X	
Rhode Island	X	X
South Carolina	X	
South Dakota	X	
Tennessee	X	X
Texas	X	
Utah	X	
Vermont	X	
Virginia	X	
Washington	X	X
West Virginia	X	
Wisconsin	X	
Wyoming		
Totals	42	14

Source: General Accounting Office, *Legislative Mandates: State Experiences Offer Insights for Federal Action*, Washington, D.C., GAO, 1988.

of 1965—which provided funds to local school districts to design and implement new compensatory education programs. Similarly, state general education aid grants are designed to assist local school districts in implementing overall K–12 education programs.

Different designs of state or federal grants can have quite different local fiscal impacts. Some grants simply replace local funds with state or federal funds. Other grants produce higher education expenditures than would occur if only local districts provided revenues. Still other grants both increase educational expenditures and focus the new spending on services for specific students or for specific areas within education. A key objective in establishing a school finance grant is to decide on the purpose of the grant and then design it on the basis of intergovernmental grant principles to maximize those objectives.

The theoretical literature on intergovernmental grants is substantial and reveals general agreement about the effects of different grant types on local expenditure decisions (Break, 1980; Musgrave and Musgrave, 1989; Oates, 1972; Wilde, 1968 and 1971). This work is based on the theory of consumer behavior, which analyzes the consumption decisions of an individual on the basis of preferences, income, and the prices of the goods to be purchased.

Intergovernmental grant theory views the recipient government as the consumer, with preferences being the priorities assigned to different public goods and to the trade-offs between public and private consumption. In general, the price of public goods is represented by a composite of goods purchased for a certain tax rate or tax price. The income constraint is the portion of community income devoted to the public sector, i.e., the level of local taxes.

A local government or school district must make decisions in two areas: (1) dividing total community income between public and private consumption by setting local tax rates, and (2) given this allocation, determining the combination of public and private goods that will maximize the welfare of local taxpayers—specifying within the tax revenue constraint (i.e., the local budget) the quantity and quality of education, police and fire protection, and other local services. These two decisions must be addressed simultaneously, since the division between public and private sector allocations cannot be separated from the specific quantity and quality of public and private goods actually chosen (Tsang and Levin, 1983, p. 331).

A local government or school district chooses the mix of services it provides from its budget by attempting to maximize the satisfaction of its constituents, given a set of preferences and prices for those public goods. Grant theory assumes a local government is in equilibrium, that it will allocate its local resources in a fashion that maximizes its own welfare. However, the level of expenditure, i.e., the range, quantity, and quality of education services decided on, may not be optimal from the view of the state or federal government, which may move to alter the local government's behavior (Tsang and Levin, 1983, pp. 331–332). For example, becoming first in the world in science and mathematics is a nationwide education goal. Consequently, both states and the federal government will probably want local districts to spend more resources on mathematics and science education.

Altering local behavior can be accomplished in part by providing intergovernmental education grants to local governments, i.e., school districts. Intergovernmental grants from states or the federal government to local school districts can take one of two general forms: (1) general or block grants and (2) categorical aid. In addition, either of these mechanisms may or may not include requirements for matching expenditures on the part of the recipient government—the local school district. Decisions on these dimensions, i.e., the specific design of the grant or funds formula, together with programmatic requirements, affect how local districts respond to the state or federal grant initiative.

Unrestricted General Aid

Unrestricted general aid or block grants increase a school district's revenue but do not place restrictions on the use of that revenue. General aid formulas provide additional revenues that districts can use in any way they want—to reduce local revenues and thus reduce local tax rates, to increase overall education spending and thus increase the quantity or quality of education services, to increase education spending in specific areas such as mathematics and science, or some combination of these options. General grants are most effective when the state's goal is fiscal capacity equalization, that is, to provide districts with additional revenue to offset their varying ability to raise local education revenues. A flat grant is a school finance mechanism that provides an equal amount of per-pupil revenue to each school district based solely on the number of students. On the other hand, foundation and guaranteed tax base programs provide general aid to districts in inverse proportion to their property wealth per pupil.[4]

General grants are the least effective in getting school districts to change their behavior to conform with state expectations, precisely because such grants carry no restrictions. Districts can use general aid to supplant local revenues and thus reduce tax rates, or to increase overall education spending and thus provide more or better educational services. Without restrictions, there likely will be no clear pattern to local district response. In particular, if the state provides general aid and hopes that the new funds will be used for specific purposes— for example, to increase spending for mathematics and science education—the likelihood of a uniform local response is low. This is because local governments attempt to maximize their local welfare, and in the process they are likely to make spending decisions different from the ones the state wants them to make.

Past research on the effects of intergovernmental grants for education has shown that school district spending increases by only a portion of the increase in general aid, with the balance devoted to local property tax relief. In an early study, using a sample of districts from 23 states, Miner (1963) found that total per-pupil educational expenditures were negatively related

---

[4] Chapter 7 provides a detailed description of how flat grants and foundation programs operate. It also provides examples of the effects of these programs using fiscal capacity equalization criteria.

to state education aid as a proportion of total educational expenditures. This finding is not as surprising as it might seem at first. At the time of Miner's study, most state school aid systems used a form of the traditional Strayer-Haig (Strayer and Haig, 1923) foundation formula (see Chapter 7) to distribute funds to local school districts. Miner's finding is consistent with the fact that under foundation programs, property-poor districts commonly have lower levels of educational expenditures, even though they receive relatively more aid than wealthier districts.

Somewhat later, in a New Jersey study of 1965–66 data, Struyk (1970) found that a dollar increase in state general aid resulted in an increase in local educational expenditures of 65 cents, with the balance returned to local taxpayers. In a Massachusetts study using 1968–69 data, Stern (1973) found that between 45 and 55 cents of each dollar of increased state general aid was used to reduce the needed amount of locally raised funds. Using the same data, Grubb and Michelson (1974) found that each dollar of general state aid led to a reduction in local revenues of between 74 and 85 cents. Ladd (1975) found that an additional dollar of state general aid resulted in increased educational spending of approximately 50 cents in 1969–70 in Massachusetts.

A 1974 study by Cohn in Pennsylvania found that general grants to local school districts increased educational expenditures by 88 cents for each dollar. By comparison, in a 49-state study conducted using data from 1967–68, Cohn found that state aid increased local educational expenditures by only 35 cents for each additional dollar of aid. In West Virginia, Bowman (1974) found that school districts reduced taxes by 50 cents for each additional dollar of unrestricted aid in 1969–70.

Grubb and Osman (1977) found that California school districts increased spending by 78 cents for every dollar of increased state general aid in 1971–72, six years before Proposition 13 passed. In Delaware, Black, Lewis, and Link (1979) found that educational block grants increased educational expenditures by 78 cents for each dollar distributed to school districts.

Using pooled regression techniques, Park and Carroll (1979) found very little response on the part of Michigan school districts to state general grants between 1973–74 and 1975–76. Vincent and Adams (1978), using a methodology that related changes in Minnesota school district response between 1972 and 1976, estimated that school districts would spend 49 cents of each additional dollar of state block grant assistance. In New York, Adams (1980) found that total educational expenditures increased by 59 cents for each additional dollar of unrestricted state aid, although she found that upstate (low-wealth) districts were more likely to spend a higher proportion of the grant on education, whereas downstate (high-wealth) districts were more likely to use the funds to reduce local tax burdens.

These studies of unrestricted or general state aid grants to school districts consistently found that districts used a portion of the grant for tax reductions and a portion for increased education spending. In reviewing numerous studies of local school district response to general aid, Tsang and Levin (1983) found that, on average, local school districts spend about half of the increases in state general aid on educational programs and about half to reduce local tax rates.

Thus, if the state's goal for general aid programs is fiscal capacity equalization, unrestricted grants generally succeed in meeting those goals. Since districts low in property wealth per pupil generally have above-average tax rates and below-average expenditures per pupil, increases in general aid let them reduce their tax rates and also increase education spending, thus addressing both disadvantages that exist with heavy reliance on local education financing.

If one accepts the notion that local districts are better able to determine the program needs of the local population (in this case, student educational needs), then unrestricted grants offer advantages in terms of economic efficiency. Unrestricted grants provide local districts with increased revenues and let each district decide how to use those revenues, drawing on local needs and priorities. Unrestricted grants also are effective tools for maintaining an equitable but decentralized decision making system.

Unrestricted general grants can be used to provide some equity in service distribution, either to establish some minimum level of service or to provide districts with some minimum level of funding. As Chapter 7 shows, flat grants and foundation programs were designed to accomplish these objectives. However, since unrestricted grants do not place limitations on district expenditures from local sources, there is no constraint on wealthy districts to increase education spending substantially above the minimum. One way to address this problems is to link a district's general aid to its willingness to spend local resources for education. The next section describes general grants that include a matching component.

Matching General Grants

The most common way to tie a district's general aid to its own willingness to spend is a matching grant. Matching grants link the level of state general aid assistance, at least in part, to the level of effort made by the local government, as well as to its fiscal capacity. In school finance, the most common general matching grant system is the guaranteed tax base (GTB) program.[5] Many state school finance programs are called percentage-equalizing, guaranteed-yield, or district-power-equalizing. Although the specific operating details of each of these systems vary, they are all designed to achieve the same goal, namely, to equalize the revenue raising ability of each school district, at least to some point. Chapter 7 contains a detailed discussion and simulation of the operation of a GTB program.

Intergovernmental grant theory analyzes matching grant programs differently than non–matching grant programs. Rather than assessing the grant's

---

[5] Although a foundation program also involves a local match—the local required tax effort—it functions more as a flat grant than a more open-ended matching program, such as the GTB.

impact on a district's income, or total tax revenues, intergovernmental grant theory analyzes matching grants in terms of how they change the relative tax prices[6] districts pay for educational services. A GTB program, for example, lowers the tax price of educational services for districts low in property wealth per pupil, because with the GTB they are able to levy a lower tax rate, and thus pay less, for a certain level of education services. Indeed, property-poor districts are able to substantially lower their tax rates to provide the same level of services as they did before a GTB program. In other words, the price to local citizens—taxpayers—is substantially decreased. Economic theory predicts that individuals faced with choices are price-sensitive and will purchase more of lower-priced items, all other things being equal.

As it plays out in school finance, a GTB gives a district with low property value per pupil the ability to raise as much money at a given tax rate as the wealthier district with a per-pupil property value equal to the tax base guarantee. Thus, with the same tax rate or tax effort, the poor district will be able to raise substantially more revenue than it could before the GTB. Based on the preceding discussion, a district would be expected to use part of this new money to increase expenditures and part to reduce its tax rate. Thus, the impact of a general matching grant is similar to that of an unrestricted general grant.

As Chapter 7 shows, a major difference between unrestricted and matching grant programs is that under an unrestricted general grant, such as a flat grant program, even property-wealthy districts receive state aid funds, whereas under a GTB-type matching grant program, the amount of state aid a district receives is inversely related to its property wealth per pupil. In fact, depending on the level of the GTB, there may be districts that do not receive any state aid at all.

Categorical Grants

In contrast to general unrestricted grants, categorical grants have limitations on how they can be used. Categorical grants are provided to school districts for a specific purpose and often come with strict application, use, and reporting requirements. Categorical grants are used to ensure that school districts provide services deemed important by the state or federal governments. These services often are provided more efficiently locally; but without assistance, school districts may choose not to provide them, or at least not to provide the level of such services desired by the state or federal government.

There are a variety of categorical grant mechanisms used by states and the federal government. Some categorical grants are used to help local school

---

[6] The tax price generally is the tax rate a district must levy to purchase a given level and quality of school services. Poor districts generally have to levy a higher tax rate and thus pay a higher tax price to purchase a given bundle of school services than a wealthy district because, at a given tax rate, the poor district would raise less per pupil than the wealthier district.

districts meet the needs of specified populations; for example, Chapter 1 assistance is provided to districts with large numbers of poor children. Other categorical grant programs are designed to support specific district functions, such as pupil transportation. The manner in which a district receives categorical grant funds also varies. Many categorical grant programs are designed to be available to recipient districts automatically: dollars flow by formula. Others have specific application rules and procedures: districts must write proposals to receive funds.

States provide school districts with categorical grants using a variety of formula designs. Districts might receive categorical grants on the basis of some sociodemographic characteristic, such as incidence of poverty or degree of urbanization. Alternatively, districts might be eligible for categorical grants on the basis of the number of children meeting a specific criterion, such as a handicapping condition. Finally, districts could simply be reimbursed for expenditures devoted to a specific function. District fiscal response to a categorical program will depend on the specific nature of the grant's distribution mechanism.

Like general grants, categorical grants increase the recipient's income. Funds allocated on the basis of the number of students meeting a specific criterion, but with no spending requirements, would be expected to create a district response similar to that for a general grant—a portion of the funds would be expended for their intended purpose, with the balance either returned to the taxpayers in the form of lower property taxes or spent on other district functions. For example, some states weight poor students in the general aid formula but do not require that districts use the extra money to expand compensatory education services for poor students. Thus, it is likely that the portion of these funds used for compensatory education will be smaller than if they were accompanied by requirements mandating their expenditure on such education.

Since one purpose of a categorical grant is to encourage specific actions on the part of local school districts, the federal government and most states that appropriate funds for categorical programs usually also issue rules and regulations to resolve this problem and restrict district use of these resources for their intended purpose.

A commonly used fiscal enforcement tool is the maintenance-of-effort provision. This provision requires districts to prove that spending on the supported program from its own funds does not decline as a result of the grant. The early Title 1 "supplement, not supplant" requirement is an example of a maintenance-of-effort provision. Other enforcement provisions include audits and evaluations to ensure that recipient districts establish programs designed to meet the purpose or goals of the grant program. Many categorical grants have specific reporting requirements that help the contributing government monitor use of the funds.

Unlike general grants, categorical grants stimulate educational expenditures by at least the level of the grant, and sometime by more than the amount of the grant. Grubb and Michelson's (1974) study of Massachusetts found that local school district expenditures increased by $1.21 for each dollar of state categorical aid distributed to local school districts, implying that for each dollar a district received from the state, it increased its own source revenues for those purposes by 21 cents. Ladd (1975) found in Massachusetts that a dollar of categorical aid resulted in increased spending of $1.10 for education. In their cross-sectional analyses of Colorado and Minnesota, Vincent and Adams (1978) found consistently stimulative effects of categorical grants. They estimated that educational expenditures increased in response to categorical grants by $1.33 and $1.07 in 1972 and 1976, respectively, in Minnesota and by $1.60 and $1.80 in 1973 and 1975, respectively, in Colorado.

Categorical grants thus appear to be more stimulative than general grants. The primary explanation is that the strings and requirements attached to categorical grants make it difficult for districts to spend the funds elsewhere (Tsang and Levin, 1983) and virtually force districts to increase spending by at least the amount of the grant. Another explanation is that categorical grants are provided for specialized programs on which local districts would spend less, if anything at all, in the absence of the categorical aid (Ladd, 1975).

Categorical grants present a different trade-off between equity and efficiency compared to general grants. Categorical programs encourage districts to treat different students differently by making additional resources available to needy students in the hope of producing similar achievement outcomes. Any time resources are devoted to a needy student, it implies a loss of what could have been produced if the resources were distributed among all students evenly (Monk, 1990). As a result, categorical grants trade economic efficiency for equity in the provision of services.

Categorical programs, by their nature, are more centralized than general grants since it is the state or federal government that determines what population needs extra services. Moreover, some federal programs, such as the program for handicapped children, include very specific requirements for identifying and serving eligible students. Although the final determination of what services to provide is left to local district and parental discretion, very specific identification and service procedures are stated in the law and accompanying regulations.

Finally, since categorical grants are designed to provide assistance to groups of students, or to districts on the basis of some characteristic (such as expensive transportation needs in a small, sparsely populated rural district), they are not generally designed to equalize fiscal capacity. Nevertheless, both special service provision and fiscal capacity equalization can be accomplished with well-designed grant schemes. These issues are discussed in more depth in Chapter 8.

Final Comments on Grants

As this discussion shows, states can use a variety of grant mechanisms to finance schools and a variety of specific educational services. The type of grant instrument chosen, as well as its specific design features, can affect how the funds are used by local districts. General grants are the most effective when the state's goal is to provide the recipient with additional revenue to meet its service obligations (a flat grant or minimum foundation to provide at least some education program) or to equalize fiscal capacity (such as a guaranteed tax base program). These grants, however, leave all specific spending decisions to local school district discretion and are not as effective in getting districts to provide specific services as targeted, categorical grant instruments.

Categorical grants can induce school districts to serve a specific population or to implement a particular program. In the first case, the district would be expected to treat the funds much as general assistance, and local spending patterns may not match the state government expectations. These grants are treated as categorical rather than general grants because they are distributed to a limited number of districts, whereas general grants are available to all districts. Categorical grants designed to meet a specific purpose frequently come with one or more mechanisms designed to ensure compliance with the grant's goals. These grants are more successful in getting the recipient district to implement state goals, but usually at a loss of efficiency.

ALTERNATIVE MEASURES OF FISCAL CAPACITY

School finance typically assumes that a district's fiscal capacity, i.e., its ability to raise local tax revenues, is measured by its property value per pupil. But research has identified additional factors that should be considered in measuring comprehensively a district's fiscal capacity: the mix of property types within a district, or the composition of the property tax base, and average household income within a district. Fiscal capacity should include the major economic variables that affect a school district's ability to raise revenues for educational purposes. Although total property value per pupil is the major fiscal capacity component, research also shows that household income, as well as the composition of the property tax base in terms of residential, commercial, and industrial property, also impact local revenue raising decisions.

Consider, for example, two districts with the same property wealth per pupil but very different property tax base composition. In district A, all of the property value is in residential housing and commercial development, but in district B, there are a number of industrial plants. Since the same tax rate will raise the same revenue per pupil, one might expect roughly similar tax effort to fund the schools. However, in district A, homeowners and local businesses pay the full property tax, whereas in district B, a very large portion of the total property tax bill is paid by the industrial plants. But the plants can "export" the tax payments to individuals outside the district—either consumers, through higher prices, or stockholders, through lower profits. In district B, then, voters might be willing to raise higher levels of property taxes, knowing that a portion of the tax bill is financed by individuals outside the district who pay the tax on the industrial plant. Since the owner of the industrial plant has at most one vote (assuming he or she actually lives in close proximity and in the same school district), there is little the industrial plant can do to reduce its tax burden.

In her 1975 Massachusetts study, Ladd found that total property value per pupil, composition of the property tax base, and household income had separate and independent impacts on school district education spending. She used her results to weight the value of commercial industrial and residential property to adjust for these factors. She found that if the weight for residential property were set at 1.0, commercial property should be weighted at 1.26 and industrial property at 0.55. The weighted property value, then, was a more accurate indicator of fiscal capacity as reflected in the local property tax base.

Ladd also found a major effect for household income. Her research, as well as research by several others (Feldstein, 1975; Vincent and Adams, 1978; Adams, 1980; Adams and Odden, 1981), found that the willingness to raise local taxes by local school district voters was also affected by income—even if income could not be taxed. In other words, even if total property value per pupil and the weighted property value per pupil were the same, higher-income households were willing to exert a higher tax effort for schools compared to lower-income households. Intrinsically, this finding makes sense. Although property taxes are attached to a capital asset (see Chapter 5 on property taxes), homeowners pay their property taxes out of current income. As a result, the impact of a tax increase on disposable income seems likely to have an impact on school funding decisions.

This finding on household income is especially important since there is not always a strong correlation between property value and income. For example, large cities frequently contain high percentages of low-income children. Yet, because of the high value of downtown commercial property and other industrial property, the city itself may appear to have average or above-average wealth in terms of property value per pupil alone. An "income factor" adjustment to the property value measure could compensate for these realities.

All studies on the relationship of income to spending for education found the effect to be "multiplicative" in nature. Thus, the appropriate income adjustment would be to multiply property value per pupil by an income factor, usually the ratio of the average household income in a school district to the average statewide household income. Many states simply add household income to the property value measure and use property plus income per pupil as the fiscal capacity measure. Such measures have peculiar and unattractive properties (Harris, 1978) and do not reflect the research on the impact of income on school revenues (Figure 4.2).

Adams and Odden (1981) reported that when a multiplicative income factor was simulated in New York state, three effects were discernible:

1. Relatively more aid was allocated to low-income districts, which were primarily large urban districts and small rural districts.
2. The cost to the state increased.
3. The equity of the school finance system improved.

FIGURE 4.2   Appropriate and inappropriate income factors

Appropriate income adjustment: $(PV/Pupil) \times (PIH/SIH)$
Inappropriate income adjustment: $(PV + PI)/Pupil$

where

PV	=	total property value
PI	=	total personal income
Pupil	=	number of students in the district
PIH	=	personal income per household (or per capita) in the district
SIH	=	statewide average personal income per household or per capita

In summary, a comprehensive measure of school district fiscal capacity would include three factors: total property value; a weighted total property value, with different weights for the residential, commercial, and industrial components of the property tax base; and a multiplicative household income adjustment. Although states have considered these more comprehensive measures of fiscal capacity, only Minnesota addresses the composition of the property tax base. Further, although approximately 20 states have an income adjustment in their school aid formula, most of these adjustments, unfortunately, are additive, not multiplicative.

Chapter 5

Sales, Income, and Other Tax Revenue Sources

This chapter analyzes sources of revenue for education, particularly individual income and sales taxes. The major reason for studying taxes is that these are the primary source of dollars for public schools. Although the focus of the chapter is on raising tax revenues, taxes can be used for other purposes as well. For example, they can be a means to redistribute income from the wealthy to the poor. Taxes also can be used to implement regulatory goals; for example, taxes could be placed on companies that pollute the environment beyond acceptable levels. In other words, taxes can be used for a variety of purposes, but this chapter focuses on taxes as a source of public revenues for schools.

The chapter has six sections. The first provides an overview of trends in federal, state, and local taxes from 1957 to 1987. The second summarizes the major structural changes in federal and state taxes over this same period. The third section of the chapter presents the public finance criteria commonly used to evaluate specific taxes. In the next two sections these criteria are used to assess the individual income and sales taxes. The final section addresses lotteries, which are increasingly popular mechanisms for raising governmental revenues.

OVERVIEW OF TRENDS
IN FEDERAL, STATE, AND LOCAL TAXES

During the past 30 years, there have been significant changes in the tax revenues raised by different governmental levels. Figure 5.1 exhibits tax revenues by type of tax for all levels of government, including school districts, from 1957 to 1987. Several trends in this table are worth noting. First, total tax revenues for all levels of government roughly doubled in each of the three decades presented in the chart; these figures reflect government growth over that time period. Second, state government revenues have increased at a faster rate than revenues for either the federal government or local governments, rising more than 17-fold between 1957 and 1987.

Another notable feature in this table is that property taxes are the primary source of tax revenues for local governments. The federal government does not

FIGURE 5.1   Tax Revenue by Source and Level of Government, 1957 to 1987

Fiscal Year	Total–All Governments	Federal Governments	State Government	Local Governments	School Districts
Total Tax Revenue (millions)					
1957	$ 98.6	$ 69.8	$ 14.5	$ 14.3	$ 4.5
1967	176.1	115.1	31.9	29.1	10.8
1977	419.8	243.8	101.1	74.9	27.1
1987	944.5	539.4	246.9	158.2	51.8
Property Taxes (millions)					
1957	$ 12.9	—	$0.5	$ 12.4	$ 4.4
1967	26.0	—	0.9	25.2	10.6
1977	62.5	—	2.3	60.3	26.4
1987	121.2	—	4.6	116.6	50.5
Sales, Gross Receipts, and Customs (millions)					
1957	$ 20.6	$ 11.1	$ 8.4	$ 1.0	—
1967	36.3	15.8	18.6	2.0	—
1977	83.8	23.2	52.4	8.3	$0.2
1987	192.7	48.4	119.9	24.5	0.5
Individual and Corporate Income Taxes (millions)					
1957	$ 59.5	$ 56.8	$ 2.5	$0.2	—
1967	103.5	95.5	7.1	0.1	—
1977	250.0	211.6	34.7	3.8	0.2
1987	582.8	476.5	96.7	9.7	0.4

Source: Advisory Commission on Intergovernmental Relations, *Significant Features of Fiscal Federalism, 1988 Edition,* vol. II, Washington, D.C., ACIR, 1988, p. 64; and U.S. Bureau of the Census, *Government Finance in 1986–87,* Washington, D.C., U.S. Bureau of the Census, 1988, p. 7.

collect any property taxes, and state governments collect a small amount of property taxes. Further, nearly 50 percent of all property taxes are collected by school districts.

The numbers also show that most sales and gross receipts taxes are raised by state governments. Customs revenues are raised primarily by the federal government. Local sales taxes, though, rose rapidly between 1977 and 1987. Sales taxes constitute the largest single source of tax revenues for state governments. School districts raise very little revenue through sales taxes.

Finally, individual income taxes raise the largest amount of governmental tax revenues, and the bulk of income taxes are raised by the federal government. But income taxes are rising at both state and local levels. Federal individual income taxes approximately doubled between 1967 and 1977, and then doubled again between 1977 and 1987, but both state and local income taxes roughly tripled during those time periods. Income taxes represent a minuscule amount of local school district revenues.

In short, sources of tax revenues have been changing over the past 30 years, and tax revenues today probably exceed $1 trillion. Despite the changes, the individual income tax is still the primary tax source for the federal government, the sales tax the primary revenue source for state governments, and the property tax the prime revenue producer for local governments, including school districts.

OVERVIEW OF CHANGES IN TAX STRUCTURES

Federal, state, and local tax structures experience significant structural changes over time. At the federal level, there are shifts in taxes on individuals versus businesses; shifts in the number and level of marginal income tax rates; additions and subtractions of various deductions, exemptions, and tax-sheltered items; and a host of other modifications that alter the functioning of the federal tax system—primarily the federal personal and corporate income tax and the Social Security tax. At the state level, tax structures experience similar flux. Over time, states have added taxes, such as a state income or sales tax; changed rates; enacted a variety of mechanisms to reduce the burden of taxes on low-income families; conformed their tax structures to the ever-changing federal tax structure; and modified their tax systems to buffet increases and decreases in federal intergovernmental aids. Although public finance economists urge governments to create stability in the tax structure so that households and the business community can make decisions in a more stable fiscal environment, political leaders have difficulty heeding such advice. Change seems to be a hallmark of the country's tax structure, catalyzed by both economic and political variables.

At the federal level, changes in the income tax structure can be divided into two periods: pre-1940 and post-1940. Individual income taxes were low prior to 1940, consuming only 1 percent of personal income in 1939, compared with nearly 13 percent today. Rates were sharply increased after 1940, with top rates of 90 percent. Federal income tax rates were somewhat reduced in 1964, 1981, and 1986, and modestly reduced in 1971 and 1975. The most fundamental changes occurred in the 1980s—first in 1981, when rates were reduced to produce a long-term decrease of 23 percent, and then in 1986, when the entire federal income tax structure was overhauled. The Federal Tax Reform Act of 1986 broadened the income tax base by closing loopholes and preferences, reduced the number of brackets to three, and reduced the rates themselves to 15, 28, and 33 percent. The standard deduction and earned income tax credits were raised to shield the working poor from paying income taxes. The intent was to keep the amount of revenues produced the same while improving the equity of the tax itself. Most would agree that those goals were accomplished, even though the federal income tax is far from perfect.

The federal tax structure was modified again in 1990. The three-rate structure was retained, but the top rate was lowered to 31 percent.[1] The earned income tax credit was increased, further sheltering the working poor from federal income taxes.

At the state and local levels, changes in the tax structure divide into about three periods, roughly corresponding to the 1960s, 1970s, and 1980s. State tax structures underwent significant structural change during the 1960s as the country experienced both continued economic growth and government growth, the latter spawned, in large part, by the War on Poverty programs. Between 1965 and 1971, for example, seven states enacted an income tax for the first time, and eight states enacted new sales taxes. The bulk of the new funds were linked to rising state support for public elementary and secondary schools, to relieve pressure on the local property tax that the baby boom generation had caused in the 1950s and early 1960s. School funding had been primarily a function of local governments, and thus the local property tax, but the large property tax increases necessary to build schools and provide operating funds for the baby boom generation led in the late 1960s to the growing unpopularity of the property tax and to pressures on states to relieve high property tax burdens. This new role for state school finance complemented the general expansion of state and local governments into a variety of domestic policy areas beginning in the mid-1960s.

During the 1970s, at least up to 1978, there was very little structural change in state taxes. Only one state—New Jersey—enacted a new income tax, and no state enacted a new sales tax. Most tax reform focused on the local property tax. This tax underwent several changes, from simple reduction in its use, to increased numbers of exemptions, to administrative reform as computer technologies allowed assessment practices to keep pace with market

---

[1] Technically, the 1986 tax reform created a four-rate structure: 15, 28, and 33 percent, and then, above a certain income level, back to 28 percent. The 1990 changes eliminated the 33 percent bubble by making it a uniform 31 percent.

values, and finally to new programs, such as "circuit breakers," to protect low-income households from excessive property tax burdens. The focus on property tax change was reinforced by the school finance reforms of the 1970s, during which nearly two-thirds of the states changed the way public elementary and secondary schools were financed, generally by increasing the state role and decreasing the local (and, thus, local property tax) role.

The period from 1978 to the present includes a variety of fast-paced state tax structure changes. In 1978, Proposition 13 inaugurated the tax limitation and tax cutting movement. In June of that year, voters in California approved an initiative that cut the property tax rate from over 2 percent, on average, to a constitutional limit of 1 percent of market value. Several states followed with a variety of tax limitations, spending limitations, or outright tax cutting measures. At the state level, 32 legislatures reduced income taxes between 1978 and 1980. The "tax revolt" was thus spawned.

Between 1980 and 1987, states enacted few structural changes in their tax systems, although the legacy of the late 1970s and early 1980s tax revolt left 17 states with some sort of tax or spending limitation, and another 10 states with some inflation indexing feature in their individual income tax systems. The incremental changes that were made tended to reduce the progressivity of state tax systems, narrow the bases for the major taxes, and make the tax systems more volatile and closely linked to national economic up- and downturns.

Then tax reform fever hit states in 1987. The major factor was the 1986 federal tax reform because, without structural tax reform change, most states would experience either a major increase or a decrease in their income tax receipts.

Indeed, the themes involved in the 1986 federal income tax reform also became salient themes at the state level, since at both levels two decades of incremental change had produced tax systems that were perceived as overly complex, unfair, and burdensome. The following themes characterized state tax reform beginning in 1987 (Gold, 1986a):

- *Broadening tax bases*. Just as the federal government had eliminated several deductions, exemptions, and special treatments, states considered similar changes in state income and sales taxes, as well as local property taxes. Thus, complexity could be reduced, fairness enhanced, and revenue yields stabilized.
- *Flattening and reducing tax rates*. By broadening the base, tax rates could be reduced and revenues held constant (or increased moderately). Thus, base broadening offered the possibility of reducing the number of tax rates (the federal income tax was reduced to just three rates) and flattening the overall structure.
- *Shifting burdens from individuals to the business community*. Just as the federal government had, prior to 1987, increased taxes on individuals and reduced them on corporations and businesses, and then shifted some of that tax burden back onto businesses in the 1986 reform, that option also existed for state governments.

- *Treating different industries more uniformly.* The federal tax reform eliminated the investment tax credit, extended depreciation schedules, and cut most tax shelters, changes that placed capital-intensive and goods-producing industries on a more equal basis with knowledge-intensive and service-producing industries. For states, more uniform treatment of the business community would mean similar changes, as well as fundamental changes in the sales tax—either eliminating it altogether for businesses or further expanding exemptions. More uniform treatment of all business was especially important in the increasing interstate competition for business enterprises.
- *Eliminating tax burdens on the poor.* The federal tax reform took most poor households off the federal income tax rolls, and states could do the same for their income tax, but the more common state response was to eliminate sales and property tax burdens on the poor, which exceeded state income taxes on the poor. Although the 1986 and 1990 federal tax reforms tended to reduce the overall progressivity of the tax structure, it was accompanied by a complementary focus on eliminating altogether tax burdens for households falling below the poverty level.
- *Imposing minimum taxes on both individuals and businesses.* This feature of the new federal tax reflected the value that wealthy individuals and businesses should pay some minimum amount of tax, even though other features of a reformed structure could reduce their burden to zero.

Twenty-seven states reformed their income tax system. Twenty states increased the standard deduction, and 17 states increased the personal exemption. Both of these structural changes enhanced progressivity and eliminated poor families from the income tax rolls. Only five states enacted more thorough reforms. The state and local tax reform that began in 1987, however, is just in its infancy and still has a large unfinished agenda (Gold, 1988).

PUBLIC FINANCE CRITERIA FOR EVALUATING TAXES

Public finance economists use several analytic criteria to evaluate taxes. These criteria are commonly accepted as both the economic and policy assessment bases needed for analyzing any tax (see Musgrave and Musgrave, 1989, for example). These criteria include the tax base, yield, equity, economic effects, and administration and compliance issues. This section discusses each of these in some detail. They are used to assess income, sales, and lottery taxes in this chapter and property taxes in the next chapter.

Tax Base

The tax base is the entity to which a tax rate is applied. For example, a tax could be based on the number of cars or television sets a person owns. The rate, then, would be a fixed dollar amount per car or television. Usually tax bases are related to some economic category, such as income, property, or consumption. Broad-based taxes, such as property, income, and sales taxes, are taxes with broad or comprehensive bases. There are four major tax bases: wealth, income, consumption, and privilege.

Wealth.   There are many forms of wealth, some typically taxed and others not. Wealth economically represents an accumulation of value, or a stock of value, at any point in time. Net worth, i.e., the sum of all economic assets minus all economic liabilities at some fixed point in time, could be one measure of wealth. Then a wealth tax could be based on net worth; indeed, proposals for net worth taxes have been made for years but have never been enacted into law.

One common measure of wealth is property. Property is divided into two general categories: real property and personal property. Real property includes land and buildings. For individuals, personal property includes household items, such as furniture, video equipment, computers, rugs, and appliances. For businesses, personal property includes machinery and equipment, furniture and other office supplies, and inventories. Stocks, bonds, and other financial instruments (certificates of deposit, notes, bank accounts, etc.) are other forms of wealth. The value of an inheritance is another form of wealth.

A pure tax on wealth would tax all of these different categories of wealth. The United States does not have and never has had a wealth tax. Financial instruments rarely have been taxed. Large portions of real property owned by the government and religious organizations are not taxed. And there has been an increasing tendency to exempt types of both real and personal property, for both businesses and individuals, from taxation.

The property tax comes closest to a wealth tax in this country. But the property tax generally covers real property only; the trend during the past two decades has been to eliminate both individual and business personal property from the tax. As the property tax is analyzed more closely in the next chapter, both its advantages and its disadvantages in covering a narrow definition of wealth will be discussed.

Income.   Income is another tax base. Compared to wealth, which is a measure of economic worth at one time, income is a measure of economic flow over time. The net value of income minus expenses over a time period represents the change in net worth over that period. Income includes salaries, interest from financial instruments, dividends from stocks, gifts, money from the sale of an item of wealth (including property and financial instruments), and other forms of money flow. Earned income typically refers to salaries; earned income is money earned by doing work. Unearned income money, by contrast, consists of returns from financial assets and investments.

Income from salaries is rather easy to identify, but income from business activities is more complicated, since net income is determined by subtracting legitimate expenses from gross receipts or sales. Although these terms are conceptually straightforward, defining gross receipts, sales, and legitimate expenses is technically complex, and income can vary substantially depending on the specifics of the definition.

However it is technically defined, income is typically viewed as the measure of one's ability to pay not only an income tax, but any tax. For example, if the value of a person's wealth is fixed, such as the value of a home, some current income is needed to pay a tax on that element of wealth. If current income is insufficient to pay the tax, the element of wealth would need to be sold or partially sold, or the individual would need to take out a loan to pay the tax or alter his or her consumption patterns to pay more taxes and purchase less of other items. The same is true for a sales or consumption tax: that tax is paid from an individual's current income, so the greater the tax, the less an individual can purchase with current income sources.

Another factor in assessing income as a measure of ability to pay is the time period over which income is measured. Typically, income is measured in yearly amounts, and most tax structures accept annual income as both the tax base and the measure of ability to pay. However, both individuals and businesses purchase capital items such as plants, factories, equipment, homes, and cars on a longer-term basis, and often on the assumption that average income will increase over a longer time period. For example, assuming that income will rise over the next decade, an individual might purchase a home that costs more, on average, based on current income but that falls to an average or even a below-average burden over a longer—5- to 10-year—time period. Thus, some measure of long-term, or lifetime, income might be a better measure of income as it relates to ability to pay. Economists have argued for such an income measure for years (Musgrave and Musgrave, 1989, for example), but current income politically wins as the most commonly accepted measure of ability to pay.

Consumption. Consumption technically includes all items individuals or businesses purchase, whether they are products or services. A consumption tax is usually called a sales tax if it applies to a broad range of items that can be purchased, as is the case for most state and local sales taxes. A consumption tax is usually called an excise tax if it applies to specific items, such as beer, alcohol, cigarettes, furs, or jewelry.

The United States does not have a broad-based consumption tax. The base for such a tax would be income less savings, i.e., all income spent on purchases for current consumption. Although most state sales taxes come close to this definition, they generally exclude services that are both a large and an increasing component of current consumption, and products such as food, prescription medicine, and homes. Thus, sales taxes in this country are more aptly described as broad-based selective sales taxes.

Privilege. A small portion of revenues for federal, state, and local government services are raised by granting individuals or businesses a privilege and charging a fee for that privilege. An automobile license fee is paid for the privilege of driving a car, a car license plate fee is paid for the privilege of owning a car, and other privilege fees are paid for a variety of other purposes, including franchise fees for running certain businesses, fees for using park facilities, fees for a permit to operate a taxi cab, and fees for using port facilities. A privilege tax is similar to an excise tax, the major difference being that the former is paid for the privilege of engaging in some activity, whereas the latter is paid for the privilege of purchasing and owning or using some product.

Yield

The yield is the amount of revenues a tax will produce. Yield is equal to the tax rate times the tax base. Rates are usually, but not always, given in percentage terms, such as a 5 percent sales tax, a 10 percent gasoline tax, a 33 percent marginal federal income tax rate, or a 4 percent state income tax rate. Given a defined tax base, it is easy to determine the yield for each percent of tax rate on that tax base. Knowing the general revenue raising or yield potential of a tax (with a defined tax base) is important information. Just in terms of yield, it is preferable to be able to raise substantial revenues at low or modest rates.

Broad-based taxes, by definition, can produce high yields even at modest rates, whereas selective taxes, such as a cigarette tax, are limited in terms of the amount of revenue they can produce. A tax that produces a large amount of revenues, such as a property tax, is difficult to eliminate (a proposal often made for the unpopular property tax) because to do so would require either large cuts in governmental services or large raises in other tax rates, and both of those options are politically unpopular. Thus, once in place, a broad-based tax is difficult if not impossible to eliminate. Indeed, it becomes easy to raise new revenues with small tax rate increases.

Other aspects of tax yield are stability and elasticity. Stability is the degree to which the yield rises or falls with national or state economic cycles. Stable tax revenues decrease less in economic downturns but also increase less during economic upturns. The property tax historically has been a stable tax since property values consistently increase over time and fall only in deep, major recessions. Sales taxes on products tend to rise and fall more in line with economic cycles, as do income taxes. Corporate income taxes follow economic cycles even more closely and thus tend to be a more volatile revenue source.

Elasticity measures the degree to which tax revenues keep pace with growth in personal income. Elasticity formally equals the ratio of the percentage change in the tax yield to the percentage change in personal income. An elasticity less than 1 indicates that tax revenues do not keep pace with income growth, an elasticity equal to 1 indicates that tax revenues grow at the same rate as incomes, and an elasticity greater than 1 indicates that tax revenues increase faster than income growth. Since prices and demands for governmental (and hence school) services at least keep pace with income growth, a desirable tax feature is to have an elasticity at least equal to 1. Individual income taxes, especially if marginal rates are higher for higher incomes, have an elasticity greater, but not substantially greater, than 1. Sales tax revenues generally track income growth. Over time, property taxes have exhibited elasticities around 1.

To some degree, a trade-off exists between stability and elasticity. Elastic taxes tend to be less stable since their yield falls in economic, and thus personal income, downturns. Stable taxes might not be so elastic since their yields remain steady when the economy and personal income grows or declines.

Tax Equity

Tax equity addresses the issue of whether the tax is fair, whether it treats individuals or businesses equitably. Again, although conceptually simple, the issue of tax equity is technically complex, and it is difficult to determine with preciseness the degree to which a tax treats all fairly. There are two primary aspects of tax equity: horizontal equity and vertical equity.

Horizontal equity concerns equal tax treatment of individuals in the same, or equal, circumstances. For example, if an income tax meets the horizontal equity test, individuals with the same taxable income, say $20,000, would pay the same amount of tax, $2,000, for example. Or two families who own homes with the same market value would pay the same amount of property tax. But, as will be discussed later, these two simple examples mask a variety of technical issues. In the income tax case, the issue is determining taxable income. At both the federal and state levels, and even with recent income tax reforms, there are various exemptions, deductions, and adjustments made to gross income in determining taxable income. If there is disagreement about any of those modifications, the conclusion about horizontal equity could be challenged. Hence, even horizontal tax equity is difficult to attain.

The fact is that individuals are generally not equally situated. Vertical equity is the principle used to describe how a tax treats individuals in different economic conditions. Determining vertical equity, it turns out, is even more complex than determining horizontal equity. The first issue is to decide on the criterion for differentiating tax treatment. That is, if taxes burden some individuals more than others, what variable should determine those differences? The degree to which the tax should vary is a value judgment. But determining on what basis a tax should vary is an important tax policy decision.

An obvious criterion is that taxes should vary with benefits received—the more the benefits, the higher the taxes. A gas tax burdens drivers but meets the benefits-received criterion since individuals who drive benefit from use of public roads and highways. A fee-for-service tax by definition meets this principle; the fee is simply the tax for the service (or benefit) received. Appealing as the benefits-received criterion is, it is simply difficult if not impossible to measure the individual benefits received for provision of services on a broad scale. Police and fire services, for example, generally benefit the individuals within the locality where such protection is provided. But education, which is another locally provided service, provides benefits not only to individuals in the form of higher incomes but also to society in general in the form of economic growth and lower needs for social services (Cohn and Geske, 1990). Even if education benefits accrued only to individuals within the given locality, today most individuals move away from where they are educated, making it difficult to have anything other than a national tax related to those benefits.

At broader levels, a benefits principle is further problematic. For example, how would one measure individual benefits for defense spending, public transportation systems, interstate highway systems, a statewide higher education system, or an interstate system of waterways for transit and agriculture? Also, it would be foolish to increase the taxes for individuals receiving welfare benefits since that would defeat the purpose of the welfare program. Thus, a benefits principle, although appealing to economists, has not been implemented as a basis for differential tax treatment, at least for broadly based income, sales, and property taxes.

Ability to pay has been adopted in this country as the criterion for vertical tax equity. Ability to pay generally is measured by income. So if taxes differ among individuals, they should differ in relation to their ability to pay, i.e., to income. However, there remains the issue of whether to use annual income or some average income measure over a longer time period.

Vertical tax equity is measured by taxes expressed as a percent of income and is characterized as progressive, proportional, or regressive. Progressive tax burdens increase with income, i.e., are higher for individuals with higher incomes. In a progressive tax structure, taxes as a percent of income are highest for the top income categories, average for the middle income categories, and lowest for the bottom income categories. Proportional tax burdens impose the same tax percentage regardless of the level of income. With a proportional tax, a higher-income individual would pay a larger amount of taxes, but based on the same percentage of income, as a low-income taxpayer. Regressive taxes are the reverse of progressive taxes in that they represent a larger percentage of lower incomes; regressive taxes burden the poor more than the rich. If all individuals were assessed the same dollar amount of taxes, the burden would be regressive, since it would represent a lower percentage for an above-average income and a higher percentage for a below-average income.

In this country, it is generally agreed that regressive tax burdens should be avoided. It is widely felt that the low-income individual or household should not pay a larger percentage of income in taxes than individuals with average or above-average income. It is also generally agreed that the tax system should be at least proportional, and probably progressive, although support for progressive tax burdens has waned in recent years as initiatives at both federal and state levels have reduced the degree of progressivity of many taxes. Put differently, although a progressive tax burden has generally been sanctioned in the past, the present consensus still supports a progressive tax burden but to a lesser degree. For example, there is still support for a progressive federal income tax, although the level of progressivity as measured by the top marginal tax rates has been reduced substantially during the past 20 years—from 90 percent in the 1960s to 31 percent today—and many still would prefer a flat federal income tax rate. And, as discussed previously, states have enacted several policies during the past decade reducing progressive elements in state and local tax structures.

Measuring vertical tax equity entails an additional series of technical problems. First, one needs to distinguish tax impact from tax incidence or tax burden. That is, one needs to differentiate who actually pays the tax to the tax collector from who actually bears the burden of the tax. For example, merchants submit sales tax payments to governments, but individuals who purchase products actually bear the burden of the sales tax. Likewise, companies or organizations usually remit income tax payments to state and federal governments, but working individuals bear the burden of that tax since income taxes are withheld from periodic salary payments. The issue of tax incidence or tax burden for other taxes is not so clear-cut.

Tax incidence is most complex for the property tax. Property taxes have four components: owner-occupied homes, residential rental property, business and industrial property, and commercial property. The property tax on individuals who own homes is not only paid by homeowners, but they bear the full burden of the tax. Property taxes on the other components can be shifted. For example, property taxes on rental property might be shifted to renters in the form of higher rents. Depending on competitive conditions, property taxes on industries and corporations could be shifted forward to consumers in the form of higher prices, or backward to workers in the form of lower wages, or they could be borne by stockholders in the form of lower dividends and stock prices. A similar issue exists for corporate income taxes: are they shifted forward to consumers in the form of higher prices, or backward to stockholders and/or workers in the form of lower dividends and wages, respectively? Likewise, depending on competitive conditions, property taxes on local commercial activities could be shifted forward to consumers or backward to owners. It turns out that shifting assumptions and patterns produce widely varying conclusions about property tax and corporate income tax incidence, from being steeply regressive to steeply progressive.

Another issue to consider in assessing tax equity is income transfers. The country and many states have programs that transfer income from the broader group of taxpayers to the poor. Welfare programs, income tax credits, food stamps, rental supplements, and child care supports are just some examples of income transfer programs. Thus, a comprehensive assessment of tax equity would consider taxes as well as income transfers, for although the poor might pay a large percentage of their incomes in sales taxes and in assumed shifted property taxes, that regressivity could be counterbalanced by receipt of income from a variety of transfer programs. Likewise, average- and above-average-income individuals pay more taxes to support income transfer programs but receive no or few income transfer benefits, the largest being Social Security.

Pechman (1985, 1986) conducted analyses of the overall equity of the country's federal, state, and local taxes over several years. His analysis indicates the tax burdens that result under a variety of assumptions about property tax shifting. Figure 5.2 shows tax burdens by population decile (ranked by income) for several years from 1966 to 1985 under more progressive as well as under more regressive sets of assumptions about the property and corporate income taxes, but without adjustments for transfers. The more progressive assumptions place half of the burden of the corporate income tax on those who receive dividends and half on property income in general. All property taxes on improvements (houses and buildings) are allocated to

FIGURE 5.2   Total Burden of Federal, State, and Local Taxes by Population Decile, Selected Years

Population Decile	1966	1970	1975	1980	1985
More Progressive					
First[a]	16.8%	18.8%	19.7%	17.1%	17.0%
Second	18.9	19.5	17.6	17.1	15.9
Third	21.7	20.8	18.9	18.9	18.1
Fourth	22.6	23.2	21.7	20.8	21.2
Fifth	22.8	24.0	23.5	22.7	23.4
Sixth	22.7	24.1	23.9	23.4	23.8
Seventh	22.7	24.3	24.2	24.4	24.7
Eighth	23.1	24.6	24.7	25.5	25.4
Ninth	23.3	25.0	25.4	26.5	26.2
Tenth	30.1	30.7	27.8	28.5	26.4
All deciles[b]	25.2	26.1	25.0	25.3	24.5
More Regressive					
First[a]	27.5%	25.8%	27.9%	25.9%	24.0%
Second	24.8	24.2	21.7	22.2	20.1
Third	26.0	24.2	21.0	22.5	20.7
Fourth	25.9	25.9	24.0	23.5	23.2
Fifth	25.8	26.4	25.4	24.7	24.4
Sixth	25.6	26.2	25.5	25.1	25.0
Seventh	25.5	26.2	25.8	25.8	25.5
Eighth	25.5	26.4	26.1	26.7	26.2
Ninth	25.1	26.1	26.6	27.4	26.7
Tenth	25.9	27.8	25.9	26.8	25.0
All deciles[b]	25.9	26.7	25.5	26.3	25.3

[a] Includes negative incomes not shown separately.
[b] Includes units only in the sixth to tenth deciles.

Source: Joseph Pechman, "Who Paid the Taxes in 1966–1985," Washington, D.C., Brookings Institution, 1986 (revised tables).

FIGURE 5.3   Tax Burden before and after Transfer Payments, by Population Decile, 1986

Population Decile	More Progressive			More Regressive		
	Taxes	Transfers	Taxes less Transfers	Taxes	Transfers	Taxes less Transfers
First	32.8%	262.5%	−229.7%	50.8%	267.2%	−216.5%
Second	22.6	106.0	−83.4	28.3	109.8	−81.5
Third	23.8	30.5	−6.7	28.3	32.4	−4.1
Fourth	25.1	12.5	12.5	28.4	13.2	15.2
Fifth	25.9	7.6	18.3	28.9	7.8	21.0
Sixth	26.1	4.8	21.3	28.6	5.2	23.5
Seventh	26.4	3.5	22.9	28.9	3.6	25.4
Eighth	27.4	2.9	24.5	29.8	2.9	26.9
Ninth	28.3	1.8	26.5	29.9	1.7	28.2
Tenth	28.6	1.4	27.2	26.3	1.4	24.9
All classes	27.5	10.0	17.4	28.5	9.9	18.6

Source: Joseph Pechman "Who Paid the Taxes in 1966–85," Washington, D.C., Brookings Institution, 1986 (revised tables).

recipients of property income in general. The more regressive assumptions allocate half the corporate income tax to property income and half to consumers, and allocate all property taxes to shelter (i.e., those who pay rent) and consumption.[2]

The figure shows that the country's taxes are mildly progressive under the more progressive assumptions and about proportional under the more regressive assumptions. The table also shows that there has been little overall shift in the pattern of total tax burdens over this two-decade period.

Figure 5.3 shows tax burdens by population decile for 1986 under these two different incidence assumptions, with adjustments for transfer payments. Transfer payments include such government programs as welfare and Social Security, under which the government actually writes checks to citizens, i.e., transfers money to them, as well as programs such as food stamps that increase individual—primarily low-income individual—purchasing power. When these adjustments are made, the country's tax and income transfer system is found to be strongly progressive, regardless of incidence assumptions used. Tax burdens are at least −200 percent for the poorest 10 percent of the population, that is, poor individuals receive from the government income transfers totaling at least 200 percent more than they earn. In the middle and upper income ranges, the tax burden is mildly progressive.

[2] See Pechman (1985), pp. 24–37 for additional explanation of incidence assumptions and allocations.

Economic Effects

Taxes are imposed by governments and thus, by definition, distort the free functioning of the competitive market, but some taxes and specific tax design mechanics distort economic decision making more than others. The general goal is for taxes to have neutral economic impacts. So this represents another criterion for assessing a specific tax structure.

Most taxes have some elements that are not economically neutral. The federal income tax allows homeowners to deduct interest on home mortgages, thus encouraging housing consumption over other kinds of consumption. Since interest from savings is taxed at both the federal and state levels, consumption is encouraged over saving. Since most sales taxes cover only products, consumption of services is favored over consumption of products. Since business purchases, even of equipment and items that will be put into products for resale, are often subject to the sales tax, vertical integration[3] is somewhat encouraged if those costs are less than the costs of paying the tax. In California, property taxes are based on market value at the time of purchase rather than current market value; thus, moving entails a high cost and is discouraged, and remaining in one's home is thus encouraged.

Differences in taxes across state borders also can encourage business investment and individual location. In metropolitan areas near state boundaries, individuals are economically encouraged to live in the state with the lower sales and/or income tax rates so they can maximize their income benefits.

In short, almost all tax structures have elements that encourage or discourage a variety of economic behaviors. The goal is to structure the tax to neutralize its economic incentives or at least to minimize its economic distortions.

Administration and Compliance

Finally, both the administration of the tax and individual or business compliance with tax requirements should be as simple and low-cost as possible. Often simplicity is gained at the cost of some tax equity and vice versa. Further, the more complex the tax, the greater the costs of both administration and compliance.

An example of a revenue source with huge administration costs is a lottery, which is becoming increasingly popular across the country. The fact is that lotteries are poor revenue sources in large part because of the high costs of administration. To sell lottery tickets, a wide variety of prizes are required. In most states, prizes make up 50 percent of all lottery revenue. Put differently, for every $1 raised through lottery sales, a full 50 cents is allocated to prizes. Further, most merchants who sell lottery tickets earn a 5 percent commission,

---

[3] Vertical integration refers to a company that owns or produces the items needed for production, the production facilities, and the sales outlet, as is the case for many, but not all, oil companies.

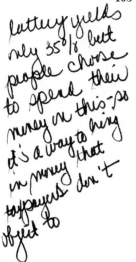

lottery yields only 35% but people chose their to spend their money on this - so it's a way to bring in money that taxpayers don't object to

which takes another nickel. Other administrative costs generally add an additional dime to expenses. After expenses, then, only 35 cents remains for each dollar of sales, a net yield of only 35 percent!

All other broad-based taxes, such as the income, sales, and property taxes, require administrative costs for both the government and individuals but provide a much higher net yield, somewhere in the high 90 percent range. To be sure, there are ways of increasing and decreasing administration costs of these taxes, but they still are dramatically lower than that those of a lottery.

States could nearly eliminate income tax administrative costs if they simply made the state income tax a fixed percent of federal tax liability. States could eliminate sales taxes altogether, and thus sales tax administrative costs, by adopting a general consumption tax that could be administered entirely through the income tax. Short of these more dramatic choices, streamlining federal and state tax administration is an important objective for any specific tax structure, as well as change in tax structure.

THE INCOME TAX

The individual income tax is the largest revenue producer for the federal government and is also used by 40 states. Another 3 states apply the income tax only to interest, dividends, and/or capital gains, i.e., on income from capital assets but not on earned income. Eleven states allow local governments to levy income taxes. In 1987, the individual income tax produced $392.6 billion for the federal government, $76.0 billion for state governments, and $7.7 billion for local governments (U.S. Bureau of the Census, 1988). Combining tax revenues from all sources, income taxes raise the largest amount and percentage of revenues. State income tax structures increasingly are being adapted to conform to the federal tax structure enacted during the 1986 federal income tax reform; the following analysis relates primarily to the federal income tax. This section ends with comments on trends in state income taxes and needed changes for the 1990s.

Basis

Income obviously is the base for both federal and state income taxes. But defining income and determining taxable income is a complex activity driven by federal and state tax codes that, even though revised recently, still consume hundreds of pages of law. Defining gross income and determining taxable income requires a series of modifications, including income adjustments; deductions, both standard and itemized; and exemptions. An income tax generally meets the horizontal equity standard since individuals with the same taxable income pay the same amount of tax, but horizontal equity is violated if any of the income modifications is deemed unjustified. In addition, both the federal and state governments have different tax schedules for individuals and for households. Since there is disagreement over what constitutes fair tax treatment of individuals versus families, horizontal equity is also violated if there is disagreement over the particular mechanism for differential treatment of individuals and families incorporated in either the federal or state income tax structure.

Income adjustments, standard and itemized deductions, and various exemptions at first blush seem reasonable modifications to make to determine taxable income. Most would agree that two families each with an income of $30,000, for example, should pay a different amount of tax if one family consists of just husband and wife with few medical expenditures and the other consists of husband, wife, four children, and a live-in parent and experiences large medical costs. But a deduction or adjustment that is reasonable to one person can seem unreasonable or unfair to another. For example, in the past, several types of investments provided large deductions for individual taxpayers, often exceeding the dollar amount of investment made. Although such tax shelters encouraged investment in those activities, some having beneficial social value, such as low-income housing, the proliferation of tax shelters and their use primarily by higher-income individuals led to perception over time that they were simply unfair.

The 1986 federal income tax reform streamlined the tax by eliminating most income adjustments, deductions, and tax shelters. Nearly all tax shelters were eliminated. Several deductions were eliminated, including state sales taxes; the original proposal called for eliminating the deduction for all state and local taxes, including the property tax. Interest deductions, except for interest on homes with a mortgage up to $1,000,000, were phased out.[4] Even medical and other deductions were reduced because such expenses had to exceed a higher percentage of gross income in order to qualify for deduction.

Several income adjustments also were eliminated. All capital gains had to be included in income, whereas in the past a percentage had been excluded; investments in individual retirement accounts were no longer exemptible in determining federal taxable income; medical deductions had to exceed 3 percent of income; and other deductions were eliminated. The personal exemption was increased by more than 100 percent, to $2,000 per individual, and its level was indexed to inflation so that it will rise in the future.

In short, the 1986 federal tax reform made several changes in the determination of gross and taxable income, which can be characterized as broadening the base by excluding numerous adjustments that had been allowed in the past. The changes substantially increased the horizontal equity of the tax.

From an economic perspective, though, additional changes could have been made to improve equity. For example, economists suggest that imputed rent for owner-occupied homes should be included as income. The rationale is that homeowners have an asset—a home—that could produce a return—rent—if

---

[4] The home mortgage interest deduction reflects the American value of individual home ownership.

it were placed on the market, and that a true economic picture of homeowners should include that potential rent. Renters not only do not have that imputed rent, but they cannot deduct mortgage interest even if it is shifted to them in higher rents. This argument never succeeds in the political arena for at least two reasons. Policymakers do not like to include unrealized economic gains—such as imputed rent—in determining a base that can be taxed. Indeed, one factor behind the unpopularity of the property tax is that when property values rise faster than incomes, the tax can become less and less related to ability to pay. Second, encouraging home ownership is a strong American value. Excluding imputed rent in determining income and including home mortgage interest as an allowable deduction both contribute to that value, even though those policies entail economic distortions.

Yield

The individual and corporate income tax have produced large amounts of revenues, in 1987 equaling $476.5 billion for the federal government and $106.9 billion for state and local governments. State and local individual income taxes total only 22.3 percent of federal individual income taxes.

Figure 5.4 shows income taxes as a percent of personal income over 20 years. These data reveal interesting trends. First, income taxes rose rapidly between 1957 and 1987, from $59.5 billion in 1957 to $582.8 billion in 1987, nearly a ten-fold rise. Second, total individual and corporate income taxes dropped as a percent of personal income over this 30-year period, from 16.7 percent in 1957 to 15.4 percent in 1987. But the last column in Figure 5.4 shows that individual income taxes rose as a percent of personal income from 10.5 percent in 1957 to 12.6 percent in 1987. These two trends are the result of a rapid drop in corporate income taxes and a rise in individual income taxes. Thus, although income taxes overall have dropped as a "bite" of personal income, there has been a shift in which individuals pay more and corporations pay less. This shift could be one reason that income taxes are still not very popular taxes.

The income tax also is an elastic tax. As income rises, income taxes also rise. Figure 5.5 shows, in fact, that the simple individual income tax elasticity itself has risen in each of the past three decades, from 1.02 between 1957 and 1967 to 1.12 between 1977 and 1987. Although these figures are not adjusted for rate and other changes, they show nevertheless that as income has grown, individual income tax revenues have grown slightly more rapidly. In other words, individual income taxes tend to be an elastic tax source.

Federal and state income tax rates have changed substantially over this 30-year period, and new income taxes have been enacted in many states. More economically pure elasticity figures adjust for these structural changes. Research shows that these purer elasticity figures range between 1.5 and 1.6, higher than the figures in Figure 5.5 (Gold, 1986b).

Income taxes, although elastic, also are quite stable. Even in economic downturns, personal income does not drop much. As a result, individual income taxes drop little, if at all. Since corporate profits fluctuate much more in

FIGURE 5.4 Income Taxes as a Percent of Personal Income, 1957 to 1987 (amounts in billions)

Fiscal Year	Total Individual and Corporate Income Taxes	Total Individual Income Taxes	Personal Income	Total Individual and Corporate Income Taxes as Percent of Personal Income	Total Individual Income Taxes as Percent of Personal Income
1957	$ 59.5	$ 37.4	$ 356.3	16.7	10.5
1967	103.5	68.3	644.5	16.1	10.6
1977	250.0	189.5	1,607.5	15.5	11.8
1987	582.8	476.5	3,780.0	15.4	12.6

Source: Advisory Commission on Intergovernmental Relations, *Significant Features of Fiscal Federalism, 1988 Edition,* vol. II. Washington, D.C., ACIR, 1988, p. 64, Table 59; U.S. Bureau of the Census, *Government Finance in 1986–87,* Washington, D.C., U.S. Bureau of the Census, 1988, p. 7; and *Economic Report of the President,* January 1989, p. 333.

FIGURE 5.5 Income Tax Yield Elasticity, 1957 to 1987 (amounts in billions)

Year	Individual Income Taxes	Personal Income	Percent Change from Previous Decade		Elasticity: Ratio of Percent Changes
			Income Taxes	Income	
1957	$ 37.4	$ 356.3	—	—	—
1967	68.3	644.5	82.6	80.9	1.02
1977	189.5	1,607.5	177.5	149.4	1.19
1987	476.2	3,780.0	151.3	135.1	1.12

Source: Advisory Commission on Intergovernmental Relations, *Significant Features of Fiscal Federalism, 1988 Edition*, vol. II, Washington, D.C., ACIR, p. 64, Table 59; U.S. Bureau of the Census, *Government Finance in 1986–87*, Washington, D.C., U.S. Bureau of the Census, 1988, p. 7, *Economic Report of the President*, January 1989, p. 333.

recessions and economic growth periods, corporate income taxes tend to be less stable than individual income taxes. Thus, the trend toward making individual income taxes a larger portion of the total of individual and corporate income taxes works to make the tax more stable. The price might be less popularity.

Equity

Horizontal equity was discussed earlier. In terms of vertical equity, the federal individual income tax is clearly progressive, as are most state individual income tax structures. Since individuals cannot shift the income tax, tax impact and tax burden are identical, i.e., those who pay the tax also bear its burden or economic incidence.

Progressivity exists largely because of the structure of the federal income tax. First, in 1989 the personal exemption was $2,000 for each individual, the individual's spouse, and each dependent. Thus, for a family of four, $8,000 was exempt from taxation. Second, the standard deduction for married individuals filing a joint return was increased to $5,200, an additional exemption. Third, the maximum earned income credit was increased to $910. The net effect of these changes was to eliminate federal income taxes completely for a family of four with an income below $19,250.

In addition, federal income tax rates are quite, though not steeply, progressive. The rates, which increase with income, are 15, 28, and 33 percent and cut in at different income levels depending on filing status. For married individuals filing jointly in 1989, the rate was 15 percent for taxable income up to $29,750, 28 percent for income between $29,750 and $71,900, 33 percent for income between $71,900 and $149,250, and then 28 percent for income over $149,250.[5] Further, the income brackets are now indexed

[5] In 1990 the law was again changed to produce a three-rate structure, with the first two rates unchanged and the top rate changed to 31 percent for all incomes above $71,900.

to inflation; thus, inflation will not automatically push individuals into higher tax brackets, and the Congress will have to raise rates if more income tax revenues are needed than the indexed structure produces. State income tax rates are not nearly as progressive overall, ranging from flat rates to top rates that equal 10 percent, as shown in Figure 5.6. Only 10 states have indexed income brackets.

Pechman (1986) has conducted the most comprehensive analysis of the actual burden of individual income taxes, and his results are displayed in Figure 5.7. The data show that income taxes have a progressive incidence pattern, regardless of incidence assumptions. The data also show that the income tax bite increased from 1975 to 1980 and from 1980 to 1985 for population deciles 2 through 9, i.e., for 80 percent of all taxpayers. For the richest 10 percent, the burden rose between 1975 and 1980 but then dropped between 1980 and 1985, probably the effect of the 1981 tax cuts.

State tax burden studies have not been as detailed as the Pechman national studies, in large part because gathering such data for all 50 states is very costly. Nevertheless, Phares (1980) calculated indices of progressivity for state individual income taxes for 1977 and found state individual income taxes to be the most progressive state tax. Indeed, Phares found that only state tax structures with a major individual income tax were progressive overall.

Economic Effects

To the degree that deductions and income adjustments are limited, the income tax can be quite neutral in its economic effects. Nevertheless, there are several economic impacts created by both the federal and most state income taxes. First, as stated previously, the deduction of home mortgage interest encourages home purchases more than would be the case if the deduction were eliminated. Second, including interest earned from savings as well as returns from investments in taxable income produces some deterrent to savings. Although there is reasonable debate over these tax provisions, if neither were taxed, savings and investments probably would increase and arguably would help improve the productivity of the country's economic system. Recent evidence (Long, 1988) suggests that savings increased when IRA investments were deductible and tax rates were higher, and they have fallen somewhat since 1986, when they were eliminated as a deduction and tax rates were lowered. Similarly, investments in tax shelters have decreased since 1986 and probably have been diverted into more fruitful activities. One of the greatest economic impacts has been the overall rate reduction enacted in 1986, which has both increased disposable income and decreased the value of any deduction. For example, charitable contributions can still be deducted, but prior to 1986 they produced a 50 percent saving for an individual in the top tax bracket and now produce just a 31 percent saving, thus increasing the real cost of such contributions.

FIGURE 5.6 State Tax Rates as of July 1, 1989

State	Income Taxes Corporate	Income Taxes Individual	General Sales and Use Tax	Gasoline Tax (per gallon)	Cigarette Tax (per pack of 20)	Property Tax
Alabama	5% (F)	2 to 5% (F)	4% (a)	11 cents	16.5 cents	X
Arizona	2.5 to 10.5 (F)	2 to 8 (F)	5 (a)	17	15	X
Arkansas	1 to 6	1 to 7	4 (a)	13.5	21	X
California	9.3 (d)	1 to 9.3 (d)	4.75 (a)	9	35	X
Colorado	5 to 5.4	5 (d)	3 (a)	12	20	X
Connecticut	11.5 (c)	1 to 14 (b)	8	20	40	X
Georgia	6	1 to 6	4 (a)	7.5 + 3% of retail	12	X
Hawaii	4.4 to 6.4	2 to 10	4	16 to 22.5	40% wholesale	
Idaho	8	2 to 8.2	5	18	18	X
Illinois	4	2.5	5 (a)	13	20	X
Indiana	3.4	3.4	5	15	15.5	X
Iowa	6 to 12 (F, c)	0.4 to 9.98 (F, d)	4 (a)	20	31	X
Kansas	4.5 (c)	3.65 to 8.75 (F)	4.25 (a)	15	24	
Kentucky	4 to 8 (F)	2 to 6 (F)	4 (a)	16	16	
Maine	3.5 to 8.93 (d)	2 to 8	5	17	28	X
Maryland	7	2 to 5	5	18.5	13	X
Massachusetts		5	5	11 (d)	26	X
Michigan	2.35	4.6	4	15	25	X
Minnesota	9.5 (d)	6 to 8.5 (d)	6 (a)	20	38	X
Mississippi	3 to 5	3 to 5	6	18	18	
Missouri	5 (F)	1.5 to 6 (F)	4.225 (a)	11	13	X
Nebraska	4.75 to 6.65	3.1 to 4.8 (d)	4 (a)	22.3 (d)	27	
New Jersey	9 (c)	2 to 3.5	6	10.5	27	X
New Mexico	4.8 to 7.6	1.8 to 8.5	4.75 (a)	16.2	15	X
New York	9 (d)	4 to 7.875	4 (a)	8	33	
North Carolina	7	3 to 7	3 (a)	15.7 (d)	2	X
North Dakota	3 to 10.5 (F, d)	3.24 to 14.57 (F)	6	20	30	X

State						
Ohio	5.1 to 8.9	0.743 to 6.9	5 (a)	15.1 (d)	18	X
Oklahoma	5	0.5 to 10 (F)	4 (a)	16	23	X
Pennsylvania	8.5	2.1	6	12	18	X
Rhode Island	9	22.96% of federal income tax	6	20 (d)	35	X
South Carolina	5	2.75 to 7	5	16	7	X
Tennessee	6	6 (b)	5.5 (a)	20	13	X
Utah	5	2.6 to 7.35 (F)	5.094 (a)	19	23	X
Vermont	5.5 to 8.25	25% of federal income tax	4	16	17	X
Virginia	6	2 to 5.75	3.5 (a)	17.5	2.5	X
West Virginia	9.45	3 to 6.5 (d)	6	15.5	17	X
Wisconsin	7.9	4.9 to 6.93 (d)	5 (a)	20.8 (d)	30	X
Florida	5.5 (d)	These seven states have no individual income tax	6 (a)	4	24	X
Nevada	These five states have no corporate income tax		5.75 (a)	16.25	15	X
South Dakota			4 (a)	18	23	X
Texas			6 (a)	15	26	X
Washington			6.5 (a)	18	34	X
Wyoming			3 (a)	9	12	X
Alaska	1 to 9.4 (d)		These five states have no general sales tax	8	16	X
Delaware	8.7	3.2 to 7.7		16	14	X
Montana	6.75 (c)	2 to 11 (F)		20	16	X
New Hampshire	8	5 (b)		14	21	X
Oregon	6.6	5 to 9 (F)		16	27	X

(X) Indicates state levies a property tax.
(F) Allows federal income tax as a deduction.
(a) Local taxes are additional.
(b) In Connecticut, New Hampshire, and Tennessee, rates apply to income from interest and dividends only. Capital gains are taxed at 7 percent in Connecticut.
(c) Corporate surtax is imposed: Connecticut, 20 percent; Kansas, 2.25 percent; Montana, 4 percent; New Jersey's rate is 0.375 percent beginning July 31, 1989.
(d) Tax rate is periodically adjusted administratively.
(e) Alternative minimum tax is imposed.

Source: Tax Foundation, *Tax Features,* 1989.

FIGURE 5.7   Individual Income Tax Burden by Income Class, 1975, 1980, 1985

	Individual Income Taxes as a Percent of Income		
Population Decile	*1975*	*1980*	*1985*
More Progressive Assumptions			
First[a]	2.4	2.4	3.8
Second	2.8	3.5	3.5
Third	3.9	5.1	5.2
Fourth	5.9	6.1	7.4
Fifth	7.4	7.8	9.2
Sixth	8.1	8.8	9.9
Seventh	8.7	9.9	10.9
Eighth	9.5	11.3	11.9
Ninth	10.9	12.9	13.3
Tenth	12.6	14.7	13.5
All deciles[b]	9.3	10.8	10.9
More Regressive Assumptions			
First[a]	2.3	2.8	4.0
Second	2.7	3.2	3.4
Third	3.8	5.1	5.1
Fourth	5.6	5.9	7.1
Fifth	7.0	7.5	8.7
Sixth	7.7	8.3	9.5
Seventh	8.3	9.4	10.4
Eighth	9.1	10.8	11.5
Ninth	10.6	12.6	13.0
Tenth	13.5	15.6	14.5
All deciles[b]	9.3	10.7	10.9

[a] Includes negative incomes.
[b] Includes only sixth to tenth deciles.

Source: Joseph Pechman, "Who Paid the Taxes in 1966–86," Washington, D.C., Brookings Institution, 1986 (revised tables).

Administration and Compliance

The federal income tax, although probably fairer than it was before 1986, is still complex and costly to administer for businesses and most individuals. Many individuals use accountants and other services to fill out income tax forms, and businesses have large accounting departments that spend considerable time keeping tax records. Tax requirements often differ from good accounting requirements, and new requirements for reporting interest from savings have forced banks to incur administrative costs over the past few years.

Major changes in the income tax structure also have caused large compliance costs. The income tax not only was overhauled in 1986 but was further modified in 1987, 1988, and 1990, and it had experienced several major changes during the early 1980s. States also continuously enact incremental changes in their individual income taxes. This stream of changes adds to compliance burdens since new rules have to be learned and then applied correctly. Nevertheless, high as administration and compliance costs are, they are quite small as a percent of total revenues.

Income Tax Trends and Issues at the State Level

Although state sales tax increases received most attention during the mid-1980s, the state income tax increased both as a percent of personal income and as a percent of total state taxes, as shown by the data in Figure 5.8. Between 1957 and 1977, state income taxes rose from 0.7 percent to 2.2 percent of personal income, and from 17.2 to 34.3 percent of total state taxes. The increases continued through 1987, with taxes rising to 2.6 percent and 39.2 percent, respectively.

These trends emerged in part because few states have reformed their income tax structures. Maximum tax rates were reached in nearly half the states when taxable incomes reached only $10,000 and the value of personal exemptions was low. Thus, inflation in the late 1970s together with general wage increases pushed individuals into the top income tax brackets. These realities interacted with rate increases in the early 1980s to combat revenue losses caused by recession and federal aid cuts, and income tax revenues rose. An unanticipated result, in part also due to unchanged income tax structures, was that increasing numbers of low-income households faced income tax burdens for the first time.

Although a few states began to reform their income tax codes in 1987, reform in most other states is needed to produce a state income tax structure sufficient for the 1990s, and one more in line with the 1986 federal tax changes. Four major themes characterize the need for state income tax reform:

FIGURE 5.8   State Income Taxes as a Percent of Personal Income and as a Percent of Total State Taxes

Year	State Income Taxes as a Percent of Personal Income	State Income Taxes as a Percent of Total State Taxes
1957	0.7	17.2
1967	1.1	22.2
1977	2.2	34.3
1987	2.6	39.2

Source: Advisory Commission on Intergovernmental Relations, *Significant Features of Fiscal Federalism, 1988 Edition,* vol. II, Washington, D.C., ACIR, 1988, p. 64; and U.S. Bureau of the Census, *Government Finance in 1986–87,* Washington, D.C., U.S. Bureau of the Census, 1988, p. 7.

- Broadening the base to improve horizontal equity, increase political and popular perceptions about the fairness of the tax, and negate the trend to narrow the base through exclusions, while also allowing for rate reduction
- Rate reduction in both numbers and levels, which will enhance public perception of the tax and help improve the business climate
- Increasing the values of personal exemptions, standard deductions, and earned income credits to eliminate the poor from income tax rolls
- Indexing the entire structure to require political votes to increase revenues rather than allowing tax revenue increases to occur as a by-product of inflation

Conclusions about the Income Tax

The income tax historically has been perceived as a fair tax and is the most progressive tax at the federal level and in most states. During the 1970s and 1980s, it was increasingly viewed as unfair as proliferating exclusions, special tax shelters, inflation, and privileged treatment drove most individuals into higher tax brackets, put the poor on the income tax rolls for the first time, and allowed many rich individuals and corporations to avoid paying any income taxes. The 1986 and 1990 federal income tax reforms began to reverse those trends and to restore the income tax as a fair and continued high-revenue-producing tax. States began to reform state income taxes in 1987. If the income tax reform fever continues, the individual income tax can be restored as the basic progressive feature of most states' tax structures, and the recent trend for states to rely somewhat more heavily on the income tax would be a sound policy to pursue.

THE SALES TAX

The general sales tax is used by 45 states and Washington, D.C. About 31 states allow local governments to augment the state rate with a local add-on. No state has added a sales tax since Vermont did in 1969. Only Alaska, Delaware, Montana, New Hampshire, and Oregon do not have a sales tax, and few predict that any of those states will enact one soon. The sales tax is the largest revenue source for state governments. Except for selective excise taxes on such products as liquor, telephones, and cigarettes, the federal government does not use the sales tax or a value-added tax as do federal governments in several other countries.

In 1987, the general sales and gross receipts tax produced $79.6 billion for state governments and $17.1 billion for local governments. State governments began to increase sales tax rates in the mid-1980s, in part to compensate revenue losses caused by the early 1980s recession and in part to finance education reforms spawned by the *Nation at Risk* report (National Commission on Excellence in Education, 1983). Further, states began to consider whether to expand the sales tax to include services; Florida enacted such a law and then quickly repealed it. The last part of this section reviews the arguments surrounding a sales tax on services.

Basis

In most states, the general sales tax covers purchases by both individuals and businesses but does not cover all purchases of either. Food, prescription drugs, and clothing are exempt from sales taxes in many states, allegedly to reduce regressivity. Neither homes nor rental payments are included in the sales tax base. Most public finance economists argue that the sales tax should cover all consumer expenditures, including food and clothing, and that regressive elements caused by such inclusion should be handled with income tax credits.

Many business purchases, including equipment, machinery, and products used in making other products for resale (i.e., business wholesale purchases), are exempt from the sales tax. Products consumed in the conduct of business, though, are generally subject to the income tax. But there is considerable debate about whether a sales tax should apply at all to businesses. Public finance economists argue that the sales tax should apply only to consumer purchases, and to all consumer purchases, including services as well as products, and not to any business purchase. Taxing business purchases increases the costs of production and encourages more vertical integration, which generally carries a degree of production inefficiency. Further, taxing some business purchases and not others discriminates against businesses that must use a large percentage of those items taxed.

With respect just to those items that are subject to the general sales tax, the sales tax provides horizontal equity. It is virtually impossible for an individual or business that purchases an item subject to the tax to avoid paying the sales tax. Including all consumer expenditures, on products as well as services, would improve the horizontal equity of the sales tax; these issues are discussed more fully later in this section.

Yield

In 1987, the sales tax produced $79.6 billion for state governments and $17.1 billion for local governments. On average, the sales tax produced about $16 billion nationally for each 1 percent levied. Sales tax rates have increased during the past decade. The median sales tax rate has risen from 3 percent in 1970 to 5 percent in 1989. In 1970, only one state had a sales tax rate over 6 percent; in 1989, 11 states had a sales tax rate that exceeded 6 percent. Not only do sales tax rates differ widely across the states, but some states allow local sales tax add-ons which further increase the rates (see Figure 5.6).

Nominal rates, though, do not indicate the actual bite taken out of personal income, since not all expenditures are subject to the sales tax. Figure 5.9 shows sales, gross receipts, and customs taxes as a percent of personal in-

FIGURE 5.9   Sales, Gross Receipts, and Customs Taxes as a Percent of Personal Income, by Level of Government, Selected Years

Year	Total	Federal	State	Local
1957	5.8	3.1	2.4	0.3
1967	5.6	2.4	2.9	0.3
1977	5.2	1.4	3.3	0.5
1987	5.1	1.3	3.2	0.6

Source: Advisory Commission on Intergovernmental Relations, *Significant Features of Fiscal Federalism, 1988 Edition,* vol. II, Washington, D.C., ACIR, 1988, p. 64, Table 59; U.S. Bureau of the Census, *Government Finance in 1986–87,* Washington, D.C., U.S. Bureau of the Census, 1988, p. 7; and *Economic Report of the President,* January 1989, p. 333.

come over several years. First, sales-type taxes consumed about 5.1 percent of personal income in 1987, down from 5.8 percent in 1957. Second, the federal share, primarily the customs tax, dropped from 3.1 to 1.3 percent of personal income between 1957 and 1987. Third, the state share has grown from 2.4 to 3.2 percent, although state sales and gross receipts taxes as a percent of income remained steady in the decade between 1977 and 1987. Fourth, the local share is growing but is still less than 1 percent. Interestingly, the overall sales tax "bite" out of personal income is about equal to the median sales tax rate.

The sales tax is both an elastic and a somewhat unstable revenue source. Figure 5.10 shows that the simple sales tax elasticity was 1.31 between 1967 and 1977, but it dropped to just 1.02 between 1977 and 1987. More sophisticated studies also show a drop in the sales tax elasticity, from about 1.1 in the early 1970s to 0.9 in the mid-1970s (Gold, 1986b). At best, it seems that sales tax revenues increase at about the same rate as personal income. The sales tax is somewhat less elastic than the income tax, in part since expenditures in items subject to a sales tax decreases as incomes rise. Nevertheless, consumption is very dependent on personal income, so as incomes rise, consumption rises, and thus so do sales tax revenues.

Likewise, in economic downturns when personal incomes fall, sales tax revenues also fall, making the sales tax a somewhat unstable revenue producer. Put differently, the sales tax is closely attuned to economic cycles, and sales tax revenues rise and fall pretty much in line with economic up- and downturns. Thus, although the sales tax is the major state revenue producer and, it turns out, the most popular revenue producer, it can cause revenue shortfalls during poor economic times; careful state monitoring is therefore needed to keep overall expenditures within revenue limits when the economy stagnates.

Equity

The sales tax is generally acknowledged to be a regressive, though not steeply regressive, tax. Since retailers actually collect the tax and physically submit the

FIGURE 5.10 State and Local Sales Tax Simple Elasticity

Year	Total State & Local General & Selective Sales & Gross Receipts Taxes (billions)	Personal Income (billions)	Percent Change in Sales Taxes	Personal Income	Elasticity: Ratio of Percent Changes
1957	$ 9.5	$ 356.3	—	—	—
1967	20.5	644.5	116.8	80.9	1.44
1977	60.6	1,607.5	195.6	149.4	1.31
1987	144.3	3,780.0	138.1	135.1	1.02

Source: Advisory Commission on Intergovernmental Relations, *Significant Features of Fiscal Federalism, 1988 Edition*, vol. II, Washington, D.C., ACIR, p. 64, Table 59; U.S. Bureau of the Census, *Government Finance 1986–87*, Washington, D.C., U.S. Bureau of the Census, 1988, p.7; *Economic Report of the President*, January 1989, p. 333.

revenues to the state, they bear the impact of the sales tax. However, individuals bear the burden or economic incidence since they pay the sales tax amount to the retailer and there is no way individuals can shift the sales tax to someone else. But because records are not kept of individual purchases, data do not exist to directly track individual sales tax payments. Thus, determining vertical equity, i.e., the incidence of the sales tax by income categories, requires a series of analyses.

The reason the sales tax is regressive is that individuals purchase declining amounts of items subject to sales tax as income rises. High-income individuals might spend more of their income on housing (which is not subject to sales taxation), investments, and savings. At the other end, lower-income individuals must spend more for food and other essential items. Although all individuals pay the same sales tax rate, as a percent of family income lower-income families purchase more items subject to the sales tax than middle- or upper-income families. As a result, the tax is regressive in incidence.

To calculate the sales tax burden, data are needed on individual consumption by income class. The consumption data must be detailed enough to distinguish those expenditures on items subject to the sales tax from those that are not. The data in Figure 5.11 show such consumption expenditures for 1986. There are several interesting patterns in these numbers. First, the data show that the highest income groups do not spend all of their income; a portion is left over for savings and investment. The lowest income groups, by contrast, spent more than their income, suggesting that they receive income supports such as welfare or food stamps or, for those temporarily poor, spend some of their savings. Second, for all six expenditure categories presented, consumption as a percent of income falls as income rises. Thus, a sales tax on consumption should show a regressive incidence pattern.

Pechman (1986) has conducted the most comprehensive analysis of the actual burden of sales taxes, and his results are displayed in Figure 5.12. The

FIGURE 5.11   Consumer Expenditure as a Percent of Income, 1986

Selected Expenditure Category	Total Income before Taxes					
	Lowest Quintile	*Second Quintile*	*Third Quintile*	*Fourth Quintile*	*Highest Quintile*	*Average*
Food	49.5	23.0	16.6	13.2	9.5	13.9
Housing	104.0	45.0	33.0	25.8	21.7	28.9
Clothes	17.1	7.3	5.8	5.3	4.4	5.4
Transportation	53.1	25.3	21.7	19.1	15.2	19.2
Health	20.2	9.3	6.3	3.7	2.3	4.5
Entertainment	13.3	5.2	5.0	4.7	3.9	4.6
Total expenditures[a]	301.0	136.0	108.0	91.0	75.0	96.0

[a] Includes categories not shown above.

Source: Bureau of Labor Statistics, *Consumer Expenditures Integrated Survey Data,* Washington, D.C., U.S. Department of Labor, August 1989.

FIGURE 5.12 Sales and Excise Tax Burden by Income Class, 1975, 1980, 1985

Population Decile	Sales and Excise Tax Rates		
	1975	1980	1985
More Progressive Assumptions			
First[a]	9.2%	8.4%	7.0%
Second	7.1	7.0	5.9
Third	6.1	5.9	5.0
Fourth	6.0	5.5	4.6
Fifth	5.7	5.1	4.3
Sixth	5.5	4.9	4.1
Seventh	5.2	4.8	3.9
Eighth	5.0	4.5	3.7
Ninth	4.5	3.9	3.3
Tenth	2.4	2.1	1.9
All deciles[b]	4.5	4.0	3.4
More Regressive Assumptions			
First[a]	9.6%	8.7%	7.2%
Second	6.8	6.8	5.7
Third	5.9	5.8	4.9
Fourth	5.9	5.4	4.6
Fifth	5.6	5.0	4.2
Sixth	5.3	4.8	4.0
Seventh	5.1	4.5	3.8
Eighth	4.8	4.3	3.7
Ninth	4.3	3.9	3.2
Tenth	2.5	2.1	1.9
All deciles[b]	4.5	4.0	3.4

[a] Includes negative incomes.
[b] Includes only sixth to tenth deciles.

Source: Joseph Pechman, "Who Paid the Taxes in 1966–86," Washington, D.C., The Brookings Institution, 1986, (revised tables).

results show that, indeed, the sales tax is regressive under both incidence assumptions. The incidence pattern is mildly regressive for middle income groups and steeply regressive for the lowest income groups (i.e., the incidence rises dramatically) and for the highest income group (i.e., the incidence falls dramatically). Interestingly, the average sales tax burden has been falling, from 4.5 percent in 1975 to 4.0 percent in 1980 and 3.4 percent in 1985.

State tax burden studies have not been as detailed as the Pechman federal studies, in large part because gathering such data for all 50 states would be a very costly exercise. Nevertheless, Phares (1980) calculated indices of progressivity for state sales taxes for 1977 and generally found the sales tax to be mildly regressive.

Sales Tax Exemptions

As mentioned previously, several items are typically exempt from a state's general sales tax. The argument for such exemptions primarily hinges on vertical equity, that exemption is needed to reduce regressivity. For example, lower-income households spend a greater portion of their incomes for food. Thus, including food in the sales tax base injects a substantial regressive element into the tax structure. Although it would be economically "cleaner" to address this type of regressivity through an income tax credit for the poor, which would protect them from regressive sales taxes and still require the nonpoor to pay sales tax even on food, income tax credits have not been popular measures for dealing with these obvious regressive sales tax elements. Most individuals do not make the connection between the two taxes; they simply see that they are paying sales tax on food, which is a necessity. Even above-average-income individuals feel they should not have to pay tax on food. Thus, most states have exemptions for items such as food and prescription drugs. Exemptions make clear the differential treatment of these items.

This part discusses several items that are usually treated specially in state sales tax structures, reviews the conclusions of their impact on sales tax incidence, and makes suggestions for how states could better treat them in their tax systems.

Food.   It is widely agreed that including food in the sales tax base injects a steeply regressive element. As the data in Figure 5.11 show quite strongly, lower-income households spend more on food than either average- or above-average-income households. If food is eliminated from the sales tax base, though, both the poor and the rich benefit. Thus, a preferred solution is to enact a sales tax credit on a state's income tax in an amount that would approximate the sales taxes paid on food (Mikesell, 1986). But 28 states and Washington, D.C., have chosen to exempt food from the sales tax. Income tax credits, although pristine in public finance eyes, are viewed as too indirect in most policy arenas. Only 8 states have income tax credits; 28 states exempt food from the sales tax.

Prescription Drugs.   All states with a sales tax exempt prescription drugs from the sales tax base, except for Hawaii and New Mexico. The general feeling is that extra tax burdens should not be caused simply by illness, that the only reason individuals purchase prescription drugs is to alleviate sickness. The incidence effects of this exemption, however, are not quite so clear, since the poor generally have a higher incidence of illness but less access to medical services. Nevertheless, it is generally conceded that illness should not increase tax burden, so nearly all states exempt prescription drugs from sales taxes.

Clothing.   Only six states—Connecticut, Massachusetts, Minnesota, New Jersey, Pennsylvania, and Rhode Island—exempt clothing from the sales tax, and some of these are the most recent states to adopt a sales tax. It seems that state politics made the clothing exemption one of the trade-offs for enacting a major new broad-based tax.

As shown by the data in Figure 5.11, though, clothing expenditures also decrease with income. Clearly, the poor spend a higher portion of their income on clothing, as is the pattern for food expenditures. Thus, exempting clothing from the sales tax would reduce sales tax regressivity but again would benefit rich and poor alike. Thus, just as for food, an income tax credit for the poor would be the preferred approach to redress this regressive element.

Items generally subject to special excise taxes.   Alcohol (including beer, wine, and liquor), cigarettes, motor fuel, and residential fuel and electricity are treated differently in most state sales tax structures. As a group, these items are usually subject to special excise taxes and then often excluded from the sales tax.

There seems to be little justification for exclusion, even though full inclusion would add modestly to the regressivity of the sales tax. Beer, wine, liquor, and cigarettes usually are targeted for special excise taxes, popularly called "sin taxes." But although there is reason to tax these purchases more, there is little reason not to subject them to the general sales tax as well. Most states include cigarettes in the sales tax base, and the most common practice is also to include alcohol products. The general policy prescription for all states would be to include them in the general sales tax base.

On the other hand, few states include motor fuel in the general sales tax base, and when energy prices rose in the late 1970s, half the states exempted residential fuel and electricity from the general sales tax base. Neither practice can be justified on economic or tax equity grounds (Mikesell, 1986). A state gasoline tax should continue, with the proceeds being used for highway construction and maintenance, but motor fuel also should be added to the sales tax base. Likewise, it may be time to add residential fuel and electricity back to the sales tax base. Both additions would broaden the base, increase sales tax revenues, and improve both the horizontal and vertical equity of the sales tax.

Generally, exemptions for individual purchases should be limited severely. Except for food, they rarely improve vertical equity, they erode the base and thus reduce revenues, and they erode vertical equity.

Economic Effects

In general, the sales tax does not have many adverse economic effects aside from the general issue, discussed earlier, of whether businesses should be subject to any sales tax burden. Differential sales tax rates can affect, to some degree, purchasing behavior. For example, if one county has a local add-on to a state sales tax, individuals might travel outside that county for major purchases. Likewise, if the sales tax rate differs at state borders, as is the case between

New York and New Jersey or New York and Connecticut, individuals might travel across state borders to the low-tax state for major purchases. Empirical data supporting these economic predictions, however, is inconsistent.

Administration and Compliance

Administration and compliance costs for the sales tax are neither complex nor costly. Generally, retailers who sell items subject to the sales tax need to register with the state and follow procedures for collecting the tax and submitting those revenues to state or local authorities. Although technicalities arise in determining which items are in the tax base—such as food for preparation (usually exempt from the base) versus food for consumption (usually included in the base)—those details get worked out over time. Both administrative and compliance costs are less than those for the income tax.

Expanding the Sales Tax to Services

Expanding the sales tax to services could be one of the most basic sales tax structural changes debated during the 1990s. Currently, most states include some services in the sales tax base, and the trend is to add services incrementally to the base. Pet services and haircuts, for example, have been added in several states during the past five years. It could be that services will be added one by one so that, in the near future, a wide range of services will be included.

Few states have attempted to change the sales tax to a tax on all individual purchases—products as well as services. In the mid-1980s, Florida extended the sales tax to services and then repealed the change, all within a 12-month period, and ran into political difficulties. But Florida's treatment of national firms and specifics of internal politics had as much to do with defeat of its sales tax initiative than did the general idea of taxing services. In 1990, Massachusetts extended a 5 percent sales tax to 600 services. Most states tax some services— before Massachusetts, the number of services taxed ranged from 2 in Alaska to 158 in Delaware—but most services escape sales taxation.

This part discusses several aspects of how expanding the sales tax base on services would change the basic nature of the general sales tax.

Basis.   Currently, services are not included in most state sales tax structures; only products are taxed. This not only narrows the base and reduces the potential yield from a sales tax, but it also violates horizontal equity. Individuals who purchase more products than services pay more sales taxes than individuals who purchase more services than products. Put differently, in terms of consumer purchases, the typical general sales tax blatantly fails the horizontal equity test and injects inequities into consumer expenditure behavior.

Yield.   If the state sales tax were expanded to include services, Fox and Murray (1988) estimate that revenues would increase by about 46 percent on average.

Because state economies differ dramatically, however, the potential revenue increase varies substantially about that average, being only 14 percent in West Virginia and a full 104 percent in Washington, D.C. Thus, general comments made here must be analyzed for the specific impact in any one state, and substantial variation by state should be expected.

This potential revenue hike, though, requires additional scrutiny because the bulk of the new revenues—73 percent—would come from taxing business services and construction. Indeed, 45 percent of new sales tax revenues would be derived from construction and another 28 percent from business services. As noted previously, there is debate as to whether any business purchase should be subject to the sales tax. Thus, policies to extend the sales tax to services must address this issue directly, since the business sector would produce nearly 3 of every 4 new sales tax dollars.

The revenue implications of not including the business sector are dramatic. Potential revenue increases would fall from about 45 percent to between 10 and 15 percent. Indeed, some argue for expanding the sales tax to services and simultaneously eliminating all sales taxes on businesses, a move that would actually reduce sales tax revenues (Quick and McKee, 1988).

If the sales tax were expanded to services purchased only by individuals, revenues would be somewhat more stable, since purchases of goods are more volatile than purchases of services. On the other hand, if the extension includes business services as well, sales tax revenues could become more volatile. Since the business sector would produce the bulk of new revenues and the business sector by definition is more tied to economic cycles, extending the sales tax to services of both individuals and businesses probably would decrease the stability of sales tax revenues.

Equity.   As with the sales tax on products, the equity impacts of extending the sales tax to services hinges on service expenditures by income class. Figure 5.13 displays those data for the mid-1980s. One characteristic of these data is the diverse nature of the service sector of the economy. The numbers show the wide range of industries that now elude sales taxation of what they offer. Three important findings emerge from these data. First, service expenditures are somewhat higher for incomes below $30,000 and are about proportional for all but the highest incomes above $30,000. Thus, a services tax would be mildly regressive below $30,000 and proportional above it. Second, medical, insurance, and personal services decline with income; thus, taxes on those services would produce a regressive impact. On the other hand, transportation and professional services are more proportional to income and would be proportional, not regressive, in income. Third, in comparing the consumer behavior patterns in Figure 5.13 to those in Figure 5.11 on expenditures of products, service expenditures are found to vary less by income than do goods expenditures. Thus, even though simply expanding the sales tax to all services would produce a regressive incidence pattern, in combination with the current sales tax on goods, it would reduce the degree of regres-

FIGURE 5.13   Selected Service Sector Expenditures as a Percent of Current Income, by Income Class

	Income Class ($)												
Service Sector	*5,000*	*10,000*	*15,000*	*20,000*	*25,000*	*30,000*	*35,000*	*40,000*	*45,000*	*50,000*	*55,000*	*60,000*	*65,000+*
Utilities													
Natural gas	1.85	0.66	0.42	0.34	0.30	0.25	0.21	0.20	0.17	0.16	0.18	0.15	0.12
Telephone	3.27	0.90	0.65	0.51	0.40	0.35	0.33	0.30	0.26	0.25	0.25	0.27	0.19
Electricity	4.27	1.32	0.89	0.71	0.61	0.52	0.49	0.46	0.40	0.40	0.31	0.34	0.28
Other	1.30	0.41	0.26	0.24	0.23	0.19	0.18	0.19	0.17	0.15	0.14	0.14	0.11
Household services													
Nonautomotive repair services	1.08	0.32	0.19	0.16	0.18	0.12	0.11	0.09	0.14	0.11	0.20	0.12	0.11
Other household services	1.49	0.35	0.24	0.21	0.19	0.19	0.17	0.18	0.19	0.18	0.16	0.21	0.23
Medical													
Prescription drugs	0.78	0.39	0.24	0.18	0.12	0.09	0.08	0.07	0.06	0.05	0.05	0.04	0.04
Doctors and nurses	1.98	0.71	0.50	0.43	0.35	0.25	0.28	0.31	0.24	0.28	0.26	0.27	0.21
Equipment and accesories	0.31	0.08	0.05	0.05	0.04	0.05	0.06	0.03	0.03	0.03	0.05	0.03	0.02
Hospitals	0.74	0.19	0.11	0.10	0.13	0.05	0.07	0.00	0.03	0.03	0.07	0.02	0.04
Insurance													
Property	2.25	0.80	0.60	0.55	0.48	0.43	0.41	0.38	0.41	0.38	0.37	0.34	0.26
Health	1.90	1.06	0.54	0.38	0.31	0.18	0.16	0.14	0.12	0.11	0.11	0.11	0.10
Personal	2.54	0.36	0.27	0.24	0.27	0.27	0.26	0.23	0.25	0.23	0.24	0.24	0.22

Lodging away from home	0.80	0.18	0.13	0.11	0.11	0.12	0.11	0.12	0.12	0.11	0.13	0.13	0.14

Transportation services excluding rentals

Local transportation	0.43	0.12	0.09	0.06	0.07	0.03	0.04	0.02	0.02	0.04	0.02	0.03	0.02
Nonlocal transportation	0.15	0.03	0.03	0.02	0.03	0.02	0.02	0.03	0.02	0.02	0.02	0.03	0.03
Other transportation	1.52	0.03	0.03	0.02	0.03	0.02	0.02	0.03	0.02	0.02	0.02	0.03	0.03
Admissions and entertainment	1.70	0.34	0.28	0.29	0.26	0.25	0.24	0.22	0.26	0.25	0.25	0.30	0.29
Personal services	1.15	0.33	0.24	0.19	0.17	0.15	0.14	0.15	0.15	0.12	0.12	0.11	0.11
Private educational services	4.73	0.41	0.30	0.32	0.19	0.26	0.23	0.23	0.23	0.29	0.24	0.32	0.23

Professional services

Legal	0.37	0.29	0.09	0.05	0.05	0.05	0.05	0.01	0.02	0.03	0.04	0.07	0.04
Other	0.29	0.08	0.06	0.05	0.05	0.05	0.04	0.03	0.04	0.04	0.04	0.04	0.04
Automotive repair services	1.75	0.46	0.41	0.33	0.34	0.25	0.23	0.24	0.22	0.22	0.19	0.16	0.16

Rentals

Recreational rentals	0.03	0.01	0.00	0.01	0.01	0.01	0.01	0.00	0.01	0.01	0.01	0.01	0.01
Automotive rentals	0.16	0.04	0.02	0.02	0.03	0.03	0.01	0.04	0.03	0.03	0.04	0.06	0.06
Other rentals	0.21	0.05	0.04	0.02	0.02	0.02	0.02	0.02	0.02	0.02	0.01	0.04	0.02
Total	37.05	9.92	6.68	5.59	4.97	4.20	3.97	3.72	3.63	3.56	3.52	3.61	3.11

Source: Robert A. Bahm and Eleanor Craig, "Sales Tax Base Modification, Revenue Stability and Equity," *Proceedings of the Eightieth Annual Conference*, Columbus, Ohio, National Tax Association–Tax Institute of America, 1988, pp. 167–174.

sivity, i.e., would make the overall incidence pattern somewhat more proportional.

Thus, on both horizontal and vertical equity grounds, it would be good public policy to extend the sales tax to services. It would both reduce regressivity and raise revenues.

Economic Effects. Two major categories of economic effects should be considered—those on price and those on inefficiencies. First, if the tax applies only to individual purchases, prices for all items—whether products or services—would increase. But if the tax also applies to business services, price distortions would enter the market because some industries must purchase more services (as well as goods) to make and market their product than others. Those industries would incur higher costs of productions and thus would have to lower their prices or lose market share, either of which would lower profits. Thus, a sales tax on business services treats different businesses differently and is unfair.

Second, a sales tax on business services (as well as purchased goods) encourages businesses to incur the diseconomies of vertical integration to the degree that such inefficiencies are less than the cost of paying the tax. In this sense, such a tax distorts economic efficiency in production.

Compliance and administration. Extending the sales tax to services would increase the number of vendors that would have to report and remit sales tax revenues and thus would increase administrative costs. More vendors would be included, and there would be more work for current vendors, since several vendors currently sell both goods and services and thus already are active in sales tax administration. Administrative efficiency also would decrease marginally. Most studies show that sales tax revenues per vendor are less for service providers than for goods-selling vendors (Fox and Murray, 1988). Thus, adding services would reduce the overall average sales tax revenue per vendor.

Further, there would be a need for new technical regulations to define what is and what is not included in new service definitions. For example, if pet services are to be taxed, dog grooming obviously would be included. But what about alligators? Are alligators pets? Although such a question may seem foolish, this and similar issues already have been raised and adjudicated in states that have added pet services to the sales tax base. But, just as for goods, such technical details get worked out through regulations and court action in the short run. All told, the sales tax still would be a highly efficient tax, with relatively small administration and compliance costs, even if services were added to the base.

Conclusions about the Sales Tax

The sales tax likely will remain the largest producer of state revenues, even though reliance on the income tax might increase. The sales tax is currently the most popular tax (Advisory Commission on Intergovernmental Relations, 1989a) and has been for several years. As currently structured, the sales tax produces substantial revenue and provides horizontal equity, at least with respect to the goods and services taxed; moreover, its revenues generally keep pace with economic (and thus income) growth, and its egregious regressive elements can be almost eliminated by exempting food or providing a state income tax credit. With the latter adjustments, it approximates a tax with a proportional incidence pattern.

States should be encouraged to limit additional exemptions for individuals and to seriously consider expanding the sales tax to include services. Such an expansion not only would raise new revenues but would lessen remaining regressive elements in the sales tax burden.

Finally, states should rethink their entire approach to taxing the business sector. Although a sales tax on business currently produces substantial revenues, it promotes substantial differential treatment of different businesses, and nearly all public finance economists recommend eliminating the sales tax on business purchases of both goods and services. Replacing such a tax, as well as the property and income taxes on businesses, with a value-added tax on business, as only one state—Michigan—has done, is a preferred alternative. It produces substantial revenues from the business sector and at relatively low rates; makes business tax revenues stable (indeed, much more stable than both corporate income taxes and corporate sales taxes); increases both horizontal and vertical equity for businesses; is easy to administer since it uses federal corporate income tax data; and allows businesses to deduct all state and local taxes on their federal income tax, whereas with the 1986 federal income tax changes, sales taxes are no longer deductible. (See Gold, 1986b, for a discussion of these issues.)

LOTTERIES

State lotteries as a mechanism for raising revenues to support public services are a relatively modern innovation, although lotteries have a history spanning hundreds of years (Thomas and Webb, 1984). New Hampshire, rarely an innovator in state finance, began the modern use of lotteries in 1964. It was followed by New York in 1967, which dedicated lottery revenues to public education. For both, tickets cost several dollars, players registered to participate, and there were few drawings per year; also, yields were low. In 1971, New Jersey continued the trend and initiated wide and aggressive marketing to increase lottery sales, and was successful beyond expectations. California enacted a lottery in 1985, with the revenues again dedicated to education, and Minnesota enacted a lottery in 1989. At the end of 1989, 29 states had lottery programs. In most states, lottery revenues were dedicated to particular public services—usually education—so modern school finance is intertwined with state lotteries and their fate.

Basis

The base of lotteries is simply the number of lottery tickets or chances sold, minus, of course, administrative costs, which are discussed later in this section. The ability of lotteries to raise revenues is largely tied to sales: the more lottery chances sold, the higher the revenues. When lotteries were initially created as new state revenue sources, they often were viewed as legalized gambling; thus, marketing and advertising to expand sales were frowned upon. Over time, however, the negative connotations of gambling have given way to the imperatives to make them stalwart state revenue raisers.

In 1971, New Jersey broke new ground by developing an aggressive marketing campaign to bolster lottery sales. Today, these techniques are accepted as common practice. To maximize lottery sales, and thus lottery revenues, the following structural elements are necessary:

- Cheap tickets—$1 to $3
- Many winners, i.e., a large percentage of winning tickets even though the prize might be small
- High payout ratios, i.e., close to 50 percent of sales dedicated to prizes
- Frequent drawings for "big" winners
- Attractive prizes, with some very large, multimillion-dollar prizes
- Convenient locations and ticket outlets to facilitate mass public buying
- Simple procedures to help all individuals play

Yet even with these elements, lotteries have low payout ratios compared to other forms of gambling. Lotteries typically pay out at most 50 cents on the dollar. Numbers games generally pay out 50-60 percent, racetracks 80 percent, slot machines 80 percent, casinos 90 percent, and bookmakers 95.5 percent. Nevertheless, research shows that lotteries make a slight dent in illegal gambling (Hybels, 1979).

Yield

Lotteries are not major revenue raisers, even when characterized by the preceding structural elements and accompanied by aggressive marketing campaigns. In 1986, total lottery sales were $11.1 billion and net proceeds only $4.7 billion, about 42 percent of total sales. Prizes and administration thus consume about 58 percent of all lottery sales. Although not large, such proceeds nevertheless represent revenues. In the most productive states—Massachusetts, Maryland, New Jersey, and Pennsylvania—lottery revenues produce about the equivalent of a 1 cent sales tax.

As a proportion of state general revenues from internal sources, lotteries are modest overall contributors. In 1978, lottery contributions to state revenues ranged from a low of 0.33 percent in Delaware to a high of 3.71 percent in Maryland. By 1984, the low dropped to 0.19 percent in Vermont, and the high had risen to 4.21 percent in Maryland. The average in 1984 was about 2 percent.

In 1986, these figures were about the same, ranging from a low of 0.4 percent in Vermont to a high of 5.3 percent in Maryland. In short, lotteries are not robust revenue raisers, even with aggressive marketing.

Lottery revenues also are unstable. The typical pattern is high revenues in the first year, usually exceeding initial projections, and then lower yields after the initial euphoria wears thin and many discontinue playing or play only occasionally, with corresponding rises and falls in yields. For example, Pennsylvania's lottery yields rose 98 percent between 1977 and 1978, rose only 7 percent between 1980 and 1981, and rose just 4.5 percent between 1983 and 1984. Declines also occur, ranging from −1 to −50 percent (Mikesell and Zorn, 1986).

Further, most would argue that lottery revenues supplant rather than supplement allocations to targeted functions. Although lotteries might be "sold" as a mechanism to add money to schools, the arts, or programs for the elderly, in time the extra funds produced are "rolled into" the regular budget. That is, over time state legislators allocate less in general revenues for the targeted function than they might have had the lottery not targeted that function for fiscal support. In other words, over the medium to long term, lotteries (and most other mechanisms that target specific general functions for financial support) do not produce net additional funding.

Equity

Since lower-income households spend greater portions of their incomes on lotteries, lotteries are universally recognized as regressive in their incidence (Mikesell and Zorn, 1986). In reviewing studies of tax and gambling incidence, Thomas and Webb (1984) showed that lotteries have a −.31 index (with −1 indicating extreme regressivity and +1 indicating extreme progressivity). The index was −.44 for numbers, −.40 for sports cards, and −.7 for horse racing. The index was +.29 for sports books and +.26 for casino games, indicating that some forms of gambling are progressive. By comparison, the sales tax index was −.15 and the federal income tax index was +.19. Thus, lotteries are twice as regressive as the sales tax.

Some argue that the lottery is simply an excise tax on a form of entertainment—gambling. As such, its impact by income class is less of an issue since it is considered a discretionary activity. However, most states now enact a lottery to raise new state revenues. Thus, viewing it as a governmental tax mechanism and analyzing its incidence by income class is appropriate, and there is no disagreement that it is regressive.

Administration

One reason a lottery is such a marginal revenue producer is that it is very expensive to run and administer. First, a large portion of sales are dedicated to winnings—up to 50 percent for most states. Second, vendors who sell lottery tickets usually retain a nickel for each dollar sold. Thus, prizes and selling costs typically consume 55 percent of sales. Finally, there is some administration—printing tickets, holding drawings, and running computer systems for the new, computerized lotto games. Thus, net receipts generally are less than 50 percent of sales, usually around 35 percent. Put differently, every dollar of lottery sales typically yields only 35 cents of revenues. This makes lotteries one of the most inefficient revenue sources. In contrast, the typical yield from tax revenues is greater than 95 percent, i.e., administration costs less than 5 percent of total tax yields. But not so for the lottery. Although not administratively complex, an effective lottery is very costly to run and net yields are usually around just one-third of sales. The problem is that the public hears about total sales; few understand that little of total lottery sales are used to support public services.

Conclusion

Lotteries are popular new ways to raise public revenues. But they are inefficient, burden the poor more than the rich, and do not produce large amounts of new revenues. They certainly do not represent a new broad-based tax that produces revenues like the income, sales, and property taxes (Clotfelter and Cook, 1989).

SUMMARY

Tax revenues provide the bulk of dollars for public schools. Different taxes have different economic properties, produce varying levels of tax revenues, impose different burdens relative to family income on households, and differ in administrative and compliance costs. As this chapter has shown, broadly based income and sales taxes produce large amounts of revenues, are progressive or proportional in their incidence,[6] and are elastic revenue producers (see Figure 5.14). These taxes likely will continue to provide the bulk of state education revenues. Although lotteries are popular and are increasingly being enacted, they do not produce large revenues, they are unstable revenue providers, and they are regressive in incidence (Figure 5.14).

[6] The low-income regressivity of the sales tax can be eliminated with appropriate exemptions or tax credits.

FIGURE 5.14 Comparative Assessment of Income, Sales, and Lottery Taxes

Evaluation Variables	Income Tax	Sales Tax	Lottery Tax
Tax base	Income	Purchases (except food and prescribed drugs)	Lottery tickets
Yield	Elastic Stable	Elastic Unstable	Inelastic Unstable
Equity	Horizontal: OK Vertical: progressive	Horizontal: OK Vertical: regressive (low-income regressivity can be reduced with exemptions or tax credits)	Horizontal: generally OK Vertical: regressive
Economic effects	Neutral	Neutral	Neutral
Administration cost	Large	Small	Extremely large —about 65% of sales
Compliance cost	Large	Small	Not applicable

The Property Tax

The property tax has been and remains the mainstay of local government financing. Currently, the property tax is the major local tax in 48 states. Alabama and Louisiana rely more on the sales and gross receipts tax, and the District of Columbia relies more on the income tax. For the entire country, the property tax accounted for 74 percent of local revenues in 1987, excluding state and federal aid.

For years, the property tax produced the largest percentage of revenues for schools, but that role was ceded to state governments during the flurry of school finance reforms enacted in the 1970s. Nevertheless, the property tax produces large amounts of steady local revenue and, except for the few local governments that can levy sales and income taxes, is the only broad-based tax that most local governments, including school districts, can use to raise funds. This chapter analyzes the property tax in terms of its base, yield, equity, economic effects, and administration and compliance costs. It ends with a summary of state approaches to property tax relief for the poor and a discussion of the impact of California's Proposition 13, enacted in 1978.

BASIS

The basis of the property tax generally is wealth. Except for the inheritance tax, which is being lowered or eliminated in many states, the property tax is the closest approximation to a wealth tax in this country. But because so many elements of wealth are not included in the property tax, and because the elements of wealth that are included are primarily property, the tax historically has been called a property tax.

There are three categories of wealth or property: (1) real or land, (2) tangible, and (3) intangible. Referring to land as real property dates to medieval times, when all land was owned by royalty; *real* actually is a derivative of *royal*. Tangible property includes improvements on land, such as buildings, homes, business establishments, factories, and office buildings, as well as personal property such as automobiles, furniture, other household items, and business inventories. A value can be placed on all forms of tangible property. Intangible property refers to items that represent a value but that themselves have no value, such as bank deposits, certificates of deposit, stock certificates, and bonds. The property tax base usually includes the bulk of real property or land; portions of tangible property, primarily land improvements but usually not personal property; and little if any intangible property.

In terms of horizontal equity, then, the property tax does not treat all wealth holdings equally. An individual with greater amounts of financial investments than real estate would pay less property tax than an individual with a portfolio mostly in real estate. Similarly, individuals with larger portions of their wealth invested in personal property exempt from the property tax base are better off than those with larger portions in land and buildings. In short, the property tax treats holders of wealth differently, primarily based on the distribution of their wealth across real, tangible, and intangible property.

These generalizations, however, mask other aspects of the property tax. A considerable amount of real property and land improvements escapes property taxation, thus driving up the tax rate for the portion that is taxed. Property and buildings owned by government—federal, state, or local—are exempt from the property tax, as are land and buildings owned by religious and some charitable organizations. Further, there is a substantial number of additional exemptions. Many states provide a homestead exemption eliminating a certain amount of a home's value from the property tax. There are also exemptions for certain kinds of business activities. Several localities, especially cities, have enacted property tax abatements under which new business buildings are exempt from the property tax rolls for a fixed number of years, ranging up to 20. These exemptions or exclusions add up to large amounts over time. Thus, although all property on the tax rolls is taxed equally (except for the issues described next), the large portions of property not on the tax rolls avoid the property tax altogether, further violating horizontal equity.

Additional issues complicate the picture because property is taxed on the basis of what is called assessed valuation, and the assessment process is riddled with technical challenges and problems. The assessment process basically involves three steps. First, all parcels of land across the country are plotted and recorded by local taxing jurisdictions, usually city or county government agencies. Second, those parcels subject to the property tax are given a value, usually approximating the market value;[1] both land and their improvements (buildings) are included in assigning a value. Third, an assessed valuation is

---

[1] The market value generally is the price at which a piece of property could be sold.

assigned, which is some percentage of true or market value. The assessed valuation is the local property tax base. But determining assessed valuation is a complex technical and political process.

Determining Market or True Value

Determining a true value for a piece of land and its improvements is conceptually straightforward. True value is the market value, what an individual would have to pay to buy the piece of property. The market value of a home, for example, is the value for which it would sell. Since records are kept of home sales, determining the market value of homes that sell is simple.

But what about placing market values on homes that are not sold? Technically, that also is fairly simple, as most real estate agents would attest, but keeping up-to-date market values on the tax rolls requires a process of continually updating figures on the tax records. Computer programs exist to provide such updating, but political pressures often mitigate against full record updating. Some feel it is unfair to tax a homeowner on unrealized home value gains, which happens when updating of tax files occurs regularly. Another issue is how often tax rolls should be updated—every year, every other year, once a decade, etc. If annual updates do not occur, horizontal equity may be violated as homeowners who do not move pay a decreasing portion of the local property tax. But annual updating costs money and creates some public displeasure.

Valuing homes is simple compared to placing values on other properties. Consider small commercial buildings or small businesses that use land and buildings that are rarely sold. Since a market value does not exist, a process called capitalizing income or capitalizing rents is commonly used. If net income or profits are 10 percent, the value is total sales divided by 10 percent (which would be total sales multiplied by 10). That is, the value is linked to the profits earned by using the land and buildings. Similarly, the value of commercial buildings is usually related to the rents that can be charged for using the building. Rents are divided by an average rate of return to determine true or market value; indeed, this process often determines the building's market price if the owner decides to sell. Capitalized values are thus determined by two critical variables: sales and net profit, or rents and assumed rate of return. Values can be increased or decreased by changing either of these two figures.

Determining market value for factories or plants provides more complex challenges. Capitalized valuation is one possible approach, but it is difficult to allocate profits and sales to just one plant for a business with multiple plants. So an alternative process, replacement costs less depreciation, is often used. Replacement costs are an estimate of what it would cost to rebuild the plant completely. In many respects, replacement costs simply updated each year would indicate the true value of such property. But, unlike homeowners, businesses are allowed to depreciate plants and factories in order to reinvest and improve properties over time. So true values for a plant or factory would be replacement costs minus accumulated depreciation.

Utilities, such as gas and electrical lines, represent yet an additional technical challenge. Although such lines have little worth in themselves, they represent a distribution network allocated by governments to utility companies, and the distribution networks have substantial value. States have taken a variety of approaches to valuing utilities and commonly use a combination of capitalized valuation and replacement costs less depreciation.

Farmland presents another set of issues. Although a market value usually exists for farmland, often the actual selling price exceeds the farming value of the land, even for farms far from growing urban areas. In addition, even if the market value of farmland equals the farming capitalized price, a drought or other natural disaster could reduce a farmer's income to zero in any one year, making it quite difficult to pay property taxes on farmland that still retained a value. Further, for farmland that does not turn over, if the selling price of nearby farmland is used as the basis for identifying a value, care must be taken to compare similar types of land. Land that can be used for only grazing should not be compared with land used for agriculture, and different types of agricultural use, which often depends on the specific characteristics of the soil, produce different net returns for farmers. All of these factors must be considered in valuing farmland. Several states use some type of market value, and several others use the lower of market value or actual use value.

Valuation of farmland near growing urban areas raises a broader issue for assessing land. Public finance economists argue that land should be valued according to its best and highest use; such a process prevents inefficient use of valued land, which is in fixed supply all over the world. For farmland near growing urban areas, such valuation would be based on its use in residential or commercial development for the growing urban area; that value usually is substantially higher than one based on farm use. But if that valuation is used, the farmer essentially is driven out of business and must sell the land, and therefore the farm, to a developer. Economically that might make sense, but socially and politically it often creates dissatisfaction.

States commonly allow a farmer to choose the valuation standard, so as long as the farmer chooses to farm the land, its valuation is related to farm use. This, however, decreases the amount that can be raised from a given local property tax rate and shifts the financing of local government services to other taxpayers. Moreover, when the farmer ultimately decides to sell the farm, it is usually sold at the highest and best use value to an urban developer, and the farmer reaps a substantial financial reward. The solution is to allow the farm use valuation as long as the land is used for farming but, once the farm is sold, to collect back taxes on the basis of the highest and best use valuation to recoup lost property tax revenues. Although economically sound, this solution also risks social and political rejection.

Actually, the same issue exists for land in an urban area. Take a downtown parking lot, for example. Based on capitalized value on its actual use, its value is quite low, and far below its market value if it were sold to someone wanting to build a tall office building. The question is whether to use a capitalized value on actual use so as not to drive out the parking lot owner, thus reflecting a social and political goal, or to use highest and best use, which would force the owner to sell to a developer or to build an office building. The latter would also provide increased tax revenues for the city. Further, just as for the farmer, if valuation is based on actual use, the parking lot owner reaps a huge windfall at the time of sale. Again, there are mechanisms that could be used to recoup lost property taxes, but they are rarely invoked.

In short, determining property values is conceptually straightforward but technically, socially, and politically complex. In many cases, there is no "right" process; technical approaches interact with value judgments. As a result, whether horizontal equity is met is both a technical and a political/social conclusion.

Determining Assessed Valuation

Once a value is given to a piece of property, an assessed value must be ascribed, because that is the value that officially becomes part of the tax base. In the best of all worlds, this step would be eliminated and the determined value would be the measure that becomes part of the property tax base. But, for a variety of reasons, fractional assessment practices exist across the country. That is, property is assessed at some fraction or percent of actual value from as low as 10 percent to as high as 100 percent, which is the actual market or true value. Public finance economists argue for 100 percent valuation and that should be the goal for most state property tax systems.

Fractional assessments have no inherent economic justification; they are simply a complicating factor, and one often fraught with substantial inequities. Fractional assessments have been used primarily to hide some of the realities of the property tax, since most individuals are not aware of the details of the local assessment process. For example, if the practice is to assess property at 25 percent of market value, a homeowner with a $100,000 home receives a tax notice showing the assessed value to be just $25,000. The homeowner typically thinks the house is undervalued since it is assessed so far below market value. To raise a fixed amount of revenue the tax rate applied to this assessed valuation would need to be four times the rate applied to full or market value, but the homeowner usually takes more comfort in a perceived valuation below market levels than in a lower tax rate. In addition, tax rates are often limited to some maximum level, so if assessment levels are artificially low, the government reaches the maximum rate more quickly and local taxes are also kept artificially low. But this gives the power of political decision making to the local assessor and not the local policy-making bodies, where tax rate decisions should be made.

Also, fractional valuations can conceal a host of related inequities. If the popular assumption is that most homes are assessed far below market value, two individuals with the same $100,000 homes, one with an assessed value of $25,000 and the other with an assessed value of $20,000, might both feel they are being given a "deal" when in fact the latter is being unfairly assessed 20 percent less than legal requirements. This situation is common as homes grow older and families do not move, and such differences often are popularly accepted as fair.

Such valuation differences lead to what are called intraclass assessment dispersions, which indicate differences in actual assessments within a class of property, such as owner-occupied homes. Different assessment practices across classes of property, such as between business property and homes, are measured by interclass assessment dispersions. Differences across areas within a local assessing jurisdiction are measured by interarea assessment dispersions. Each is a measure of the degree to which actual assessments of property differ. High coefficients of dispersion indicate low levels of horizontal equity, i.e., that similarly situated property owners are being treated differently.

Differential assessment practices create significant problems for state school finance systems designed to provide relatively more state education aid to districts low in assessed value of property per pupil. For two districts alike in all characteristics, the district assessed at the lower fraction of market value would look poorer and thus be eligible for more state aid. That would be unfair, and state school finance systems need to adjust for such inequities. Consider two districts, A and B, with assessed valuations of $34,500,000 and $50,000,000, respectively. These numbers alone would suggest that district B is wealthier in terms of total valuation than district A. But further assume that district A assesses property at 25 percent of true value, and district B assesses at 50 percent. To determine the true or market value, or adjusted or equalized assessed value, as it is called in school finance, the assessed valuation figures must be divided by the assessment ratios. Thus, the true valuation for district A is $138,000,000 ($34,500,000 \div .25$), and the true valuation for district B is $100,000,000 ($50,000,000 \div .50$), which shows that district A actually has more wealth than district B. In other words, the unadjusted assessed valuations do not give an accurate picture of relative total wealth between these two districts.

For school finance purposes, the property tax base is divided by the number of students to determine relative ability to raise property tax dollars. Assume that district A has 2,500 students and district B 1,500 students. If the state used just assessed valuation per pupil, district A would have a value of $13,800 ($34,500,000 \div 2,500$) and district B would have a value of $33,333 ($50,000,000 \div 1,500$); district B would appear nearly three times as wealthy as district A. But if equalized or adjusted assessed valuations are used, as they should be, district B would appear only slightly wealthier than district A, at $66,667 and $55,200, respectively.

Thus, it is important for the state to recognize that local assessing practices can vary from required state practice, to collect data to identify the variations, and to make adjustments in school finance formulas to adjust for the differences. Usually, this adjustment is accomplished through what is commonly called a state equalization board, which monitors local assessing performance. The monitoring generally consists of gathering sales data, comparing them to assessed valuations, and calculating assessment/sales ratios to determine the degree to which local assessment practices reflect state requirements. Since assessment/sales ratios are available, the state legislature can and usually does use them to adjust local assessed valuations in determining state aid calculations.

In summary, numerous issues are associated with determining the local property tax base. The property tax base is primarily land and improvements on the land, although land owned by government, religious, and charitable organizations is exempt. Tax abatements and homestead exemptions further erode the local property tax base. Determining true or market value for many types of property is a technically complex undertaking, and it raises social and political issues as well. Fractional assessments are widely practiced but serve only to obscure the actual functioning of the property tax. Actual property assessments tend to differ within classes of property, across classes of property, and across areas within local taxing jurisdictions, leading to horizontal inequities. And differential fractional assessments across local taxing jurisdictions require state adjustments for state education aid to be allocated in an equitable manner.

YIELD

The property tax is a stalwart revenue producer, providing $121.2 billion in revenues for state and local governments in 1987. Figure 6.1 shows total property taxes and property taxes as a percent of personal income over several years. Property tax yields rose from $12.9 billion in 1957 to $121.2 billion in 1987. Between 1957 and 1967, and between 1977 and 1987, property tax revenues roughly doubled; property tax revenues more than doubled between 1967 and 1977.

But as a percent of personal income, property taxes represent less today than they did 30 years ago. Property taxes as a percent of personal income rose from 3.6 percent in 1957 to 4.0 percent in 1967, but during the next decade, when property taxes more than doubled, they dropped slightly relative to personal income. In 1987, property taxes consumed only 3.2 percent of

FIGURE 6.1   Property Taxes as a Percent of Personal Income, 1957 to 1987

Fiscal Year	Total Property Taxes (billions)	Personal Income (billions)	Property Taxes as a Percent of Personal Income
1957	$ 12.9	$ 356.3	3.6
1967	26.0	644.5	4.0
1977	62.5	1,607.5	3.9
1987	121.2	3,780.0	3.2

Source: Advisory Commission on Intergovernmental Relations, *Significant Features of Fiscal Federalism, 1988 Edition.* vol. II, Washington, D.C., ACIR, 1988, p. 64, Table 59; and *Economic Report of the President,* January 1989, p. 333.

personal income. The drop since 1977 probably reflects the tax and expenditure limitation fever after 1978. It is difficult to predict the future for this variable. Although the tax limitation push is still with us, many states increased property taxes to help fund the 1980s education reforms, so the property tax bite out of personal income could rise in the future.

Property Tax Rates

Expressed as a percent, a property tax rate is easily used to determine the property tax yield. If the tax rate is 1.5 % and assessed valuation is $50,000, the yield is .015 times $50,000, or $750.

Unfortunately, the property tax rate is not always given as a percent of assessed valuation. Property tax rates are usually stated in mills or in dollars-per-hundred dollars of assessed valuation. These units add to the complexity surrounding the property tax. A tax rate in mills indicates the rate applied to each $1,000 of assessed valuation. Thus, if the tax rate is 15 mills and assessed valuation is $50,000, the yield is 15 times $50, or $750. The mill rate is useful because it can be multiplied by the assessed valuation, with a decimal point replacing the comma that indicates thousands. Technically, a mill is one-thousandth, so a tax rate of, say, 15 mills expressed as a decimal would be $15 \times 1/1,000$ or 15/1,000 or .015. If that representation of the rate is used, the yield would be just the rate times the base, or $.015 \times $50,000$ or $750.

The same tax rate given in units of dollars per hundred would be $1.50. Thus, the yield would be the rate, $1.50, times the number of hundreds of dollars of assessed valuation ($50,000 \div 100$, or $500) again, $750. Notice that this rate is similar to the rate given as a percent; for both, the number 1.5 is used.

Mills and dollars per hundred are used in part because assessed valuation figures are so large. Such a rate helps reduce the number of figures needed to calculate results. But these two rates are confusing, especially in comparing rates across jurisdictions and across states. Shifting to a simple percentage rate, as California has done, would simplify matters. Then all tax rates—income, sales, and property—would be given in the same units and could be compared.

Average property tax rates for single-family homes with FHA-insured mortgages are displayed by state in Figure 6.2. These data document two important facts about property tax rates on homes. First, they vary substantially, ranging in 1987 from a low of 0.22 percent in Louisiana to a high of 2.38 percent in New Jersey. In other words, property taxes vary widely by geographical location. Second, property tax rates dropped between 1977 and 1987, falling by 20 to 40 percent in many instances.

Property Tax Elasticity

The property tax has been a somewhat elastic tax, but its elasticity may be changing. As Figure 6.3 shows, the simple property tax elasticity fell between

FIGURE 6.2 Average Effective Property Tax Rates on Single-Family Homes with FHA-Insured Mortgages

State	1987	1977
Alabama	0.39%	0.74%
Alaska	0.81	NA
Arizona	0.66	1.72
Arkansas	0.64	1.49
California	1.05	2.21
Colorado	0.93	1.80
Connecticut	1.46	2.17
D.C. (Washington)	1.17	NA
Delaware	0.68	0.88
Florida	0.92	1.13
Georgia	1.03	1.27
Hawaii	0.51	NA
Idaho	0.87	1.46
Illinois	1.55	1.90
Indiana	1.25	1.66
Iowa	1.96	1.76
Kansas	1.11	1.37
Kentucky	0.87	1.25
Louisiana	0.22	0.61
Maine	1.22	1.65
Maryland	1.22	1.69
Massachusetts	0.84	3.50
Michigan	2.10	2.63
Minnesota	1.00	1.39
Mississippi	0.76	1.10
Missouri	0.83	1.59
Montana	1.34	1.31
Nebraska	2.01	2.48
Nevada	0.69	1.71
New Hampshire	1.55	NA
New Jersey	2.38	3.31
New Mexico	0.88	1.65
New York	2.07	2.89
North Carolina	1.01	1.35
North Dakota	1.38	1.26
Ohio	1.06	1.26
Oklahoma	0.76	0.95
Oregon	2.26	2.25
Pennsylvania	1.40	1.85
Rhode Island	1.49	NA
South Carolina	0.72	0.82
South Dakota	2.17	1.79
Tennessee	0.89	1.40
Texas	1.41	1.84
Utah	0.97	1.03
Vermont	NA	NA
Virginia	0.98	1.21
Washington (state)	1.10	1.75
West Virginia	0.69	NA
Wisconsin	2.03	2.22
Wyoming	0.57	0.87

Source: Advisory Commission on Intergovernmental Relations, *Significant Features of Fiscal Federalism,* 1989 Edition, vol. 1, Washington, D.C., ACIR, 1989.

FIGURE 6.3 Property Tax Simple Elasticity, 1957 to 1987

Year	Percent Change from Previous Decade		Elasticity: Ratio of Percent Changes
	Property Taxes	*Personal Income*	
1957	—	—	—
1967	101.6	80.9	1.26
1977	140.4	149.4	0.94
1987	93.9	135.1	0.70

Source: Calculated from data in Figure 6.1.

1957 and 1987, from 1.26 between 1957 and 1967 to just 0.70 between 1977 and 1987. These numbers show that, for several reasons, property tax revenues did not keep pace with income growth after 1967. The simple elasticity does not adjust for rate changes, however, and property tax rates also fell after 1977. If adjustments were made for rate changes and a host of other factors, research shows the property tax elasticity would be higher. Although it is important to know the "true" property tax elasticity, the simple elasticity also has meaning because it shows just how property tax revenues track personal income. The figure indicates that in the recent past, property tax revenues simply have increased more slowly than income.

Property Tax Stability

In terms of stability, the property tax has some ideal characteristics. In economic slowdowns, it produces a steady revenue stream, largely because property values maintain their levels except in very deep recessions. On the other hand, in times of economic growth and/or inflation, property values rise, so property tax revenues rise. In other words, property tax revenues relative to the business or economic cycle are stable on the downside and increase on the upside.

EQUITY

For years the property tax was considered a regressive, actually a steeply regressive, tax (Netzer, 1966). In the 1970s a new view of the property tax incidence was developed indicating a progressive incidence pattern (Aaron, 1975; Mieszkowski, 1972). Since the mid-1970s, analysts have essentially divided into two camps: those claiming a progressive incidence pattern and those claiming a regressive incidence pattern. This section summarizes both arguments, presents research results, and makes the important conclusion that property tax incidence is steeply regressive in the low income ranges regardless of the conceptual framework used to determine incidence.

Estimating Property Tax Incidence

For estimating property tax incidence, the tax is usually divided into four basic components:

- The land component
- The owner-occupied residential component
- The rented residential component
- The nonresidential component

The conventional view uses a framework that analyzes the impact of the property tax on users rather than owners, and the new view focuses on owners rather than users, but both views must address these different components.

First, under both views of property tax incidence, the land component is assumed to fall on landowners. Both views make the assumption that land is in fixed supply, i.e., the amount of land is given and cannot be changed. The price of something that is fixed in supply is the same with or without the tax. There is virtually no way landowners can shift the tax to some other party. Thus, the property tax on land falls exclusively on landowners. This portion of the tax is distributed across income classes by using data either on land ownership by income class or on income from all forms of capital by income class. Since land ownership (as well as income from capital) is concentrated in the upper-income tax brackets, this component of the property tax is progressive in incidence.

Second, under both views, the owner-occupied residential component is assumed to fall on homeowners. Again, at least in the short term, it is nearly impossible for a homeowner to shift the tax to some other party. Even if the homeowner should move, the price of the house would not increase or decrease because of the tax (assuming the negative effect of increased tax revenues was perfectly offset by the positive value of new services). In short, homeowners pay the property tax on owner-occupied homes. This portion of the property tax is distributed according to housing consumption by income class. Since housing consumption is concentrated in the middle and upper income ranges, this portion of the tax is proportional or mildly progressive, clearly not regressive. So essentially there is no difference in the two views about the burden of the first two components of the property tax.

Property tax incidence under the conventional view   The two views differ over the burden of the rented residential component and the nonresidential—or business, commercial, and utilities—component. Under the conventional view, these components of the tax are assumed to be shifted to the final consumers of the goods and services produced by the taxed structures—renters in the case of rented residences and consumers in the case of business structures.

How are these taxes shifted? Consider an increase in the property tax, and take the case of a landlord who, before the tax increases, was earning what is considered an adequate rate of return on the investment in rental housing. The property tax increase causes an increase in costs and, thus, a decrease in profits or net rate of return. The landlord has the following options: (1) accept the lower rate of return, (2) increase rents in the amount of the new tax (or decrease maintenance in the same amount), or (3) shift the investments out of rental property.

If rents are increased or maintenance decreased, the result is the same for the renter: a lower quality of rented property for a given price. This impact would encourage renters to either consume less rented property or consume the same amount but of lower quality. In both cases, the rent increase is shifted to the renter. If the landlord shifts some capital investment away from rental structures, in the long term the supply of rental structures would decrease, which would increase rents. As the market adjusted to this new equilibrium point, the property tax increase would again be shifted to the renter. The more inelastic the demand, i.e., the more that demand for rental housing is insensitive to prices, and the more elastic the supply, the greater the extent of shifting. It is usually assumed that, in the long run, supply is quite elastic, so that nearly full shifting occurs (Deleeuw and Ekanem, 1971; Grieson, 1973; Orr, 1968; Hyman and Pasour, 1973).[2]

A similar argument is made for property tax increases on commercial, industrial, and utilities properties. Over both the long and short runs, the tax is shifted to the users of the products produced by the taxed structures, i.e., the tax is shifted to consumers.

The shifted property tax on residential rental property is distributed according to rental payments by income class. Since these tend to decrease with income, this portion of the property tax is usually regressive. The shifted property tax on nonresidential property is distributed according to consumer expenditures by income class. Since these decrease sharply with income, this portion of the property tax has a steeply regressive incidence pattern.

Empirical studies of property tax incidence under the conventional view consistently show very regressive incidence patterns (Brownlee, 1960; Musgrave and Daicoff, 1958; Netzer, 1966).

Property tax incidence under the new view   The new view holds that the property tax is, at heart, a uniform tax on all property. This view proceeds by analyzing the tax within a framework that focuses on the impact of the tax on owners rather than users of capital, i.e., consumers of goods and services produced by capital.

The new view involves two steps. Assuming a fixed supply of capital and a fixed level of consumption for all goods, the first step considers the property tax as a uniform tax on all property. The burden of such a tax is borne by owners

[2] Inelastic demand means that the demand for rental housing stays about the same even if prices rise. By contrast, elastic demand indicates that as prices rise, demand falls. Elastic supply in this case means that as taxes or costs rise (thus perhaps dropping profits), the supply of rental housing falls. Inelastic supply indicates that the amount of rental property provided (by investors or landlords) will stay about the same even if taxes or costs rise.

of all capital, whether property or otherwise. As property taxes are increased, owners will move capital out of areas subject to the property tax. This will reduce the supply, increase the price, and thus decrease the consumption of goods and services produced by capital subject to the property tax. The shift of capital to areas not subject to the property tax, however, will increase the supply of goods and services produced by this capital and thus decrease their prices. As the entire system moves to a new equilibrium point, the net rate of return on investment in both sectors shifts to a new, lower level. The final effect is a decrease in the net rate of return to capital investment in all sectors. In the long run, a uniform property tax is assumed to be borne entirely by capital owners. Since the ownership of capital is higher for upper-income groups, the burden of the property tax tends to be quite progressive in nature.

Studies on this portion of the new view show strong progressive property tax incidence patterns (Aaron, 1975; Musgrave and Musgrave, 1989: Pechman and Okner, 1974; Pechman, 1985).

The second step of the new view recognizes the nonuniformity of the property tax that is caused by varying tax rates across state and local governments. These differentials tend to increase rents and prices in high-tax locations and to decrease them in low-tax locations. The precise nature of these effects is difficult to determine because they depend on the mobility of capital and the shifts in demand for goods and services caused by differential tax rates. Adherents of the new view argue, however, that the central tendency of property tax incidence, even after adjustment for these differentials, will still be progressive.

A policy issue approach to assessing property tax incidence   It is difficult simply to choose a particular incidence perspective. The problem with the conventional view is that it ignores nationwide average impacts. The problem with the new view is that the tax is not a nationwide tax but a tax with varying rates across thousands of local taxing jurisdictions. If the policy issue is average nationwide property tax incidence, the new view is appropriate. If, for example, the issue were the degree to which the federal income tax offsets any regressivity from the local property tax, or regressivity from all state and local taxes together, the new view would be appropriate. However, policy implications would be hard to draw for the property tax per se, since it is a local and not a national tax.

Another policy approach is to try to minimize regressive elements in any tax. Under this approach, the policy question is whether property tax regressivity exists regardless of the perspective used to analyze incidence. Indeed, several studies have taken this approach and documented persistent regressivity (Pechman and Okner, 1974; Odden, 1975; Odden and Vincent, 1976; Pechman, 1986; Musgrave and Musgrave, 1989). These studies investigated property tax incidence under a variety of assumptions, from most regressive to most progressive, both nationally and for several states, including Connecticut, Minnesota, Missouri, and South Dakota. All except the 1986 Pechman study, which was a nationwide estimate, show persistent regressivity in the low income ranges. Further, these studies document regressivity for the income ranges that include the bulk of taxpayers.

FIGURE 6.4   Property Tax Burden by Income Class, 1975, 1980, 1985

	Property Taxes as a Percent of Income		
Population Decile	*1975*	*1980*	*1985*
More Progressive Assumptions			
First[a]	3.5	2.3	2.2
Second	2.6	1.9	1.9
Third	2.3	1.6	1.5
Fourth	2.0	1.5	1.4
Fifth	1.8	1.3	1.3
Sixth	1.7	1.2	1.1
Seventh	1.8	1.3	1.2
Eighth	1.9	1.4	1.3
Ninth	1.9	1.4	1.3
Tenth	4.2	3.1	3.1
All deciles[b]	2.8	2.0	2.0
More Regressive Assumptions			
First[a]	5.6	4.1	3.9
Second	4.1	3.1	3.0
Third	3.3	2.5	2.4
Fourth	3.2	2.3	2.3
Fifth	3.0	2.2	2.1
Sixth	3.0	2.2	2.1
Seventh	3.1	2.2	2.1
Eighth	3.0	2.2	2.1
Ninth	3.0	2.1	2.1
Tenth	3.1	2.1	2.2
All deciles[b]	3.2	2.3	2.3

[a] Includes negative incomes.
[b] Includes only sixth to tenth deciles.

Source: Joseph Pechman, "Who Paid the Taxes in 1966–86," Washington, D.C., Brookings Institution, 1986. (Revised tables).

Indeed, these studies suggest that the major impact of the new view is to shift understandings of property tax incidence primarily for the upper income categories, for which property tax burdens shift from regressive to progressive. In short, even accepting new understandings for analyzing property tax incidence, the property tax exhibits a regressive incidence pattern in the lower income ranges, thus justifying policy mechanisms to stem that regressivity.

Pechman has conducted the most recent study of nationwide property tax incidence; his revised results are presented in Figure 6.4. The data show that the property tax is regressive under both incidence assumptions in the first to fifth population deciles. Thus, for policy purposes, the property tax can be assumed to produce a greater burden in middle- and lower-income households. Second, under both incidence assumptions, the nationwide property tax burden is primarily proportional in the middle income categories. Third, under the more progressive incidence assumptions, the property tax is progressive mainly for the top 10 percent; it is proportional through the middle- and high-income ranges. Fourth, even under the more regressive incidence assumptions, the property tax is less regressive on average across the nation than is the sales tax (see Figure 5.12).[3] Fifth, overall property tax burdens have fallen since 1975 and are lower than average sales tax burdens. Finally, the data in these tables have been adjusted to reflect federal income tax deductibility of property taxes; when these adjustments are made, the property tax bite drops from about 3 to about 2 percent of personal income.

ECONOMIC AND SOCIAL EFFECTS

For homeowners, the property tax is a tax on housing consumption. As such, it raises the price of housing and thus discourages housing investments. On the other hand, the property tax, which consumed 3.2% of personal income in 1987, is a smaller burden than the sales tax, which consumed about 5% of personal income, and thus is a much smaller burden than if housing consumption were simply rolled into the sales tax base, a policy for which good arguments could be made. Further, property tax payments can be deducted from federal income tax payments. In addition, as discussed throughout this chapter, states have enacted a wide-ranging array of adjustments designed to reduce the property tax impact on homeowners and to encourage housing consumption. Although all of these mechanisms may not fully offset the regressive effect of the tax, they probably come close.

The costs of property taxes are further offset by the benefits in local services that they support. Indeed, both taxes and services get capitalized into the price of property, with taxes decreasing the price and services increasing them. Research shows that the capitalized impact of services is substantial (Wendling, 1981b).

Property taxes on the business sector raise a series of additional economic issues. A general issue is that businesses that rely more heavily on physical capital (land, buildings, equipment, and machinery, including inventories) than on human capital (lawyers, accountants, computer service vendors, etc.) bear the impact of higher costs from property taxation and thus have some economic disadvantages in the marketplace. This raises the overall question of how businesses should be taxed, which was briefly discussed in the previous chapter. During the past several years, states have generally exempted business inventories as well as machinery and equipment from the property tax rolls, thus including only land and buildings owned by the business sector.

---

[3] Property tax burdens in a particular state generally will be very different from these national averages.

ADMINISTRATION AND COMPLIANCE

The administration burdens of the property tax primarily consist of recording all property parcels, maintaining a record of changing ownership, and assessing property, which is fraught with technical and political challenges. Technically, tools exist to keep up-to-date values on just about any kind of property, and thus to maintain assessed values pretty close to current market values. But, as noted, practice generally is otherwise. The minimal requirements for good property tax administration are appointed rather than elected local assessors, with clear specification of the skills needed to qualify for appointment; some degree of funding for the local assessment process, with computer facilities to store, maintain, and update records; and a state board of equalization to conduct periodic assessment-sales studies and provide equalization ratios for state school aid purposes.

Individual compliance is probably more straightforward for this tax than for any other. A tax bill is submitted once a year, and property owners pay, sometimes in annual and sometimes in semiannual payments. Some homeowners have the bank collect property tax liabilities monthly along with the mortgage payment; in these cases, the bank pays the bill annually. The annual nature of property tax bills contributes to the unpopularity of this tax. Individuals would rather pay taxes in little bites, as they do for the sales tax.

LOW-INCOME
PROPERTY TAX RELIEF PROGRAMS

For years, states have enacted a variety of programs that ostensibly provide property tax relief, sometimes to all homeowners but often only to low-income homeowners, the elderly, veterans, or the disabled. Public finance economists generally criticize these programs on a variety of grounds, but the programs remain and are actually proliferating. Ebel and Ortbal (1989) recently summarized these programs based on a detailed update by the Advisory Commission on Intergovernmental Relations (1989b).

Generally, property tax relief includes a variety of programs designed to reduce reliance on the tax to raise local revenues. As such, the programs are intended to benefit all local property tax payers as well as to target additional relief to low-income households to reduce property tax regressivity. There are two categories of property tax relief programs: direct and indirect. Direct programs include homestead exemptions or credits, circuit breakers, tax deferral plans, and classification of the property tax base. These programs reduce property tax bills directly. Indirect programs include intergovernmental aid programs (which include school finance equalization programs at the state level), tax and spending limitations (for a review, see Gold, 1984), and local option sales and income taxes. This section reviews only the direct programs. Key elements of these programs are listed in Figure 6.5.

FIGURE 6.5 Direct Residential Property Tax Relief

States	Classification		Differential by:	Circuit Breakers	Homestead Exemption or Credit	Residential Deferral
	Number of Classes	High/low				
Alabama	3	3:1	Value			E
Alaska					EHR, W	
Arizona	9	20:1	Value	AR, EH		
Arkansas				EH		
California	2		Value	EHR	AH, DV	LIE
Colorado	2	1.38:1	Value	DHR, EHR	LIED	E
Connecticut				EHR	D, DV	D
D.C. (Washington)	4	1.67:1	Rate	EHR	AH	AH
Delaware					E, LI	LIE
Florida					AH	AH
Georgia					AH, LIE, V	LIE
Hawaii	8		Rate	AR	AH, B, D, DV, E	
Idaho				D, EH	AH	
Illinois				D, EHR	AH, E, V	LIE
Indiana					AH, DV, LIE	
Iowa	4		Value	DHR, EHR	AH, DV	
Kansas	4	2.5:1	Value	B, D, EHR		
Kentucky					E, D	
Louisiana	4	2.5:1	Value		AH	
Maine				AHR	B, V	V
Maryland				AH, D, ER	B, DV	DV
Massachusetts					AH, EV, LI	LIE
Michigan				AHR	DV	LIE
Minnesota	34	27.5:1	Value, Credit	AHR	AH	
Mississippi	2	2:1	Value			
Missouri	3	2.67:1	Value	EHR	AH, D, EH	
Montana	6	10:1	Value	EHR	DV, LI	
Nebraska					D, DV, EH	

State				Circuit-breaker / relief	Exemption beneficiaries
Nevada				EHR	B, DV, O, V, W
New Hampshire					B, DV, E; E
New Jersey					AH, D, DV, E; AH, DV, E
New Mexico				EHR	AH, V
New York	4,2		Value	AHR	AH, V
North Carolina			Value		DV, LIE, D
North Dakota	4	1.11:1	Value	DHR, EHR	B, E, D
Ohio	2		Rate, Credit	D, EH	AH
Oklahoma				D, EH	AH, V
Oregon	2		Value	AHR	DV; LIE
Pennsylvania				D, EHR	B, D, DV; D
Rhode Island				EHR	V
South Carolina	5	2.63:1	Value		B, D, DV, E
South Dakota	3	2.2:1	Value	DHR, EHR	
Tennessee					DV, EDH; LIE
Texas					AH, D, EH; E
Utah	3	1.67:1	Value	EHR	B; LIE
Vermont				AHR	V
Virginia					D, EH
Washington					LIED
West Virginia	4	4:1	Rate	EHR	D, E; LIE
Wisconsin				AHR	
Wyoming				D, EHR	

Key:

AHR	All homeowners and renters	LIE	Low-income elderly
AH	All homeowners	LIED	Low-income elderly disabled
AR	All renters	O	Orphans
B	Blind	V	Veteran homesteaders
D	Disabled homeowners	W	Widows or widowers
DV	Disabled veterans	AV	Assessed valuation
DHR	Disabled homeowners and renters	NA	Not available
E	Elderly		
EDH	Elderly disabled homeowners		
EH	Elderly homeowners		
EHR	Elderly homeowners and renters		
ER	Elderly renters		
EV	Elderly veterans		
LI	Low-income		

Source: Robert D. Ebel and James Orthal. "Direct Residential Property Tax Relief," *Intergovernmental Perspective*, 15(2):9–14, Spring 1989.

Classification of the Property Tax Base

As of 1989, 19 states and the District of Columbia legislated some type of property tax base classification. Five states allowed local choice in creating a classification system. The basic goal of a classification program is to tax different elements of the property tax base—residential, commercial, industrial, farm, utilities, etc.—at different effective rates. Typically, the goal is to tax non-residential (i.e., business) property at higher effective tax rates. A classification system is often called a "split roll" system.

The usual procedure is to assess different components of the property tax base at different levels, with residential property usually assessed below the levels of other property, and to apply a uniform tax rate to total assessed valuations. West Virginia and the District of Columbia, though, assess all property at the same level and apply different tax rates to the different property classes. Although obviously less popular, the latter approach is preferred since it maintains assessment accuracy. Differential assessments add further cloudiness to what is already a complex set of assessment practices across the country.

The number of classifications of property varies substantially, from a low of 2 to a one-time high of 34 in Minnesota. Minnesota's system was so complex that some analysts suggested the state actually had created 70 property classifications (Bell and Bowman, 1986). In 1989, Minnesota changed its classification system, reducing the number of classes to about 10.

Circuit Breaker Programs

As the name suggests, a circuit breaker program is designed to protect homeowners from property tax overload, which could result if current income fell in a year due to illness or unemployment or dropped for several years due to retirement. Circuit breakers typically relate property tax bills to a taxpayer's income; the relief is then some portion of the property tax bill that exceeds a given percentage of income. Such programs can directly control regressive residential property tax burdens.

Most states link the circuit breaker program to the state income tax through a separate schedule, but several states administer the program separately and send cash refunds to those who qualify. Still other states have the local government provide the property tax relief and then reimburse the local government for the total amount.

In 1989, 32 states had some type of circuit breaker program. Wisconsin enacted the first program in 1964; Michigan currently has the most comprehensive program. All 32 states make all homeowners eligible, and 28 states make renters eligible (assuming that property tax bills are shifted forward by landlords to renters). Some states target relief to the elderly or disabled. The costs vary, from a high of $60 per capita in Michigan to a low of less than $1,000 total dollars in West Virginia.

Homestead Exemptions and Credits

Again reflecting the value this country places on home ownership, 41 states have some type of homestead exemption or homestead credit, which simply reduces the property tax for individuals who own homes. Homestead exemptions or credits are one of the oldest property tax relief programs. For the homestead exemption, the assessed valuation is reduced by a fixed amount, often several thousand dollars. This reduces the property tax bill, and the cost is borne by local governments. Some, but not many, states reimburse local governments for these revenue losses through a homestead credit, whereby the local government reduces the homeowner's property tax bill by the homestead exemption amount times the tax rate and then bills the state for the total amount for all local taxpayers. Since several of the programs are financed locally, the total cost of these programs has not been calculated.

Interestingly, 20 percent of the 41 states that provide this type of property tax relief do not link it to income, i.e., do not have a "needs" test: all homeowners, rich or poor, benefit from the homestead exemption or credit. Further, only 18 of the 41 states extend the program to all homesteads; 20 states limit the program to the elderly (again, both rich and poor), 13 limit it to the disabled, and 24 limit it to veterans or disabled veterans.

Tax Deferrals

A tax deferral program extends the time period over which property taxes can be paid. The taxpayer is given the option of paying the current tax bill or deferring the payment to some future time, usually when the property is sold. At that time, past property tax payments plus interest are due. Legally, these deferred property tax payments are liens on the property.

Tax deferrals are the most recently enacted property tax relief programs. In 1979 only nine states had such programs; the number increased to 21 by 1989. Tax deferral programs have the "best" economic characteristics of all the property tax relief programs because they entail minimal governmental interference in housing consumption, they reflect the social goal of home ownership and staying in one's home even when income drops, and they maintain governmental revenues, at least over time. Unfortunately, as with most tax relief programs that have the best economic features, they are not very popular. Deferral programs have few participants; it seems that the negative feature of placing a lien on one's home for deferred tax payments is not outweighed by the positive features of location stability and continued home ownership.

Final Comments

As this discussion suggests, property tax relief programs for all homeowners, as well as programs targeted at the elderly, the poor, veterans, or the disabled, are popular and increasing in numbers. There are several major policy as well as economic benefits associated with these programs. The first is that most provide aid or relief to all homeowners—regardless of income level. Classification systems in which all residential property is taxed less than nonresidential property, along with general homestead exemptions and credits, provide aid to the rich and poor alike. Other programs target certain groups (the elderly, veterans, and the disabled) for protection, usually without needs (i.e., income) tests and exclude other groups with low property tax burdens and low incomes from assistance. On economic grounds, such programs can be challenged; these programs clearly place the social goals of home ownership above the economic goals of a good tax system. A public finance economist would argue that all of these programs should be linked to income, i.e., that the overall policy objective should be to reduce regressivity, and thus relief should be targeted in increasing amounts to low-income property tax payers. Most public finance economists, however, go beyond this recommendation and argue that housing goals should be excluded completely from property tax adjustments and handled through other public policies (Musgrave and Musgrave, 1989).

Further, many of these programs, especially circuit breaker programs, make it easier for local governments to raise property taxes; the circuit breaker effectively cuts in for all taxpayers if residential property tax payments exceed the fixed percent of income. Thus, the programs become indirect state support for local choices either for more services or for higher-quality services.

Finally, except for state-financed circuit breakers, most of these programs reduce the local property tax base. Thus, they make it more difficult to raise local tax revenues for schools as well as other functions.

There are other economic and policy questions that can be raised about these mechanisms, as well as about other special property tax adjustments. Gold (1979) provided the most recent comprehensive analysis. It probably is time for a new look at the economic and policy impacts of these costly and expanding property tax relief programs.

THE CALIFORNIA APPROACH TO PROPERTY TAXATION: WHAT NOT TO DO

In 1978, California dramatically changed the process for determining assessed valuation for property taxation. Proposition 13, enacted by initiative in June 1978, rolled back assessed valuations to the 1975–76 market value. Growth in assessed value was limited to 2 percent a year, with reappraisal to market value occurring only when property was sold. The tax rate was fixed at 1 percent of assessed evaluation. Analytically, California shifted to an acquisition-based assessment system, under which property is assessed at market value at different intervals—namely, when it exchanges ownership. Drawing on data over 10 years, Phillips (1988) recently analyzed the effects of this approach.

Basis and Horizontal Equity

In the first year, assessments were dropped to market value (as of 1975–76), and the tax rate was 1 percent. Further, all property—residential and nonresidential—was assessed at the same level, producing a high degree of horizontal equity, i.e., all property on the tax rolls was assessed at the same ratio to market value. But within a few years, horizontal equity began to deteriorate rapidly. By 1981, Phillips (1988) showed that the tax base relative to market value dropped by nearly 50 percent. Median assessment–market value ratios ranged between 0.38 and 0.77 in most metropolitan areas and did not exceed 0.75 in any nonmetropolitan area. In short, between one-quarter and one-half of the tax base appeared to escape property taxation.

These overall drops, which differed across as well as within local government jurisdictions, were paralleled by growing differences across and within categories of property. First, single-family homes tended to have higher assessment to market value ratios than nonresidential property, in part indicating a higher turnover rate among homes than business property. Second, using data for San Francisco, Phillips showed that for residential property, homes were underassessed relative to rental apartments and condominiums. Finally, again using data for San Francisco as an example, Phillips showed that the average difference between the assessed value of a home and the average assessment was 60 percent, suggesting large intraclass assessment differences.

The differences for homes were essentially related to the year of acquisition, that is, two identical properties could have dramatically different assessed values depending solely on the year they were acquired. These assessed valuation differences translated directly into tax impact differences, with recent buyers burdened with substantially larger tax payments than long-term owners. By 1986, the effective tax for a long-term owner was just 0.31 percent of market value, whereas a recent buyer faced a burden more than three times higher, at 1.0 percent.

Such differential assessments and the effective overall tax impacts had peculiar benefit patterns. First, elderly homeowners—both rich and poor—benefited. Their property tax burden fell, according to Phillips, from 8 to 3 percent of income. But young families with children, who tend to buy new homes, did not benefit. In fact, their effective property tax rate increased from 1978 to 1986, and their property taxes as a percent of income ranged between 3 and 4 percent, compared to 2 percent for long-term owners.

Further, assessment/market values were inversely related to property value, meaning that individuals with the higher-valued homes had lower relative assessed valuations, so that the rich benefited more than the middle- or lower-income household. Finally, Phillips showed that big business benefited more than small business.

The major factors behind these differential impacts were year of acquisition (the primary culprit), differential rates of market value increase, and the rate of new building. The data show that the "winners" from Proposition 13 were high-income individuals, senior citizens rather than young families, long-time homeowners rather than new home buyers, and big rather than small businesses. In nearly all cases, the difference related mainly to turnover rates, a variable with absolutely no economic value.

In summary, Proposition 13, an acquisition-based system of property tax assessment, significantly lowered the base over time and violated horizontal equity in directions that make the tax even more regressive overall.

Yield

When enacted, Proposition 13 reduced the property tax yield by about $7 billion, but the state had about the same level of surplus funds and was able to bail out local governments in the immediate aftermath. Over time, though, the property tax yield has fallen relative to market value; up to 50 percent of the yield has been lost. Although the result has been to reduce further the impact of the property tax in California, the reduction has been at the cost of substantial inequity: many still pay 1 percent of market value, but others now pay as little as 0.25 percent of market value. Nevertheless, when statewide figures are compared, the ratio of property taxes paid by residential versus nonresidential property has stayed about the same, increasing slightly for small nonresidential property. It seems that business expansion and new construction has kept the ratio of property taxes paid between the two sectors at about the same level.

Summary

California's approach to property tax reform through Proposition 13 is bad public policy. The result is a property tax that violates all economic standards for horizontal and vertical equity, produces a much smaller level of tax revenues, and is under state rather than local control. California's experience shows that a property tax structure that pegs assessed values to the price at the time of purchase is an ill-conceived way to administer the property tax.

CONCLUSIONS ABOUT THE PROPERTY TAX

The property tax has never been a popular tax; for most of this century, it has been the most unpopular tax. Yet it has been and continues to be the pillar of local government and school finance. It likely will continue to play this role. It produces large amounts of revenues, maintains those revenue levels in economic downturns, and produces revenue increases during economic growth periods. Its burden is proportional in the middle income ranges, and its regressivity can be reduced by circuit breaker and other income tax credit programs (see Figure 6.6). Although its unpopularity engendered property tax relief and reform during the 1970s, it also contributed to the tax and spending limitation drive

FIGURE 6.6 Overall Assessment of the Property Tax

Tax base	Wealth; generally, assessed value of real and land property
Yield	Elastic in general Stable on the downside of economic cycle and increasing on the upside
Equity	Horizontal: varies by type of property, degrees of exemptions, and assessment valuation methods; generally not met
	Vertical: • regressive across all income levels under "conventional" view • progressive in upper income levels under "new" view • proportional in middle income levels under both "conventional" and "new" views
Economic effects	More neutral as tax rates across jurisdictions are more uniform
Administration	Complicated; technically can be good, but in actual practice, there is wide variation across states and localities within states
Compliance costs	Small

in the late 1970s. But, as the federal government cut real federal aid during the 1980s and education improvement became a national imperative, states tapped the property tax for substantial new revenues. Property taxes are crucial for funding local government services but are not popular taxes. They are needed even though they are not liked.

—Chapter 7————————————

School Finance Formulas

School finance is concerned with the interrelated issues of raising, distributing, allocating, and using revenues for the purpose of educating children. This chapter moves from the issues of raising revenues, discussed in the preceding two chapters, to the issues involved in distributing revenues. The chapter reviews the major types of fiscal equalization formulas states have used during the twentieth century to distribute general education aid to local school districts. To emphasize the characteristics and impacts of various school finance formulas, all discussion in this chapter assumes that student needs are the same, or uniform across districts. The next chapter discusses special-purpose, or categorical, state aid programs and focuses on how to make formula adjustments for special student and district needs.

Four types of formulas are analyzed: (1) flat grants, (2) foundation programs, (3) guaranteed tax base programs,[1] and (4) combination foundation and guaranteed tax base programs. Full state funding and other types of state-determined spending programs also are discussed briefly. For each formula, three issues are discussed:

- The intergovernmental aid properties
- The reflection of school finance values
- The impact on fiscal equity

[1] Guaranteed tax base programs are algebraically equivalent to district power equalization, percentage equalization, and guaranteed yield programs. The latter programs are not discussed individually in this chapter.

The school finance computer simulation that accompanies the text should be used with this chapter. Although the text includes some printouts from that simulation, a more in-depth understanding of the different school finance formulas, how they work, and what impacts they have on both the state and local districts will be developed by using the simulation to analyze variations in the funding formulas.

At this point, readers should familiarize themselves with the operation of the school finance simulation that accompanies the book. The appendix describes how to install the simulation on your computer system and how to use it. This chapter encourages readers to simulate and assess versions of formulas different from those discussed.

SCHOOL FINANCE EQUITY AND POLICY GOALS

Chapter 3 developed a comprehensive equity framework that can be used to assess the equity of a state's school finance structure. If the group of concern is students, the chapter showed that distributional equity can relate to several particular objects, such as current operating expenditures per pupil, state and local revenues per pupil, teacher/pupil ratios, the enacted curriculum, and student achievement. The chapter also identified four equity principles: (1) horizontal equity, which requires equal distribution of the object; (2) vertical equity, which allows for extra amounts of the object to be distributed on the basis of special student or district needs; (3) fiscal neutrality, which requires that the object not be related to local fiscal capacity, such as property value per pupil; and (4) effectiveness, which requires that a level and use of resources produce a fixed amount of student performance.

This chapter uses this framework to analyze a representative 10-district sample of school districts. The text shows how various school finance objectives can be in conflict, as well as how politics might intervene to constrain the amount of equity a state political system can produce. In general, a school finance structure is designed to: (1) compensate for the varying amounts of local tax capacity, generally property value per child; (2) reduce disparities in state and local revenues per pupil (indeed, some programs seek to eliminate disparities); (3) allow for local fiscal decision making, which can produce decisions to spend at different levels; (4) keep the local and state costs within reasonable limits; (5) increase state aid to a sufficient number of districts to produce a positive majority vote in both houses of a state's legislature to enact the program; and (6) encourage efficiency and effectiveness in local school operations. At times, providing property tax reduction and relief are also policy objectives. Some of these objectives may conflict, specifically, local fiscal decision making and equality of revenues per pupil (even allowing for adjustments for special needs). Thus, school finance formula design is both a substantive and political task that seeks to balance these many objectives; "perfect equity" is generally not possible (Brown and Elmore, 1982).

THE SIMULATION: SAMPLE DISTRICTS

In designing new school finance structures, analysts and policymakers begin with state education finance systems that have evolved over several years. Local districts have real property tax rates, and state general aid has been distributed according to some mechanism, usually with the goal of reducing spending disparities caused by unequal distribution of the local per-pupil property tax base.

Figure 7.1 displays data for a representative sample of 10 districts that will be used throughout the chapter to demonstrate the impact of various new school finance structures. The data have been taken from a real state and reflect the typical school finance situation across the country. The numbers indicate several characteristics of the impact of the extant school finance system in the state from which the sample was selected.

First, there are large differences in property value per pupil. The richest district has $306,766 in property value per pupil, which is almost nine times the value in the poorest district ($36,670). The weighted average[2] property value per student is $71,277, which is about twice the value of the poorest district and about half the value of the second wealthiest district ($135,496).

Second, household income varies from a low of $14,435 to a high of $22,569, a difference of nearly 1.5 to 1. The average household income is $17,544, with the lowest-income district having 18 percent less than the average and the highest-income district having 29 percent more. These disparities are much less severe than those for property wealth per pupil. As is usually the case, income varies less than wealth, largely because income is an annual flow of economic value whereas wealth is the accumulation of economic value over a multiple-year period. As such, one would expect wealth to be larger than and vary more than income.

Another feature of these numbers is that income and property value are not perfectly related. Although income generally increases as property value increases, the district with the highest household income is not the district with highest property value. Several factors account for this imperfect relationship. For example, big cities typically have large amounts of commercial and industrial property and low proportions of students relative to total population; together, these drive up average property value per child. They also often have concentrations of families in poverty, which drives down average household income. Similarly, new suburban bedroom communities often have

---

[2] All statistics in the table and in the computer simulation are calculated in a manner that weights each district value by the number of students in the district. Thus, the values for district A, with 10,040 students, contribute more to the weighted average than the values for district J, which has only 848 students. Using student-weighted statistics has become the usual way to present statistics in school finance analyses. The results thus indicate the impact of the funding structure on students. In the past, school finance analysis treated each district value equally, giving equal weight to districts with large and small numbers of students.

FIGURE 7.1 Ten-District Sample: Base Data

					Pupil weights			
					Regular 1.00		Compensatory 1.00	
					Handicapped 1.00		LEP 1.00	
District	Pupils	Property Value per Pupil ($)	Household Income ($)	Property Tax Rate (mills)	Local Revenue per Pupil ($)	State Revenue per Pupil ($)	Total Revenue per Pupil ($)
A	10,040	36,670	14,435	30.43	1,116	978	2,094
B	7,028	46,845	15,674	28.33	1,327	888	2,215
C	7,985	55,203	17,229	26.86	1,483	794	2,277
D	4,152	64,875	16,290	25.61	1,661	620	2,281
E	5,148	71,762	17,074	24.39	1,750	572	2,322
F	6,216	81,913	19,390	23.54	1,928	477	2,405
G	3,666	92,949	21,551	23.28	2,164	437	2,601
H	2,961	106,195	20,769	21.72	2,307	411	2,718
I	3,472	135,496	22,569	19.52	2,645	388	3,033
J	848	306,766	19,146	10.52	3,227	366	3,593
Weighted average		71,277	17,544	25.69	1,688	686	2,374
Standard deviation		40,819	2,534	3.73	484	218	292
Median		64,875	17,074	25.61	1,661	620	2,281

Totals

Pupils	51,516
Local revenue	$86,946,800
State revenue	$34,017,243
Total revenue	$120,964,043

Equity Measures

Horizontal equity	
Range	$1,499
Range ratio	.369
Coef. of variation	.123
McLoone index	.959
Gini coefficient	.060
Fiscal neutrality	
Correlation	.965
Elasticity	.199

primarily residential property on the tax rolls and high proportions of children relative to total population. Together, these factors drive down the average property value per child, even though the suburban areas often have families with above-average incomes.

The fifth column in Figure 7.1 shows that property tax rates also vary considerably, from a low of 10.52 mills to a high of 30.43 mills, a difference of 3 to 1. Interestingly, it is the lower-property-value districts that have the higher property tax rates and the higher-property-value districts that have the lower property tax rates. Because of differences in the tax base, the second wealthiest district raises $135 dollars per pupil for each mill levied and thus takes in $2,645 per pupil in local revenues at its tax rate of 19.52 mills. On the other hand, the second poorest district receives only $47 for each mill levied and thus raises just $1,327 at its 28.33-mill tax rate. Even though the poorer district exerts a higher tax effort, it produces a much lower level of revenues because its tax base is so low. On the other hand, the wealthier district raises a much higher level of local revenues per pupil even though it exerts a lower tax effort, because its tax base is so much larger.

State aid is distributed in inverse relationship to property value per pupil, i.e., the poorest districts receive the largest amounts of per-pupil state aid, and aid declines as property value per pupil rises. In fact, the poorest district receives almost three times as much state aid per pupil as the wealthiest district. This pattern of state aid provides fiscal capacity equalization. But even the wealthiest districts receive some state general aid, nearly $400 per pupil for this sample. This distribution of state aid is characteristic of most states. All states use some type of fiscal capacity–equalizing school finance formula to distribute general aid, and all districts receive some minimum level of general aid.

But the difference in state aid allocations, although in the right direction (higher amounts to property-poor districts), is not sufficient to offset the 9-to-1 difference in property value per pupil among districts. Thus, the poorest district, even though it receives three times the aid of the wealthiest district and exerts three times the tax rate, has revenues per child that total only 58 percent of total revenues for the highest-spending district. The figures document a consistent pattern: the lower the property value per child, the lower the total revenues per pupil, even though per-pupil state aid and property tax rates are higher.

Figure 7.1 also includes statistical measures of the fiscal equity of this school finance system. In terms of horizontal equity for students, the coefficient of variation for total revenues per pupil is 12.3 percent, which means that two-thirds of these districts have total revenues per pupil within 12.3 percent (or $292) of the weighted average, and 95 percent of districts have total revenues per pupil within 24.6 percent (or $584) of the average. The relatively low coefficient of variation indicates that the fiscal capacity–equalizing distribution of state general aid substantially offsets the differences in local ability to raise property taxes. To understand the impact of state general aid, compare Figure 7.1 with the results of the "no state aid" model in the simulation. You can do this by selecting the **No State Aid** option from the **Model** menu. Notice that the coefficient of variation more than doubles; state aid clearly has helped to reduce differences in total revenues per pupil.

The McLoone index in Figure 7.1 indicates that total revenues per pupil for the bottom 50 percent of students are quite close to the total for the student at the median. Again, state aid has helped push this statistic toward 1.00, which would indicate full equity for the bottom 50 percent, as compared to the McLoone index of 0.784 in the "no state aid" case (again, choose **No State Aid** from the **Model** menu in the simulation).

In terms of fiscal neutrality, i.e., the degree to which total revenues per pupil are linked to property wealth per pupil, Figure 7.1 shows a high correlation, 0.965, but a relatively low elasticity, 0.199. This means that revenues are strongly related to wealth but that wealth increases produce only small increases in revenues—specifically, a 1 percent increase in wealth produces only about a 0.2 percent increase in revenues. This means that as wealth increases about 100 percent from the poorest district to the average-wealth district (district E), for example, revenues per pupil would increase about 20 percent, which is slightly less than the actual total revenue increase from $2,094 to $2,322. The very large wealth value of the top district skews the statistic upward, even though that district has few students.

Figure 7.2 shows graphically the relationship between revenues per pupil and property value per pupil for this sample, and Figure 7.3 shows the same

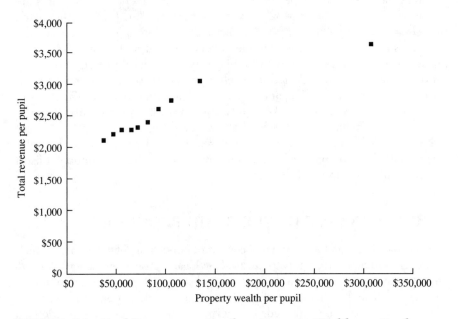

FIGURE 7.2 Total Revenue per Pupil vs. Property Wealth per Pupil: Base Data

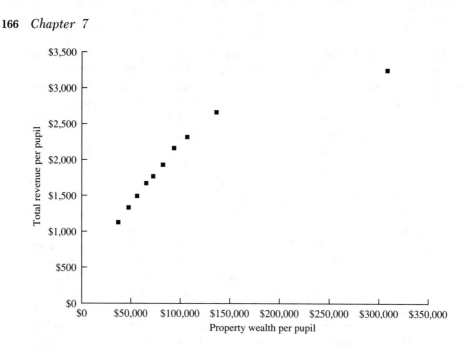

FIGURE 7.3   Total Revenue per Pupil vs. Property Wealth per Pupil: No State Aid

data with no state aid. For both, there is a linear relationship between the two variables; however, the "slope" of the graph is much steeper for the "no state aid" case. Thus, state aid has reduced the magnitude but has not eliminated the role of property value per pupil in producing revenue-per-pupil disparities.

In short, the 10-district sample reflects the current context of school finance in many states. There is wide disparity in the local per-pupil property tax base. State aid is distributed inversely to property wealth and is somewhat fiscal capacity-equalizing, but not sufficiently equalizing to offset differences in property wealth. As a result, the equity statistics reflect a system that needs further improvements to meet either horizontal equity or fiscal neutrality equity standards. This chapter discusses how different types of school finance formulas for general school aid produce equity improvements in the distribution of fiscal resources for this sample of districts.

SCHOOL FINANCE GENERAL AID PROGRAMS

School finance general aid programs consist of education "block grants," which provide unrestricted revenues to be used by local districts and schools for any education purpose. Sometimes they require districts to spend a minimum percentage on teacher salaries or a maximum on administration, but generally they are completely unrestricted. Furthermore, they do not carry restrictions for "maintaining local effort," so districts can even use large increases in general aid revenues to help roll back local property tax rates. Indeed, as discussed in Chapter 4, half of each general aid dollar, on average, is used to increase local education spending, and half is used to reduce local property tax rates.

Although the 1980s' history of education "block grants" is associated with attempts to consolidate, deregulate, and fund categorical programs for special students (handicapped or low achievers), the generic nature of a block grant is attractive to local educators. Block grant funds are "money on the stump," i.e., funds given to local school districts to spend as they wish.

Flat Grant Programs

In the very early years of this country (i.e., during the late eighteenth and early nineteenth centuries), there were few public schools. Most schools were private, many run by churches. Only a small proportion of the population received formal schooling. As the country developed and interest emerged not only in formally educating citizens but also in forging a common culture, local governments began to create public schools.

As discussed in Chapters 1 and 2, these schools were not part of state systems of education, as exist today, but were independent creatures of local governments. Through various means, including taxation and "in kind" contributions, localities built schools (often one-room), hired teachers (who commonly lived in the schools and were paid in food, housing, etc. rather than money), and educated increasing numbers of children.

From the beginning through at least the middle of the nineteenth century, the inequities associated with this laissez faire approach to creating and financing schools were recognized. Some localities were too poor to create any type of public school. Larger and wealthier localities not only were able to create schools but even levied local taxes to finance them. Recognizing these different circumstances, states began to require each locality to have at least one public elementary school and often provided a lump sum—a flat grant, usually on a per-school basis—to help support some type of local elementary school program. This approach obviously remedied the problem of the poorest locality not being able to create a school on its own; in many of these communities, state funds were the only fiscal support for the school.

But the flat grant approach also provided funds to localities that had been able to create a school with their own resources, thus providing them with even more dollars. The overall impact was to expand education and boost the average level of schooling, and perhaps even education quality, but the flat grant program benefited poor and rich districts alike.

Over time, states increased the level of flat grants, in part to match rising costs. The growing numbers of students, moreover, required shifts in the formula structure from flat grants per school to flat grants per classroom or per teacher in order to finance schools and classrooms that had outgrown the initial one-room school format. As the education system continued to grow, it became clear that the level of the flat grant, always quite low, would need to be increased to finance the type of education system needed for an emerging industrial society. The school finance response is described in the next section, on foundation programs.

Today, states do not use flat grants as the major formula to apportion state general school aid. However, until 1974, Connecticut's school aid formula was a flat grant—$250 per pupil. Nevertheless, flat grant programs have several intriguing characteristics, some of which are quite attractive.[3]

From the perspective of an intergovernmental grant design, flat grants are general-purpose operating funds. They are based solely on some measure of local education need—such as number of schools, classrooms, teachers, or students. They have no local matching requirements. Flat grants also flow to local districts in equal amounts per unit of educational need, regardless of differences in local fiscal capacity, i.e., property wealth per pupil or household income. They are therefore unlikely to have a major impact in improving the fiscal neutrality of a school finance system, i.e., of reducing the connections between local fiscal capacity and expenditures per pupil. Moreover, flat grants are blunt instruments for raising local education spending, since districts could use the funds to reduce their own levels of spending and thus to reduce local property tax rates.

The flat grant formula.   Flat grants are simple. State aid per pupil (SAPP) for a flat grant is algebraically expressed as:

$$SAPP = FG,$$

where

$$FG = \text{amount of the flat grant.}$$

Total state aid (TSA) is defined as:

$$TSA = SAPP \times Pupils,$$

where

$$Pupils = \text{number of students in the school district.}[4]$$

---

[3] Some states, such as California, have constitutional requirements to provide a minimum amount of per-pupil state aid to local districts. These minimums function as flat grant programs for the very wealthy districts. California must provide a minimum $120 per pupil in state aid to all districts even if the formula calculation would provide for no state aid.

[4] In this example, pupils are the unit of need. Today most states finance schools on a per-pupil basis. But there are other measures of local need, such as teachers, classrooms, and schools. This book uses pupils as the basic unit of need, but the formulas also could be used with these other need measures.

Once the unit of need is identified, which today usually is pupils, a flat grant will provide an equal number of dollars for each unit of need in all districts. Such a program can be easily understood by all education policy leaders, at both state and local levels. Furthermore, because a flat grant treats all districts "equally," it has an aura of fairness. State education revenues are raised by taxing citizens across the state and are then returned to localities in a "fair" manner by providing an equal number of dollars for each unit of need.

Flat grants reflect the traditional American concern with the "bottom half." A flat grant implements the value of providing a bare minimum level of support for those students and districts at the bottom, which is usually defined in terms of relative fiscal capacity. Education flat grants were created to ensure that even the poorest localities could offer some type of education program. Since the amount of the flat grant historically has been very low, the most recent being only $250 per pupil, flat grants fall short of ensuring a minimum level of quality; the best that can be said is that they provide some level of support. Although they impact all school districts, they have emerged as a mechanism to help the poorest, i.e., the least fiscally able, localities to provide an education program.

Figures 7.4 and 7.5 depict graphically the impact of a flat grant program on the ability of school districts to raise funds for education purposes. Figure 7.4 represents the situation before a flat grant program. The solid lines show the revenues per pupil raised at different tax rates, 30 and 40 mills in this example, for districts with different levels of property value per pupil. For example,

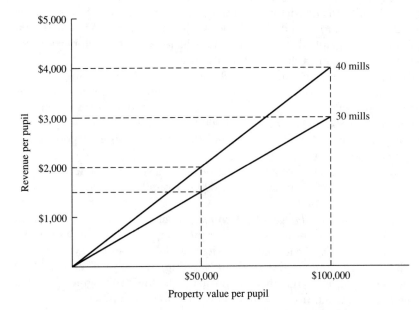

FIGURE 7.4   Graphical Representation of the Impact of No State Aid

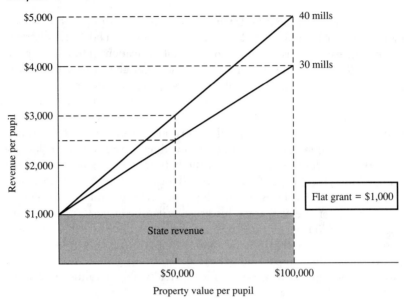

FIGURE 7.5 Graphical Representation of the Impact of a Flat Grant

at 30 mills, the district with a property value per pupil of $50,000 raises just $1,500 per pupil, whereas the district with a property value of $100,000 raises $3,000. At 40 mills, the district with a property value per pupil of $50,000 raises more—$2,000 per pupil—and the district with a property value of $100,000 raises $4,000. The graph shows that revenues increase both as property value per pupil increases and as the local tax rate increases.

Figure 7.5 depicts the impact of a flat grant. The result is simply that the amount of the flat grant—$1,000 in this case—is added to local revenues per pupil; the slopes of the lines do not change. So the district with a property value per pupil of $50,000 now raises $3,000 ($2,000 of local revenues plus the $1,000 flat grant) at a 40 mill tax rate, and the district with a property value per pupil of $100,000 raises $5,000 ($4,000 of local money plus the $1,000 flat grant) at the same tax rate. Wealthier districts still raise more money, but with the flat grant all districts have at least $1,000 per pupil.

Fiscal equity impacts of flat grant programs.   Figure 7.6 shows the result of replacing the current state aid system for the sample of districts with a flat grant of $800 per child. That amount is slightly higher than the average state aid in the original sample, and is about one-third the level of average total revenues per pupil, although there is no magic in the $800 figure. This flat grant increases state aid from $34 million to just over $41 million.

FIGURE 7.6 Ten-District Sample: Flat Grant (amount of flat grant: $800)

						Pupil weights			
						Regular 1.00			
						Handicapped 1.00		Comp. LEP 1.00	
District	Pupils	Property Value per Pupil ($)	Property Tax Rate (mills)	Local Revenue per Pupil ($)	State Revenue per Pupil ($)	Change in State Revenue per Pupil ($)	Total Revenue per Pupil ($)	Total Gain (Loss) per Pupil ($)
A	10,040	36,670	30.43	1,116	800	(178)	1,916	(178)
B	7,028	46,845	28.33	1,327	800	(88)	2,127	(88)
C	7,985	55,203	26.86	1,483	800	6	2,283	6
D	4,152	64,875	25.61	1,661	800	180	2,461	180
E	5,148	71,762	24.39	1,750	800	228	2,550	228
F	6,216	81,913	23.54	1,928	800	323	2,728	323
G	3,666	92,949	23.28	2,164	800	363	2,964	363
H	2,961	106,195	21.72	2,307	800	389	3,107	389
I	3,472	135,496	19.52	2,645	800	412	3,445	412
J	848	306,766	10.52	3,227	800	434	4,027	434
Weighted average		71,277	25.69	1,688	800	114	2,488	114
Standard deviation		42,185	3.45	460	0	218	460	195
Median		64,875	25.61	1,661	800	180	2,461	180

	Totals	Change
Pupils	51,516	
Local revenue	$86,946,800	$0
State revenue	$41,212,800	$7,195,557
Total revenue	$128,159,600	$7,195,557
State aid		
Number of winners	8	
Number of losers	2	

Equity Measures

Horizontal equity
Range	$2,111
Range ratio	.764
Coef. of variation	.185
McLoone index	.854
Gini coefficient	.107

Fiscal neutrality
Correlation	.931
Elasticity	.297

The flat grant completely erases the fiscal capacity–equalizing impact of the original state aid, actually decreasing state aid in the poorest two districts and increasing it in the wealthier eight districts (see the last column). All the equity statistics indicate a less equal distribution. The range ratio increases,[5] the coefficient of variation increases, and the McLoone index decreases. Further, both fiscal neutrality statistics increase, showing a stronger and more significant relationship between total revenues per pupil and property value per pupil. Indeed, the graph of this flat grant (use the simulation to view the graph) is very similar to the graph for the "no state aid" case (Figure 7.3). The difference is that revenues per pupil are about $800 higher with the flat grant; the graph has been shifted upward by the level of the flat grant. At low levels, in short, a flat grant is not a viable option for enhancing the fiscal equity of a state's school finance system.

As the flat grant grows, though, it begins to have a positive impact on the fiscal equity. For example, a flat grant of $1,600 per pupil reduces the coefficient of variation from .185 to .14 and the fiscal neutrality elasticity from .297 to .225 (use the simulation to confirm these figures). A flat grant of $2,400 further improves these statistics, lowering the coefficient of variation to .113 and the property wealth elasticity to .181 (again, use the simulation to confirm these figures). If the flat grant were increased over time to $10,000 and local tax rates and property value per pupil stayed the same, the flat grant would be the major source of school revenues. At this level, the coefficient of variation would be negligible, .039, and the wealth elasticity also would be negligible, at .063. Put a different way, a low-level flat grant would have a deleterious impact on the fiscal equity of the sample districts, but a very high flat grant would swamp the current inequities and produce a highly equalized system.[6]

Of course, as the level of the flat grant rises, so does the total or state cost of the program. The positive impacts on fiscal equity, in other words, are achieved only at significant cost. Nevertheless, the point of this example is that although low-level flat grants are unattractive, except for their simplicity, higher-level flat grants can reduce the fiscal inequities characteristic of most state school finance structures.

Finally, a few technical statistical points can be noted by reviewing the equity measures and the means and standard deviations of the major variables. First, the standard deviation of total revenue per pupil ($460) stays the same irrespective of the level of the flat grant. That is, adding a constant amount to all

[5] The range ratio in this example is the value of revenues per pupil for the ninth district minus the value for the second district, divided by the value of the second district. The federal range ratio is the preferred range statistic, but there are no 95th and 5th percentile observations in a 10-district sample; thus, the values for the districts at the 90th and 10th percentiles were used.

[6] Readers are encouraged to run these flat grant amounts on the computer simulation and to review the results on the computer screen as well as perhaps print them out. In addition, the reader should view the scatterplots for each run. The scatterplot for the flat grant at $10,000 shows that the graph of total revenues per pupil vs. property wealth per pupil is almost a straight, horizontal line.

variables in a sample does not change the standard deviation. This helps explain why the coefficient of variation decreases as the flat grant increases. Since the coefficient of variation is the standard deviation divided by the mean, the numerator (standard deviation) remains constant while the denominator (mean or average revenues per pupil) increases. Second, the correlation coefficient also stays the same irrespective of the level of the flat grant. Again, adding a constant amount to all variables in a sample does not change their correlation.

Flat grants were early attempts to involve the state in redressing local differences in the ability to support public schools. Flat grants are easy-to-understand intergovernmental aid programs, but they provide assistance to poor and rich districts alike. They are expensive, even at relatively low values. And at the affordable low values, they tend to worsen measures of school finance equity. They are not used as general aid policy instruments today.

Foundation Programs

As the shortcomings of flat grant programs became increasingly obvious at the turn of this century, there was a search for a new and more powerful formula. At about that time, the state of New York created a commission to study its school finance system with the specific charge to create a new school finance structure that went beyond the flat grant approach. George Srayer and Roger Haig, professors at Columbia University, were hired as the consultants to this commission. Their new creation was a formula that would come to dominate school finance during the rest of the century. Indeed, most states today use some variation of the Strayer-Haig foundation program, or minimum foundation program, as it originally was called. Indeed, in many states, the synonym for "school finance formula" is "minimum foundation program"; the state role in school finance is defined, as it were, as providing a minimum foundation program.

Strayer and Haig ingeniously incorporated several school finance issues into their new foundation program formula. First, the foundation program addressed the issue of a minimum-quality education program. Although flat grants provided financial assistance for localities to provide some level of local school funding, the low level of the flat grant was rarely sufficient to finance what could be called a minimum-quality education program. A driving feature of the minimum foundation program, however, was that it set an expenditure per pupil—the minimum foundation—at a level that would provide at least a minimum-quality education program. The idea was to put a fiscal "foundation" under every local school sufficient to provide an education program that met minimum standards. Thus, the foundation program was designed to remedy the first major defect of the low-level flat grant.

But what about the cost? The reason flat grants remained low was that to increase them would require more funds than the state could afford. The foundation program resolved this dilemma by financing the foundation expenditure per pupil with a combination of state and local revenues. A foundation program requires a minimum local tax effort as a condition of receiving state aid. The required local tax effort is applied to the local property tax base. State aid per pupil is the difference between the foundation per-pupil expenditure level and the per-pupil revenues raised by the required local tax rate.

The foundation formula.   Algebraically, state aid per pupil (SAPP) for a foundation program is:

$$SAPP = FEPP - (RTR \times PVPP),$$

where

$$FEPP = \text{foundation expenditure per pupil,}$$

$$RTR = \text{local required tax rate, and}$$

$$PVPP = \text{local property value per pupil.}$$

A district's total state aid (TSA) would be:

$$TSA = SAPP \times Pupils,$$

where

$$SAPP = \text{state aid per pupil, and}$$

$$Pupils = \text{number of students in the school district.}[7]$$

Thus, the total cost of the foundation program is shared by the state and local school district. A state could afford to enact such a program, and therefore substantially raise the minimum expenditure per pupil, because a large portion of the increase was financed by local tax revenues. Indeed, the advent of foundation school aid formulas formally underscored the joint and interrelated state and local roles in financing public elementary and secondary schools.

Foundation policy issues.   From an intergovernmental aid design perspective, the foundation program has several attractive features. First, it links local school districts with the state in a sophisticated structure of intergovernmental fiscal relationships. Second, it continues to provide large sources of general aid to local school districts, but through a mechanism by which local and state revenues are formally combined in the general aid "pot." Third, it formally requires a

---

[7] Again, teachers, classrooms, or schools could be used as the need measure. Indeed, South Dakota uses a foundation program with the classroom as the unit of need. Several states have used a foundation program with teachers as the need measure; Texas used such a program up to 1984.

"local match" in order for a district to receive state aid; the district must levy the required local tax rate as a condition of receiving state foundation aid.[8]

Fourth, per-pupil state aid also is related to fiscal capacity. Since the required local tax rate produces less money in a district with low property value than in a district with high property value, state aid becomes higher in the poor district. In fact, there is nearly a linear relationship between the level of state aid and the level of local property value per pupil: as property value decreases, state aid increases. Thus, a foundation program finances a minimum base education program in each school district, provides general aid in a manner that is fiscal capacity–equalizing (i.e., aid increases as property value per pupil decreases), and requires a local contribution as well. As discussed in Chapter 4, these are all attractive features of intergovernmental aid formulas.

The foundation program goes one or two steps beyond the flat grant, reflecting the American concern with the less well off and the importance of providing at least a minimum-quality education program. Foundation programs were designed, in fact, to ensure that there would be sufficient revenues from state and local sources to provide such a program in each school district. Viewed from today's education objectives, this does not seem a very lofty goal. But viewed from the perspective of the beginning of the twentieth century, it was a major and bold step forward. The foundation program allowed states to implement an education finance structure that substantially upgraded the education systems in the lowest-spending schools to a level that at least met a standard of minimum adequacy.

Three major shortcomings of foundation programs have emerged over the years. The first is that a foundation program typically allows districts to spend above the minimum foundation level. This fiscal leeway, or local add-on, is financed entirely by local revenues, however. As a result, districts with a high property value per pupil can levy a tax rate slightly above the required local effort and take in large amounts of supplemental revenues, whereas districts with a low property value per pupil can levy a substantial extra tax rate and still see only a small amount of additional revenue per pupil. In fact, this feature of foundation programs ultimately led to the court cases discussed in Chapter 2; over time, the local add-on component of education revenues far surpassed the foundation program revenues, producing a system which, although more equitable than a system with no state aid, still left education revenues per pupil strongly linked to local property wealth per pupil. Further, this local add-on feature is the "Achilles' heel" of the finance structure in all states that

---

[8] Historically, states have "hedged" on this requirement. Although most districts levy a tax rate above the minimum required local tax rate, a few do not. The policy issue for most states is whether to force these districts to raise their tax rates. The dilemma is that most of these low-tax-effort districts are usually the districts lowest in property wealth and lowest in household income, i.e., the poorest of the poor. States usually have not ultimately required these districts to raise their tax rates. Sometimes, as in New York State, the districts receive state aid as if they were levying that minimum tax rate. Other states, such as Texas, reduce state aid by a factor equal to the ratio of the actual local property tax rate to the foundation program's required tax rate.

today have a foundation program as their system for providing general school aid. In 1986–87, 30 states had such a foundation program as the basis or as a component of their school-aid program (Salmon et al., 1988).

Second, although foundation programs initially boosted the minimum level of local school spending, in many cases this minimum quickly proved inadequate to meet basic requirements. Put another way, after the initial years, many minimum foundation programs did not provide sufficient revenues per pupil to fund an education program that would meet the lowest standards. The inadequate level was due in part to technical problems (the law gave a specific dollar amount as the foundation expenditure and required legislative action each year to increase it) and in part to fiscal constraints (the state could not afford to raise it significantly). Over time, the low level forced districts who wanted to provide a higher-quality education program to expand the local add-on, which gradually transformed the overall system to one based more and more on local property value per pupil.

Third, although foundation programs usually increased total education revenues in property-poor districts and helped them enhance their education programs, strict state aid formula calculations for wealthier districts yielded a negative number. This result meant that these districts could raise more than the minimum foundation expenditure at the required tax rate. In a world of perfect fiscal equity, the state would require such districts to send a check in the amount of negative aid to the state, which the state would put in the general fund for redistribution to poorer districts. But states did not enact this "recapture" component; if state aid calculations produced a negative figure, the state simply provided no aid to that district. This meant that even under a minimum foundation program, districts high in property value per pupil were able to raise more funds at the given required tax rate just with local funds than other districts could with a combination of state and local funds.

All of these characteristics of a foundation program are depicted in Figure 7.7 for a foundation program with an expenditure per pupil of $2,000 and a required tax rate of 20 mills. For the first 20 mills, all districts with a property value per pupil less than $100,000 receive a total of $2,000 per child; districts with a property value per pupil above $100,000 raise more than the foundation level, as the slope of the 20-mill line shows. If districts decide to levy a tax rate above the required rate, as most districts do, the additional funds are raised solely from the local property tax base. So at 30 mills, the district with a property wealth per pupil of $50,000 would produce $2,000 per pupil for the first 20 mills and only $500 per pupil for the next 10 mills, or $2,500 per pupil in total, whereas the district with a property wealth per pupil of $100,000 also would produce $2,000 per pupil for the first 20 mills but would produce $1,000 for the next 10 mills, or $3,000 per pupil in total.

The fiscal advantage for districts high in property value per pupil was further enhanced by prior receipt of flat grant state aid, which had been distributed to all districts, irrespective of property wealth per pupil. For these districts, the state faced a dual policy dilemma: whether, under the foundation

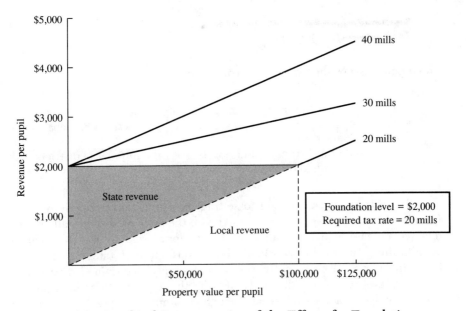

FIGURE 7.7 Graphical Representation of the Effect of a Foundation Program

aid calculation, to require them to send checks in the amount of negative aid to the state, which was rarely if ever invoked; and whether to take away the flat grant aid and thereby reduce their state aid to zero. Most states took a political route to solving this dilemma and distributed an amount that was the larger of the new amount under the foundation formula or the previous level of aid, i.e., they did not take away the old flat grant aid. This "hold harmless" approach has typified school finance structures (as well as most other intergovernmental aid structures) for years. Not only were the wealthiest districts not forced to send negative aid amounts to the state, but they also kept some minimum level of per-pupil state aid. Indeed, states often gradually increased the minimum amount over the years.

Such policy dilemmas and ultimate policy decisions blunted the ability of minimum foundation programs substantially to impact the fiscal equity of a state's school finance structure. New minimum foundation programs clearly boosted the fiscal resources of the lowest-spending districts, which was a clear objective and a definite positive feature, but their shortcomings, especially over time, severely limited their role as an adequate school finance mechanism.

Districts in the base sample show the residue of these incremental approaches to school finance (see Figure 7.1); even the districts highest in property value per pupil receive state aid. Thus, the school finance policy question is, what type of foundation program can enhance the fiscal equity of the financial condition of the sample districts? In addressing this question, two policy decisions must be made:

- The foundation expenditure level
- The required local tax rate

Three policy issues then have to be considered:

- The impact on the fiscal equity of the sample
- The total costs (usually in state revenues, but also including changes in local revenues)
- The number of "winners" and "losers," i.e., the number of districts with increases versus those with decreases in state aid

There is no magic solution to setting the foundation expenditure level. Usually, states set a level that, combined with the amount raised locally by the required tax rate, equals the amount of state appropriations available. This is a politically grounded but substantively vacuous approach, although it seems to be the norm. More recently, states have simply determined a particular spending level, deemed sufficiently high by the appropriate cross section of political and education leaders, and sought to fund that spending level over time. To ensure that the level stayed "current" or increased with inflation, states often legislated a mechanism automatically increasing the foundation per-pupil expenditure level each year. Inflating it by the increase in the consumer price index or using the deflator for state and local governmental services is a common approach.

A more robust approach is to set a specific policy target such as 50 percent, 100 percent, or some other percentage of the statewide average expenditure. The policy target could even be to bring the foundation level up to match the spending in some district above the average; a late-1970s bill in California set the expenditure level of the district at the 75th percentile as the foundation expenditure target. Whatever the level, this approach provides a clear policy target as to what the foundation base spending level will be.

Another approach is to define the education program that should be provided with a given level of revenues from a foundation program. Washington took this approach by specifying a pupil/teacher ratio with an average teacher salary, an administrator/teacher ratio with an average administrator salary, and a specific level of funds for other instructional and school costs. The combination then translated into a foundation expenditure level per pupil. Chambers and Parrish (1983) used a resource-cost model that identified in even greater detail numerous aspects of local education programs, put a price on each aspect, and summed them up for each district. This is another possible approach, but it has yet to be enacted by any state.

An advance, at least conceptually, on the Washington approach would be to identify the level of spending needed for students in all districts to, on average, meet national or state student achievement goals. Translating this conceptual target to a specific money figure is not straightforward, but it provides another policy benchmark for substantively determining foundation per-pupil expenditure levels in the 1990s.

Once the foundation expenditure level is determined, setting the required tax rate raises another set of interrelated issues. First, if the required tax rate is above the tax rate for some poor school district, it will require that district to raise its tax rate. That often is politically difficult to enact. Second, and related, the level of the required tax rate determines the state cost of the program: the higher the required local effort, the less the state cost.

Third, the foundation expenditure level and required tax rate are connected in a way that determines which districts are eligible for at least some aid and which districts receive zero (or negative) aid. The zero-aid district is defined as:

$$\text{SAPP} = \text{FEPP} - (\text{RTR} \times \text{PVPP}) = 0.$$

Solving this equation for PVPP identifies the property value per pupil below which a district will receive some foundation aid and above which it will not. The solution becomes:

$$\text{FEPP} = \text{RTR} \times \text{PVPP},$$

or, transposing and dividing by RTR,

$$\text{PVPP (zero-aid district)} = \text{FEPP/RTR},$$

where

$$\text{FEPP} = \text{foundation per-pupil expenditure level,}$$

$$\text{RTR} = \text{required tax rate, and}$$

$$\text{PVPP} = \text{property value of the zero-aid district,}$$
$$\text{in thousands of dollars of assessed valuation.}$$

Thus, if the foundation level is \$3,000 and the required tax rate is 30 mills, the zero-aid district has a property value per pupil of \$100,000.

The zero-aid district is an important policy variable to consider. Districts with property value above this level will not be eligible for any state aid (or, at best, will be "held harmless" with their previous level of state aid); therefore, their legislative representatives might vote against the proposal if self-interest is the only motivating variable. Another policy aspect of the zero-aid district is that it identifies a level up to which the state provides some fiscal capacity equalization. The policy issue is whether the state wants to equalize fiscal capacity up to just the statewide average, the 75th percentile, the 90th percentile, the property value per pupil of the wealthiest district, or some other selected level.

In other words, setting the foundation expenditure level and the required tax rate determines simultaneously the level of education program that becomes the base, the state and local costs, the zero-aid district, the level up to which the state seeks to equalize fiscal capacity, and the numbers of state aid gainers and losers. In short, it determines several key aspects of the political economy of the foundation program itself.

Fiscal equity impacts of foundation programs.   Setting these parameters determines the impact of the new foundation program on the fiscal equity of the finance structure. Figure 7.8 shows several figures for a foundation program with the expenditure level set at $2,400, about the average level for the base sample, and a required tax effort of 24 mills.[9] This means that the zero-aid district has a property value per pupil of $100,000, which in the sample is between district G and district H. This also means that this program would provide fiscal capacity equalization for districts that enroll 86 percent of the students (which is the cumulative enrollment of districts A–G). The program increases state aid by 25 percent—$9.1 million. It also positively impacts fiscal equity, reducing the coefficient of variation from 12.3 percent for the base sample down to 8.9 percent, and reduces the wealth elasticity from .199 to .135. It raises spending up to the foundation level in the five poorest and lowest-spending districts. This impact can be seen by using the simulation to view the graph of the results: the left-hand portion of the graph from Figure 7.2 (the base data) has been rotated up (clockwise) at about the wealth value of the zero-aid district to form a horizontal line at the foundation expenditure level of $2,400. But this foundation program also reduces aid to half the districts. Districts F and G, which receive some foundation aid, have a net loss of aid from their base context, and districts H, I, and J lose all of their state aid.

A foundation program with the expenditure level set at $2,400 and the required tax rate at 33.33 mills, which provides for fiscal capacity equalization

---

[9] For the foundation, guaranteed tax base, and combination simulations, state aid has been set equal to zero if the calculation produces a negative figure, but districts are not "held harmless"; i.e., they lose state aid if the calculation produces a zero aid figure. Further, a local tax response has been built into the simulation. If a district's original tax rate was below that of the foundation required tax rate and has wealth below that of the zero-aid district, the simulation only increased the tax rate to the required level. At times, this produces some loss of total revenues. In reality, a district might increase its rate to a level that compensates for all lost revenues. For districts with property value per pupil above the zero-aid district, the response model increases their local property tax rate to "cover" the lost aid. For these districts, the last column of the results shows no total revenue loss, but this is a result of a loss of state aid and an equal increase in local revenues. There also is a response model for districts that have state aid increases. These districts use half the state aid increase to raise spending and half to reduce local property tax rates. For the foundation part of the program, though, tax rates cannot be reduced below the required tax rate.

FIGURE 7.8 Ten-District Sample: Foundation Program (foundation level: $2,400; required tax rate (mills): 24)

Pupil weights			
Regular	1.00	Comp.	1.00
Handicapped	1.00	LEP	1.00

District	Pupils	Property Value per Pupil ($)	Old Property Tax Rate (mills)	New Property Tax Rate (mills)	Old Local Revenue per Pupil ($)	New Local Revenue per Pupil ($)	State Revenue per Pupil ($)	Change in State Revenue per Pupil ($)	Total Revenue per Pupil ($)	Total Gain (Loss) per Pupil ($)
A	10,040	36,670	30.43	24.00	1,116	880	1,520	542	2,400	306
B	7,028	46,845	28.33	24.19	1,327	1,133	1,276	388	2,409	194
C	7,985	55,203	26.86	24.31	1,483	1,342	1,075	281	2,417	141
D	4,152	64,875	25.61	24.00	1,661	1,557	843	223	2,400	119
E	5,148	71,762	24.39	24.00	1,750	1,722	678	106	2,400	78
F	6,216	81,913	23.54	24.00	1,928	1,966	434	(43)	2,400	(5)
G	3,666	92,949	23.28	24.00	2,164	2,231	169	(268)	2,400	(201)
H	2,961	106,195	21.72	25.59	2,307	2,718	0	(411)	2,718	0
I	3,472	135,496	19.52	22.38	2,645	3,033	0	(388)	3,033	0
J	848	306,766	10.52	11.71	3,227	3,593	0	(366)	3,593	0
Weighted average		71,277	25.69	23.85	1,688	1,647	837	151	2,484	110
Standard deviation		40,819	3.73	1.68	484	679	528	316	222	137
Median		64,875	25.61		1,661				2,400	

	Totals	Change
Pupils	51,516	
Local revenue	$84,870,921	($2,075,879)
State revenue	$43,118,318	$9,101,075
Total revenue	$127,989,239	$7,025,196

State aid

Number of winners	5
Number of losers	5

Equity Measures

Horizontal equity
Range	$1,193
Range ratio	.264
Coef. of variation	.089
McLoone index	1.000
Gini coefficient	.030

Fiscal neutrality
Correlation	.910
Elasticity	.135

181

up to a property wealth of $72,000, the statewide average, produces a net drop in state aid and also a reduction in state aid for 9 of the 10 districts. (Use the simulation to assess the broader impacts of these parameters.) On the other hand, a foundation of $2,400 with a required tax rate of 17.5 mills, which provides for fiscal capacity equalization up to $136,000, provides at least some state general aid for 9 of the 10 districts and further enhances fiscal equity (the coefficient of variation drops to 6.2 percent and the wealth elasticity to .082), but the cost to the state is nearly $28 million more. (Again, use the simulation to assess the broader impacts of this set of parameters.) In short, these results indicate that the foundation expenditure level, required tax effort, level of fiscal capacity equalization, state costs, numbers of winners and losers, and school finance fiscal equity all are interrelated. These interrelations suggest why getting legislatures to enact complicated school finance reforms is not an easy task; several variables—educational, political, and fiscal—need to be balanced.

In summary, foundation programs have several attractive features. They began as programs designed to provide a minimum-quality education program but today can be used to guarantee a higher-quality program, perhaps one sufficient to enable the average student to meet state or national education goals. Foundation programs are unique in having this base program guarantee as a critical variable. Second, they are funded by a combination of state and local funds and therefore link states and school districts inextricably in a fiscal partnership for funding public schools. Third, they are fiscal capacity–equalizing; that is, they provide state aid in an inverse relationship to local property value per pupil, and consequently they address the key structural problem of school finance—the disparity in the local property tax base. Their key defect is that they allow local spending above the foundation program, and if the base program is low, these local fiscal add-ons—financed entirely with local property tax revenues—increase the linkages between property wealth and education spending, the Achilles' heel of school finance and the central issue targeted in school finance litigation. As will be shown later in this chapter, this defect can be easily remedied.

Guaranteed Tax Base Programs

Guaranteed tax base (GTB) programs, surprisingly, are a recent phenomenon in school finance structures. The first guaranteed tax base programs were enacted in the early 1970s after the initial rounds of school finance litigation. The late arrival of these programs is perplexing because, as the name suggests, this type of school finance program addresses the primary structural flaw in traditional approaches to local financing of public schools, namely, the unequal distribution of the local property tax base. A GTB program simply erases this inequality by guaranteeing, through state aid allocations, that each local district can function as if it had an equal property tax base per pupil. A GTB program is conceptually simple, and, it attacks and remedies the basic inequity in school finance—unequal access to a local property tax base.

The simple and straightforward guaranteed tax base program, however, had a somewhat complicated evolution. The early forms of GTB programs were called percentage-equalizing programs. Percentage-equalizing formulas were introduced in the 1920s and were proposed for two major reasons. First, foundation program levels remained low, and most districts enacted local add-ons financed entirely from the local property tax base. Local add-ons came to dominate the level of total revenues, and consequently there was a search for a school finance mechanism that went beyond foundation programs and provided state fiscal capacity–equalizing aid for the overall spending levels in local school districts.

Second, because the state fiscal role remained small as the level of the minimum foundation programs remained low, policy pressure grew to increase the state role. Over time, in fact, many states sought to increase the state role to some fixed target—often 50 percent. Since most state aid was distributed in a fiscal capacity–equalizing manner, the assumption was that the fiscal equity of the school finance system would improve as the state role increased toward, or even surpassed, 50 percent.

The percentage-equalizing formula was designed to address both of these policy concerns. First, the state share (in percentage terms) of total costs was directly included in the formula. The formula was designed to provide a larger state role in lower-property-wealth districts, thus providing a fiscal capacity equalization thrust to the program. The formula resulted in a state aid ratio for each district. The ratio was higher in property-poor districts and lower in property-wealthy districts. The state role policy target, say 50 percent, was usually set for the district with statewide average property value per pupil.[10]

To determine state aid, the ratio was applied to the local spending level, which was a policy decision of each district. The aid ratio times the spending level produced the amount of state aid per pupil for each district. State aid, therefore, varied with both the level of wealth and the level of locally determined spending. During 1986–87, five states had percentage-equalizing

---

[10] State aid per pupil for a percentage-equalizing program is equal to:

$$SAPP = [1 - LR(PVPP_d/PVPP_k)]TREVPP,$$

where

$\quad SAPP$ = state aid per pupil,

$\quad LR$ = local role, in percent terms (the state role is $(1 - LR)$,

$\quad PVPP_d$ = property value per pupil for each district,

$\quad PVPP_k$ = property value per pupil in the comparative district, usually but not necessarily the statewide average, and

$\quad TREVPP$ = total (state and local) revenue per pupil.

The zero-aid district is $PVPP_k/LR$. The aid ratio is $1 - LR(PVPP_d/PVPP_k)$.

programs. The percentage-equalizing formula is more complicated than but algebraically equivalent to a guaranteed tax base program.

Guaranteed tax base programs were first enacted in the early 1970s, at the time of the first successful school finance court cases. These court cases had directly challenged the relationship between expenditures and wealth caused by the unequal distribution of the local tax base per pupil. The book that developed the "fiscal neutrality" legal theory for these cases (Coons, Clune, and Sugarman, 1970) also discussed the design and operation of a new "district power-equalizing" school finance structure, a system that would "equalize" the "power" of local districts to raise funds through the property tax. The mechanism was for the state to "guarantee" a "tax base" that all districts would use in deciding school tax rate and expenditure levels. Subsequently, these approaches became known as guaranteed tax base programs. They are also called guaranteed yield or resource-equalizing programs in some states.

The GTB formula. The formula for calculating state aid for a guaranteed tax base program is:

$$SAPP = DTR \times (GTB - PVPP),$$

where

$$SAPP = \text{state aid per pupil},$$

$$DTR = \text{local district property tax rate},$$

$$GTB = \text{tax base guaranteed by the state, in thousand dollars of property value per pupil, and}$$

$$PVPP = \text{local district property value per pupil}.$$

Total GTB state aid, therefore, is:

$$TSA = SAPP \times \text{Pupils},$$

where

$$TSA = \text{total state aid},$$

$$SAPP = \text{state aid per pupil from the GTB formula, and}$$

$$\text{Pupils} = \text{number of students in the school district}.$$

During 1986–87, six states had guaranteed tax base programs (Salmon et al., 1988).

Several interesting features of the GTB state aid formula should be mentioned. First, the amount of state aid a district receives varies with the size of the local tax base: the greater the local tax base (PVPP), the smaller the factor (GTB−PVPP) and, thus, the smaller the amount of per-pupil state aid. In other words, state aid varies inversely with property wealth per child.

A second feature is that local expenditures (or revenues) per pupil are equal to the tax rate times the GTB. This can be shown algebraically:

$$\text{Local revenue} = \text{DTR} \times \text{PVPP},$$

$$\text{State aid} = \text{DTR} \times (\text{GTB} - \text{PVPP}),$$

$$\text{Total revenues} = \text{local revenue} + \text{state aid},$$

or, substituting,

$$\text{Total revenues} = (\text{DTR} \times \text{PVPP}) + [\text{DTR} \times (\text{GTB} - \text{PVPP})].$$

Combining terms on the right hand side and factoring out DTR yields

$$\text{Total revenues} = \text{DTR} \times (\text{PVPP} + \text{GTB} - \text{PVPP}),$$

$$= \text{DTR} \times \text{GTB}!$$

In other words, the GTB operates exactly as designed.[11] Districts can function as if they had the GTB as their local tax base. Once they determine their desired spending level, they divide it by the GTB to determine the local tax rate they must levy. Or, conversely, by multiplying their local property tax rate by the GTB, they identify their per-pupil spending level. As a corollary, by multiplying their local property tax rate by the local property tax base, they also identify the amount of local revenues they must raise.

A final feature is that state aid also is a function of the local school tax rate: the higher the tax rate, the greater the state aid. This feature has two implications. First, if local districts increase their property tax rate, they not only raise more funds locally, but they also become eligible for more state aid. This can be an attractive component for a campaign to increase the local school property tax rate. Second, and related, the total amount of revenues the state needs to appropriate is in part determined by local action. Put differently, the state is not in complete control of the level of revenues needed to finance the general aid school finance formula; if districts unexpectedly increase local tax rates to a higher level than anticipated, additional state funds will be needed to fund fully the GTB formula.

[11] Strictly speaking, this holds for all districts only if the state has a total recapture plan. In the absence of such recapture, this applies only to districts with property wealth at or below the GTB level.

This feature has been troublesome when the GTB formula has been considered by legislatures who themselves want to be in complete control of the level of funding needed for the general aid program. Many states reject a GTB because of this feature. But, over time, local tax rates usually "settle" into fairly predictable patterns, and states can pretty much predict the level of appropriation needed to fund the formula. Michigan, for example, has had a GTB program for several years and has no more difficulty predicting the level of appropriations needed than do other states with different school aid distribution mechanisms. Many other factors complicate estimation of state aid, for example, enrollment projections, property value projections, and estimates of state tax revenues. Many additional factors beyond the design of the general aid formula make state aid prediction an imperfect art.

GTB policy issues.   A guaranteed tax base program has several attractive features as an intergovernmental grant mechanism. First, a GTB requires a local match, which is equal to the district tax rate times its property value per pupil. Indeed, as GTB aid increases along with the local tax rate, thus requiring more state funds, the local tax rate applied to the local tax base must also increase. In other words, more GTB aid does not come without additional local effort. Indeed, the local match feature helps keep both local tax rates and state aid at acceptable levels over time.

district must put up amount of money accepted by state or they don't get funding

Second, the GTB program equalizes fiscal capacity. As local property wealth decreases, GTB aid as a percent of local expenditures increases, and vice versa. This generally is a desired feature for school finance formulas. But, in a way, the GTB program is almost "perfectly" fiscal capacity–equalizing because, as stated in the introduction to this section, it directly addresses the key structural problem of school financing—the disparity in the local property tax base per child. The GTB program simply makes the tax base equal for all districts, or at least for those districts with a property value per pupil less than the GTB. If the primary school finance problem is unequal distribution of the property tax base, the GTB program is the school finance structure that remedies the problem.

The GTB program reflects the American values of choice, local control, and equal education opportunity, defined as equal access to a tax base. The GTB program provides equal access to a school tax base. For districts with a property value per pupil less than the GTB, it provides for equal dollars per pupil from state and local sources for equal school tax rates. A pure GTB program, moreover, implements the value of local control since it allows local districts to decide on the tax rate they want to levy for schools, and thus the level of per-pupil school spending. If localities want a higher-quality program, they are free to impose a higher school tax rate. The GTB ensures that all districts levying that tax rate will receive the same revenues per pupil from the general fund. If districts want just an average program, they need only levy an average school tax rate.

Put a different way, a GTB program allows—even encourages, some would say—different local decisions on per-pupil spending levels. Or, put bluntly,

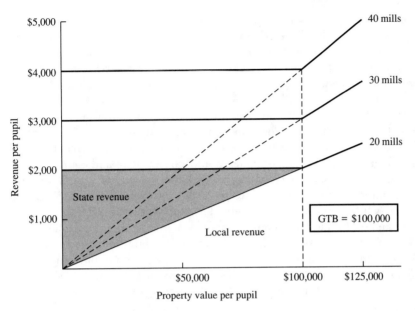

FIGURE 7.9 Graphical Representation of the Effect of a Guaranteed Tax Base Program

GTB programs are not focused on equal per-pupil spending. Indeed, without a requirement for a minimum school tax rate, GTB programs do not even require a minimum education expenditure level, although in most situations where GTB programs have been enacted, they increase expenditures in all but the lowest tax rate school districts.

Nevertheless, it should be emphasized that a GTB program is incompatible with the horizontal equity principle for students because it does not require, nor is it focused on, equal spending per child. A GTB program provides equal access to the local tax base—a key structural problem with local financing of schools—but allows local districts to decide on the specific per-pupil expenditure level. For districts with a property value per pupil below the GTB, the GTB provides equal spending for equal tax rates but allows tax rates, and thus expenditures per pupil, to vary.

Figure 7.9 indicates graphically some of these characteristics of a GTB program, for a GTB set at $100,000. The graph shows that for districts with a property value per pupil below the GTB, revenues differ according to the tax rate, but that all districts have the same revenues per pupil (from state and local sources) if they levy the same tax rate. As the 20-mill example shows, the higher a district's property wealth per pupil, the greater the share of total revenue provided from local sources. If the tax rate is raised to 30 mills, all districts get $3,000 per pupil, and the proportion of state aid is inversely related to the district's property wealth. The graph also shows that districts above the GTB raise higher revenues per pupil at any given tax rate.

In implementing a GTB program, there is one primary policy issue to resolve: the tax base level the state wants to guarantee. There are no absolute standards by which to assess this policy issue, but there are several benchmarks. The state could seek to guarantee the tax base up to the 50th percentile of students, the statewide average, or to a higher percentile, such as the 75th or 90th percentile, or even higher. A GTB program in response to a typical fiscal neutrality court suit would need to hit at least the 75th percentile, and probably the 90th. The legal question would be, what constitutes "substantial" equal access to raising education dollars? At least the 75th percentile, and probably higher, but how much higher would vary by state and court.

There are two secondary policy issues. One is whether a minimum tax rate is required. A minimum tax rate translates into a minimum expenditure per pupil (which equals the minimum tax rate times the GTB). Requiring a minimum would allow a smoother transition from a minimum foundation program, for which the state policy goal includes a minimum base program, to a GTB program, which in its pure form does not have a minimum expenditure requirement. A later section of this chapter shows that the minimum tax rate conceptually links the GTB and foundation programs, a linkage that in practice may be complex.

A second issue is whether to cap GTB aid at some tax rate or whether to cap local school tax rates at some level. Under the first type of cap, GTB aid would be available only up to a set tax rate. As tax rates rose above the set level, the state would no longer participate, leaving the districts with only local funds from the extra tax effort. This would give the GTB an unequalized local add-on element, as exists for all foundation programs. Over time, non-fiscal capacity–equalized add-ons would dominate the structure and produce a system, as currently exists in most states, in which expenditures per pupil are strongly related to the level of local property value per child.

The second type of cap is an absolute cap on the local tax rate. Not only would GTB aid not be available above this tax rate, but districts would not be allowed to levy a tax rate above the cap. This tax rate cap would have the effect of an expenditure cap, since the maximum expenditure would be the tax rate cap times the GTB. Thus, a state also could limit local expenditures per pupil, which would be the same as limiting the tax rate. Either type of cap certainly puts a major constraint on local control, but it also limits the variation in expenditures per pupil that would be allowed by a GTB program.

Fiscal equity impacts of GTB programs. Figure 7.10 displays the simulation results for a program where the GTB is set at $100,000, which is about the 90th percentile for the sample of districts. Interestingly, this level of GTB would require a one-third increase in state aid but would still leave the state share of the total at only 34 percent ($45 million divided by $131.8 million). Relative to total revenues, this is a modest state aid increase.

This level of GTB would have major, positive impacts on fiscal equity. It reduces per-pupil revenue disparities. In terms of horizontal equity for students,

FIGURE 7.10 Ten-District Sample: Guaranteed Tax Base (guaranteed tax base: $100,000)

District	Pupils	Property Value per Pupil ($)	Old Property Tax Rate (mills)	New Property Tax Rate (mills)	Old Local Revenue per Pupil ($)	New Local Revenue per Pupil ($)	New State Revenue per pupil ($) Regular 1.00 / Handicapped 1.00	Change in State Revenue per Pupil ($) 1.00 / 1.00	Total Revenue per Pupil ($) Comp. / LEP	Total Gain (Loss) per Pupil ($) 1.00 / 1.00
A	10,040	36,670	30.43	25.68	1,116	942	1,627	649	2,568	475
B	7,028	46,845	28.33	25.24	1,327	1,182	1,342	454	2,524	309
C	7,985	55,203	26.86	24.81	1,483	1,370	1,112	318	2,481	205
D	4,152	64,875	25.61	24.21	1,661	1,571	850	230	2,421	140
E	5,148	71,762	24.39	23.81	1,750	1,708	672	100	2,381	58
F	6,216	81,913	23.54	24.05	1,928	1,970	435	(42)	2,405	0
G	3,666	92,949	23.28	26.01	2,164	2,417	183	(254)	2,601	0
H	2,961	106,195	21.72	25.59	2,307	2,718	0	(411)	2,718	0
I	3,472	135,496	19.52	22.38	2,645	3,033	0	(388)	3,033	0
J	848	306,766	10.52	11.71	3,227	3,593	0	(366)	3,593	0
Weighted average		71,277	25.69	24.55	1,688	1,684	874	187	2,558	183
Standard deviation		40,819	3.73	1.91	484	671	564	350	207	178
Median		64,875	25.61		1,661				2,524	

	Totals	Change
Pupils	51,516	
Local revenue	$86,753,491	($ 193,310)
State revenue	$45,004,424	$10,987,181
Total revenue	$131,757,914	$10,793,871
State aid		
Number of winners	5	
Number of losers	5	

Equity Measures

Horizontal equity
Range $1,213
Range ratio .... .261
Coef. of variation .... .081
McLoone index .... .965
Gini coefficient .... .036

Fiscal neutrality
Correlation .... .833
Elasticity .... .110

the coefficient of variation drops to 8.1 percent, and the McLoone index increases to .965.

In terms of fiscal neutrality, it reduces the correlation between total revenues per pupil and property value per pupil to .833 and the wealth elasticity to just .11, which is very low. The latter should be expected since the GTB provides equal access to a tax base for districts with 90 percent of all students. This simulation shows the powerful impact a GTB at the 90th percentile can have on the equity of the school finance structure. Use the simulation to view the graph of the GTB results.

Although the GTB is focused on providing equal tax bases and not equal spending, it is nevertheless effective in helping to reduce overall revenue disparities, as these horizontal equity statistics indicate. This occurs because the GTB raises substantially the effective tax base in low-wealth districts, which usually have above-average tax rates. Thus, when a GTB program is implemented, these districts qualify for substantial new amounts of state aid—due both to their low wealth and to their high tax rates—and so can both increase their school spending (thus reducing per-pupil expenditure disparities) and reduce their tax rates to more average levels. In short, although a GTB allows for differences in spending based on tax effort, when implemented in most states it also reduces overall revenue disparities.

The data in Figure 7.10 reveal several other aspects of this GTB, as well as of the sample districts before application of the GTB. First, the GTB covers 90 percent of the students, but it provides state aid for only 70 percent of the districts—specifically, districts A to G—and increases in aid for only 50 percent of districts.[12] In the real world, a school finance program that, at best, would provide "hold harmless" aid for 50 percent of all districts would be very difficult to enact politically, even if these districts were small and enrolled only a tiny percentage of children.

Second, even though 7 of the 10 districts are eligible for some state aid, only 5 districts would be eligible for greater amounts of state aid; in other words, two of the districts eligible for at least some GTB aid would receive less state aid than under the old structure used by the sample state. Thus, five, or fully half, of the districts would lose some or all of their state aid.

These realities would reduce the chances of having such a program being legislatively enacted—half the districts would lose state aid. Although it could be argued that the old school finance program allocated too much aid to districts high in property wealth per pupil, and a GTB at the 90th percentile "ought" to be good enough, these results suggest that the politics of enactment in the sample state would be difficult at best.

These effects of a relatively high GTB are not dissimilar to the impact of such a GTB in many states today. Most states allocate some general state aid in

---

[12] Recall that the fiscal response model built into the simulation increases the local property tax rate to a level where local funds replace lost state funds for state aid "losers," and it increases expenditures and reduces the tax rate each by half the amount of the state aid increase for state aid "winners."

sufficiently large amounts to even the wealthiest districts, so that a transition to a GTB—even at a reasonably high level—becomes problematic politically. Although a "hold harmless" provision would blunt the loss of state aid, it also would present most districts with the likelihood that their general state aid would not increase in the short to medium run, a not-so-attractive scenario. These realities also mean that unless a state that wants to enact a GTB program enacts one soon, the transition problems related to the level of state general aid provided to the highest-wealth districts could worsen over time, making it more complicated to enact a high-level GTB program.

These dilemmas are more drastic for a GTB of $72,000, which is about the statewide average property value per pupil and is just above the wealth of the fifth poorest district (district E), representing a percentile that includes two-thirds of the students. (Readers should run this GTB on the simulation and review the results.) Under this program, nine of the ten districts would lose state aid, and state aid itself would drop by almost a third. This level of GTB (which, incidentally, is higher than the level of the GTB component of the general aid formula in most states[13]) would not likely be politically popular in the sample state!

A GTB of $136,000, on the other hand, which exceeds the per-pupil property value for 9 of the 10 districts, districts that enroll over 98 percent of the students, would push the state role to 58 percent ($102 million divided by $174 million) and also lower the coefficient of variation to just .051. The wealth elasticity is actually negative, at .024, almost negligible. These are substantial impacts.

For such a high-level GTB, however, the simulation probably indicates a higher expenditure level for the lower-wealth districts than might occur in practice. It would be unlikely for districts to increase local spending by nearly 50 percent, as the current simulation response model assumes. With a GTB this high, such districts probably would use more than half of their state aid increase to reduce property tax rates. (Again, readers should run this GTB using the simulation and review the results, as well as the scatterplot. Indeed, readers should run GTB programs between $100,000 and $136,000 to find a level that reduces some of the political drawbacks of the former and is less costly than the latter.)

In summary, GTB school finance formulas are relatively straightforward structures that address the primary problem behind local financing of schools: unequal access to a school tax base. The GTB remedies this defect by making the tax base equal for all districts with a property value per pupil below the GTB. The primary policy target is the level at which to set the GTB; courts likely would require the GTB to be set at a level that would provide "substantial" equal access to a school property tax base. This would equate to the level of

---

[13] Most state GTB programs do not guarantee the wealth of the district for which the cumulative proportion of students is 66 percent; the guarantee level is usually lower than the 66th percentile.

the district for which the property value per pupil is at or close to the 90th percentile.

GTB programs reflect the value of local control, allowing different districts to spend different amounts per pupil. Such interdistrict spending differences, however, are not related to differences in property value per pupil but to differences in tax effort—the higher the tax effort, the higher the expenditure per pupil. For policymakers and educators who hold the horizontal equity principle above local choice, the GTB is not the appropriate school finance program.

Finally, although GTB programs are fiscal capacity–equalizing, the level of state aid is determined both by the GTB level, which is set by state policy, and by local property tax rates, which are set by local policy. Thus, the amount of state aid is not under the complete control of state policymakers. This feature has made several states skittish about enacting a GTB program, even though they may prefer it as the school general aid structure. States that have enacted GTB programs, however, have devised several phase-in mechanisms that allow them to control the level of state aid. These states have found that, over time, local tax rates settle to a steady state that makes predicting the level of state aid appropriations no more difficult than for other types of formulas.

Finally, guaranteed tax base programs are the most straightforward form of school aid formulas designed to equalize the tax base. As discussed previously, though, there are several different GTB formulas including percentage equalizing, guaranteed yield, district power equalizing (Coons, Clune, and Sugarman, 1969), guaranteed valuation, and resource equalizing. All of these are variations on the same theme. The major new element in district power equalizing is that it can include negative aid, often called recapture, when the local property value per pupil is greater than the tax base guaranteed by the state. This negative aid feature also could be invoked in a regular GTB formula, but it rarely has been.

Combination Foundation and Guaranteed Tax Base Programs

For several reasons, states increasingly are enacting combination school finance formulas. These plans usually include two different formulas in the overall approach to providing general education aid through the fiscal capacity–equalizing program. One type of formula is used for the base, or the tier 1 program, and another type of formula is used for spending above the base, or the tier 2 program.

Missouri has had a two-tiered, combination foundation and guaranteed tax base program since the late 1970s. Like many states, Missouri had a minimum foundation program before it enacted a school finance reform in 1977. The new program retained the foundation program to ensure a base spending level, a key feature of the foundation approach. The 1977 bill set the foundation expenditure level at 75 percent of the previous year's statewide average expenditure per pupil, thus ensuring that the foundation level also would increase every year. To remedy the major defect of foundation programs—fiscal add-ons above the base that are financed solely with local funds—the legislature put a GTB program on top, so that districts wanting to spend above the foundation level would be allowed equal extra spending for equal extra tax rates. The reform bill set the GTB at the wealth of the district for which, with all districts rank-ordered on the basis of property value per pupil, the cumulative percentage of students was 90 percent (i.e., the 90th percentile).

Combination or two-tiered school finance formulas are rising in popularity. In 1987, Salmon et al. (1988) indicated that about a dozen states had combination programs. The combination approach also typified new school finance formulas enacted during the early months of 1990. Both Texas and Kentucky, which were under court orders to revise their school finance structures, enacted combination foundation and guaranteed tax base programs. In Texas, the 1989–90 foundation program provided a base spending level of $1,477, which was about 42 percent of the statewide average expenditure per pupil. The guaranteed tax base program was set at $182,500, the wealth of the district just below the statewide average district wealth of $191,300. Unfortunately, Texas placed a tax rate cap on the GTB component of the formula, providing GTB aid for just an extra 3.6 mills above the foundation-required tax rate. Moreover, districts are not prohibited from levying even higher tax rates, which means that additional revenues will derive solely from the local tax base.

Kentucky enacted a similar combination program. The 1989–90 foundation base was set at $2,305, which was about 77 percent of the statewide average district wealth. Kentucky also put a GTB on top of the foundation program, setting it at about 150 percent of the statewide average. The GTB program, however, includes two types of tax rate caps. The first limits the additional tax rate for which districts can receive GTB aid; *school boards* can increase spending (and thus the local tax rate) by 15 percent over the foundation base and receive GTB aid. *Taxpayers* by a local vote can increase spending (and thus the local tax rate) by another 15 percent, but this second 15 percent spending boost is not eligible for GTB aid. Thus, expenditures above the foundation base are limited to an additional 30 percent, half of which is fiscal capacity–equalized by a GTB.

The combination approach merges the best features of the foundation and GTB programs and also redresses the major defects of each. The foundation portion ensures a base spending level, usually above what is considered a minimum adequate level. This base spending level, a key feature of foundation programs, is financed with a combination of local and state funds. This remedies a possible shortcoming of pure GTB programs, which do not require a minimum spending level.

The GTB portion of the combined program guarantees equal education spending per pupil for equal tax rates above the foundation-required tax rate. This component remedies the major defect of a foundation program: unequalized spending above the foundation base.

The combination foundation and GTB program formula.   The formula for calculating the foundation portion of the combination program is the same as for the regular foundation program:

$$SFAPP = FEPP - (RTR \times PVPP),$$

where

$$SFAPP = \text{state foundation aid per pupil,}$$

$$FEPP = \text{foundation expenditure per pupil,}$$

$$RTR = \text{local required tax rate, and}$$

$$PVPP = \text{local property value per pupil.}$$

Total foundation state aid is:

$$TFSA = SFAPP \times \text{Pupils,}$$

where

$$TFSA = \text{total foundation state aid,}$$

$$SFAPP = \text{state foundation aid per pupil, and}$$

$$\text{Pupils} = \text{number of students in the school district.}$$

For the GTB portion, state aid is:

$$SGTBAPP = (DTR - RTR) \times (GTB - PVPP),$$

where

$$SGTBAPP = \text{state guaranteed tax base aid per pupil,}$$

$$DTR = \text{local district property tax rate,}$$

RTR = required tax base for the foundation program (GTB aid is provided only for tax rates above the foundation-required tax rate),

GTB = tax rate guaranteed by the state, in thousand dollars of property value per pupil, and

$$PVPP = \text{local district property value per pupil.}$$

Total GTB state aid, therefore, is:

$$\text{TGTBSA} = \text{SGTBAPP} \times \text{Pupils},$$

where

$\qquad$ TGTBSA $=$ total guaranteed tax base state aid,

$\qquad$ SGTBAPP $=$ state guaranteed tax base aid per pupil
$\qquad\qquad\qquad$ from the preceding formula, and

$\qquad$ Pupils $=$ number of students in the school district.

Total state general aid for the combination program, therefore, is:

$$\text{TSA} = \text{TFSA} + \text{TGTBSA}.$$

Combination foundation and GTB program policy issues.   A combination foundation and GTB program is a fairly attractive package. Both components of the program require local matching funds and provide for fiscal capacity equalization. A base spending level is guaranteed. The ability to spend above the base is possible on an equal basis for rich and poor districts alike, ensuring a fiscally neutral system. And two American values—concern for the bottom half and local choice—are uniquely wrapped together in a single general aid program.

$\qquad$ The only fault is that the GTB program allows for different spending levels and thus is not in keeping with the horizontal equity principle for students. But the fact is that this principle conflicts with the value of local choice; pure versions of both cannot be included in any one formula. The two-tiered foundation-GTB program is about the closest a school finance formula can come to combining these values. There is an expenditure equality dimension, in terms of a base program that is mandated for all students. But there is local choice to spend above this base. If a state enacted a cap on the level of extra expenditures, such as the 30 percent cap in Kentucky, the program might be more appealing to those who champion horizontal equity for children.

$\qquad$ Figure 7.11 depicts graphically how a combination foundation-GTB program works. The lowest horizontal line shows that the minimum revenues per pupil are the foundation expenditure level of $2,000. The upper two horizontal lines reflect the impact of a GTB at $75,000 for total tax rates of 30 and 40 mills (with 20 mills being the required tax rate for the foundation portion of the program). Note that the zero-aid district level for the foundation portion of the program is $100,000 and, obviously, $75,000 for the GTB portion of the program. For each tax rate level, the revenue per pupil line is initially horizontal and then slopes upward only beyond the level of the zero-aid district, indicating that districts with a property value per pupil above this level will raise more per pupil than is provided even by the GTB.

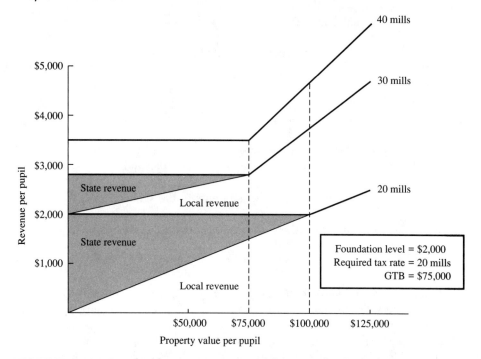

FIGURE 7.11 **Graphical Representation of the Impact of a Combination Foundation and Guaranteed Tax Base Program**

Several issues need to be addressed in implementing a combination foundation-GTB program. The first two are the general policy targets of:

- The level of base spending in the foundation program
- The level of the GTB

The same considerations raised earlier in the chapter for each individual program can be applied to the combination program. States in the 1990s, for example, might set the base expenditure at a level sufficiently high for districts, on average, to meet nationwide and state student performance goals. This type of policy target could become a new rationale for setting the base spending in state foundation programs. Although not exactly stated in its new legislation, this approach was used by Kentucky in its 1990 school finance reform.

The GTB also needs to be set at a relatively high level, such as the 90th percentile of property wealth per pupil. On the other hand, there may be some "wiggle" room for the GTB level. For example, if the base spending level is set high—sufficient for the average student to meet ambitious student achievement objectives—the state might want to limit local add-ons, for example, to 30 percent, as Kentucky has done, or even to a smaller amount. At this point, since all students on average have been educated to some new high performance level, one could argue that local add-ons are much more an element of local choice as to how to spend discretionary income. Thus, setting a GTB at just the statewide average, or the 50th percentile, which would focus it on equal access to a tax base just for the bottom half, might be viewed as sufficient. How these policy dimensions will play out during the 1990s remains to be seen.

The key conceptual point in the preceding discussion is that there potentially is an implicit trade-off between the level of the foundation base spending and the level of the GTB. If the base spending level is high, and sufficient for students on average to meet bold new achievement levels, that will itself require substantial new education funds and will greatly raise school spending for all students. Fewer districts will feel they need to spend above the base. Thus, GTB-aided spending becomes, in effect, discretionary spending, and the GTB level could be focused just on districts below the average. Extra spending could even be capped, since spending levels already would be at much higher levels.

On the other hand, if the base spending level is much lower (an argument for such a strategy follows), then the GTB component becomes a much larger portion of the overall program, and its level becomes much more critical to the fiscal equity impact of the system. If the base spending level is low, more districts—undoubtedly, more than half of the districts—would want to spend more. Thus, local add-ons become a larger part of the overall system. To make the system fiscally neutral, the GTB would have to be set at a high level, such as the 90th percentile.

There are two rationales for having a lower foundation base spending level and a higher GTB level, one substantive and one political. The substantive argument concerns differences in educational needs and costs between metropolitan (urban and suburban) and nonmetropolitan (rural) districts. In most states, foundation expenditure levels per pupil are too low for most districts to provide an "adequate" education program. But a modest increase in the foundation level may be sufficient to allow most nonmetropolitan school districts to provide an adequate program.

However, raising the foundation expenditure to a level that would be sufficient for metropolitan districts, which usually face educational prices 10 to 20 percent higher than those for nonmetropolitan districts, usually is too expensive for the state. Moreover, raising the foundation expenditure to such a level would also allow nonmetropolitan districts to provide a much higher-level program. Indeed, it might provide so much money for rural districts that some local education leaders and their legislatures would argue that excessive funds were being allocated to schools.

Although the divergence between the resource needs of urban and rural districts should not be overdrawn, it is an implicit issue that arises in nearly all states that seek to raise the foundation base to some level deemed sufficient to provide an "adequate" education program. In the most ambitious states, the expenditure level usually is more than rural districts need and less than urban districts need, an "average" solution that is not efficient for either.

The dilemma could be remedied by setting the base at an adequate level for the lowest-cost districts and then adjusting it by a price index (Chambers,

1981; Wendling, 1981b) for districts facing higher costs. However, a sound education price index, although technically straightforward to develop, has yet to be enacted by any state, except perhaps Texas, although a number of states have versions of price indexes. Education price indexes are discussed in Chapter 8.

The second rationale for keeping the foundation base low relative to the GTB concerns the politics of shifting from a low-level minimum foundation program, the situation in most states, to a GTB or combination foundation-GTB program. Even for minimum foundation programs, most states require a very low district tax rate as a condition for receiving the foundation aid. This means that the property value per pupil of the zero-aid district is quite high. Put differently, most districts receive at least some state aid under the minimum foundation program. Further, as discussed earlier, most high-property-value districts have been "held harmless" in their receipt of flat grant aid over the years. The result, as indicated in Figure 7.1 for the sample of districts, is that all districts— including the wealthiest ones—receive some level of general state aid.

Thus, the transition issue becomes somewhat political. In a new school finance program, focused resolutely on making specific fiscal equity impacts, how many districts can have their general state aid reduced? Even though a new per-pupil state aid "hold harmless" provision always can be the final compromise, policymakers representing these districts, even the wealthiest ones, will be concerned about the loss of "formula aid."

The combination foundation-GTB program can become a mechanism for blunting the state aid loss for districts in the transition from a minimum foundation program to a GTB program. The foundation portion is viewed as a mechanism to minimize the state aid loss for all districts, not to ensure a base spending level per pupil, although it could be rhetorically described as that. Then the GTB program becomes the dominant element of the new general aid program.

Fiscal equity impacts of combination foundation and GTB programs.   In structuring a combination program with this rationale, the first step is to identify the lowest-level, lowest-cost foundation program that produces minimum state aid losers. Figure 7.12 shows such a program. The foundation program is low, at $1,500, and the local required tax rate is just 10 mills. At this step, the GTB is set at zero so the second tier does not play a role. This makes the "zero-aid" district the one with property value per pupil of $150,000 ($1,500 divided by 10, the result multiplied by 1,000). Indeed, the data show that 9 of the 10 districts receive state foundation aid, all with a wealth below $150,000. Although district I receives some state aid, it receives less than it had been receiving. Nevertheless, this structure for a foundation is low-cost: it requires an extra $8 million in state aid, about a 23 percent increase. Only two districts, which happen to enroll only 8 percent of students, lose state aid; and of the two, only one is ineligible for any state general aid. This formula mechanism, then, reduces state aid losers to a minimum. (The reader might want to try other simulations, such as a foundation expenditure level of $1,650 and a local required tax rate of 11.67 mills.)

FIGURE 7.12 Ten-District Sample: Combination (foundation level: $1,500; required tax rate (mills): 10; guaranteed tax base: $0; GTB rate cap above foundation level (mills): 99)

Pupil weights: Regular 1.00 Handicapped 1.00 Comp. LEP 1.00 1.00

District	Pupils	Property Value per Pupil ($)	Old Property Tax Rate (mills)	New Property Tax Rate (mills)	Old Local Revenue per Pupil ($)	New Local Revenue per Pupil ($)	State Found. Revenue per Pupil ($)	State GTB Revenue per Pupil ($)	Change in State Revenue per Pupil ($)	Total Revenue per Pupil ($)	Total Gain (Loss) per Pupil ($)
A	10,040	36,670	30.43	28.31	1,116	1,038	1,133	0	155	2,172	78
B	7,028	46,845	28.33	26.80	1,327	1,255	1,032	0	144	2,287	72
C	7,985	55,203	26.86	25.47	1,483	1,406	948	0	154	2,354	77
D	4,152	64,875	25.61	23.83	1,661	1,546	851	0	231	2,397	116
E	5,148	71,762	24.39	22.92	1,750	1,645	782	0	210	2,427	105
F	6,216	81,913	23.54	22.30	1,928	1,826	681	0	204	2,507	102
G	3,666	92,949	23.28	22.56	2,164	2,097	571	0	134	2,668	67
H	2,961	106,195	21.72	21.59	2,307	2,293	438	0	27	2,731	14
I	3,472	135,496	19.52	21.31	2,645	2,888	145	0	(243)	3,033	0
J	848	306,766	10.52	11.71	3,227	3,593	0	0	(366)	3,593	0
Weighted average		71,277	25.69	24.50	1,688	1,636	813	0	127	2,449	75
Standard deviation		40,819	3.73	2.95	484	558	291	0	128	270	32
Median		64,875	25.61		1,661					2,397	

	Totals	Change
Pupils	51,516	
Local revenue	$84,261,967	($2,684,833)
State revenue	$41,884,111	$7,866,868
Total revenue	$126,146,078	$5,182,034
State aid		
Number of winners	8	
Number of losers	2	

Equity Measures

Horizontal equity
Range $1,422
Range ratio .326
Coef. of variation .110
McLoone index .945
Gini coefficient .055

Fiscal neutrality
Correlation .992
Elasticity .157

With this foundation program as a base, the GTB program becomes the dominant element of the general aid formula, and whatever level of GTB is set, the result simply is that some districts receive more state aid. Since this combination program really is a GTB program with an element (the low foundation base) added to ease the transition, the GTB should be set at a relatively high level. Figure 7.13 shows this combination program with a GTB of $100,000, which is about the 90th percentile. Note that 9 of the 10 districts receive some state aid; 8 of those 9 have state aid increases.

The fiscal equity impacts are very impressive. First, per-pupil expenditure disparities have been reduced substantially. The coefficient of variation is down to only 5.4 percent, which is probably lower than in any state except for California, Florida, Hawaii, and New Mexico which have the equivalent of state-set, equal spending levels for all districts. The McLoone index is higher, at .979, which means that the spending of the bottom five districts (i.e., the bottom half) is almost equal.

Fiscal neutrality is also strong, although the figures show an anomaly with the correlation coefficient and wealth elasticity. The correlation coefficient is still quite high, at .921. This means that revenues per pupil and property value per pupil are strongly related. But the elasticity is low, at .071, which means that the relationship between the two variables is not that significant, that although revenues might increase with property wealth, the increase is very small; a 100 percent increase in property wealth per pupil (from the average of $72,000 to $144,000, higher than all but the top district) would produce only a 7 percent increase in revenues per pupil.

Put another way, when the correlation is high, it means that two variables have a strong linear relationship. When the elasticity also is high, it means that the slope of the relationship is high; when the elasticity is low, it means that the slope of the relationship is low. This is shown by comparing the graph in Figure 7.14, for the combination program, to the graph in Figure 7.3, for the base data with no state aid. The former shows a low slope for the combination program, whereas the latter shows a high slope between revenues per pupil and property value per pupil. This combination program produces a system that is very fiscally neutral.

The total cost of the program also is relatively modest, at only $21 million, a total increase of just 17 percent ($21 million/$121 million). Of course, this is a combination of a $30 million increase in state money and a $9 million drop in local revenues caused by the use of some state aid increase for lowering local property tax rates in the low-wealth districts.

Indeed, the average local property tax rate drops by about 3.7 mills (25.69−21.69 mills). Thus, the program also produces substantial local property tax relief in the low-wealth districts. These districts had previously suffered from the "double whammy" of high tax rates and low revenues per pupil. With this program, they have average or slightly above-average revenues per pupil and average or slightly above-average tax rates. The double whammy has been eliminated!

FIGURE 7.13 Ten-District Sample: Combination (foundation level: $1,500; required tax rate (mills): 10; guaranteed tax base: $100,000; GTB rate cap above foundation level (mills): 99;

Pupil weights	
Regular	1.00
Handicapped	1.00
Comp.	1.00
LEP	1.00

District	Pupils	Property Value per Pupil ($)	Old Property Tax Rate (mills)	New Property Tax Rate (mills)	Old Local Revenue per Pupil ($)	New Local Revenue per Pupil ($)	State Found. Revenue per Pupil ($)	State GTB Revenue per Pupil ($)	Change in State Revenue per Pupil ($)	Total Revenue per Pupil ($)	Total Gain (Loss) per Pupil ($)
A	10,040	36,670	30.43	23.18	1,116	850	1,133	835	990	2,818	725
B	7,028	46,845	28.33	22.74	1,327	1,065	1,032	677	821	2,774	559
C	7,985	55,203	26.86	22.31	1,483	1,232	948	552	706	2,731	455
D	4,152	64,875	25.61	21.71	1,661	1,409	851	411	643	2,671	390
E	5,148	71,762	24.39	21.31	1,750	1,529	782	319	530	2,631	308
F	6,216	81,913	23.54	21.30	1,928	1,744	681	204	408	2,630	224
G	3,666	92,949	23.28	22.14	2,164	2,058	571	86	219	2,714	114
H	2,961	106,195	21.72	21.59	2,307	2,293	438	0	27	2,731	14
I	3,472	135,496	19.52	21.31	2,645	2,888	145	0	(243)	3,033	0
J	848	306,766	10.52	11.71	3,227	3,593	0	0	(366)	3,593	0
Weighted average		71,277	25.69	21.97	1,688	1,511	813	436	563	2,760	386
Standard deviation		40,819	3.73	1.50	484	622	291	291	366	148	238
Median		64,875	25.61		1,661		291			2,731	

Totals

		Change
Pupils	51,516	
Local revenue	$77,830,331	($ 9,116,469)
State revenue	$64,367,012	$30,349,769
Total revenue	$142,197,344	$21,233,300

State aid

Number of winners	8
Number of losers	2

Equity Measures

Horizontal equity
Range	$964
Range ratio	.153
Coef. of variation	.054
McLoone index	.979
Gini coefficient	.024

Fiscal neutrality
Correlation	.921
Elasticity	.071

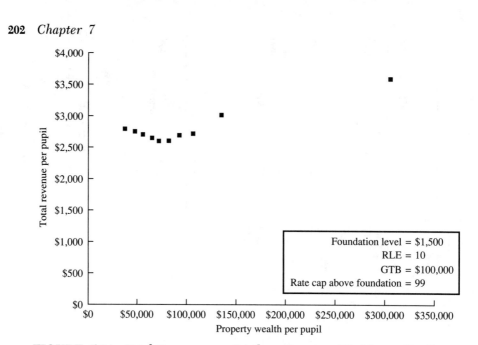

FIGURE 7.14   Total Revenue per Pupil vs. Property Wealth per Pupil: Combination Foundation Program and Guaranteed Tax Base

In summary, a combination program links the best features of a foundation program and a GTB program and also remedies the major flaws of each. The combination program can be used to implement the goals of more equal spending and local choice, although there are constraints on each. The foundation program, moreover, can be structured to serve quite different purposes, including providing a very high spending base (high to allow average students to meet new, ambitious performance goals) and allowing some local spending add-ons. Also, the combination program can serve as a transition from a minimum foundation program that provides aid to all districts, including even the very wealthy districts, to a system that minimizes state aid losers and provides equal access to a school tax base.

Full State Funding and State-Determined Spending Programs

The final category of school aid program is generally referred to as full state funding. A full state funding program simply sets an equal expenditure level per pupil for all districts. Districts cannot spend less than this amount, nor can they spend more. Indeed, if a state wants to implement the objective of horizontal equity for students, i.e., a program that provides for equal spending, a full state funding program is the only choice.

One key issue is how full state funding programs are financed. As the words connote, such a program in pure form is fully funded with state revenues, which is the case in Hawaii. But that is not a necessary characteristic. The key characteristic is that a full state funding program requires equal spending per pupil in all districts. The revenues, however, could be derived from a combination of state revenues and local property tax revenues. Indeed, the state could require a uniform statewide property tax rate for schools and set state aid as the difference between the revenues that would result and the total revenues needed to provide the equal spending level. This is the approach taken by New Mexico.

California has a version of full state funding called a revenue limit program. The state sets a base spending level per pupil for each district and finances it with a combination of state and local property tax revenues. Since local property taxes are constitutionally set at 1% of assessed value, this is conceptually equivalent to a full state funding program.

Florida has a different system that also functions like a full state funding program, financed with a combination of state and local revenues. Florida has a combination foundation and GTB program. The GTB program has an absolute maximum tax rate cap. Since most districts are at the cap, and since the GTB is higher than the wealth of most districts, the structure comes close to being the equivalent of a full state funding program.

In summary, full state funding will be used in this book to indicate a school finance program that requires equal per-pupil spending across all school districts. The program can be financed solely with state funds or with a combination of state and local funds, usually property tax revenues. The key element of a full state funding program is that a district cannot spend less or more than the level set by the state. A full state funding program is the only type of school finance formula that implements the horizontal equity principle for students.

SUGGESTED PROBLEMS AND OTHER STRATEGIES FOR USING THE SIMULATION

PROBLEM 7.1

Assume that the base data for the 10-district sample on the school finance simulation represents the condition of school finance in your state. A taxpayer rights group has conducted an analysis of that system and, based on that analysis, has sued in state court, arguing that school spending levels are a function of district wealth. They have asked the court to invalidate the state's funding structure. You are the chief of staff of the state legislature's school finance committee. Looking at a printout of the base data from the simulation, you see that per-pupil revenue ranges from $2,094 to $3,593 and that the tax rate in the lowest-revenue district is 30.43 mills compared with 10.52 mills in the highest-revenue district. The state share of total educational revenues is under 30%. Moreover, you note that the correlation of revenue and wealth per pupil is .9665 and the elasticity is .199. Looking carefully at a graph of revenue versus wealth per pupil for the base data, you conclude that there is a substantial likelihood the court will invalidate the state finance structure.

Additionally, a number of years ago, the state's voters approved an expenditure limitation. As a result, it is unlikely that more than $9 million in additional state funds will be available for education next year.

Using the simulation, design a school finance system using a foundation program that reduces the fiscal neutrality of this system without increasing *state* spending by more than $9 million. Experiment with different combinations of foundation level and required levy effort (RLE). Experiment with combinations of high and low foundation levels and high and low RLE. Can you find more than one foundation level/RLE combination that costs the state $9 million or less? Note the number of "winners" and "losers" for each option. Once you have three or four possible options, answer each of the following questions:

a. How does each of these combinations affect the fiscal neutrality criteria being considered in the lawsuit?
b. What impact does each of these options have on the horizontal equity of the system?
c. How does total revenue for education change under each of these options? How does the state's share of total revenue change?
d. How will you address legislative questions about districts that gained and those that lost state aid? In other words, how would you assess your programs politically?
e. Which option would you recommend to the legislature? Why?
f. If the state suddenly found that it could devote $15 million to education next year rather than $9 million, how would you change your recommendations?

PROBLEM 7.2

Using the same information as presented in Problem 7.1, remove the restriction that you must use a foundation program to design a new school finance system. Experiment with the GTB option, and find a model that meets the $9 million state spending increase limitation. How does this model compare to the foundation program you recommended to the legislature in Problem 7.1? Specifically:

a. How does *total* spending change under the GTB compared to the foundation program?
b. How do local district tax rates compare?
c. Are there more winners or losers under the GTB? How does the magnitude of each district's gain or loss in state aid compare

between the two options? Which program do you think is more politically viable?

d. Which model, the GTB or the foundation program, does a better job of minimizing the relationship between wealth and revenue?

e. Which of the two models better meets horizontal equity standards?

f. How does the state's share of total educational revenue compare between the two models?

g. Which model would you recommend to the legislature? Describe the trade-offs that policymakers will have to make in choosing one option over the other.

h. How would your analysis change if there were $15 million available for education instead of $9 million?

PROBLEM 7.3

A number of states have opted to use two-tier programs, relying on a foundation program to provide a base level of revenue for all districts and a GTB to equalize district decisions to supplement that base. Using the same $9 million limitation, design a combination (two-tier) school finance system for your state. How does this model compare to the two previous models? What would you now recommend to the legislature? Why? What happens if the state is willing to increase its commitment to $15 million?

PROBLEM 7.4 [14]

Divide the class into groups of one, two, or three so that each group represents one of the school districts in the 10-district sample.

First have each group design the foundation program, with an increased state cost of $20 million, that gives their district the greatest increase in state aid. Have each group discuss in class why their plan should be the one proposed to the legislature. Each group should argue on the basis of the impacts of their program on school finance equity.

Second, have each group design the foundation program, with an increased state cost of $20 million, that they feel is the best for their particular district and that they think two-thirds of the class would support. Compare the programs designed.

[14] Problem 7.4 and all subsequent problems could be used as class exercises utilizing the 10-district sample simulation, after the issues in Chapter 7 have been covered. These problems all raise the interrelated issues of school finance equity goals; state, local and total costs; and the particular interests of districts with below-average and those with above-average property wealth per pupil.

PROBLEM 7.5

Divide the class into two groups. Members of group 1 represent superintendents from districts low in property value per pupil, i.e., districts A–E. Members of group 2 represent superintendents from districts high in property value per pupil, i.e., districts F–J. Ask each group to run a combination foundation-GTB program with total extra costs (i.e., the sum of the changes in local and state revenues) of $34 million.

For this exercise, have each group consider school finance equity as well as political feasibility. Have each group decide whether their interest is better served by a relatively low foundation program and a relatively high GTB or a relatively high foundation program and a modest GTB, and have them explain why.

Compare the different designs. Some should have large increases in state aid combined with large decreases in local revenues for a total increased cost of $34 million. Others should have increased state costs much closer to $34 million and much less property tax relief.

PROBLEM 7.6

Again divide the class into groups—of two, three, or four depending on the size of the class—representing different types of districts: below-average wealth, average wealth, and above-average wealth.

Have each group design a combination foundation-GTB program with an increased *state* cost of $30 million.

Again compare the programs designed. Have the class discuss the merits of each and vote on the one they would enact into legislation if they made up the state legislature.

Endnote

To compare the various designs and impacts of simulation programs, it is sometimes helpful to create a summary chart so that all important figures may be reviewed at a glance. Figure 7.15 is an example of such a chart, using data from the school finance programs simulated in Chapter 7. The chart gives the values of all key parameters for each formula simulated and summarizes impacts in terms of state aid losers; changes in state, local, and total revenue; and the horizontal and fiscal neutrality equity statistics.

FIGURE 7.15   Summary Chart for Comparing Simulated School Finance Programs

	Formula Parameters					Impacts	
Simulation	Flat Grant	Foundation Level	Required Tax Rate	Zero-Aid District	GTB	Number of State Aid Losers	Change in State Revenue (millions)
Base data	—	—	—	n.a.	—	—	—
1	$800	—	—	None	—	2	$ 7.2
2	—	$2,400	24	$100,000	—	5	9.1
3	—	—	—	100,000	$100,000	5	11.0
4	—	1,500	10	150,000	0	2	7.9
5	—	1,500	10	150,000	100,000	2	30.3

Source: Figures 7.1, 7.6, 7.8, 7.10, 7.12, and 7.13.

FIGURE 7.15   Summary Chart for Comparing Simulated School Finance Programs (Continued)

		Impacts				
Change in Local Revenue (millions)	Change in Total Revenue (millions)	Coefficient of Variation	McLoone Index	Gini Coefficient	Correlation Coefficient	Elasticity
—	—	.123	.959	.060	.965	.199
$0.0	$ 7.2	.185	.854	.107	.931	.297
-1.3	7.8	.089	.997	.033	.936	.140
-0.2	10.8	.081	.965	.036	.833	.110
-2.7	5.2	.110	.945	.055	.992	.157
-9.2	21.2	.054	.979	.024	.921	.071

Source: Figures 7.1, 7.6, 7.8, 7.10, 7.12, and 7.13.

Chapter 8

Adjustments for Student Needs, Education Level, Scale Economies, and Price

Chapter 7 analyzed the basic school finance formulas and the variety of policy and political issues associated with each. But the discussion implicitly assumed uniformity along several dimensions, and in the real world, such an assumption does not hold. For example, some students have special needs and require additional educational services above those provided through state and local general funds. Further, some argue that it is wise to spend more on students at different education levels. Traditionally, states spend more on secondary students, although there is an increasing trend to spend more on students in kindergarten through grade 3. Many states still have small schools that experience diseconomies of scale or schools in rural isolated areas, both of which incur higher costs. Finally, the price of purchasing educational goods varies across districts in a state, especially large, diverse states such as Florida, New York, or Texas. This chapter discusses these issues and the types of vertical equity adjustments to basic school finance formulas that reflect legitimate reasons for providing unequal resources.

ADJUSTMENTS FOR DIFFERENT
PUPIL NEEDS

If different pupil needs requiring extra educational resources were evenly distributed across school districts, neither special adjustments to regular school finance formulas nor separate categorical programs would be needed; the extra amounts could be included, at least implicitly, in the spending levels set for the regular program. But the distribution of different pupil needs is not even across all school districts. Students from homes with incomes below the poverty level tend to be concentrated in large, urban districts and in small, rural, isolated school districts; these students are much less prevalent in suburban school districts. Similarly, students for whom English is not the primary language are also not found in equal percentages in all types of school districts; these students too tend to enroll in greater percentages in urban and rural school districts. Likewise, students with physical or mental handicaps are not found in equal concentrations in all school districts; indeed, some suburban school districts that have developed especially effective programs for handicapped children see the percentage of such students rise as parents move to that district for access to the outstanding program.

In short, the demographics of students with different types of special educational needs vary from school district to school district. Indeed, the proportions of students who need extra educational services approach 50 percent in the largest districts in the country, such as Chicago, Dallas, Los Angeles, and New York City.

Furthermore, the prices districts face in providing these extra services also vary, intensifying the fiscal burden caused by special-needs students. Large, central cities face the highest prices and, usually, have the highest concentration of these students. Many rural districts, which generally have lower prices, usually face high costs for the special needs of these students because the low incidence dramatically increases the per-pupil costs of needed services. For example, if there is only one blind student in a rural school, the cost for providing appropriate services is spread over just that one student, whereas in more populated areas, the incidence of blindness among children is higher and the costs of providing needed additional services can be spread over all blind children.

If states required districts to provide the needed extra services solely from local funds, they would be imposing an extra financial burden that would vary substantially by district. Further, since the incidence of special student needs is not necessarily related to local fiscal capacity, such a state requirement could worsen school finance fiscal inequities. In short, because of demographics and price differences, a state role is needed to make the provision of extra services for special-needs students—the poor, handicapped, or limited-English-proficient (LEP)—fair across all schools districts. This section discusses school finance programs to accommodate these vertical equity adjustments.

Development of Special-Needs Student Programs

There is a rich developmental history associated with the major special-needs student programs: compensatory education programs for low-income students; language acquisition programs for LEP students (Hodge, 1981), and special education programs for physical and mentally handicapped students. Both the federal government and the states have been major actors in this history.

Compensatory education.   The federal stimulus was inaugurated in 1965 with passage of the Elementary and Secondary Education Act (ESEA); Title I provided grants to local school districts on the basis of the number of students from families with incomes below the poverty level. Within districts, schools were to use the funds to provide extra educational services for low-achieving students. Initially, the per-pupil grant was funded at about $200, which was about 37 percent of the national average expenditure per pupil. Although this federal compensatory education program has a long history of implementation, by the early 1980s the program was firmly in place across the country (Odden, 1991).

Further, as discussed in Chapter 3, although in the early years a substantial portion of Title I dollars "supplanted" (i.e., replaced) local dollars, by the end of the 1970s each dollar of Title I funded produced a minimum of an extra dollar of expenditures on compensatory education programs (Odden, 1988). A series of rules and regulations developed during the 1970s, focused primarily on funds allocation and use, helped produce these end-of-the-decade fiscal outcomes. "Comparability" required districts to allocate district and state funds equally among schools before allocating Title I dollars. "Supplement and not supplant" required districts to ensure that Title I dollars provided extra educational services and did not merely replace local funds. And "children in greatest need" requirements guaranteed that only the children with the lowest student achievement were eligible to receive extra educational services provided by Title I funds.

In 1981, ESEA was amended by the Education Consolidation and Improvement Act (ECIA), and Title I was replaced by Chapter 1. In 1989, ECIA was replaced by a new Elementary and Secondary Education Act. The compensatory education program became Chapter 1 of Title 1 of the new ESEA. In 1990, approximately $4.76 billion were provided for Chapter 1 services. Dollars are allocated to states, and to local districts within states on a flat grant basis, depending on the number of students from families with incomes below the poverty level.

Title I and, later, Chapter 1 stimulated many states to enact their own compensatory education programs. Most were designed to complement the federal program. California and New York were among the first states to enact compensatory education programs. A major issue for many state programs, and an issue also raised for the federal program, was whether to distribute funds on the basis of poverty, an indirect measure of student need, or student achievement, a direct measure of student need. The New York program allocates funds on the basis of student achievement criteria, whereas the California program uses a poverty index.

The politics surrounding the enactment of Title I (Bailey and Mosher, 1968; Ravitch, 1983) favored poverty as the measure of need because it ensured that funds flowed disproportionately to large cities, primarily those in the Midwest and Northeast, and to rural areas, primarily in the South. Representatives of these areas were the strongest supporters of ESEA, and their districts were felt to have the greatest need for federal support. A student achievement measure would drastically alter the distribution of federal compensatory education funds; dollars would flow out of rural and urban areas and into suburban areas, since all districts have low-achieving students. Similarly, in most states, use of a poverty index to distribute compensatory education funds channels relatively more aid into rural and urban areas; a student achievement measure spreads the dollars across more districts and increases the relative proportion allocated to suburban districts, which usually are the wealthier districts. Whatever educational argument is used to rationalize the allocation of compensatory education funds, these political dimensions also affect the final program design.

In the early 1980s, nearly 20 states had compensatory education programs and/or pupil weights in their general aid formula, with about half using pupil weights (McGuire, 1982). Student eligibility was determined by a mixture of poverty and student achievement measures. In 1986–87, the number of states with compensatory education programs and/or compensatory education pupil weights increased to 28. Figure 8.1 lists the different state approaches to funding compensatory education.

Although both federal and state compensatory programs provide opportunities for low-achieving students to receive additional educational services, the programs do not establish a "right" to such extra services. The services are available solely because of the federal and state programs.

Bilingual education.   Services for students with limited English proficiency emerged in the mid-1970s primarily in response to the 1974 *Lau v. Nicholas*[1] case in California. This case was brought in San Francisco, where students who did not speak English were "immersed" in classes taught in English. The case was filed as an equal protection case, but it was decided on the basis of Title VI of the federal Civil Rights Act of 1964. The court held that it was discriminatory to place non-English-speaking students in classes where the language of instruction was English. As a result, districts created bilingual programs that provided instruction in English as a second language (ESL) and instruction in subject matter classes taught in the student's native language until the student learned enough English to be instructed in English only.

Although debates have surrounded various approaches to bilingual education, the key finding of *Lau* is that the language capability of students must be considered in designing an appropriate instructional environment. Today,

[1] 414 U.S. 653.

FIGURE 8.1   State Approaches to Funding Compensatory Education

State	Compensatory Program Description	1986–87 Funding (millions of dollars)	
California	Funds distributed for marginal costs of compensatory programs not funded thorugh revenue limit, on the basis of a variety of poverty measures	Economic Impact Aid Urban Impact and Meade Aid	197.5 86.6
Colorado	Districts with over 15% low-income pupils receive $125 per low-income pupil in excess of the 15%	Low income/ADC	4.35
Connecticut	Half of grant on basis of number of low-income pupils, half on basis of low achievement; weight of 0.5 in general aid formula	Compensatory education grants	8.63
Florida	Categorical grant distributed on basis of number of children scoring in lowest quartile on statewide assessment tests	State compensation education program	38.35
Georgia	Weight of 1.314 for pupils with low achievement test scores in reading and math	Remedial education Program	13.3
Hawaii	Full state funding for educationally disadvantaged, immigrant children with limited English, alienated youth, and other targeted groups with educational programs	Compensatory education	10.28
Illinois	Chapter 1–eligible children are given a variable weight from 0 to 0.625 depending on the concentration of low-income students relative to the state average concentration of 19.19%; a district with 19.19% concentration has an additional weight of 0.53 per low-income pupil	Unknown	
Louisiana	Flat grant for approved programs	Unknown	
Maryland	25% of foundation amount per Chapter 1–eligible pupil, with requirement that a minimum portion of that amount be devoted to Chapter 1–eligible students	Compensatory education	44.36

(Continued)

FIGURE 8.1 (Continued)   State Approaches to Funding Compensatory Education

State	Compensatory Program Description	1986–87 Funding (millions of dollars)	
Massachusetts	Pupil weight of 0.20 for Chapter 1–eligible children	Unknown	
Michigan	Aid for districts with large number of pupils in need of improvement based on state test	Compensatory education	32.14
Minnesota	Pupil weight range of 0.5 to 1.1: pupil weight of 0.5 for AFDC pupils, plus districts with more than 6% AFDC students receive an additional 0.1 weight per pupil up to an additional 0.6 limit	Unknown	
Missouri	AFDC and orphan students weighted 0.25	Unknown	
Nebraska	Culturally deprived students weighted an additional 1.0; only districts that receive equalization aid qualify for funding	Unknown	
New Jersey	Weight of 0.18 for pupils currently enrolled in remedial programs	State compensatory education	110.2
New York	Weight of 0.25 for students scoring below minimum competence on state reading and math tests	Unknown	
North Carolina	60% of remediation funds based on high school competency test failures; 40% of funds distributed on basis of number of students scoring below 35th percentile on 8th-grade CAT test	Unknown	
Ohio	Varying amount per pupil based on the percentage of AFDC children in the district; per-pupil payment increases as percent of AFDC pupils increases	Disadvantaged pupil impact aid	212.7
Oklahoma	Pupils who qualify and participate in reduced-price and free lunch program are weighted 0.25	Unknown	

(Continued)

FIGURE 8.1 (Continued)   State Approaches to Funding Compensatory Education

State	Compensatory Program Description	1986–87 Funding (millions of dollars)	
Oregon	Disadvantage funds provided to Portland school district	$1 million in 1987–88	
Pennsylvania	Districts with 10–39.9% of ADM from AFDC families receive payments of $100 per ADM; districts with 40% or more receive $300 per ADM The number of pupils in grades 3, 5, and 8 who fail the TELLS examination receive a pro rata share of appropriation for the Agenda for Excellence program	Poverty Payment Agenda for Excellence	85.5 28.0
Rhode Island	Ratio of Chapter 1 entitlement in district to statewide total times appropriation	$2 million in 1988	
South Carolina	Pupil weights: Grades 1–6 compensatory 0.26 Grades 2–6 remediation 0.114 Grades 7–12 remediation 0.114	Remedial and compensatory	56.8
Texas	0.2 pupil weight based on number of pupils eligible for free or reduced-price lunches	Unknown	
Utah	District share based on ratio of AFDC students to statewide total AFDC students	Unknown	
Vermont	Weight of 0.15 for students from families receiving food stamps	Unknown	
Virginia	Additional payments for students scoring below grade level on state achievement tests	Remedial education payments	17.5
Washington	Flat grant to districts on the basis of the number of students scoring in the lowest quartile on the statewide basic skills test	Remedial assistance program	11.0

Source: Deborah Verstegen, *School Finance at a Glance*, Denver, Colo., Education Commission of the States, 1988; and Richard Salmon, Christina Dawson, Steven Lawton, and Thomas Johns, *Public School Finance Programs of the United States and Canada: 1986–87*, Blacksburg, Virginia, Virginia Polytechnic Institute and State University, and American Education Finance Association, 1988.

for example, when one class might comprise students with many different native languages, bilingual instruction is not possible, and a "sheltered English" instructional approach may be an acceptable option (Krashen and Biber, 1988). In all instructional approaches, lessons have dual objectives: development of English language skills as well as content knowledge. The *Lau* decision made access to a language-appropriate classroom environment a legal right of all LEP students.

In 1967, just before the *Lau* ruling, Title VII was added to the federal ESEA program. Title VII provided funds for districts to design and implement bilingual education programs. Funds were available on a proposal basis only; districts wrote proposals, and a review process determined which proposals received funding. In 1990, the federal government provided about $189 million for bilingual education.

States also began to provide bilingual education programs, in part as a response to *Lau*. In 1975, 13 states had bilingual education programs. By the early 1980s, the number had risen to 22. By 1986–87, 22 states had bilingual education programs or bilingual education pupil weights. Figure 8.2 lists states' approaches to funding bilingual education programs.

Special education. For years, most states have supported special education programs for physically or mentally handicapped students at some level. But during the late 1960s and early 1970s, it became apparent that many handicapped students were being prohibited from attending local public schools. Whether certain handicaps were so severe they required very costly services or because of blatant discrimination against handicapped individuals, these exclusions were challenged under equal protection litigation. One of the first legal actions occurred in the *Pennsylvania Association of Retarded Children v. Pennsylvania* (PARC) case in 1972. This case, settled by a consent decree, held that district actions prohibiting handicapped students from attending local public schools violated the equal protection clause of the U.S. Constitution. The case spawned several other court cases as well as a spate of new federal and state policy initiatives.

In 1975, Congress enacted the federal Education for All Handicapped Children Act, P.L. 94-142. This sweeping new federal program essentially made access to a free public education program a legal right of all children. To receive any federal education dollars, states had to provide appropriate special education services to all handicapped children. The services had to meet a series of new, detailed federal requirements, many of which were written into P.L. 94-142 itself. Although several states initially responded negatively to the detailed federal requirements, and some states refused all federal education aid for a few years, today all states comply with the mandates of this federal law.

P.L. 94-142 authorizes the federal government to fund up to 40 percent of nationwide costs for special education services. In the year it was enacted, Congress appropriated $300 million, or about $74 per handicapped student—much less than the 40 percent authorized. In 1985–86, federal support totaled

FIGURE 8.2   State Approaches to Funding Education for Limited-English-Speaking Children

State	LEP Program Description	Program Operating Characteristics	
Alaska	Bilingual program costs included in state support program as additional instructional units	*ADM*	*Inst. Units*
		1–12	1
		13–18	2
		19–42	3
		43 and over	3 plus 1 for each 24 weighted ADM or fraction of 24
Arizona	Weights included in block grant calculations	*Weights*	
		K–8	1.158
		9–12	1.268
California	Funds distributed through Economic Impact Aid program, based on measures of poverty, limited English proficiency, and pupil transiency		
Colorado	English Language Proficiency Act provides funding to build English proficiency for under-achieving K–12 pupils of limited English profiency	$2,000,000 in 1986–87	
Florida	Pupil weighting program	Bilingual students weighted at 1.657	
Georgia	Grants based on need		
Hawaii	Full state funding		
Illinois	Excess cost for approved programs	$18,632,300 in 1986–87	
Kansas	Payments for approved programs	$150 per pupil in approved programs	
Louisiana	Additional instructional units provided for full-time second-language instructors at elementary level		
Massachusetts	Pupil weighting program	Weight of 1.4 for transitional bilingual program	

(Continued)

FIGURE 8.2 (Continued)   State Approaches to Funding Education for Limited-English-Speaking Children

State	LEP Program Description	Program Operating Characteristics
Michigan	Reimbursement to districts on basis of number of LEP students	$4,212,000 in 1986–87
Minnesota	State categorical program	Lesser of 61% of salary of FTE teacher or $17,000 per 45 LEP students with 1/2 teacher in districts with less than 23 LEP students
New Jersey	Pupil weights	Additional 0.23 times state average net current expense per pupil for LEP students
New Mexico	Pupil weights	FTE LEP students weighted an additional 0.3
New York	Pupil weights	LEP students weighted an additional 0.12
Oklahoma	Pupil weights	Weight of an additional 0.25 in foundation program
Rhode Island	Incentive program for bilingual pupils	$1.8 million in 1986–87
Texas	10% of adjusted allotment per pupil enrolled in a bilingual or special language program	
Utah	Categorical appropriation distributed proportionately based on number of LEP students	
Washington	Transitional bilingual program	$4,291,000 in grants to school districts in 1986–87
Wisconsin	State reimburses 63% of approved costs	$4,608,000 in 1986–87

Source: Deborah Verstegen, *School Finance at a Glance*, Denver, Colo., Education Commission of the States, 1988; and Richard Salmon, Christina Dawson, Steven Lawton, and Thomas Johns, *Public School Finance Programs of the United States and Canada: 1986–87*, Blacksburg, Virginia, Virginia Polytechnic Institute and State University, and American Education Finance Association, 1988.

$869 million, about 7.8 of total nationwide costs.[2] In 1990, federal support for special education services totaled about $2.7 billion, a large increase from 1985–86.

Federal funds are allocated on a per-pupil flat grant basis. The federal law requires that states identify students in the following 12 special education categories:

1. Deaf
2. Deaf and blind
3. Hard of hearing
4. Mentally retarded
5. Multiply handicapped
6. Orthopedically handicapped
7. Other health impaired
8. Seriously emotionally disturbed
9. Specific learning disabilities
10. Speech impaired
11. Visually handicapped
12. Autistic

Further, the category of learning disabled is limited to 2 percent of all students in a state. In 1987–88, the incidence of handicapped students averaged 6.74 percent across the nation, with individual state figures ranging from 4.03 percent in Hawaii to 10.3 percent in Massachusetts. Many states use the federal student categories to structure their state programs for the handicapped. Even though the per-pupil costs of providing services varies substantially by category, the federal program allocates the same flat grant amount for each identified student, regardless of category.

In the late 1980s, a "regular education initiative" was begun by a group of individuals who believed that a focus on fitting handicapped students into a diverse set of special categories and pulling students out of regular classrooms for instruction was doing more harm than good for many handicapped students. This initiative reinforced earlier views that labeling students was not the best approach to providing extra services; indeed, many argued that all students had particular needs and that schools, given their student populations, should identify the different types of services to provide, and that funding should be determined by the service levels needed. States such as Iowa and Massachusetts, in fact, structured their state programs for the handicapped on this basis. Nevertheless, the federal student labeling requirements have not changed

---

[2] In 1985, special education costs (excluding related services) totaled $11.466 billion, with $0.87 billion from the federal government, $6.92 billion from states, and $3.68 billion from local districts.

and are used, in some form, by most states (see also Chambers and Hartman, 1983).

Issues in Determining Costs of Special-Needs Programs

Four major categories of issues must be addressed in assessing and calculating costs for any special-needs program; (1) defining student eligibility, (2) identifying appropriate services, (3) determining the appropriate placement, and (4) calculating state and local cost shares.

Student eligibility. Since most states allocate special-needs funds on the basis of the number of eligible students, regulations on student eligibility are quite important. As mentioned previously, compensatory education program guidelines define eligibility in two ways: (1) based on poverty measures, such as household income, eligibility for free or reduced-price lunch, or eligibility for Aid to Families with Dependent Children (AFDC); or (2) based on achievement measures, including the type of tests used, the content areas to be tested, and the degree of divergence from the average or grade norm. Special education programs need guidelines on the number of discrete handicapping categories, assessment procedures, and whether there are "caps" on eligibility in any one category, such as the federal 2 percent cap on the learning disabled (see Moore, Walker, and Holland, 1982, for example). Bilingual education programs need to identify the types of language examinations that can be used and criteria for determining partial or full English proficiency, i.e., criteria for determining the transition into "sheltered English" instruction or into the regular, English-taught classroom. In each area, these issues can be quite complex. Finally, there is pressure to move away from narrow definitions of student eligibility to broader categories, such as requirement for a low, medium, or high level of extra services.

Eligible age ranges also need to be identified. In many states, handicapped children from birth to age 21 are eligible for public education services; other states limit eligibility to conventional school age. Only school-age children are eligible for compensatory and bilingual education services, although for these programs most money is spent at the elementary level. A service and policy issue is whether secondary students also should have these extra services.

Finally, the incidence of special-needs students varies widely overall and by program. Although the incidence of handicapped students is about 6.7 percent nationwide, some estimate that the total number of at-risk students might be as high as 25 percent (Pallas, Natriello, and McDill, 1988).

Appropriate services. Program guidelines also need to identify the range of services on which funds can be spent. Some programs restrict spending to current operating activities, and others allow capital expenditures—for buildings and equipment—as well. Within operating expenditures, some programs allow only instructional expenditures, whereas others provide spending for additional functional categories, such as transportation, which generally is costly. Within instructional expenditures, some programs limit spending to certain subject areas, such as reading and mathematics; others allow spending on all academic content areas, including art, music, and physical education.

Another issue is the degree to which program funds can be spent on administration. Because many categorical programs need special management and have reporting requirements—to ensure that only eligible students are served and that funds are spent as intended—many districts have created a special categorical program administration staff to manage the program and meet reporting and compliance requirements. Many programs specify the maximum portion of program funds that can be spent for administration.

Other service issues include student assessment and the level of assessment that can be employed (i.e., the diagnostic activities to determine placement), class size policies, and length of school day and year for special programs. For special education, a major issue is "related services," such as counseling, medical services, occupational therapy, and parent counseling. The guideline has been that such services are required if they are related to educational need. Related services can be costly for students with multiple physical handicaps, so the interpretation of these guidelines can have a substantial impact on the "bottom line" of special education costs.

Another issue is the comprehensiveness and quality of special services. The *Rowley*[3] court decision held that handicapped students were required access to an adequate educational program, but not the educational program of the quality needed to optimize their intellectual growth. In this case, a deaf individual sued a district to force employment of a teacher to read materials in a one-to-one tutoring situation, arguing that such a service was needed to maximize her learning. The district refused, and the court upheld the district's action, stating that P.L. 94-142 required provision of only adequate educational services, not services to maximize student performance.

Educational placement. The way educational services are provided can produce substantial cost variations for students at the same grade level and with the same special education need. There are five basic placement categories: (1) preschool, (2) resource program, (3) self-contained classroom, (4) home or hospital program, and (5) residential care. Most compensatory education and bilingual education programs are provided through resource programs, as are special education services for handicapped students who are "mainstreamed" in the regular program. Moore et al. (1988) and Chambers and Parrish (1983) show how costs vary widely—by a ratio of 2 to 1—across different educational placements.

Costs. Once decisions are made about student eligibility, types of services required or eligible for reimbursement, and educational placement, program

---

[3] 485 U.S. 176 (1982).

costs are relatively easy to calculate. One of the most sophisticated mechanisms for determining special-needs program costs is the resource cost model (Chambers and Parrish, 1983), which also can determine the most cost-effective educational placement depending on special-need condition and size and location of the school district. Such a program conceivably could be used by a state to determine the levels of cost that should be associated with numerous, local special-needs programs, but no state has yet adopted such a model.

Of course, after total costs have been determined, the next task is to identify the state and local shares of those costs. These issues are discussed next.

General Approaches to Special-Needs Formula Adjustments

States have adopted several different mechanisms to finance programs for special-needs students. These strategies divide into two general approaches. The first is for the state to cover the entire extra costs of providing the services. This approach certainly has strong appeal to local districts and eliminates fiscal inequities caused by requiring local districts to finance these services by raising local revenues. Under this approach, local districts document the extra costs and submit a reimbursement claim to the state each year. Alternatively, if the program costs are "forward-funded," districts submit an application for reimbursement of estimated costs. The state then needs a reconciliation mechanism to ensure that payments equal actual costs. Modifying the next year's payment by the difference between predicted and actual costs is a straightforward example of such an adjustment.

Full state funding of special-needs program costs requires rigorous state oversight or an audit mechanism to verify that only legitimate local costs are reimbursed. With the state paying the full tab for extra services, local districts have a fiscal incentive to develop and implement comprehensive, expansive, and high-quality programs. If the state has neither cost controls nor regulatory guidelines to monitor local programs and their financial needs, state costs could soar. Any state reimbursement program for special students needs some regulatory and program guidelines, but such mechanisms are an absolute requirement for a state program that reimburses 100 percent of local costs.

Over the long term, it is difficult for states to fully fund all special services. When service provision is mandated, as for special education, a drop in state funding forces districts to "encroach" on the general fund to cover the full costs of the special programs.

Thus, over the years, most states have devised some means of sharing the costs with local school districts, the second approach to funding special services. States have created several types of specific financial structures to implement state-local sharing. The simplest approach has been to provide a flat grant per eligible pupil. Sometimes the flat grant is based on the number of teachers or classroom units instead of pupils. Very few states currently use this approach, but it is the mechanism the federal government uses to distribute both Chapter 1 funds and funds under P.L. 94-142 for handicapped students. The obvious drawback to this approach is that it provides the same per-pupil level of financial assistance to rich and poor districts, and if the amount does not cover all costs, districts low in property value per pupil need to levy a higher incremental tax rate to make up the difference. Additionally, if all program-eligible students generate identical grades, these grants don't take different needs into account.

A second state-local cost sharing program is "excess cost reimbursement," in which the state reimburses a percentage (less than 100 percent) of excess local costs. This ensures that local districts finance at least some portion of the costs of the programs they create and implement. The local match is in part a fiscal incentive for local districts to control costs; if program costs soar, the local match requirement puts a direct strain on local budgets, as well as the state. Since, under this program, the local share is raised by increasing the local tax rate (or encroaching on the general fund budget), this approach also somewhat disadvantages property-poor districts, which have to exert a higher incremental local tax rate to make up the difference between full program costs and the costs shared by the state.

A third state-local sharing strategy includes some fiscal capacity–equalizing component in the state reimbursement program. For example, the state could turn a flat grant into a foundation-type grant. Or the state could use a separate guaranteed tax base program for the tax rate needed to raise the extra revenues to finance the total costs of the special-needs program.

The most prevalent form of special-needs student program that includes a fiscal capacity-equalizing element emerged in the 1970s and is called pupil weighting. Under this strategy, each special-needs pupil is given an extra weight that indicates, relative to some norm expenditure (usually the statewide average), how much funding for additional services is required. For example, if the extra weight for a compensatory education student is 0.5, such a student would be counted as 1.5 students in determining state aid. The advantage of a pupil weighting approach is its simplicity in incorporating into the school aid formula the level of extra need for each student and in structuring the state share to make it higher in low-wealth districts and lower in high-wealth districts. Another advantage is that only one finance formula is used to provide all state aid to local districts; the weighted pupil count may be used in place of the unweighted pupil count for all state aid calculations.

A weighted pupil approach also indicates very directly the degree of vertical equity in the school finance system; the weights are the vertical adjustments. The adequacy of the vertical equity adjustments may be determined by evaluation of the specific pupil weights. In calculating the fiscal equity of the resultant distribution of educational resources, moreover, equity statistics are calculated using the number of weighted pupils.

A pupil-weighted system can be used with any type of school finance formula. Technical issues, however, arise in the following ways. If the weight for a particular type of student is determined by comparing the excess costs required with the statewide average expenditure per pupil, this expenditure must then be included in the state aid program for the weight to be accurate. Often, states with foundation programs set the foundation expenditure below the statewide average expenditure per pupil but use a pupil weight that has been calculated using the statewide average. In this situation, the level of extra resources provided is less than that required. On the other hand, if a state has a guaranteed tax base program together with a pupil weighting system, districts that tax at an above-average level will have expenditures above the statewide average, and thus the pupil weight might generate more additional revenues than are needed to cover excess costs.

In addition, there are shortcomings in labeling students as needing extra resources, and some have argued for systems that identify service levels necessary for schools to educate students. Despite these technical concerns, pupil weighting programs are rising in popularity.

In short, there are two generic approaches states can use to provide assistance to local districts for educating students with special needs. Under the first, the state picks up the entire amount of excess costs. Under the second, the state shares in the excess costs through one or more mechanisms. Pupil weighting programs have become popular as a way for a state to identify directly, through an extra weight, the degree of extra service to provide, and then to share in financing that extra support by allocating state aid through the general aid formula using a weighted count of pupils. This strategy also conditions the level of extra aid received on local fiscal capacity; for a given number of special-needs students, districts low in property value per pupil will receive larger amounts of special funds than districts high in property value per pupil.

The reason some states do not adopt a weighted pupil strategy, despite its many attractions, is precisely because that approach makes it difficult to funnel state aid to property-wealthy districts. If the state uses a categorical program approach (i.e., devises a separate program formula for distributing financial support for special-needs students, usually some form of excess cost reimbursement) all districts—rich and poor—become eligible for some state aid. At first blush this might seem inequitable, but the politics of state aid distribution often requires this approach. If the state has a strong fiscal capacity–equalizing general aid program, districts high in property wealth per pupil receive little or no general state aid, which squares with fiscal equity principles. But politics can intervene in two ways. First, many legislators feel that all districts should be eligible for at least some state aid. And providing state support for special-needs students—even in the wealthiest districts—has surface appeal as a rationale for distributing aid to all districts, including wealthy ones. Second, it is difficult to maintain political support for strongly redistributive programs, such as robust fiscal capacity school finance formulas. Thus, providing at least some state aid for all districts, even if it is just for special-needs students, helps legislators maintain political support for a general aid program that provides aid in amounts inversely related to property value per pupil.

Unfortunately, just as with the basic school finance formulas, states have used a variety of names for programs implemented using these generic approaches, and the different terms may make the school finance programs sound like fundamentally different approaches. But just as many basic school finance formulas are algebraically equivalent, so also are many formulas for addressing special pupil needs. Berstein, Hartman, and Marshall (1976) show how the various approaches states use to help local districts provide extra services for special-needs students are simply variations of the general types of programs discussed in this chapter.

Finally, the interaction of the specific funding formulas and the regulations accompanying them provide incentives and disincentives for student identification, program placement, and dollar use. At the local level, districts sometimes classify students in higher reimbursement categories and place them in lower-cost instructional programs to increase revenues and reduce costs. Although some "play" in these interactions is desirable, the limits of such flexibility need to be understood and addressed. Hartman (1980) discusses such issues for special education.

Costs and Formulas for Financing Compensatory Education Programs

The federal government has provided funds to local school districts for compensatory programs since 1965. Under Chapter 1 of the 1988 Elementary and Secondary Education Act, funds are allocated to students in five distinct steps. First, the federal government allocates funds to states based on the number of low-income children and the state's per-pupil expenditures for elementary and secondary education.[4] Second, the state allocates funds to counties within the state. Third, if county and school district boundaries are not coterminous (which is the case in most states), the state uses a subcounty allocation formula to distribute funds to local school districts, based on the number of low-income students in each district. Fourth, local school districts decide which schools will receive Chapter 1 funds based on the number of *low-achieving* students. Finally, each district decides how the resources will be divided among the schools and the students in those schools.

Federal regulations on the use of Chapter 1 funds focus on ensuring that districts use the money they receive to "supplement and not supplant" local funds, but they provide little guidance about how the resources should be divided among eligible students. Consequently, there is considerable variation in how local districts choose to allocate compensatory funds. Goertz's (1988) study of Chapter 1 funds allocation in 17 school districts confirmed variations among districts in the type and level of services provided to eligible schools and students.

---

[4] Currently, Chapter 1 is *authorized* at 40 percent of the state's average expenditures per pupil. Each state's amount per pupil, however, cannot be less than 80 percent or greater than 120 percent of the national average expenditure per pupil. Dollar amounts are proportionately reduced each year since appropriations usually provide a total that is less than that needed to fund the authorized levels.

Generally, school districts have greater latitude in determining the kind of compensatory programs they offer; thus, determining compensatory education costs is not straightforward. Programs for other special-needs students are better defined. Districts are required by law, for example, to provide appropriate services to all handicapped children. Once a child's handicap has been identified and an appropriate level of service agreed upon, it is relatively straightforward to determine the costs of that service. Although there may be variations in costs and instructional techniques across districts, it is possible to estimate an "average" cost for each special service provided within a region or state.

The problem of determining compensatory education program costs is more complex. A district receives a funding level according to the federal program requirements, and those are the funds used to provide extra services. Chapter 1 and most state compensatory programs require that program funds be expended on low-income or low-achieving children but specify neither how they should be served nor whether all eligible children must receive services. As a result, local districts have considerable flexibility in determining the breadth and intensity of services provided.

For example, one district may choose to offer intensive services to a subgroup of eligible low-income students, and another district may elect to serve all of the eligible student population with a less intensive program. In fact, a number of different allocation procedures or rules are possible. Goertz (1988) found that among 17 large districts across the United States, allocation rules included:

- Uniform allocation to each eligible building
- Allocations based on the number of low-achieving students in a building
- Allocations based on the relative size and/or poverty of the building's student body

Even among districts with similar allocation rules, Goertz found a wide range in the breadth and intensity of compensatory services. In the 17 districts analyzed, the percentages of children in poverty served through Chapter 1 programs ranged from a low of 19 percent to a high of 81 percent, and the average caseload per teacher ranged from 35:1 to 100:1.

The study also found considerable differences in instructional expenditures per pupil within districts and among Chapter 1 programs. Goertz reported these figures on the basis of the range of expenditures across schools within each district. One district had a Chapter 1 expenditure range of $300 to $2,500 per pupil; in another district, expenditures ranged from $450 to $625. The lowest per-pupil Chapter 1 expenditure identified in the 17 districts was $175 (in a district with an expenditure range of $175 to $1,070); the highest was the $2,500 per pupil identified above.

Other studies have had similar difficulties identifying the costs of compensatory programs. The New York State Special Task Force on Equity and Excellence in Education (Gaughan and Glasheen, 1979) found that the state's accounting system for schools made it very difficult to track the costs of programs for special-needs students. The task force found that compensatory programs increased per-pupil costs between 25 and 100 percent. At that time, compensatory aid was distributed to districts on a weighted-pupil basis, with each identified pupil receiving a weight of 0.25.

In 1985–86, the Texas State Board of Education (1986) reviewed the costs of compensatory education and recommended an extra weight of 0.2 for all eligible compensatory education students. Although subsequent studies suggested that many districts did not spend that much extra for compensatory education, in part because compensatory education services within the regular school day were provided in lieu of other services, the legislature has retained the 0.2 extra weighting.

Another problem in identifying the costs of compensatory education programs is the fact that over 90 percent of the school districts in the United States receive Chapter 1 funds (Orland, 1988). Clearly, the percentage of low-income children varies greatly among these districts. Districts with larger concentrations of low-income students have more funds available for compensatory programs, and one might thus expect more intense compensatory services. In fact, Orland (1988) found that not only did Chapter 1 generally allocate more resources to a state's high-need school districts, but that more students were more intensively served in those districts. Although Orland did not provide expenditure data for compensatory programs directly, his work implies that expenditures per pupil served might be higher in districts with concentrations of low-income students.

In summary, compensatory education funds are distributed to school districts on the basis of the number of eligible pupils. For the federal Chapter 1 program, eligibility is determined by the number of low-income students in a district. Many state programs use income measures for eligibility, and others offer compensatory aid for low-achieving students. Compensatory education programs generally include requirements that districts do not use the money to replace local funds, but they do not delineate how services should be provided, or how many of the eligible students must be served. Consequently, some districts attempt to provide compensatory services to all eligible schools and students, whereas others focus their resources at specific populations. This results in a tremendous range in the breadth and intensity of the compensatory education services provided across the United States.

Costs and Formulas for Financing
Bilingual Education Programs

Studies of the costs of providing bilingual education have produced widely varying results, from less than an extra 5 percent (Carpenter-Huffman and Samulon, 1981) to an extra 100 percent (Chambers and Parrish, 1983). There are several reasons for these variations, and they go to the heart of what a bilingual education program is and how it should be structured.

Five specific issues define the costs of bilingual education programs (Nelson, 1984): (1) student eligibility, (2) minimum number of LEP students required to trigger provision of a bilingual education program, (3) instructional approach used, (4) transition into the regular program, and (5) class size.

Student eligibility usually is determined by a score on some type of English language proficiency test. As Nelson (1984) noted, states use different tests and have selected different cutoff points for eligibility, as low as the 23d percentile, in Texas. Clearly, the higher the cutoff point, the more students eligible and the smaller the number of low-incidence programs.

Most states also require a minimum number of students in a grade level for a school or district to provide a bilingual education program. Minimums range widely, from 10 students for a school in California, to 20 students for a district in Texas (Nelson, 1984). The lower the minimum number of children and the larger the unit, the more students will qualify.

Class size in many states also is limited, sometimes to as few as 10 students. Other states do not set lower limits on class size for bilingual or ESL classes. Clearly, small class size requirements will boost per-pupil costs.

Transition policies also affect the level of services provided. Most state bilingual education policy assumes that students diagnosed as LEP will be able to make the transition into regular classes, i.e., classes taught in English, within three years. A longer transition period, i.e., the provision of extra services to students who need more than three years to make the transition and perform well in English-only classrooms, would clearly boost per-pupil costs.

Finally, the instructional approach used also is a major determinant of program costs. A few comments on bilingual education program goals and characteristics of instructional strategies that work will help provide some background for assessing the nature of the instructional approach and, thus, the results of cost studies based on different approaches.

The student who is eligible for bilingual education programs generally lives in a family in which a language other than English is spoken or is from a background in which English is not the student's native language. The key issue is the degree to which the student is proficient in English as a language for learning. Literacy—the ability to read, write, do mathematics, and think— can be developed in any language; literacy is neutral with respect to language (Office of Bilingual Education, 1984). Once literacy is developed in one language, it is easily transferred to another, once the second language is learned. Students diagnosed as LEP are those who do not have sufficient English language proficiency to learn in English. Research shows that the most effective approach for such students is to teach them regular subjects in their native language and give them an ESL class, i.e., to provide an extra class to teach them English (Krashen and Biber, 1988). The goal of such a program is to have them learn English while learning regular academic subject matter.

The same research shows that students (adults too, for that matter) learn conversational English first; this English proficiency is sufficient for socializing on the playground, playing with friends, and talking about the weather, but it is not sufficient for academic learning (see also Cummins, 1980). When this conversational level of English proficiency is learned, the student is ready for "sheltered English" instruction in subjects with a great deal of language and terminology of their own, such as mathematics and science (Krashen and Biber, 1988), but they still need both instruction in their native language for history and language arts and continuation of ESL classes. This intermediate approach helps the student learn "academic" English, i.e., English proficiency sufficient to learn academic subjects. History/social science is the next subject for sheltered English instruction; the last such class is language arts. In other words, the most effective program is to begin instruction in the native language; transit sequentially to sheltered English instruction in mathematics, science, history/social science, and language arts; and only then move to English-only, or regular classroom, instruction. ESL instruction also should continue until the full transition is made to the regular classroom.

The Krashen and Biber report does not make recommendations for major class size reductions. Nor does this report recommend the common school practice of having an English-only instructor assisted by a bilingual education aid. This configuration is quite common across the country because there are insufficient numbers of bilingual teachers to teach students in their native languages. In this circumstance, Krashen and Biber recommend ESL with a sheltered English instruction approach.

Thus, the major extra costs of bilingual education for the most effective instructional approach are threefold:

- *A teacher for the ESL class.* If the class has a normal number of students and is used for six periods a day, costs increase by about 1/6, i.e., the cost of the extra period of instruction. Other, related costs, such as materials and space, might bring the total extra cost to about 20 percent.
- *Intensive staff development in sheltered English instruction.* Clearly, this is professional expertise that can be learned by all teachers; knowledge of a second language is not required. Sheltered English instruction is good instruction mediated by a variety of mechanisms and with a conscious English language development component.
- *Additional materials both in the native language of the student and for mediating the sheltered English instructional approach.* These extras would probably add a maximum of 25 to 35 percent. Note that regular classes are taught either by bilingual teachers, by teachers using a sheltered English approach, or in a regular classroom; other than staff development, these classes entail no extra costs.[5]

Most studies of bilingual education program costs reflect these levels of extra costs. Garcia (1977) found the add-on costs for bilingual education in New

---

[5] Some states and districts pay bilingual teachers a bonus of up to $5,000. This clearly is an extra cost. The bonus is rationalized on the basis that bilingual teachers are in short supply and have an expertise—proficiency in a second language—that other teachers do not have.

Mexico to be about 27 percent. Three studies by the Intercultural Development Research Association found bilingual education to cost an extra 30 to 35 percent in Texas (Cardenas, Bernal, and Kean, 1976), an extra 17 to 25 percent in Utah (Guss-Zamora et al., 1979), and an extra 15 to 22 percent in Colorado (Robledo et al., 1978). These studies analyzed program configurations quite different from that described here, but the findings provide a range of cost estimates that are nevertheless comparable.

Finally, although districts have typically reported higher extra costs for bilingual education programs than most studies have found (Carpenter-Huffman and Samulon, 1981), the Chambers and Parrish (1983) study in Illinois produced fairly large figures for bilingual education program costs. Studies have found that bilingual program costs vary depending on the program structure. Cost estimates have ranged from an additional $848 to $5,113 per pupil. More to the point, the studies showed that additional costs amounted to between 33 and 100 percent of a district's expenditures for regular programs. The highest cost figure, moreover, was based on both a low incidence and a very low class size, the latter a characteristic absent from the Krashen and Biber studies of effective California programs.

Bilingual education continues to be controversial, but the key ingredients for an effective program structure are an ESL program to teach English and regular teachers who teach either in the native language or in a sheltered English format—either alternative entails extra costs, supplementary materials, and staff development. As the diversity of students' native language increases, as is the case in many border states and especially California, sheltered English instruction becomes the dominant instructional mode in addition to ESL. Extra costs for this program structure, as found in several research reports, range between 25 and 35 percent.

Costs and Formulas for Financing Special Education Programs

Identifying the costs of special education programs for physically and mentally handicapped students has been a major subject of study for the past two decades. Initially, studies sought to identify different costs by handicapping condition and to determine how that varied by size of district. More recently, special education cost research has focused more on excess costs as a function of educational placement (Rossmiller and Frohreich, 1979; and Moore et al., 1988).

Some of the earliest work was conducted by Rossmiller under the auspices of the early 1970s National Education Finance Project (NEFP) (Rossmiller et al., 1970; Johns, Alexander, and Jordan, 1971). This work was probably the first analysis of special education costs that produced results that could be used to create pupil weighting programs. Indeed, in 1973, Florida enacted one of the first pupil weighting programs as a new approach for financing special education.

Florida adopted the following weights for 1976–77, based in large part on the Rossmiller and NEFP analyses:

Educable mentally retarded	2.3
Trainable mentally retarded	3.0
Physically handicapped	3.5
Physical and occupational therapy, part-time	6.0
Speech and hearing therapy, part-time	10.0
Deaf	4.0
Visually handicapped, part-time	10.0
Visually handicapped	3.5
Emotionally disturbed, part-time	7.5
Emotionally disturbed	3.7
Socially maladjusted	2.3
Specific learning disability, part-time	7.5
Specific learning disability	2.3
Hospital and homebound, part-time	15.0

In addition to the general points made earlier on factors that determine program costs, three key issues are related to determining special education program costs. The first is the level of program quality. Most of the early studies sought to identify "good" special education programs and based special education cost estimates on the expenditure patterns of those programs. Few studies set a priori standards for program quality. Thus, studies have been plagued over the years by various definitions of program quality. The second issue is identification of services included in the study. The most controversial aspect of this issue is whether to include administrative services, such as general district administration, as well as noneducational related services. A third issue, especially for determining per-pupil costs, is how the number of students is determined—by headcount or by full-time-equivalent. The importance of this issue is shown by the high weights for students receiving part-time services in the early Florida program. Kakalik (1979) provides another overview of issues in determining special education costs.

Two large studies of nationwide special education costs have been conducted, one by Kakalik et al. (1981), using data from the mid-1970s, and one by Moore et al. (1988), using data from the mid-1980s. Both used a representative national sample, thus providing a picture of actual special education expenditures across all programs in the country. The results in terms of excess costs for special education programs are quite similar. Kakalik et al. presented results as ratios of special education expenditures to regular education expenditures in 1977–78 for 13 categories of handicapping conditions; the weights ranged from 1.37 for speech-impaired children to 5.86 for the blind. The overall weight across all handicapping categories was 2.17. The authors also presented data comparing special education expenditures to regular education expenditures by 10 categories of educational placement. For in-school programs, the ratios or weights ranged from 1.37 for "regular class plus related services" to 3.24 for "special day school." The "regular class plus part-time special class" arrangement had a weight of 2.85.

Moore et al. (1988) presented no pupil weights or ratios in their report, tending rather to emphasize the linkage between type of educational program or educational placement and handicapping condition. The following are their summary findings of 1985–86 special education program costs:

Handicapping Condition	Preschool	Self-contained	Resource Room
Speech impaired	$3,062	$ 7,140	$ 647
Mentally retarded	3,983	4,754	2,290
Orthopedically impaired	4,702	5,248	3,999
Multihandicapped	5,400	6,674	NA
Learning disabled	3,708	3,083	1,643
Seriously emotionally disturbed	4,297	4,857	2,620
Deaf	5,771	7,988	NA
Deaf-blind	NA	20,416	NA
Hard of hearing	4,583	6,058	3,372
Other health impaired	3,243	4,782	NA
Autistic	6,265	7,582	NA
Visually impaired	4,068	6,181	3,395

These results can be transformed into pupil weights by comparing these costs to the 1985–86 expenditure per pupil for regular students, which was $2,780. Since the preceding figures are costs just for the special education services, the $2,780 figure would have to be added to them in calculating the weight. Moore et al. found that the overall average expenditure for special education across all programs and placements was $3,649. Thus, their study produced an overall weight of 2.3 [($3,649 + $2,780)/$2,780], close to the Kakalik et al. finding of 2.17.

In short, it seems that the average expenditure for a handicapped student is about twice that for a regular student. But caution must be applied in using this figure. Significant variation in special education costs occur by handicapping condition, educational placement, type of educational program, and size of school district. McClure (1976) and Leppert and Routh (1979) further discuss issues related to developing and implementing a state weighted-pupil approach to financing special education services for handicapped students.

Simulation of Adjustments for Special-Needs Students

Adding adjustments for special-needs students to a state school finance structure clearly improves the vertical equity of the system, but it also improves both horizontal equity and fiscal neutrality, although the improvements require additional revenues. The simulation that accompanies this book can be used to analyze the impact of a pupil weighting system. Select the **pupil weights** option in the model menu. The combination foundation and GTB program analyzed in Chapter 7 (see Figure 7.8) was used to simulate a weighted-pupil program with the following characteristics:

- Compensatory education students weighted 1.3
- Limited-English-proficient students weighted 1.3
- Handicapped students weighted 2.0.

Figure 8.3 shows the results of this simulation. The impacts are substantial. First, the total state cost of the program increases from $30.3 million to $47.1 million, an increase of $16.8 million, or 55 percent. Since the parameters of the simulated program—the foundation level, the required tax effort, and the guaranteed tax base—remained the same, local costs have dropped because the extra students have reduced each district's property value per pupil and thus made it eligible for more state aid.[6] The combination of more state aid and reduced local costs produce a total cost rise of one-third, which is a large increase. Note that the total number of weighted students is 62,021—an extra 10,505 children, or about 20 percent, over the unweighted total of 51,516. All of these children require extra services that, according to the simulation, increase costs 30 to 100 percent. Thus, increased costs should be expected.[7]

Second, the bulk of the extra costs is for handicapped students. Readers should run a series of simulations, each time giving a weight to just one of the three categories of special-needs students. The results will show that the incidence of bilingual students is quite low, which is the case in most states (but not California, Arizona, New Mexico, Texas, Florida, and New York). Since the extra cost for each student is just 30 percent, the total extra costs are marginal. Extra costs for compensatory education alone are higher because the incidence of poverty-level students is about 20 percent, but the extra cost for each student is just 30 percent. The incidence of handicapped students is about 12 percent; with an extra cost of 100 percent for each student, this produces the largest extra cost for a special-needs student category.

Third, the pupil weighting in Figure 8.3 improves all the fiscal equity statistics compared with the unweighted situation in Figure 7.8. The range ratio drops by nearly one-third, from .15 to .09, the coefficient of variation drops from .054 to .042, the correlation coefficient falls from .92 to .69, the elasticity

---

[6] A policy issue in simulating weighted-pupil programs is whether the original program parameters should be lowered by using weighted pupils to determine major policy variables such as the zero-aid district and level of tax base guaranteed. For simplicity, the parameters were retained, and the simulation indicates how much extra funding all special student needs would cost.

[7] The base data include no state aid for categorical programs such as those simulated. Since most states already have some level of categorical programs, the extra costs would not be as large as indicated by the simulated results.

FIGURE 8.3 Ten-District Sample: Combination (foundation level: $1,500; required tax rate (mills): 10; guaranteed tax base: $100,000; GTB rate cap above foundation level (mills): 99)

Pupil weights		
Regular	1.00	
Handicapped	2.00	
Comp.	1.30	
LEP	1.30	

District	Weighted Pupils	Property Value per Weighted Pupil ($)	Old Property Tax Rate (mills)	New Property Tax Rate (mills)	Old Revenue per Weighted Pupil ($)	New Revenue per Weighted Pupil ($)	State Found. Revenue per Weighted Pupil ($)	State GTB Revenue per Weighted Pupil ($)	Change in State Revenue per Pupil ($)	Total Revenue per Weighted Pupil ($)	Total Gain (Loss) per Weighted Pupil ($)
A	12,277	29,988	30.43	22.17	913	665	1,200	852	1,074	2,717	826
B	8,583	38,357	28.33	21.54	1,087	826	1,116	711	940	2,654	679
C	9,555	46,132	26.86	21.10	1,239	973	1,039	598	842	2,610	576
D	5,059	53,245	25.61	20.22	1,364	1,077	968	478	826	2,522	539
E	6,171	59,868	24.39	19.86	1,460	1,189	901	396	725	2,486	453
F	7,295	69,798	23.54	19.87	1,643	1,387	802	298	623	2,487	367
G	4,451	76,549	23.28	20.24	1,782	1,549	735	240	538	2,524	304
H	3,580	87,841	21.72	19.95	1,908	1,753	622	121	332	2,495	177
I	4,054	116,041	19.52	19.94	2,265	2,314	340	0	(48)	2,653	0
J	996	261,261	10.52	11.92	2,748	3,114	0	0	(366)	3,114	0
Weighted Average		59,204	25.74	20.68	1,402	1,179	926	497	734	2,601	511
Standard Deviation		34,744	3.72	1.43	419	505	261	268	323	109	241
Median		53,245	25.61		1,364					2,524	

	Totals	Change
Weighted Pupils	62,021	
Local Revenue	$73,101,323	($13,845,477)
State Revenue	$88,230,066	$47,082,975
Total Revenue	$161,331,389	$33,237,497

State Aid
Number of winners 8
Number of losers 2

Equity Measures

Horizontal equity
Range $629
Range ratio .092
Coef. of variation .042
McLoone index .991
Gini coefficient .021

Fiscal neutrality
Correlation .692
Elasticity .034

decreases from .07 to .03, and the McLoone index rises from .979 to .991, all changes in the direction of greater fiscal equity. In short, vertical adjustments for special student needs improves equity on all fronts. Of course, costs also rise, so equity gains come at a price.

ADJUSTMENTS FOR DIFFERENT GRADE LEVELS

For years, the primary grade level adjustment in school finance formulas was for secondary students, who typically were provided an additional 25 percent of resources or weighted 1.25. The rationale for this practice was that, given current patterns of elementary and secondary school organization, costs were higher for secondary students. More specialized classes were provided, more expensive educational programs (such as vocational education) were provided, and class sizes were often smaller.

Figure 8.4 shows the grade level adjustments states made during the 1986–87 school year. As expected, most states provided more for secondary students, with the extra costs ranging from 5 to 37 percent. Interestingly, several states also weighted K–3 students, up to an additional 25 percent. This practice began in the 1970s; the rationale was that if students learned successfully in the early years, compensatory or remedial programs in the later years would not be needed, at least not at current levels.

There are strong arguments for concentrating extra educational investments in the early years. Indeed, preschool programs provide long-term achievement and other benefits (Berrueta-Clement et al., 1984). Further, extended-day kindergarten programs for low-income children help boost performance in later grades (Puelo, 1988). One-to-one tutoring in the early grades produces achievement gains on the order of one-half to a full standard deviation (Slavin, 1989a; Odden, 1990d). Finally, a small class size of about 15 also improves achievement for kindergarten and first-grade students (Folger, 1990).

Such research results firmly support investing more at the early grades, perhaps even weighting K–3 students an extra 25–30 percent. Nevertheless, current practice generally is to provide more resources at the secondary level. As productivity, i.e., the link between resources and student achievement, assumes greater importance in the 1990s, the practice of allotting extra investments for the early years might also expand.

ADJUSTMENTS FOR SIZE

There is substantial controversy over size adjustments in state school finance formulas. Conditions that could produce higher costs possibly qualifying for a size adjustment in the state aid program are: (1) small school size, (2) small district size, (3) large school size, and (4) large district size. The generic policy

FIGURE 8.4 Forms of Pupil Weighting Used by States for Grade Level Differences, 1987–88

State	Program Description	Pupil Weight
Alabama	K	1.4
	1–12	1.0[a]
Alaska	Below 80 elementary and 74 secondary ADM, instructional units allocated on basis of formulas that require a lower ADM to generate instructional units at the secondary level	
	At elementary level above 80 ADM, districts get 6 units plus 1 unit per 18 ADM or fraction	
	At secondary level, districts get 7 units plus 1 unit for each additional 16 ADM or fraction	
Arizona	K–8	1.158
	9–12	1.268
Delaware	K	1.05
	1–3	1.00
	4–6	1.05
	7–12	1.05[a]
Florida	K–3	1.121
	4–8	1.000
	9–12	1.188
Idaho	For large districts (over 300 elementary and 750 secondary), secondary students have an implicit weight of 1.24; differentials exists based on state-determined schedule for smaller schools	
Illinois	Pre-K–6	1.00
	7–8	1.05
	9–12	1.25
Kentucky	K	1.087
	1–3	1.00
	4–12	1.17[a]
Louisiana	K–3	1.14
	4–12	1.00[a]
Minnesota	K	0.5
	Elementary	1.0
	Secondary	1.4
Mississippi	1–4	1.125
	5–12	1.000[a]

FIGURE 8.4 (Continued) Forms of Pupil Weighting Used by States for Grade Level Differences, 1987–88

State	Pupil Weight Program Description	
Montana	Districts generate dollars based on number of students under a variable scale; different scales used for elementary and high school districts (higher per-pupil funding at high school level)	
New Mexico	K	1.3 (half-day)
	1–3	1.1
	4–6	1.0
	7–12	1.25
New York	K (half-day)	0.5
	K (full day)–6	1.0
	7–12	1.25
North Carolina	K–9	1.15
	10–12	1.00[a]
North Dakota	*Elementary*	
	Preschool	0.49
	K	½ elem. factor
	One-room rural	1.30
	Graded < 100 pupils	1.00
	100–999 pupils	0.90
	1000+ pupils	0.95
	7–8	1.00
	Secondary (9–12)	
	1–74 pupils	1.70
	75–149 pupils	1.40
	150-549 pupils	1.32
	550+ pupils	1.20
Pennsylvania	K (half-day)	0.5
	Elementary	1.0
	Seconday	1.36
South Carolina	K	1.30
	1–3	1.24
	4–8	1.00
	9–12	1.25
South Dakota	K–8	1.00
	9–12	1.12[a]

(Continued)

FIGURE 8.4 (Continued)   Forms of Pupil Weighting Used by States for Grade Level Differences, 1987–88

State		Pupil Weight Program Description
Tennessee	K–3	1.287
	4	1.137
	5–6	1.037
	7–8	1.137
	9	1.261
	10–12	1.371
Utah	K	0.55
	1–12	1.00
Vermont	General state aid based on pupil counts (ADM) weighted for secondary and poverty costs	
Washington	Basic aid distributed on basis of units determined by size and grade	

[a] Implicit weights calculated from variations in classroom unit allocations.

Source: Deborah Verstegen, *School Finance at a Glance*, Denver, Colo., Education Commission of the States, 1988; and Richard Salmon, Christina Dawson, Steven Lawton, and Thomas Johns, *Public School Finance Programs of the United States and Canada: 1986–87*, Blacksburg, Virginia, Virginia Polytechnic Institute and State University, and American Education Finance Association, 1988.

issue is whether small (large) schools or districts experience diseconomies of scale, i.e., whether it costs more per pupil to run a small (large) school or district. If size affects school operational costs, the policy question is whether those extra costs should be recognized in the state aid formula through a special adjustment or whether the school or district should be urged or required to consolidate (break up) into a larger (smaller) entity, thereby reducing costs.

The major focus has been on small schools and districts. The general perception is that small schools or districts are inefficient and should consolidate into larger entities. Indeed, as the data in Chapter 1 showed, school and district consolidation has been a major objective over the past 50 years. Many states have incentive programs that reward small districts that consolidate into larger ones (Salmon et al., 1988).

Analysts, however, argue that the projected cost savings from massive school and district consolidation have not been realized (Guthrie, 1979), and that consolidation might actually harm student performance in rural schools (Sher and Tompkins, 1977). If small schools or districts indeed cost more but consolidation reduces performance, the better policy choice might be to resist consolidation and provide special adjustments to compensate for the higher costs.

The research knowledge on diseconomies of scale generally does not support a consolidation policy. From an economic perspective, the concept of diseconomies of scale includes both costs and outputs. The issue is whether costs per unit of output are higher in small schools or districts, or, put differently, whether costs can be reduced and output maintained as size rises. In an extensive review of the literature, Fox (1981) concluded that little research had been done to analyze output in combination with input and size variables, and Monk (1990) concluded that the meager extant research provided little support for either school or district consolidation.

For elementary schools, research knowledge is thin, but data suggest that size economies that reduce costs by more than $1 per pupil exist up to but not beyond 200 pupils (Riew, 1986). Thus, very small schools experience diseconomies of small size and, except in rural, isolated areas, could be merged into larger ones. But the real opportunities for cost savings from such consolidation are not great. Most schools of this size today have unique circumstances that preclude their consolidating, such as lying in rural, isolated areas.

At the secondary level, the data are more mixed. No research has assessed both size and output simultaneously, so scale diseconomies have not been adequately studied. Riew (1981) found that cost savings were below $1 per pupil for middle schools with enrollments above 500, and most middle schools already enroll more than this number. In analyzing whether larger secondary schools actually provided more comprehensive programs, an additional argument for larger size, Monk (1987) concluded in a study of New York that program comprehensiveness increased consistently in secondary schools for size increases up to but not beyond about 400 students. In subsequent research, Haller et al. (1990) found that although larger schools offered more comprehensive programs, wide variation existed among both smaller and larger schools, and there is no clear "tipping point" that ensures program comprehensiveness. Further, Hamilton (1983) showed that social development is better in small high schools.

Studies of district size generally analyze expenditures per pupil as a function of size but do not include an output variable, such as student achievement (Fox, 1981). To document diseconomies of district size, however, expenditures, size, and output need to be analyzed simultaneously, since the goal is to determine if costs per unit of output change with size (i.e., decrease as the number of students in the district increases). Again, in reviewing the literature, Monk (1990) concluded that definitive statements could not be made about district consolidation.

In short, there is not a strong research base for continuing to encourage school and district consolidation. As a result, states can take some comfort in maintaining their various approaches to size adjustments in school aid formulas (see Salmon et al., 1988).

ADJUSTMENTS FOR PRICE DIFFERENCES

An issue that gained prominence in school finance during the 1970s and 1980s was the difference in prices that school districts faced in purchasing educational resources. Districts not only purchase different market baskets of educational goods (just as individuals purchase different market baskets of goods), but they also pay different prices for the goods they purchase. School district expenditures cover quantity issues (numbers of different types of educational goods purchased, such as teachers, books, and buildings), the level of quality of purchased goods, and price paid for each good. School district expenditures, what a school district spends, is determined by the variety, number, quality, and price of all educational goods purchased. Although expenditures are often referred to as costs in informal school finance talk, there is a large difference between these two economic entities.

Because prices for educational resources differ across school districts, many states have taken an interest in trying to adjust school aid allocations to compensate for price differences. For example, a teacher of a certain quality level will probably cost more (i.e., the salary will need to be higher) in an urban area, where general costs of living are higher, than in a nonurban area, where such costs are lower. But price variations also exist among school districts because of variations in the nature of the work required and the quality of the working environment and local community. Teachers might accept marginally lower salaries if, for example, they were to teach four rather than five periods a day or have smaller classes. Teachers might accept marginally smaller salaries if there were many opportunities for staff development (McLaughlin and Yee, 1988). Or teachers might want marginally higher salaries if there were few cultural opportunities in the surrounding community. The combination of differences in the general cost of living, working conditions, and the surrounding community produces differences in prices that districts must pay for teachers of a given quality.

Similarly, districts within the same state might have to allocate different amounts of general revenues for such noneducational activities as transportation and heating/cooling. Districts in sparsely populated rural areas face higher-than-average transportation costs because their students are spread over a wider region and because fuel prices and repair costs may also be higher. Districts in especially cold or unusually warm environments must spend more for heating or air conditioning. These above-average expenditures are beyond the control of the district and, holding quality constant and assuming similar technical efficiency, impose higher costs on district budgets.

These are just a few examples of factors that constrain the ability of school districts, even with the same total general revenue per pupil, to provide a constant level and quality of educational services to their students. States have recognized these price and cost variations but only recently have begun to make adjustments for them in state aid formulas.

Although several different approaches can be taken in constructing education cost indexes (Berne and Stiefel, 1984; Brazer, 1974; Chambers, 1981;

Kenny, Denslow, and Goffman, 1975), there is substantial correlation among price indexes constructed with different methodologies (Chambers, 1981). Whatever methodology is used, prices can vary substantially. In studies in California (Chambers, 1978, 1980), Florida (Kenny, Denslow, and Goffman, 1975), Missouri (Chambers, Odden, and Vincent, 1976), New York (Wendling, 1981b), and Texas (Augenblick and Adams, 1979) prices for education items varied by 20 percent (10 percent above and below the average) in California and 40 percent (20 percent above and below the average) in Texas. These are substantial differences. These results mean that districts facing higher prices in California must pay 20 percent more for the same educational goods than low-cost districts; thus, with equal per-pupil revenues, high-cost districts are able to purchase only 75 percent of what low-cost districts can purchase. The differences in Texas are even greater. Such price variation, caused by circumstances and conditions essentially outside the control of district decision makers, qualifies as a target for adjustments in state aid formulas.

States can take two different approaches in using an education price index. First, state aid could be multiplied by the price index to ensure that equal amounts of state aid can purchase equal "real" amounts of educational goods. But this approach leaves local revenues unadjusted. A better way is to multiply key factors in a school aid formula by the price index to ensure that total education revenues can purchase the same level of real resources. Thus, the price index would be applied to the foundation expenditure level in a foundation program, the tax base guaranteed by the state in a GTB program, the state-determined spending level in a full state funding program, or total current operating expenditures for a percentage equalizing formula.

Including a price index in a school finance formula is relatively simple technically. Further, price indexes tend to remain stable over time (Chambers, 1981), suggesting that states would need to develop price indexes only periodically, i.e., once every three to five years, if they were used as part of a state aid formula.

Price indexes, however, alter the distribution of state aid. In general, education price indexes are higher in urban and metropolitan areas than in rural areas. Thus, with a given amount of state aid, use of a price index would shift at the margin shares of state aid from rural to urban school districts. This distributional characteristic injects an additional dimension to constructing a state aid mechanism that is politically viable.[8] Nevertheless, because prices vary across school districts and affect the real levels of education goods and services

---

[8] Since price of education indexes also are correlated with household income, a price index alters at the margin the relative distribution of state aid toward higher-income communities. This impact is partially offset if a household income measure also is part of the fiscal capacity measure, which alters at the margin the relative distribution of state aid toward lower-income communities (see Chapter 4). It could be argued that if states incorporate a price index in their school aid formula, they also should include income in the measure of local fiscal capacity, and vice versa (see Odden, 1979, 1980).

that can be purchased, including an education price index in the school aid formula is a direct way to adjust for circumstances outside the control of school district policymakers.

CONCLUSIONS

There are many legitimate reasons for states to allocate additional revenues based on certain student or district characteristics. These vertical adjustments not only are justified, but, as they are identified, they also become required as a matter of equity. Specific levels of adjustments may be refined and changed based on new research findings, but there is strong consensus that states should share in funding services for low-achieving poor children, limited-English-proficient children, and children with physical or mental handicaps. There also is consensus that price adjustments are warranted, although states have been reluctant to use price indexes developed using standard, but quite sophisticated, econometric methods. When pupil weights recognizing special needs are used and a price index added to the formula, equity analyses should use both a weighted pupil count and price-adjusted dollars.

There is less consensus regarding adjustments for secondary and early elementary students and for small (or large) size. Most states weight high school students an extra 25 to 30 percent, but this weight reflects current expenditure patterns more than productivity findings. Indeed, the research base is stronger for investing more in the K–3 grades; utilization of K–3 weightings, including extended-day kindergarten and even preschool programs for poor four-year-olds, is increasing.

Controversy still surrounds small district size. Although policymakers generally support school and district consolidation, research undergirding that policy option is thin. In general, research does not support incentives to create larger schools and districts, but state policies providing extra resources for small schools and districts in rural, isolated areas make sense.

—Chapter 9—————————————————

The Politics and Impacts of School Finance Changes, 1970–1990

School finance reforms were enacted in virtually all 50 states over the two decades between 1970 and 1990. These reforms have altered the shape of state approaches to financing schools, as well as the politics surrounding education fiscal decision making. This chapter explores the politics and impacts of the school finance changes enacted during the 1970s and 1980s. The first section discusses how issues become part of the formal policy agenda from a political science perspective. The second section uses this framework to analyze school finance changes during the 1970s. The last section focuses on changes in the 1980s.

HOW ISSUES BECOME PART OF THE FORMAL POLICY AGENDA

Issues of school finance, as well as education improvement more generally, always have been part of the ongoing policy agendas of state, local, and federal governments. In this sense, they are part of the "systemic agenda," using the terminology of Cobb and Elder (1982). But during the 1970s and 1980s, these issues became "hot" policy issues and were catapulted up to the top of state

242

policy agendas, garnering the continued attention of most state political and education leaders.

According to Cobb and Elder (1982), issues become "hot" and are placed on the formal policy agenda through the dynamic interplay of: (1) "triggering mechanisms," or shocks to or changes in the environment, and (2) political "initiators," or individuals who respond to the triggering mechanisms and provide leadership in the political arena on the issue. For education policy, most triggering mechanisms are internal, according to the Cobb and Elder typology. Internal triggering mechanisms include such occurrences as unanticipated human events, such as a riot or assassination; technical changes that allow new approaches to solving the problem; and ecological changes, such as demographic or fiscal conditions that affect the nature of the issue.

The initiators divide into four categories, according to Cobb and Elder's structure:

- "Exploiters," who manufacture issues for their own gain
- "Circumstantial reactors," who respond to unanticipated events
- "Do-gooders," who respond in order to make better public policy
- "Readjusters," who respond to make a situation or policy more balanced in its effects on various constituencies

In the 1970s and 1980s, a number of triggering mechanisms and various types of initiators interacted across the states to put school finance on the formal policy agenda and to produce a wide array of new policies and programs.

SCHOOL FINANCE REFORM DURING THE 1970s

During the 1970s, school finance reform was a dominant force that influenced and helped change the overall state politics of education (Fuhrman, 1982). Education, largely through school finance reform, became connected to the salient and more broadly based noneducation issue of property tax relief and reform (Odden and Augenblick, 1981; Fuhrman, 1978). The politics surrounding school finance demonstrated that the dominance of the education interest groups in making education policy during the 1960s (Bailey et al., 1962) had diminished, and new coalitions involving diverse pressure groups outside the education community had to be developed in order to pass school finance reform legislation (Kirst, 1978). This section first discusses the politics that surrounded the school finance reforms enacted during the 1970s and then describes the impacts in terms of new school finance policies.

The Politics of School Finance Reform

Several political aspects of school finance reform set it apart from previous school fiscal politics, as well as previous state education politics more generally.

Nevertheless, school finance reform can be viewed within a typical political science framework of how problems get translated into issues that are pushed to the formal policy agenda for concrete action. Although school finance reform is a redistributive policy issue and the politics of redistributive issues are inherently more intense and more complicated than the politics of distributive issues (Hargrove, 1983), from a more generic perspective the political events of school finance during the past two decades have followed classical political science tracks.

Courts as a new political actor. A new actor in setting education policy agendas—the courts—entered the education finance scene during the 1970s. Indeed, court cases overturning state school finance decisions became the major "triggering mechanism" for school finance reform during this decade. The court cases, or the threat of a court case in states not affected by a court decision, took school finance inequities, which had been recognized throughout the twentieth century, and placed them on the legislative agenda for new action. By declaring school finance structures unconstitutional, state courts required legislators to address, in fundamental new ways, the inequities in school finance systems. Indeed, by enjoining districts from spending state education funds in the summer of 1976, the New Jersey Supreme Court demonstrated—if only symbolically—that it had the clout to force legislators to act. Although courts were scrupulous in not requiring a specific type of legislative response, i.e., in not mandating a specific school finance structure, court actions put school finance on legislative agendas in several states, and the threat of a court suit helped catapult school finance to a top policy position in many other states. Since that time, moreover, courts have continued to play a role in school finance policy, as discussed in Chapter 2.

Changes in the political, fiscal, and technical environments surrounding school finance helped undergird these bold court actions in placing school finance reform on the policy agenda. Three changes were particularly important: the linkage of school finance to a broader issue—property tax relief, new technical expertise, and expanded state fiscal resources.

Linking school finance reform to property tax relief. Although educators had pushed school finance reform primarily to reduce fiscal inequities, many analysts argue that the connection of school finance reform to property tax reform and relief (i.e., the use of school finance reform to reduce property taxes) was the main reason for the involvement of most political leaders in school finance issues during the 1970s (Callahan and Wilken, 1976). In Colorado, for example, the governor became a school finance reform leader when two commissions he empaneled—one on the property tax and one on school finance—suggested that his commitment to provide $50 million of property tax relief could be implemented through a reformed school finance structure and revenue limits on local school districts. Several other states also used new school finance formulas to channel property tax relief to poor districts with above-average property tax burdens.

New technical expertise. A new education policy expertise emerged that helped facilitate the policy community's working through the complexities of school finance reform and other education program change. Economists, political scientists, lawyers, and other individuals nationwide with substantive social science expertise began to analyze school finance issues with new disciplinary perspectives, both adding to knowledge about the problem and creating new alternatives to solving school finance inequities. A national reform network emerged that reinforced the overall reform thrust (Kirst, 1978; Heclo, 1978; Kirst, Meister, and Rowley, 1984). Lawyers sued states. Economists and new school finance experts, both as individuals and as staff with such organizations as the Education Commission of the States and the National Conference of State Legislators, then worked with state political leaders to design new systems. And, over time, state legislative, gubernatorial, and education department staff became peppered with experts from the national school finance reform network. Within states, moreover, new staff expertise both led to the development of common data bases so that all parties used the same numbers to analyze the system and assess the impacts of alternative reform strategies and provided in-state substantive assistance to governors and legislators who were dealing with these tough issues perhaps for the first time in their political careers.

Available state revenues. The politics of school finance reform also were aided by excess state dollars. These funds allowed the states to "level up" and provide the variety of side payments needed to form the coalitions that would produce 51 percent of the votes in both houses of the legislature, as well as the governor's signature. The new revenues were derived from three major sources: (1) a growing and healthy national economy at the beginning of the 1970s, which swelled state revenue coffers; (2) large amounts of new funds from implementation in 1973 of the federal revenue sharing program; and (3) new state taxes and tax rate hikes. These considerable resources helped fund the redistributive politics of school finance reform. And when the economy turned downward at the close of the 1970s, school finance reform came, if not to a halt, at least to a hiatus (Fuhrman, 1982).

In responding to these new challenges, a new form of political leadership emerged. General political leaders—governors and legislators—rather than school superintendents and broadly representative blue ribbon commissions, rather than just representatives of the education groups, became the new political initiators and provided school finance political leadership.

Political leadership. Political leaders assumed new leadership roles. For example, governors Wendell Anderson of Minnesota, William Milliken of Michigan, Ruben Askew of Florida, and Tom McCall of Oregon, and legislators Guilbert Bursely of Michigan, Joseph Harder of Kansas, Willy Brown of California, and Bob Graham of Florida became known as school finance leaders—not only in their states, but nationally. In fact, the 1970s marked the decline of educators in setting state public school fiscal as well as program policy. Indeed, many educators opposed legislative and gubernatorial involvement in school finance, and educators' clout in political circles dropped. Yet a key characteristic of the new politics of education was precisely the involvement and leadership of governors and legislators (Fuhrman, 1978; Kirst, 1978; Fuhrman, 1982).

Use of blue ribbon commissions.   Task forces and blue ribbon commissions as a route to reform became much more the norm. Most states empaneled such groups to identify the issues, to analyze the specific status of their state's school finance structure, and to begin the compromise and coalition building process to craft an acceptable reform package. These commissions usually represented all major interest groups, the governor and legislature, and education communities. Educators were often a small minority on these commissions.

Finally, the political process of making new school finance policy became much more complex, in part because it required allocating more resources to some districts than to others. School finance moved from being a quiet political issue, with policy designed by leading superintendents, to a complex coalition building activity. Further, legislative rather than initiative routes to reform were much more successful.

Coalition building politics.   The politics of school finance reform were accurately described as "coalition building," i.e., full of side payments required to build the political coalition needed to pass the program (Kirst, 1978).[1] All new legislative programs need to build coalitions, but the coalition needed to support school finance reform was more complex, for several reasons. First, it was a redistributive program, and inducements were needed to convince the politically powerful representatives of wealthy suburban school districts (not the big winners in a school finance reform) to vote for a program that provided most if not all of its benefits to other jurisdictions. Second, urban districts that had concentrations of low-income and minority students also often had a large per-pupil property tax base and lost state aid in a revised general aid program; some adjustments were needed to make sure they gained and did not lose revenues. Third, rural districts, which still had considerable although declining political clout, commonly had higher property wealth and also needed inducements to vote for the reform package. Fourth, state political leaders who were providing large amounts of increased revenue, sometimes with tax rate increases, wanted mechanisms to ensure that the new expenditures were justified.

Various side payments developed for these diverse groups help to explain some of the complexity of the new school finance structures that emerged. Enhanced special education programs injected increased revenues into many suburban school districts, and the "level up" approach often meant that they received at least modest increases instead of decreases in general aid. These strategies often were sufficient to convince suburban legislators to vote for the package. Compensatory and bilingual education programs and urban adjustments such as density factors or municipal overburden adjustments (discussed

---

[1] Side payments were additional education programs and policies providing funds to districts that did not fare well in a general school finance reform.

in Chapter 2) induced many urban legislators to join the coalition. Rural adjustments and income factors were sufficient to tip some rural legislators into supporting the reform. Property tax relief (which benefited all taxpayers, not just the education community) strengthened fiscal capacity equalization programs, and tax and spending limitations were reform components that helped general political leaders (i.e., governors and legislators) justify the large new state fiscal role in supporting schools. In short, the coalition politics that emerged as a characteristic of school finance reform became intertwined with the complexities of the new finance structures themselves.

Legislative rather than initiative routes. Finally, the legislative route to school finance reform was much more successful than the initiative route (Fuhrman, 1978). Several states, including California, Colorado, Oregon, and Michigan, attempted to enact school finance changes via initiative. All failed. Legislators, by contrast, enacted reforms in nearly 30 states.

The Impacts of the 1970s School Finance Reforms

Nearly 30 states fundamentally changed their school finance structures during the 1970s, either under court order, under the threat of a court order, or through legislative leadership (Odden, 1982). There were eight major impacts associated with these reforms.[2]

Increased revenues. Education revenues increased from all sources during the 1970s. As Figure 1.3 showed, total revenues rose from $40.3 billion in 1970 to $96.9 billion in 1980, a nominal rise of $56.6 billion, or 140 percent. After adjustment for inflation, total expenditures per pupil increased 36 percent.[3] In short, whatever other goals were associated with school finance reform, such as fiscal equity or property tax relief, a major effect was to boost overall funding for public schools.

Shifting governmental roles. During the 1970s, there was a shift in governmental roles in financing schools. As shown in Chapter 1, local districts entered the 1970s as the dominant provider of school revenues, but the states exited the 1970s with the largest fiscal role. In 1990, states provided about 50 cents of each public school dollar.

Restructured general aid programs. States restructured their general aid programs to create more fiscally neutral school finance systems. The new state programs were designed to more powerfully compensate for different fiscal capacities across school districts, to reduce the relationships between expenditures per pupil and local district per-pupil property value, and even to reduce

---

[2] This section is drawn from Odden and Augenblick (1981) and Odden, McGuire, and Belsches-Simmons (1983).
[3] Part of the large per-pupil increase was caused by enrollment decline.

overall spending differences. In most states, the new programs "leveled up" resources for all districts, but especially low-spending, low-wealth districts were the largest beneficiaries of these new programs.

Three major types of school finance formulas were used. Several states substantially increased the expenditure level of their foundation programs. As shown in Chapter 7, this change produces short-term improvements in fiscal equity. However, in states that continued to allow local fiscal add-ons funded solely through local property taxes, these programs began to look like the fiscally nonneutral structures they replaced. Several other states, including Colorado, Connecticut, Michigan, and Wisconsin, enacted guaranteed tax bases to create structures that produced approximately equal per-pupil revenues from state and local sources for equal school tax efforts; of course, these systems let local districts set tax rates and therefore allowed spending differences. The differences, however, largely were a result of tax effort and not the local property tax base. Finally, a number of states, including Maine, Missouri, and Utah, enacted two-tiered, combination foundation and guaranteed tax base programs. These programs provided for higher base spending across all districts but also made sure that the same extra tax effort above the foundation level produced the same extra per-pupil revenues from state and local sources.

Improved equity.   The new school finance strategies produced increased school finance equity, at least in terms of fiscal neutrality, immediately after the reforms in each state. Studies showed that equity increased in California, Colorado, Illinois, Michigan, and Minnesota, for example (Odden, Berne, and Stiefel, 1979; Carroll and Park, 1983; Hickrod, Chaudhari, and Hubbard, 1981). In several states, moreover, spending disparities themselves decreased in the short term (Odden, Berne, and Stiefel, 1979).

Expanded measures of fiscal capacity.   States expanded the measures of fiscal capacity used in school finance formulas. Income was added to the formula in several states. For example, Connecticut, Kansas, Maryland, Missouri, Ohio, Pennsylvania, Rhode Island, and Virginia added income to their measures of school district fiscal capacity. Today, almost 20 states have an income factor in their school aid formulas. Other states discussed differentiating fiscal capacity on the basis of the composition of the property tax base and considered treating residential and nonresidential property differently.[4]

Treatment of special-needs students.   States paid increased attention to special-needs students by strengthening categorical programs for the handicapped, low-income, and limited-English-proficient students or by enacting new categorical programs for these students. Many of these programs funneled relatively more dollars into urban districts at the expense of suburban districts. By the end of the 1970s, all states had enhanced special education programs, 24 states had

---

[4] See Chapter 4 for a discussion of more comprehensive measures of fiscal capacity and the role of household income in school finance.

compensatory education programs or compensatory education pupil weights, and 22 states had bilingual education programs (McGuire, 1982).

District needs. There was an expansion of categorical programs targeted at special district needs during the 1970s. Urban adjustments included cost-of-living or cost-of-education adjustments, municipal overburden factors, use of per capita wealth measures (which made some cities look much poorer on a relative basis), and density and poverty adjustments. For rural districts, sparsity and small-size adjustments were enacted, and transportation programs were enhanced. Growth adjustments often benefited property-poor, suburban bedroom communities. Some formula adjustments, such as declining enrollment factors, helped both urban and rural, but not suburban, districts.

Tax and spending limits. A number of new constraints on local fiscal decision making, including tax and spending limitation measures, were enacted. Prior to California's 1978 Proposition 13, which lowered the property tax rate to 1 percent of assessed value, 37 states had enacted expenditure increase limitations, school tax rate caps, or education budget limits. These constraints often followed the large, new sums of state dollars that flowed into the education system and were, in part, the price of an enhanced state fiscal role.

In short, state school finance structures were both more sophisticated and more comprehensive at the close of the 1970s. School finance reform began as a focused attempt to reduce the linkages between revenues and the local tax base, but ended addressing a much broader agenda. The politics of enacting new school finance programs that provided more revenues to some districts and fewer to others, i.e., the politics of redistributive programs, help explain the increased complexity of school finance at the close of the decade.

SCHOOL FINANCE CHANGES DURING THE EDUCATION REFORM ERA OF THE 1980s

Several of the broad 1970s themes are reflected in the 1980s politics of education and school finance reform. Education was again a top policy issue in the states and the nation. This time the broader policy issue to which education became linked was economic growth rather than property tax relief (Odden and Dougherty, 1984). Nearly all political actors believed that education improvement was key to maintaining state and national economic competition (McDonnell and Fuhrman, 1986). New political initiators, including for the first time the business community, began to congregate around education as a policy issue, further diminishing the role of educators in the politics of education and school finance. At the same time, education and school finance policy continued its journey into new arenas of comprehensiveness and complexity. This section first discusses the politics that surrounded school finance and education policy reform in the 1980s and then describes the impacts of those reforms.

The Politics of the 1980s
Education and School Finance Reforms

Although more distributive in nature than the clearly redistributive school finance reforms of the 1970s, the politics of education and finance reform in the 1980s nevertheless were complicated. Again, education became attached to noneducation issues—international economic competition and local economic growth—which thrust education into a priority position on state policy agendas. New actors, especially the business community, entered the politics surrounding these issues. And the policy initiatives were again triggered by an external event, this time publication of a national education reform report.

Stimulus from a "triggering event." Just as the courts were the "triggering event" that spawned the school finance reforms of the 1970s, an external event also catalyzed education reform in the 1980s. This was the April 1983 release of *A Nation at Risk,* a federal report that discussed a "rising tide of mediocrity" in the nation's public schools and called for deep and comprehensive changes. This report galvanized the entire country around the importance of improving public schools and returned education, which had been slipping from state policy agendas (Fuhrman, 1982), priority.

The courts, primarily through school finance decisions, continued its important role in education and school finance policy. In 1989, moreover, the Kentucky Supreme Court took a school finance case and used it to overturn the entire Kentucky education system—finance, program, and governance—thus using finance inequities as a lever to begin a major, state-led education restructuring venture.

Gubernatorial political leadership. Whereas previously both gubernatorial and legislative leaders were at the forefront of education reform, in the 1980s governors moved into the preeminent role (Mueller and McKeown, 1986). Governors appointed most of the state blue ribbon education reform task forces. The National Governors Association targeted education reform as its priority issue (National Governors Association, 1986). At the end of the decade, the governors had an education summit with the president and in early 1990 agreed upon nationwide education goals (White House, 1990). Indeed, by the close of the decade, governors and the course of education reform had become permanently linked (Elmore and Fuhrman, 1990a).

Nevertheless, state legislators also were active in leading education reform in the 1980s. Indeed, all reform legislation was enacted by state legislators (Elmore and Fuhrman, 1990b). And in many states, specific legislators were the primary leaders for both education and school finance reform. The federal role, however, was primarily through the "bully pulpit" (Jung and Kirst, 1986) and included few new programs and a decline in real funding (Odden, 1990a).

The business community as a new political actor. Another new actor—the business community—entered the politics of education in the 1980s. Corporate leaders had remained outside K–12 education politics prior to the 1980s.

But when education improvement became a key to economic growth, the business community joined in the K–12 public policy debate with gusto. Business roundtable groups in several states issued their own education reform reports, the national Committee for Economic Development (1985, 1987) issued reform reports, the national Business Roundtable created an education reform commission represented by CEOs from the largest American corporations, and the National Alliance for Business began a long-term process of efforts to improve the schools. Today, the business community remains involved in K–12 education and school finance policy and views education improvement as the key to the health of corporate America and the U.S. economy.

The increased role of governors and legislators in making education policy, combined with the entrance of the business community, further reduced the role of the education community in affecting either education fiscal or program policy. A major political result of school finance and education policy in the 1970s and the 1980s has been the eclipsing of educators' roles in the policy making process.

Continued use of task forces.   States continued to use the blue ribbon task force as vehicle for education and finance reform. In the wake of the early 1980s *Nation at Risk* report, states created hundreds of blue ribbon task forces (Education Commission of the States, 1984). And throughout the 1980s, education reform task forces have been created to continue the reform momentum.

Coalition building politics.   The politics of the 1980s education and school finance reforms also included coalition building and new side payments, all of which cost money. The business community extracted several new programs as the price for their support and new money, including, for example, the requirement that high school students pass an exit examination to graduate and a relaxation of teacher dismissal regulations. The business community wanted to make sure children performed at minimum levels before leaving schools and wanted educational administrators to be able to terminate non-performing teachers. Second, the education and general political communities traded big, new funding increases for the enacting of new career ladder, or pay-for-performance, programs. Teachers received large across-the-board salary increases funded through the general aid program, while political leaders had new career ladder programs enacted, in part to pay the best teachers more. Third, educators received other new sources of money but in the form of restricted or targeted categorical programs. Thus, new money was provided, but its use was directed by political and business leaders. These and other examples show how the coalition politics of education reform involved compromises and political trade-offs but also produced bold new programs, many of which came with fairly large price tags.

A new political economy for increasing education dollars.   A new political quid pro quo emerged for increasing education funding. No longer would many state political leaders provide money on the stump through the equalization formula and hope that local educators would use it to improve the education system. The new political economy directive was "more money, but only for reform" (Massel and Kirst, 1986). Indeed, many of the reforms that states enacted did not bring new funds; the expectation was that the new dollars included without restrictions in the general aid formula would be used to finance the reforms. "More money, but only for reform or improvements" continues as the political condition for increasing school financing.

The Impacts of the 1980s Education and School Finance Reforms

Nearly all states enacted some version of an education reform during the 1980s, and many included school finance modifications as well (Murphy, 1990). The policy changes shared a number of characteristics.

Increased education dollars.   In the 1980s, as in every decade since World War II, education revenues increased, in both nominal and real terms (Odden, 1990a). As Figure 1.3 showed, total revenues rose from $96.9 billion in 1980 to $195.2 billion in 1990, a nominal rise of $98.3 billion, or 101 percent. After adjusting for inflation, total expenditures per pupil increased 30 percent. In short, whatever other goals were associated with education and school finance reform in the 1980s, a major effect was boosted overall funding for public schools.

The state as the lead public school funder.   There was a solidification of the state role in funding schools. In response to the federal cutbacks during the first portion of the 1980s, states acted to protect key programs and, even during the early 1980s recession, raised tax rates to balance state budgets. During this time, moreover, states generally protected the fiscal base for education more so than for other functional areas (Gold, 1983). Further, in the mid- and late 1980s, states provided substantial new resources to fund expensive education reforms, often increasing state taxes to do so (Odden, 1990a). During the 1980s, the state role in funding education reached the 50 percent mark, making states the majority providers of school funds.

School finance reform continued.   States continued to implement school finance reforms. Arkansas, under a court order to change its school finance system, postponed action until it created a bold new education reform. The resulting school finance reform was targeted not only on creating fiscal equity but also on funding a program designed to improve the public schools. Likewise, Texas linked education and school finance reform. State legislators decided to alter the school finance structure, which was not adequate as a fiscal base for the state's ambitious 1984 education reform. Further, California enacted several important modifications to its school finance system as part of its 1983 reform package. In short, education reform dominated education policy, but school finance reform was not ignored (Odden and Dougherty, 1984).

New types of categorical programs.   States created a new series of "education reform" categorical programs focused on improving curriculum, instruction, and student achievement, rather than on special-needs students. School improvement, mentor teacher, high school writing, textbook purchasing, counseling, career ladder, and performance incentive programs proliferated across the nation, each usually funded with a separate new categorical program, and each a component of a broad strategy to improve the regular school program. These programs further expanded the comprehensiveness and complexity of state school finance structures (Odden and Dougherty, 1984).

Unfortunately, most of the funds for these programs were distributed on a flat grant basis to local school districts. Policy makers forgot that the formula structure itself, in addition to the new funds, could induce local behavior in the direction of reform objectives (Picus, 1990). Nevertheless, most new money was distributed through the regular school finance equalization formula (Odden and Dougherty, 1984), and the amount of money specifically targeted at reform programs was not large (Jordan and McKeown, 1990).

Continued attention to special-needs programs.   States also continued to expand the number of and funding for special-needs student categorical programs. For example, South Carolina enacted a large K–12 compensatory education program, and Texas included new pupil weights for students eligible for compensatory and bilingual education.

Linking money to quality improvements.   The new political quid pro quo (discussed earlier) surrounding new money for education led to a more earnest effort to link finance to education quality improvements. States created a variety of new fiscal incentives (Richards and Shujaa, 1989) to reward schools and districts for meeting education improvement objectives. These are discussed at more length in Chapter 11.

Increased revenues.   States found new revenues to finance most of these reforms. The new revenues were derived from two major sources: (1) a healthy national economy, which produced natural increases in tax revenues, and (2) tax rate increases.

Economic Growth.   Although some (Odden, 1987) have suggested that education reform produced the real education revenue increases during the 1980s, other research (Hawkins, 1989) found that economic growth was the primary factor. Hawkins analyzed whether education reform, economic conditions, or demographic variables accounted for changes in education revenues across the states. Her analyses showed that economic variables (i.e., economic growth) dominated and that none of the education reform variables were statistically significant. She concluded that the country's and, as a corollary, a state's economic health was the major factor in producing education revenue increases during the 1980s. She did not disparage the saliency of education reform and suggested that reform impetus helped to keep education on the state policy agendas. But her statistical results documented the strength of economic over political variables. The policy implication is that maintaining a healthy national and state economy is the primary route to increasing education revenues.

Tax Rate Increases.   Although a growing economy was the major factor in producing increased education revenues, hikes in tax rates also played a role, but at the state and local district level, not at the federal level. The 1980s witnessed major declines in national tax rates, particularly income tax rates.

On the other hand, many states and numerous local school districts hiked tax rates to produce new revenues to finance education reform. At the state level, increased sales tax rates were the most popular tax rate increase strategy. States such as Arkansas, Florida, South Carolina, Tennessee, Texas, and Utah all raised the sales tax rate and generally used the proceeds to help fund major education reforms. In addition, many states mandated increases in local property tax rates to produce even more revenues.

The equity of the impact of these tax changes, however, differed from the 1970s. For school finance reforms of the 1970s, more regressive property taxes were reduced and more progressive state income taxes increased, thus improving the overall progressivity of state and local tax structures. In the 1980s, however, sales and property taxes were raised and the income tax changed to make it more proportional. The result probably reduced the overall progressivity of many state and local tax structures.

Non-Broadly Based Tax Sources.   New education revenues from sources other than income, sales, and property taxes, always the hope of many, were tried in some states and local school districts but produced only small amounts of funding. There was much talk of a rise in the number of local school foundations, i.e., nonprofit fund-raising organizations for a local school. But even in affluent communities they produced very little in the way of additional revenues—less than 1 percent of the budget (Meno, 1984).

Several states also enacted lotteries during the decade. But lotteries are very inefficient revenue raisers and generally produce only small amounts of new revenue (Mikesell and Zorn, 1986). In general, every dollar of lottery sales produces only 35 cents of net revenue. In California, which dedicates the lottery to K–14 education, the lottery produces about $150 per child of a total budget of about $4,000 per child, or about 3.75 percent. Although this amounts to a large total—about 1 billion a year—it still constitutes a small percentage of the overall budget. Put differently, if big money is the goal, lotteries and local school foundations are not the answer.

Dedicated Revenue Sources.   Another strategy for producing education revenues was to "dedicate" a revenue source (such as the sales tax), a tax rate increase (such as the 1 cent sales tax increase in Arkansas and South Carolina), or even a portion of the state general budget (as mandated by California's Proposition 98) to education. The theory was that dedication would ensure that all the revenues go to education and, over the medium and long run, would mean more money for the schools. The immediate conclusion was that dedication does not work. In a recent review of this issue, Gold (1990) concluded that dedicating tax resources for education or any other function does not work; there simply are too many legislative ways around dedication requirements. Also, as educators found in California, the "floor" also became the "ceiling," as the legislature proved unwilling to appropriate any more to schools than required by Proposition 98.

PROGNOSIS FOR THE 1990s

There is no crystal ball for predicting the course of education reform or education revenues for the 1990s. Although pessimists and optimists abound, history shows that real revenues always rise in large percentages. Furthermore, if economic growth and tax rate increases are the major engines that produce school funding, there seems to be sufficient good news on these fronts to paint a modestly optimistic scenario. American industry has substantially restructured itself to be more productive, U.S. exports are rising and reducing the trade deficit, and interest rates are predicted to drop during the 1990s. In general, the economic prognosis is on the plus side, as long as international events do not interfere in deleterious ways.

Moreover, California's 1990 approval of a constitutional proposition to modify its state expenditure limit and to raise taxes to improve its highways was interpreted as a signal of the end of the tax limitation movement and the beginning of a new era of addressing pressing social needs.

Finally, education reform is still firmly entrenched in a priority spot on state and national policy agendas, supported by a broadening spectrum of the politically powerful. The business community increasingly sees elementary and secondary education improvement as key to world market economic competitiveness. The president and the nation's governors set ambitious national education goals, including our becoming first in the world in mathematics and science; these goals can be accomplished only with increased educational investments.

Accept the modest scenario that real per-pupil education revenues will rise in the 1990s at about the same rate as they did during the 1980s and 1970s—about one-third. That is substantially more than a marginal increase. The policy issue, therefore, may not be how to use a marginal increase in education dollars, which restricts the available options. The issue, simply drawing on the fiscal history of the past 40 years, may be how to use *substantially increased* education dollars. Resolving this issue in a way that substantially improves student achievement and the productivity of a state's public education system, in addition to reducing traditional school finance inequities, may become the key school finance agenda for the 1990s. This may require analyzing educational expenditure needs in a way that differs from the incremental processes used in schools today. Even if funds do not rise in large amounts, the policy issue nevertheless is how strategically and productively to invest the new revenues.

Chapter 10

Allocation and Use of Funds at the District, School, and Classroom Levels

Distributing dollars to districts in equitable ways is a first step in providing educational programs and services for the purposes of educating children. Interdistrict resource allocation has dominated the study of school finance for years. But there is insufficient information on how to put dollars to productive use in districts, schools, and classrooms. Indeed, there is considerable misinformation about how schools use money. Former U.S. Secretary of Education William Bennett implied that too much money was used for administration; he popularized the term the "administrative blob." And a recent study of New York City implied that for every dollar that reached high school classrooms, $2 were lost in four layers of "overhead" (Sarrel and Cooper, forthcoming).

As this chapter shows, little is known about what happens to dollars once they reach districts. The policy questions that require answers are:

- Where did the money go? To instruction? To administration and the alleged administration "blob"? To support services? To raise teachers' salaries? To lower class size? To lengthen the school day or year? To "overhead"?
- How was the money used? To increase instruction in the regular program? To boost instruction in the core academic programs? To teach more curriculum content? To improve mathematics and science, subjects in which the country plans to be first in the world? To provide services for special-needs students? How does resource use differ across elementary, middle, and high schools?
- What impact did the funding have on student achievement? How do resource allocation and use patterns relate to student performance? Have these patterns changed to produce more student learning? Are the linkages different at the elementary, middle, and high school levels?

School finance as a field of study cannot answer these questions very well today, but it is hoped that answering these straightforward and important questions will be a major focus of school finance research in the 1990s.

Since schools and classrooms are the "production units" in education, gathering data on resource allocation and use at these levels should guide future research. For each level of schooling—elementary, middle, and high school—the following types of data are needed:

- Expenditure by program: the regular instruction program; programs for special-needs students, such as compensatory, bilingual, and special education; administration; staff development; and instructional materials
- Expenditures by content area: mathematics, language arts (reading in elementary schools), science, history/social science, foreign language, art, music, and physical education
- For each of the preceding, expenditures by student: male, female, black, Hispanic, Asian, Anglo, other, poor, limited-English-proficient, and handicapped
- Interrelationships among these expenditure patterns
- Relationships of these expenditure patterns to student performance

The field of school finance is far from having these kinds of data. Accounting systems based on the accounting codes of Handbook II, Revised (National Center for Education Statistics, 1980) need to be changed to create these data. At the present time, few states are able to report expenditures by program area with their current accounting systems.

Nevertheless, these data are the minimum needed to address the productivity issues that policymakers will raise over the decade of the 1990s (see also Kirst, 1988). They will want to know where new money goes, what resources—especially curriculum content and instructional resources—it buys, and what impact those resources have on student performance. These are reasonable questions. If, for example, the country expects to be first in the world in mathematics and science achievement, it is important to know how much currently is spent on mathematics and science instruction at the elementary, middle, and high school levels, and whether new funds will be allocated to boost mathematics and science instruction. In the future, it will be important to know if expenditures in those content areas actually increase and, if not, where increased funds go.

Total expenditures by level for elementary, middle, and high schools across the United States and within most of the 50 states are not known. Data are not systematically collected by education level. Yet, as discussed in Chapter 8, educational investments for the early years appear to offer high yields in terms of student achievement. Perhaps one reason that student achievement is low is because our nation underinvests in education for the early years, particularly pre-K and K–3, and overinvests at the secondary and postsecondary levels.

This chapter describes what currently is known about how dollars are used. The first section describes expenditures by function and staffing patterns on national and statewide bases. The following section discusses how expenditure and use patterns vary across districts within a state, especially across different spending levels. The next, unfortunately short, section describes what is currently known about expenditures by program, school, student, and content area. The fourth section reviews current knowledge on the relationship between resources and student achievement. The last section presents a conceptual framework for analyzing how inter- and intradistrict resource level and allocation patterns can be combined with variables on students and schools to determine the linkages between traditional school finance issues and student performance.

EXPENDITURES BY FUNCTION AND STAFFING PATTERNS

All 50 states collect some kind of fiscal data from their school districts. These data include information on district revenues and expenditures and on district employees. The revenue data generally contain information on the sources and amounts of revenue received by each school district. Expenditure data are most frequently collected by object of expenditure, broken into categories such as certificated salaries, classified salaries, employee benefits, materials and supplies, and capital expenditures. Some states collect expenditure data by broad program area or function, such as instruction, administration, transportation, plant operation and maintenance, and debt service.

Staffing data usually include information on the number of certificated staff employed by each district and on job title, such as teacher, administrator, principal, librarian, and counselor. Some states maintain data bases with information on instructional aides as well. In a few states, data on teacher credentials and/or teaching assignments are also available.

Analysis of these data provides initial information on how school districts allocate resources, but to date this information has been inadequate to answer the important productivity questions raised earlier.

Staffing data usually include numbers of professional staff and, within that, numbers of administrators, teachers, librarians and counselors, instructional aides, and support staff. In some states, data on teacher credentials and/or assignments are also available. Analyzing these data provides a beginning step toward knowing how money is used, but the results are several steps removed from the data needed to answer important productivity issues. Nevertheless, these data provide a starting point for identifying how districts use money.

Expenditures by Function

Annually, the National Center for Educational Statistics (NCES) provides nationwide and individual state data on expenditures by function. But because definitions for functional categories differ across states, the NCES reports expenditures across only a few very broad functional categories. Data for 1986–87 are presented in Figure 10.1. Only three functional categories are presented: instruction; support services, which include administration, operations and maintenance, and transportation; and noninstructional. Nationally, 61.1 percent of all funds were spent for instruction, 35.4 percent for support, and 3.5 percent for noninstructional purposes.[1]

Individual state patterns differed, but not dramatically, from this pattern. Hawaii, for example, which funds public education almost entirely with state

[1] These figures are similar to unpublished data from the Educational Research Service, which show, according to Kirst (1988), that 66.1 percent was spent on instruction in 1986-87. Again, small percentage differences could be caused by definitional differences.

Figure 10.1 Current Expenditures (millions) by Function for the United States and Selected States, 1986–1987

	Total	Instruction		Support Services[a]		Noninstructional	
		Amount	*Percent*	*Amount*	*Percent*	*Amount*	*Percent*
U.S. average	$146.7	$89.6	61.1	$51.9	35.4	$5.1	3.5
California	16.5	9.3	56.1	6.7	40.8	0.5	3.1
Hawaii	0.58	0.35	61.1	0.19	33.6	0.03	5.3
Kentucky	1.6	1.2	73.2	0.35	22.0	0.08	4.8
New Hampshire	0.59	0.38	65.0	0.20	33.6	0.01	1.4
New Jersey	6.1	3.9	63.5	2.0	33.5	0.2	3.0
Tennessee	2.2	1.5	69.9	0.51	23.5	0.1	6.6
Texas	10.2	6.1	59.8	3.5	34.4	0.6	5.8
West Virginia	1.2	0.59	48.2	0.57	46.7	0.06	5.1

[a] Support services include general and school administration, operations and maintenance, and transportation, among others.

Source: National Center for Education Statistics, *Digest of Educational Statistics, 1989,* Washington, D.C., NCES, 1989, p. 154.

Figure 10.2   Percentage Distribution of Expenditures by Function, 1920–1980

	1930	*1940*	*1950*	*1960*	*1970*	*1980*
Total expenditures, all schools	100.0	100.0	100.0	100.0	100.0	100.0
Current expenditures, all schools	80.0	83.4	80.9	79.8	85.7	91.2
Public elementary & secondary schools	79.6	82.8	80.3	79.0	84.1	90.6
Administration	3.4	3.9	3.8	3.4	3.9	4.4
Instruction	56.9	59.9	53.3	53.5	57.2	55.5
Plant operation	9.3	8.3	7.3	6.9	6.2 ⎤	10.6
Plant maintenance	3.4	3.1	3.7	2.7	2.4 ⎦	
Fixed charges	2.2	2.1	4.5	5.8	8.0	12.3
Other school services[a]	4.4	5.5	7.7	6.6	6.3	8.3
Summer schools[b]				0.1	0.3	<0.05
Adult education[b]	0.4	0.6	0.6	0.2	0.3	N/A
Community colleges[b]				0.2	0.3	N/A
Community services[a]				0.4	0.6	0.6
Capital outlay[c]	16.0	11.0	17.4	17.0	11.5	6.8
Interest on school debt	4.0	5.6	1.7	3.1	2.9	2.0

Note: Beginning in 1959–60, includes Alaska and Hawaii. Because of rounding, details may not add to totals.
[a] Prior to 1959–60, items included under "other school services" were listed under "auxiliary services," a more comprehensive classification that also included community services.
[b] Prior to 1959–60, data shown for adult education represent combined expenditures for adult education, summer schools, and community colleges.
[c] Prior to 1969–70, excludes capital outlay by state and local schoolhousing authorities.

Source: National Center for Education Statistics, *Digest of Educational Statistics, 1989,* Washington, D.C., NCES, 1989, p. 151.

dollars, spent the same percentage—61.1—on instruction as the national average, and a little less on support services. New Hampshire, which has the largest local role in funding public education, spent 65 percent on instruction, slightly above the national average. Kentucky spent the largest percentage on instruction, 73.2 percent, and West Virginia spent the smallest, 48.2 percent.

As Figure 10.2, shows, moreover, these broad patterns of expenditure have not changed much over the years. Using more functional categories, Figure 10.2 indicates that between 1930 and 1980 instructional expenditures varied from a low of 53.3 percent in 1950 to a high of 59.9 percent in 1940. The 1980 figure was 55.5 percent. The portion spent for administration has increased about 1 percentage point since 1930. The largest increase has occurred in the fixed charges category, which usually includes employee benefits. These results suggest that there has not been a dramatic decline in the amount spent on instruction over the past 50 years, somewhat contrary to popular perception.

Even with these broad categories, states define instruction, administration, and support differently, so these figures might not accurately reflect instruction and noninstruction expenditure patterns, although NCES attempted to portray comparable data. California, for example, claims that its instructional

FIGURE 10.3   California School District General Fund Expenditures, 1986–87

Category	Amount (millions)	Percent
Total	$14,836.3	
Teacher salaries	6,613.2	44.6
Administrator salaries	495.1	3.3
Other certified salaries	827.9	5.6
Instructional aides	490.4	3.3
Other support personnel	2,003.6	13.5
Employee benefits	2,247.6	15.1
Books and supplies	656.0	4.4
Services and operating expenses	1,075.3	7.2
Capital outlay	427.2	3.2

Source: James W. Guthrie, Michael W. Kirst, and Allan R. Odden, *Conditions of Education in California, 1989,* Berkeley, University of California School of Education, Policy Analysis for California Education, 1990.

expenditures appear artificially low, that several categories of expenditures included in the support/administrative category really are instructional. But, as shown in Figure 10.3, California's standard functional categories are different from those used by NCES and not easily converted to the NCES categories. California's standard report does not separate district from site expenditures for administrators, other certified salaries, and support personnel. In fact, California's categories are more objects of expenditures than functions.

To adjust for different definitions of functional expenditures, NCES commissioned several studies in the late 1980s to obtain comparable expenditure patterns across the states. The preliminary nationwide figures for 1988–89 are presented in Figure 10.4. The numbers confirm the results in the previous

FIGURE 10.4   Current Expenditures by Function for the United States, 1988–89

	Amount (billions)	Percent of Total
Current operating expenditures (excluding food services and enterprise activities)	$165.53	100.00
Instruction	101.93	61.58
Support	17.27	10.43
Other direct program support	6.02	3.64
School administration	9.52	5.75
General administration	4.94	2.98
Operation and maintenance	18.70	11.30
Transportation	7.15	4.32

Source: Preliminary results from the NCES 1988–89 National Public Education Financial Survey, December 1990.

figures. First, nationwide instructional expenditures account for 61.58 percent of total current operating expenditures. Total administration represents 8.73 percent of the total, operations and maintenance 11.30 percent, and transportation 4.32 percent. Two categories of support services account for 14.07 percent of total expenditures. Although increasing instructional expenditures might be a laudable goal, the data show that other school system functions also require resources, and that for every $3 spent on direct instruction, only $2 are spent on other functions.

Staffing Patterns

Translating these broad expenditures into staffing patterns is one next step toward analyzing district spending patterns. Figure 10.5 presents national data on the number and distribution of school district staff by staffing category for fall 1987. Administrators do not appear to represent a large portion of the total. District, or central office, administrators totaled 1.7 percent and site administrators another 3.1 percent. Administrators accounted for just 4.8 percent of all staff, which about equals the percentage spent on administration in Figure 10.2.

Instructional staff represented 66.5 percent of total staff (63.4 percent if site administrators are excluded), which approximately equals the percent spent on instruction indicated in Figures 10.1, 10.2, and 10.4. One of the more interesting statistics in Figure 10.5 is that 31.7 percent of staff are in noninstructional and nonadministrative roles, such as secretaries and operation, maintenance, and transportation personnel. If policymakers and local taxpayers wonder why only 60 percent of expenditures is spent on instruction, one answer is that operations, maintenance, transportation, and a small amount of district admin-

FIGURE 10.5   Staff Employed in the Public Schools, 1987

	Number	Percent of Total
District administrators	75,134	1.7
Instructional staff	2,868,577	66.5
Site administrators	133,464	3.1
Teachers	2,278,813	52.8
Teacher aides	337,061	7.8
Counselors	71,024	1.6
Librarians	48,215	1.1
Support staff	1,368,758	31.7
Total	4,312,469	

Source: National Center for Education Statistics, *Digest of Educational Statistics, 1989,* Washington, D.C., NCES, 1989, p. 84.

istration accounts for nearly one-third of public school expenditures. Although expenditures in any category can be analyzed on efficiency criteria, it appears that noninstructional expenditures do not support the allegation of an "administrative blob."

These broad staffing categories are at best indirect indicators of how school funds are spent. Figure 10.6 disaggregates the figures a little more and shows the percentage distribution of secondary teachers by content area for 1981 and 1986. These data can be used to determine whether high school staffing patterns changed after the release of *A Nation at Risk*[2] in 1983. These figures give some indication of the amount spent by content area, important information in an era when improved student performance in the core academic content areas is a national goal. In 1981, 65.2 percent of secondary teachers were in the core academic areas of English, mathematics, science, social studies, and foreign language. That number increased to 69.3 percent in 1986. Since one objective of the 1983 era of educational reform was to increase teaching of core academic subjects (Murphy, 1990), these staffing shifts are in line with reform goals.

[2] Interestingly, secondary teachers make up about 43 percent of all teachers, a higher percentage than represented by secondary students. This is due in part to the fact that most high school students take six classes whereas secondary teachers generally teach five, and is further evidence that the country spends more on high school than on elementary school students.

FIGURE 10.6   Secondary Teachers by Content Area, 1981 and 1986

	Percent of Total	
Subject	*1981*	*1986*
Agriculture	1.1	0.06
Art	3.1	1.5
Business education	6.2	6.5
English	23.8	21.8
Foreign language	2.8	3.7
Health/PE	6.5	5.6
Home economics	3.6	2.6
Industrial arts	5.2	2.2
Mathematics	15.3	19.2
Music	3.7	4.8
Science	12.1	11.0
Social studies	11.2	13.6
Special education	2.1	3.5
Other	3.3	3.4
Total	995,000	970,000

Source: National Center for Education Statistics, *Digest of Educational Statistics, 1989*, Washington, D.C., NCES, 1989, p. 73.

Staffing changes for individual subject areas were even more impressive. Mathematics teachers rose from 15.3 percent to 19.2 percent of the total, an increase of nearly one-third. Social studies teachers increased from 11.2 to 13.6 percent of the total, probably reflecting more teaching of American History, world history, and geography. And foreign language teachers increased from 2.8 to 3.7 percent of the total, an increase of about one-third. Science teachers dropped from 12.1 to 11.0 percent, and English teachers dropped from 23.8 to 21.8 percent of the total.[3] The increase in the academic areas came at the price of a loss in other areas. The percentage of teachers in agriculture, art, home economics, and industrial arts all fell, with industrial arts teachers falling by more than 50 percent. These numbers suggest that academics "won" and vocational education "lost" in terms of resource shifts reflected by secondary teachers in the years following the publication of *A Nation at Risk*. Although not definitive, the numbers indicate that resource allocations shifted in line with 1980s education reform expectations. Unfortunately, similar staff data are not available for elementary and middle schools.

In the late 1980s, NCES began a comprehensive school and staffing survey (SASS) to produce more detailed information on how schools and classrooms

---

[3] In some states, this pattern for English teachers masked important changes within the English curriculum. Often, the number of elective and remedial teachers dropped and the number of individuals teaching English 1, 2, 3, and 4, i.e., academic English, rose.

FIGURE 10.7   Elementary and Secondary Teachers by Primary Assignment Field, 1987–88

	Percent of Total	
	Elementary	*Secondary*
English/Language arts	1.3	15.5
Mathematics	1.3	13.8
Social studies	0.8	12.0
Science	0.8	11.9
General elementary, prekindergarten, and kindergarten	78.1	—
Special education	13.4	9.0
Foreign language	0.2	3.7
Art/Music	2.0	7.0
Vocational education	0.2	18.8
Physical education	2.1	8.3
Total	14,204	19,183

Source: Sharon A. Bobbit and Marilyn Miles McMillen, "Teacher Training, Certification, and Assignment," paper presented to the annual meeting of the American Education Research Association, Boston, 1990.

are staffed across the country. The data tapes became available in late 1990 and can be used in future analyses to identify staffing patterns by state, level of education, primary field assignment, and a variety of teacher characteristics.[4] Figure 10.7 indicates for 1987–88 the distribution of teachers by primary assignment field for the overall SASS sample for both elementary and secondary schools. The data show that the majority of teachers in elementary schools were elementary school generalists, with very few having content-specific assignments. Also, 13.4 percent of elementary teachers were in special education. At the secondary level, 52.2 percent of the teachers in the sample had assignments in the academic core areas of English/language arts, mathematics, social studies, and science, somewhat below the figures in the preceding NCES reports. Only 9.0 percent of secondary teachers were in special education, but close to 18.8 were in vocational education. These nationwide data provide the beginnings of detailed information on staffing patterns, but future analyses disaggregating the data to state and local levels will provide even more useful information on how dollars relate into staffing patterns.

EXPENDITURE PATTERNS ACROSS DISTRICTS WITH DIFFERENT SPENDING LEVELS

Because education services are organized by local education systems—school districts—and provided in schools and classrooms, statewide expenditure patterns need to be disaggregated to these lower levels. This section first analyzes several studies of expenditure patterns across districts within a state, grouped according to spending levels, and then reviews the research on how districts use new money.

Expenditure Patterns across Districts within a State

Over the years, only a few detailed studies of school district expenditure patterns have been conducted. Two are discussed here, one conducted in the late 1970s for a New York task force created in response to a lower court's overturning the state's school finance structure in 1978 (Odden, Palaich, and Augenblick, 1979), and the other conducted in the late 1980s using data from Pennsylvania (Hartman, 1988). In general, the findings from the two studies are similar.

Figure 10.8 displays several expenditure categories and resources by high, medium, and low levels of operating spending levels for New York districts for the 1977–78 school year.[5] The numbers reflect several characteristics of interdistrict expenditure patterns within a state, some similar to the patterns discussed earlier and some different. First, instructional expenditures constituted about 60 percent of state/local operating expenditures per pupil, quite close to the

---

[4] Characteristics include sex, race, ethnic origin, age, marital status, level of education, major assignment field, and area of licensing.

[5] The data are for expenditures from state and local revenues only.

FIGURE 10.8 Selected Expenditures by Function and by Level of Spending in New York, 1977–78

Component of Per-Pupil Expenditures	Level of Spending[a]		
	High	*Medium*	*Low*
Operating expenditures	$2,863	$1,850	$1,325
Central district administration	80 (3%)	42 (2%)	48 (3%)
Central district services	329 (11%)	240 (13%)	156 (11%)
Instruction	1,822 (63%)	1,107 (59%)	800 (58%)
Employee benefits	559 (19%)	373 (20%)	271 (20%)
Transportation	114 (4%)	105 (6%)	104 (8%)
Instructional expenditures	1,822	1,102	800
Curriculum development and supervision	175 (10%)	116 (10%)	55 (7%)
Teacher salaries	1,303 (72%)	807 (73%)	619 (77%)
Noninstructional salaries	28 (2%)	21 (2%)	9 (1%)
Books, materials, and equipment	58 (3%)	41 (4%)	36 (5%)
Pupil services	138 (8%)	71 (6%)	47 (6%)
Special-needs students	220 (12%)	219	195
Teachers			
Pupil/classroom teachers	17.2	18.9	20.4
Median teacher salary	$22,037	$16,654	$12,716
Percent with only a B.A.	9.1	20.2	33.4
Percent with M.A. and 30 points or a doctorate	35.9	15.3	6.0
Percent with more than 10 years of experience	68.2	53.8	43.6

[a] High is highest-spending decile; middle is decile 6; low is lowest-spending decile.

Source: Allan Odden, Robert Palaich, and John Augenblick, *Analysis of the New York State School Finance System, 1977–78,* Denver, Colo., Education Commission of the States, 1979.

national average. Second, instructional expenditures per pupil as a percent of total operating expenditures increased with spending level, from 58 percent for the bottom decile, to 59 percent in the middle, to 63 percent for the top decile. This pattern was different from the Pennsylvania results, as well as results from earlier studies in Michigan and California, which will be discussed in the next part of this section.

Employee benefit expenditures, often called fixed costs, consumed about 20 percent of expenditures across all spending levels, higher than the national figures. Expenditures for central office administration and services also represented about an equal percentage of expenditures across all spending levels. Transportation, on the other hand, constituted a declining percent of the budget as spending rose.

Spending for special student needs such as compensatory and bilingual education totaled about $200 per pupil for all three spending levels. Since levels differ substantially in overall operating expenditures per pupil, this finding shows that spending for special-needs students constituted a much higher percentage of operating expenditures in low-than in middle- or high-spending districts. This finding undergirds the importance of a strong and fair state role in supporting services for special-needs students (see Chapter 8).

Although the proportion spent on instruction increased from just 58 to 63 percent, the dollar amount of the increase was large: $800 per pupil in the low-spending decile, $1,107 in the middle, and $1,822 at the high-spending decile. These differences produced different patterns in expenditures for teachers. Low-spending districts spent 77 percent on teacher salaries, compared with only 72 percent in the high-spending districts. Nevertheless, the high-spending districts spent more than twice the per-pupil amount on teachers—$1,303 compared to $619. These higher expenditures were reflected primarily in different salaries; the median salaries were almost twice as high in the high-spending districts as in the low-spending districts. Class sizes differed only marginally in New York, ranging from 20.4 in the lowest-spending districts to 17.2 in the higher-spending districts. In general, class sizes were uniformly low. Thus, differences in spending on teachers were reflected primarily in differences in teacher salary levels. These results are different from the Pennsylvania, California, and Michigan studies to be discussed, for which the bulk of differential teacher salary expenditures were used to hire more teachers in order to reduce class size.

Further, there were large differences in teacher education and experience across spending levels in New York. The higher-spending districts had substantially more teachers with doctorates, or master's degrees plus 30 additional units, than the middle- and low-spending districts, and substantially fewer teachers with just bachelor's degrees. In addition, higher-spending districts had more teachers with greater than 10 years of experience.

Thus, in New York, higher-spending districts paid teachers more and hired teachers with greater education and experience, the typical teacher quality indicators. By spending a lower percentage of their instructional budget on teachers, higher-spending districts were able to spend more on curriculum development and supervision and pupil services than the middle- and low-spending districts. Class size, however, was about the same—consistently low in all New York districts.

In Pennsylvania, the expenditure patterns across spending levels are similar to those in New York, with two major exceptions, as shown by the data in Figure 10.9. Instructional expenditures as a percent of current expenditures decreased as current spending increased, although the decline was slightly more than 3 percent; and a larger portion of teacher expenditures were spent on reducing class size than on increasing teacher salaries. In terms of other patterns, higher-spending districts had teachers with slightly more education and experience (although the differences were not as dramatic as in New York) and had more support and administrative personnel.

These two studies show that higher-spending districts purchase a different mix of educational services than low-spending districts. They hire more

FIGURE 10.9 **Expenditures by Function and Other Resources by Expenditure Levels in Pennsylvania, 1984–85**

Component of Per Pupil Expenditures	Level of Spending		
	High	*Medium*	*Low*
Current operating expenditures	$4,298	$2,759	$2,266
Instructional expenditures	2,497 (58.1%)	1,650 (59.8%)	1,389 (61.3%)
Support expenditures	1,698 (39.5%)	1,046 (37.9%)	827 (36.5%)
Noninstructional expenditures	103 (2.4%)	63 (2.3%)	50 (2.2%)
Teacher resources			
Student/teacher ratio	15.7	19.2	21.0
Average teacher salary	$28,065	$22,345	$20,474
Education level[a]	5.8	5.5	5.4
Years of experience	23.9	23.0	22.1

[a] Education level: 4(3 yrs. of college), 5(B.A.), 6(M.A.), 7(M.A. + 30 grad. units), 8(M.A. + 60 grad. units), 9 (doctorate)

Source: William Hartman, "Policy Effects of Special Education Funding Formulas," *Journal of Education Finance,* 13(4), 436–459.

teachers, administrators, and support personnel; they hire teachers with more advanced education and years of experience; they pay them more (sometimes dramatically more); they have lower class sizes; and they provide more pupil support services and a greater variety of instructionally related support services. These studies show common patterns in what higher spending districts purchase with their additional money. A reasonable assumption would be that local education leaders believe these extra purchases will produce more student learning. In a later section of this chapter, the relationships between these variables and student achievement are discussed.

How Districts Use New Money

How districts spend money generally is important knowledge for policy purposes. What they do with *increases* in budgets is also an interesting policy concern. In the early 1970s, when school finance reforms were spawned by the early school finance court cases, the policy community was interested in "how districts would use new money." The conventional view was summarized by Moynihan (1972):

> Who will benefit from this [equalization]? The question is easily answered: Teachers will benefit. Any increase in school expenditures will in the first instance accrue to teachers.

At that time, the hope was that increased dollars would not lead to increases in teacher salaries. In the 1980s, when schools received a nearly one-third real increase in revenues per pupil (see Chapter 1 and Odden, 1990a), the policy community again wanted to know "how districts would use new money." During that decade, however, increased teacher salaries was an explicit policy objective and a hoped-for result. This part first reviews the knowledge on where school finance reform dollars went in the 1970s and then examines data on where education reform dollars went in the 1980s.

Three major studies investigated how districts would use dollar increases provided through the 1970s school finance reforms, or through normal year-to-year budget changes. Two of the studies (Alexander, 1974; Barro and Carroll, 1975) analyzed cross-sectional data for districts with different spending levels in California and Michigan, respectively. Their goal, similar to the New York and Pennsylvania studies, was to determine how higher-spending districts within a state used their greater revenues. The focus of these two studies, however, was on teacher-related expenditures. The authors assumed that as district budgets increased, the new spending patterns likely would be similar to patterns in the higher-spending districts identified in a cross-sectional analysis.

The findings from both studies were very similar. Several were particularly important:

- Per-pupil expenditures for teachers increased at a slower rate than total current operating expenditures. Barro and Carroll found that as the total budget increased by 1 percent, teacher expenditures per pupil increased by 0.75 percent. Alexander found that only 41 percent of each additional dollar was spent on teachers.
- Expenditures for administrators also increased at a slower rate than total spending.
- Expenditures for specialists and for supplies and equipment increased at a much faster rate than total spending. Barro and Carroll found that as total spending rose 1 percent, spending for specialists rose 1.5 percent, and spending on other resources rose 1.6 percent.

Further, these studies found that increased expenditures on teachers did not translate into large salary hikes. Alexander found that less than half, and Barro and Carroll found that only one-third, of increased expenditures on teachers were used to increase salaries. The bulk of the new money—63 percent in the Barro and Carroll study—was used to hire more teachers, i.e., to increase the teacher/student ratio. Further, both studies found that beginning teacher salaries were quite insensitive to expenditure increases, with elasticities relative to increases in total expenditure per pupil between .1 and .15.

In short, the authors found that as district spending levels increased, districts tended to use the money to increase nonteaching aspects of the budget, and that those dollars used to increase teacher expenditures were primarily used to increase teacher/student ratios, with only a small portion used to raise average teacher salary levels. Since the policy community did not want new money simply to increase teacher salaries, these findings were viewed with favor by legislators enacting school finance reforms.

Kirst (1977) directly studied how local districts used the new dollars they received from school finance reform. He analyzed how spending changed in K–12 districts in Los Angeles County that received a 15 percent increase in state aid from a 1972 California school finance reform in response to the *Serrano* v. *Priest* suit. He too found that salary increases were marginal, in the 5–7 percent range. His study showed that the bulk of new funds were used to hire additional instructional personnel, with some funds used to reduce class size, some to add periods to the school day, and some to hire specialists. The specific roles of the new staff varied across districts, but all districts exhibited a pattern of hiring more professional personnel rather than hiking salaries or salary schedules.

Studies of how new funds received as part of the 1980s education reforms were used by districts are fewer. Descriptive studies (Odden, 1990a) showed that teacher salaries increased by substantial amounts in real terms. This was good news in the 1980s since raising teacher salaries was a core policy objective. If the 1970s and 1980s findings on average teacher salaries are compared, it seems that school systems responded to policy intention by not increasing salaries inordinately in the 1970s and then by increasing salaries in real terms in the 1980s. Whether policy intent was the reason for local behavior cannot be determined, but the result of local action on teacher salaries was in line with policy intent.

In an econometric analysis of local district response to increased funds from a major education reform, Picus (1988) found that districts increased instructional expenditures more in response to fiscal incentives to increase the length of the school day and year than in response to increases in unrestricted general aid revenue.[6] Analyzing the data over a multiple time period, Picus also found that these instructional expenditure boosts dissipated when California "rolled" the incentive funds into the district's general aid grant. Chapter 11 discusses other results of the Picus study and describes more comprehensively the role incentives might play in future school finance structures.

In a case study of local district response to Texas's 1984 reforms, Verstegen (1988–89) found in the second year after the reforms that expenditures for instruction had also increased, from 55.6 percent of the current operating expenses to 58.3 percent, a jump of 2.7 percentage points. She also found that expenditures for both central office and site administration dropped slightly, although the changes were not statistically significant. Both the Picus and Verstegen studies suggest that local leaders allocated more funds to instruction in the years immediately following a 1980s state education reform, although Picus suggested that the budget shifts might erode in the longer term.[7]

---

[6] This finding is consistent with predictions derived from intergovernmental grant theory discussed in Chapter 4.

[7] Verstegen's study also identified expenditures by function for 1986–87. The results parallel the patterns discussed earlier in this chapter. Approximately 5.8 percent was spent for central office administration, 6.9 percent for site administration, 58.3 percent for instruction, 2.2 percent for instructional support services, 12 percent for other pupil services, 2.9 percent for transportation, and 12 percent for operations and maintenance.

No other econometric studies of local response to the 1970s or 1980s real revenue increases for education have been conducted. Jordan and McKeown (1990) argue that not much money was appropriated specifically for reform programs during the 1980s, but others (Odden, 1990a) argue that large revenue increases were provided even if the level of expenditures specifically marked "reform" dollars was not high.

In short, there is limited information on how districts use increased education dollars. Hopefully, this knowledge gap will be closed during the 1990s. The fact is that, as Chapter 1 showed, real education revenues per pupil rise substantially every decade, despite predictions to the contrary. When real per-pupil revenues rise by one-third, the policy community expects a one-third rise in student performance, yet performance did not rise by that magnitude during either the 1980s or the 1970s. Knowing more about how new money is used could help explain why performance does not rise at the same levels as revenue increases.

One hypothesis is that most of the new money is spent on providing extra educational services to rising numbers of special-needs students. Empirical research analyzing expenditures by program and student is needed to show whether or not that hypothesis is true.

Drawing upon the past decade's patterns, another hypothesis is that spending patterns did not change dramatically in the 1980s, and thus increased student performance should not be expected. This has been Hanushek's (1981, 1989) argument for several years. Although his point has been misinterpreted, he argues that if increased funds are not used to alter educational practices and thus expenditure patterns, major impacts on student performance should not be expected. If changes do not occur, real spending increases simply make the system more expensive, not more effective. Odden (1990e) suggests that since education revenues increase each decade by at least 25–33%, local education leaders should assume that a similar revenue hike will occur during the 1990s. The hope is that they can create a robust vision of a restructured school system that will have a more substantial impact on student learning and, through the use of these new revenues as well as through the reallocation of current dollars, finance that vision.

There undoubtedly are other hypotheses about how school districts use new money. By the end of the 1990s, research will be needed to show how new money was spent by education program, school, student, and curriculum content area and how those patterns relate to student achievement. These data are crucial if the school finance community is to contribute to the debate about how to make the country's education system more productive, i.e., about how to use new revenues to increase student performance.

EXPENDITURES BY PROGRAM, SCHOOL, CLASSROOM, STUDENT, AND CURRICULUM CONTENT AREA

Unfortunately, little is known about how public school dollars are spent by program, school, student, and curriculum content area. Approximations for some program expenditure items can be gleaned by analyzing revenues by programmatic categories. Chapter 8, for example, provides some information on federal and state revenues for compensatory, bilingual, and special education. There are three problems with these data: the figures do not include local revenues, which in many cases are substantial; the revenue figures are not comparable across states; and the revenue figures are not available for many states.

Further approximations can be made by analyzing pupil weighting studies to get a sense of the magnitude of extra expenditures for certain programs— again the special-needs programs such as compensatory, bilingual, and special education. But few states systematically provide comprehensive expenditure data by all programmatic categories such as:

- The regular instruction program
- Content programs, such as mathematics and science
- Special programs, such as compensatory, bilingual, special, vocational, gifted, and talented
- Staff development

The culprit, in part, is the accounting system. For years, school districts tracked expenditures only by objects such as salaries, benefits, books and other instructional materials, supplies, rent, or operations and maintenance. Then, in the 1970s, accounting systems began to organize object expenditures into different functional categories such as:

1. Administration, sometimes divided between site and central office administration
2. Instruction, sometimes (but usually not) divided between direct classroom instruction and instructional support, such as staff development and curriculum development
3. Operations and maintenance
4. Transportation
5. Fixed charges, such as employee benefits (unfortunately, not linked to the different salary expenditures that induced the benefits charge)
6. Capital
7. Debt service

This grouping of expenditures represented a step forward, but it still has not been implemented in a consistent manner across all states. Indeed, for the past twenty years, NCES has worked with states to use a common accounting document, called Handbook II, followed by Handbook, II Revised (National Center for Education Statistics, 1980). But these documents have not been used, and few states have a program accounting system.

The real policy issue concerns expenditures by program, school, and curriculum content area. To produce these figures, functional expenditure items need three additional codes indicating the program, school (elementary, middle, or high school level), and curriculum content area for which the expenditure is made. The last category would be somewhat difficult for elementary schools, although studies could be made to determine school and/or district patterns (see Chapter 3). Although several states have account codes for programs and even schools, few districts and fewer states collect such data and make them publicly available. Technically, these data could be collected. Perhaps as the policy saliency of these data becomes more known during the 1990s, they will become systematically available.

Expenditures by School and Classroom

Two major studies on expenditures by school and classroom form the current information base on how funds are used below the district level. Figure 10.10 presents 1985–86 California expenditures on a school basis (Guthrie, Kirst, and Odden, 1990). The numbers represent a statewide average for all schools, merging data for elementary, middle, and high schools, for which expenditure patterns undoubtedly differ. Nevertheless, this was one of the first studies that provided information on expenditures on a school level. The figures show that 63 percent of all expenditures were spent directly on classroom services, which is close to the percentages spent on instruction specified in earlier sections. Of this total, only 50 percent was spent on classroom and specialized teachers. How was the other 13 percent spent in the classroom? Instructional aides constituted one large portion, 5 percent; pupil personnel support, such as guidance counselors, constituted another 4 percent; and books, supplies, and equipment

FIGURE 10.10   California Expenditures per School, 1985–86

Category	Expenditures per School	Percent of Total
Classroom expenditures	$1,286,000	63%
22 classroom teachers	914,000	45%
2.5 specialized instructors	102,000	5%
7.0 instructional aides	94,000	5%
2.0 pupil personnel support	84,000	4%
Books, supplies, equipment	92,000	4%
Other site expenditures	629,000	31%
Operation, maintenance, and transportation	395,000	19%
Instructional support	95,000	5%
School site leadership	139,000	7%
District/County administration	120,000	5.5%
State department of education	11,000	0.5%
Total operating expenditures	$2,046,000	100%
School facilities/Capital	$133,000	

Source: James W. Guthrie, Michael W. Kirst, and Allan R. Odden, *Conditions of Education in California, 1989,* Berkeley, University of California School of Education, Policy Analysis for California Education, 1990.

made up the remaining 4 percent. Thus, the data indicate that about two-thirds of expenditures were on direct classroom services.

What made up the one-third noninstructional elements? First, about 31 percent was spent on other site-related items—site administration; site instructional support, including curriculum support and staff development; and operations, maintenance, and transportation. Only 6 percent was spent on district, county, and state administration. Thus, 37 percent of California 1986–87 school site expenditures were spent on nonclassroom activities. Hayward (1988) shows that for many of these expenditure items, the amount spent per item (per meal served, per student transported, per square foot of physical plant, etc.) was below the norm in the private sector, suggesting that school system expenditures were not profligate.

These figures begin to take the mystery out of how educational dollars are spent. Although only 50 cents of each dollar was spent on teachers, the other 50 cents was not simply wasted. Of course, the efficiency of expenditures in all categories can be examined, but the fact is that all categories of expenditures are needed. Students must be transported to school. Schools must be operated, heated or cooled, and maintained. Some central administration is necessary, and 6 percent is not a large figure. Books, materials, supplies, professional staff development, and instructional support services are needed.

In short, nonteacher expenditures are not lost in the alleged "administrative blob." Although a dramatically restructured school might have different spending patterns and produce more student learning, current spending patterns are not unreasonable. The route to improving school productivity is not in attacking administrative costs, although such costs are probably too high in many districts. The route is determining what works to boost student learning and making sure dollars support those strategies.

National data on classroom expenditures generally confirm these California subdistrict school expenditure patterns. Figure 10.11 shows nationwide classroom expenditures for 1984–85 (Fox, 1987). These numbers also reflect a merged elementary, middle, and high school classroom. The figures show that "other" expenditures, including transportation, operation and maintenance, food services, and fixed charges, constituted about one-third (33.2 percent) of total expenditures. Nonsite administration constituted another 7.2 percent.

Instruction and site administration accounted for 58.6 percent of total expenditures, with classroom teachers and other specialist teachers making up 40.4 percent of total expenditures. Indeed, these national data show that the percentage of expenditures for teachers nationwide was lower than in California, and that the percentage spent on instruction and site administration expenditures were somewhat below that spent in California.

Despite the marginal differences, the data indicated that at the classroom level, the large portion of expenditures not directly instructionally related is not lost in some "administrative blob." These expenditures are maintenance, transportation, food services, and fixed charges, all components that must be funded in any system, education or otherwise.

FIGURE 10.11 **Nationwide Expenditures per Classroom, 1984–85**

Item of expenditure	Amount (percent of total)	
Total	$78,422	
Nonsite administration	5,646	(7.2)
District and state administration	3,058	(3.9)
Clerks (district and site)	2,588	(3.3)
Site administration	2,353	(3.0)
Principals	1,647	(2.1)
Assistant principals	706	(0.9)
Instruction	43,801	(55.6)
Teachers	23,546	(30.0)
Curriculum specialists and other classroom teachers	8,336	(10.4)
Other professional staff	1,490	(1.9)
Teacher aids	1,804	(2.3)
Library media specialists	549	(0.7)
Guidance and counseling	1,176	(1.5)
Instructional materials	6,430	(8.2)
Pupil support services, attendance, health	470	(0.6)
Other Nonadministration and instruction	26,036	(33.2)
Maintenance	8,783	(11.2)
Transportation	3,451	(4.4)
Food service	3,137	(4.0)
Fixed charges (insurance, benefits, etc.)	10,665	(13.6)

Source: James Fox, "An Analysis of Classroom Spending," *Planning and Changing,* 18 (3), 154–162.

Expenditures by Student

The country lacks systematic data on expenditures by student, including categories of students such as male and female; minority and nonminority; general, academic, and vocational education track; and special needs such as compensatory, bilingual, and special education. Such data are needed in order to understand more fully the resource distribution dimension of why some groups of students achieve at higher levels than others. Expenditure data by different student categories would help further probe the differential in mathematics and science performance between boys and girls; the achievement gap between minorities and nonminorities; and the achievement differences among students in general, academic, and vocational education tracks.

The most comprehensive information on expenditures by type of student is that for special needs students, as discussed in Chapter 8. The country has a good sense of expenditures for special education, although the data derive not from routinely collected fiscal data, but from periodically conducted special studies. There is less comprehensive and valid data on expenditures for compensatory, bilingual, and vocational education, although the types of studies discussed in Chapter 8 give some indication of expenditures for compensatory and bilingual education students.

The lack of data on expenditures by student is somewhat surprising because differential expenditures on students by income and race gave rise, in part, to the school finance reform movements in the late 1960s and early 1970s. Sexton's (1961) study of Chicago showed systematic differential expenditures between poor and nonpoor students within the district. The 1966 *Hobson* v. *Hansen* court case in the Washington, D.C., school district also focused on intradistrict resource disparities between low and high income and minority and nonminority students.

Although expenditure data are not normally tracked by student type, Ginsberg et al. (1981) conducted a study of inter- and intradistrict resource allocation among low-income and minority students on a school basis, using 1976–77 New York data. Their findings are interesting because a common prediction was that expenditures would be lower in schools with higher concentrations of poor and minority students. What these authors found was that the needier schools—those with higher concentrations of minorities, poverty, and low-achieving students—tended to have greater than average expenditures. Although individual teachers in these schools had less education and experience on average and thus lower salaries, there were both more teachers and more paraprofessional teacher aides in them. Thus, quantity offset quality difference, with the result that the needier schools had the higher educational expenditures. Surprisingly, total resource distribution patterns using local, state and federal funds actually favored low-income and minority schools.

These findings are important. A 1990 suit in Los Angeles alleged that district resource distribution patterns discriminated against schools with concentrations of low-income, ethnic, and language minority schools largely because teachers in these schools had less education and experience and thus lower salaries. If the New York findings hold for California and Los Angeles, which have a greater number of categorical programs specifically targeted on low-income, minority, and limited-English-proficient students, the results could show that total resources per pupil in these schools are above the average and exceed those in higher-income and less minority schools.[8]

Nevertheless, there is insufficient information on resource distribution and use patterns by important categories of students. The information that is

---

[8] Indeed, exactly these findings were produced in a study of mid-1970s resource allocation in Los Angeles. Choy and Gifford (1980) found that while expenditures per pupil from regular funds were about 10 percent lower in primarily black and Hispanic schools, they found that expenditures per pupil from all funds (i.e., including special needs categorical funds) was 17 percent higher in black and Hispanic schools. Their findings generally paralleled those of Ginsberg et al. that categorical program dollars more than compensated for the lower expenditures from regular funds.

available, moreover, is produced from special funded studies that occur periodically, rarely within any one state. Expanding information in this arena is another research imperative for the 1990s and another important cog in the wheel of educational productivity.

Expenditures by Curriculum Content Area

There is almost no information on expenditures by curriculum content area. The data are not collected nationally, and no state systematically collects such data. As mentioned earlier, however, such data are crucial in order to link fiscal allocations with the country's goal of being number one in the world in mathematics and science. Information on expenditures by curriculum area are also important more generally for meeting the aggressive National Goals for student achievement in all subject areas.

In addition to gathering expenditure data by content area, the types of curriculum and instruction resource data discussed in Chapter 3 will also be important for pushing the frontiers of educational productivity in the 1990s. What and how students are taught are major determinants of student learning (Porter, forthcoming). We know that (1) time provided to different content areas varies widely by teacher and school (Denham and Lieberman, 1980) and (2) curriculum content within and across subjects varies by students, especially those in different academic tracks (Oakes, 1990).

It could very well be that these curriculum and instructional resource disparities are the most critical factors behind differences in student learning. It also could be that higher-spending districts provide on average more curriculum content and instruction in thinking and problem solving than is provided by lower-spending districts, further spreading the distribution of student performance. Indeed, Murphy and Hallinger (1987) show this to be the case for effective school programs in high- and low-SES communities. In short, obtaining fiscal and other resource data by curriculum content area and student should be a key future research priority. At the minimum, these data will help further resolve the mystery behind the relationships between resources and student performance.

KNOWLEDGE ON THE RELATIONSHIP BETWEEN FISCAL AND PHYSICAL RESOURCES AND STUDENT ACHIEVEMENT

There is a fairly solid research base for answering questions about the relationship between fiscal resources and student performance. Although the research does not include the more disaggregated data on curriculum and instruction as it relates to student achievement, it does include analysis of the relationships between the types of resources on which school districts usually spend education dollars and typical measures of student achievement.

The first two sections of this chapter showed that, according to the limited research that exists, higher-spending school districts and school districts that receive large increases in resources typically spend their additional dollars on

- More teachers to reduce class size
- Teachers that have more education and experience

The impact of these variables on student achievement has been analyzed from several different research perspectives.

There is some controversy about the impact of class size, but several recent studies conclude that only dramatic reductions in class size are likely to improve student achievement. The earlier Glass and Smith (1979) meta-analysis of class size and student achievement concluded that class size below 20, and especially down to 15, produces significant gains in student performance.

Slavin (1984), however, criticized this research on three grounds. First, a meta-analysis includes all studies, both those that are methodologically sound and those not methodologically sound. Slavin argued that only studies with methodologically sound research designs should be analyzed. Second, even for such a reduced sample, the Glass and Smith meta-analysis included several studies in which student achievement was not academic achievement, but physical achievement such as learning to play tennis. Slavin argued that these studies should be excluded, and that only studies investigating class size and student academic achievement should be analyzed. Third, Slavin showed that the effects for classes with fewer than 20 students were statistical artifacts, not based on empirical examples: classes with between 14 and 18 students had very modest positive impacts on student achievement; there were no classes with between 3 and 14 students, and the classes with large achievement gains were essentially one-to-one or one-to-two tutoring programs.

Finally, the Glass and Smith review did not include any studies on the impact of class size reduction over a number of years. It is inaccurate to assume that the impact of a one-year class size reduction can simply be multiplied by a number of years to indicate the long-term effect. Indeed, the recent Tennessee class size reduction experiment showed that the small class effect was produced in the first two years and had no additional impact in the next two years (Folger, 1990).

Slavin (1989a), Tomlinson (1989), and Odden (1990d) concluded that the research evidence for small class size supports only one-to-one or small group (up to three students) tutoring. Further, Slavin, Karweit, and Madden (1989) and Odden (1990d) argue that one-to-one tutoring in grades one and two can be a powerful intervention, with achievement impacts of more than 0.5 standard deviations and up to one full standard deviation, and can keep children in these grades performing at grade level. Folger (1990) shows that substantial impacts also are produced by class sizes around 15 for just kindergarten and first grade. In short, the research on class size and student achievement does not support overall class size reductions, and it primarily supports one-to-one tutoring, especially for students in the early grades, and class size reductions just for kindergarten and first grade.

Thus, even though most districts spend increased dollars to lower class size, class size research suggests that these are not highly productive uses of those dollars. The economic production function research reinforces this conclusion about class size and also analyzes the impact of expenditures for greater teacher education and experience. Although there are major conceptual and measurement obstacles in conducting production function research (Hanushek, 1979), several studies have been conducted over the past 30 years. In reviewing these studies, Hanushek (1986; 1989) concluded that the studies did not systematically find that either class size, teacher education, or teacher years of experience were systematically related to student achievement. These conclusions have generally been reached by other reviewers of this literature (see for example, Monk, 1990; Rossmiller, 1983), but some reviewers have interpreted the data more optimistically (MacPhail-Wilcox and King, 1986b).

In addition to findings on these variables for which dollars are spent, the production function research rarely finds that higher expenditures per se are related to greater student performance (Hanushek, 1989; Monk, 1990). A major reason, of course, is that if districts generally use more dollars to hire more teachers and to hire teachers with greater years of experience and education, variables not strongly related to higher student performance, then the expenditure figure itself is unlikely to be related to student performance.

Again, there are different interpretations of the research findings. Childs and Shakeshaft (1986), for example, conducted a meta-analysis of the relationship between fiscal (i.e., expenditure) variables and student achievement, and they found that the average correlation coefficient from 45 studies with 417 correlations was positive, +0.1023. In a school-based study in New York, using data reported above on expenditure patterns (Odden, Palaich, and Augenblick, 1979), Wendling and Cohen (1981) found that student achievement was positively related to expenditures per pupil, teacher education, and teacher experience.[9] And Murnane (1983) identified five factors from the production function literature that were consistently associated with increased student learning:

- Teacher verbal ability
- At least some teacher experience, between three and five years
- Effective teaching strategies
- Teacher attitudes and expectations
- Socioeconomic composition of students

So an argument can be made that higher expenditures and some of the variables on which districts spend resources are related to higher student achievement.

---

[9] Curiously, they also found that achievement was negatively related to class size. Recall, however, that class sizes in New York were on average quite low at that time.

There are several reasons why the production function research has been relatively unsuccessful in identifying relationships between resource uses and student achievement. First, production function research assumes that all school systems are pursuing the same goals, and that those goals are related to student achievement. The fact is that school systems pursue a variety of goals, and in many cases student achievement may not be the primary goal. Increasing high school graduation rates, boosting post-secondary participation rates, enhancing self-esteem, and improving performance in the post-high school labor market are all reasonable goals, related to but not the same as student achievement. Further, the measures of student achievement are usually standardized achievement tests, but as discussed in Chapter 3, these are not good indicators of what students have learned.

Second, it is difficult to identify inputs. Moreover, production function studies seek to relate inputs to outcomes, and ignore processes. Not only is it difficult to obtain a consensus on the types of inputs to analyze,[10] and studies tend to vary widely on the inputs analyzed, but also other research in education suggests that process variables—curriculum and instruction—may be the critical factors linked to student learning (Wittrock, 1986). Inputs could be reconceptualized to mean the enacted curriculum and instructional quality, but since production function analysis ignores process, this might not be an acceptable approach for a production function study.

Third, there are difficulties in determining the functional relationship among variables. Most studies assume a linear relationship, but the linkages might be curvilinear, logarithmic, or interactive. Fourth, most literature reviews do not distinguish among production function studies by unit of analysis: district, school, classroom, or student. Not only is there more variation within districts, schools, and classrooms than across these entities, but also more positive results are found between resources and achievement as the unit becomes smaller (see, for example, Wendling and Cohen, 1981; Summers and Wolfe, 1977). Finally, most studies use cross-sectional rather than longitudinal data and thus cannot analyze "value added," the real issue in relating education to achievement. There are other issues that have limited the ability of production function research to identify patterns of relationships between resources and student achievement (see Monk, 1990 for example).

A final, important issue related to production function studies is their assumption about technical efficiency, that is, the assumption that teachers and administrators work to maximize student achievement. This assumption, which seems reasonable, is problematic for several reasons. First, as mentioned above, there is no consensus on school goals. With the creation of National Education Goals in early 1990, this dilemma perhaps can be overcome during the 1990s. Policymakers see student achievement as the primary school goal. Now that student achievement has been explicitly stated as an education goal,

[10] It also is difficult to obtain comparable measures of school inputs.

a clearer focus of local education activities on accomplishing these goals during the 1990s might evolve.

Second, however, educators might legitimately never seek to maximize student performance. This might seem counterintuitive, but maximizing student achievement would work against equity orientations that are part of most school systems. The way to maximize average student performance is to spend less time and effort with lower-performing students and more time with brighter students, even accelerating their instruction over more and more complicated curriculum content.

But the country has a 30-year history of "compensatory" school policies that focus extra attention on low achievers. This resource deployment will not result in maximum student performance. It will, however, produce more equitable student performance. Indeed, in microstudies of resource deployment within classrooms, Brown and Saks (1980; 1987) found a dominance of "leveler" over "elitist" action, i.e., use of discretionary time and resources to bring all students up to some minimum level rather than use of those resources to push the higher achievers up to their highest level, which probably would boost the overall class average by a larger amount. In short, even when school systems target student achievement as the primary goal, given current equity policy directives, they will not be likely to seek maximum average performance. Thus, production function research might have only limited utility for probing the frontiers of how resources can affect student achievement.

Nevertheless, the conventional conclusion from most educational production function research is that there are few educational resources, including higher expenditures themselves, that are consistently related to student performance, or at least large increases in student performance. The message, however, is not that money does not matter. *The important message from this research is that if additional education revenues are spent in the same way as current education revenues, student performance increases are unlikely to emerge.* The message is that the way money is used matters. New revenues need to support new strategies in order to produce significant student achievement gains. Even Hanushek (1989) argues that raising teacher salaries will likely recruit more able individuals into teaching and that more able individuals are better teachers.

APPROACHING EDUCATIONAL PRODUCTIVITY IN THE 1990s

Although research has had difficulty showing how dollars can be used to improve student achievement, education in this country is still viewed as a good public investment. Research shows that both private (individual) and social (governmental) rates of return to investments in education are sizable, ranking with other conservative or governmental investment opportunities (Cohn and Geske, 1990). Cohn (1979) showed that returns to high school education in the 1970s were far above yields of long-term governmental bonds. Murphy and Welch (1989) showed that the wage premium to college education increased dramatically in the 1980s after falling somewhat during the 1970s. In short, research evidence shows that private and social rates of return are more than comparable to those for private investments, and that rates of return to elementary education can exceed private investment rates by a factor of four to one. Thus, education investments are good investments, for both governments and individuals.

There even is some consensus on programmatic expenditures that are likely to increase student performance. There is widespread agreement that investments in programs designed to prevent school failure or enhance school success, especially for poor children, are good public investments. Research shows that preschool programs for poor children have long-term benefits (Slavin, Karweit, and Madden, 1989) and high cost-effectiveness ratios. Even when future benefits are discounted to present values, investments in comprehensive early childhood programs for poor four-year-olds have benefit-cost ratios of up to six to one (Barnett, 1985). Early childhood programs for poor three-year-olds have benefit-cost ratios of up to three to one (Barnett, 1985).

Research also shows that extended day kindergarten (i.e., full day kindergarten for poor children) helps students perform adequately in subsequent elementary grades (Puelo, 1988). In fact, extended day kindergarten can help students increase their school performance by up to half a standard deviation on achievement tests (Slavin, Karweit and Madden, 1989). Further, early childhood programs and extended day kindergarten combined help poor children improve their success rate in elementary school. Fully funding both preschool and extended-day kindergarten for children from poverty backgrounds would substantially help implement the national goal of ensuring that "all students start school ready to learn."

Almost as interestingly, intervention programs to prevent school dropouts also have relatively high benefit-cost ratios. Levin (1989) showed that programs designed to keep poor students (i.e., students at risk of dropping out of high school) in high school to earn a high school diploma have positive benefit-cost ratios. Although the ratios are lower than those for prevention programs, the positive results show that even late remediation programs pay off in the long term. A recent study of a three-year California dropout-prevention program showed that it had a two-to-one benefit-cost ratio (Stern et al., 1989).

Although it is smarter to invest in prevention programs (early childhood education for low-income three- and four-year-olds, and extended or full-day kindergarten programs for low-income children), it is also wise to invest in remediation programs that work. All such programs more than return the public expenditure of funds.

Further, there are several within-school programmatic initiatives that improve student performance, including peer tutoring, adult tutoring, and cooperative learning. The first is peer tutoring. This program includes students, usually older students, tutoring usually younger students in academic subject areas.

This type of program requires organizational mechanism at the school level to facilitate implementation and some initial staff training in structuring the program and helping students play the tutor roles. It is cost-effective (Levin, Glass, and Meister, 1987).

The second is adult tutoring, which is similar to peer tutoring except that adults with modest amounts of training perform the tutoring function. In a comparison of several programmatic interventions, Levin, Glass, and Meister (1987) found that both peer and adult tutoring were more cost-effective than extending the school day, lowering class size, or computer-assisted instruction. Other research (Slavin, 1989b; Slavin, Karweit, and Madden, 1989) has shown that peer tutoring produces large achievement gains (usually more than half a standard deviation) for both tutor and tutee.

The third is cooperative learning (Slavin, 1989), another classroom organizational strategy that produces large gains (more than half a standard deviation) in student performance. Moreover, cooperative learning entails heterogeneous groups of students (with both high- and low-achieving students in each group) working together on tasks, and research shows that achievement improves for all students, both high and low achievers. In addition, cooperative learning produces improvements in affective domains as well, including greater respect for other cultures, ethnicities, races, and dominant language use, and is thus an effective intervention strategy in situations with diverse student bodies.

The dilemma for the 1990s, nevertheless, is how to deploy overall resources in schools to produce dramatic increases in overall average achievement as well as to reduce achievement gaps between the top and bottom, males and females, and minorities and nonminorities. School finance research needs to identify (1) how districts allocate dollars across functions and programs; (2) how schools transform resources into curriculum and instruction; and (3) the impact on student achievement. Research also needs to show how the interrelationships vary by level of schooling, curriculum content area, and student characteristics.

There likely will be no one best way to develop this new knowledge. There is a general consensus that combinations of macro- and microanalyses will be needed (Monk, 1989; King, 1985; MacPhail-Wilcox and King, 1986a). Thomas (1980) suggested that research needs to take a classroom perspective and analyze resource allocation within classrooms, assessing the total effect of curriculum taught, instructional strategies used, school organization, peer effects, and home investments in education. Monk (1989) argued that it might be more fruitful to analyze broader constructs, such as the within-school strategies just discussed, time on task, curriculum delivered, and the trade-offs between teacher expertise and expertise imbedded in new computer technologies. He argued that gathering data on individual students in classrooms is expensive both in money and time, and that district and state policy implications from findings on micro-classroom behaviors are often not possible.

Finally, Porter (forthcoming) and Oakes (1989) have suggested that the most crucial data to collect are those on the enacted curriculum in order to determine what curriculum content is provided to students and with what types of instructional strategies, arguing that disparities in curriculum and instruction could well explain the bulk of variation in student performance. These suggestions complement the broader types of resource data that need to be included in future resource equity studies, as discussed in Chapter 3. These suggestions implicitly argue that expanding the knowledge base on the specific curriculum and instruction resources into which dollars are transformed in schools might be the most fruitful route to unlocking the education productivity dilemma in the 1990s.

There undoubtedly are additional approaches. As this chapter has shown, the current knowledge base of how districts and schools spend dollars on functions, programs, curricula, or students, and how that impacts student performance, is not very large. We do not know much about what happens to dollars once they are distributed to schools, or about how to get higher student achievement from new educational investments. Expanding this knowledge base during the 1990s should be a critical school finance research focus.

Chapter 11

Fiscal Incentives for Schools

The discussion of fiscal federalism in Chapter 4 described the nature of fiscal relationships between states or the federal government and local school districts. That discussion focused on the fiscal instruments used by higher levels of government to provide aid to local school districts. It also described how local districts are expected to respond to that aid. The discussion in Chapter 4 indicated that the school reform movement of the 1980s has generated considerable interest in the use of fiscal incentives to improve school performance. This chapter discusses the kinds of incentives available to educational policymakers, their use to date, and the role such incentives play in the design of a school finance system.

Incentive funding is still in its early stages of development. Little is known about how incentives work, but they are increasingly popular among education policymakers and have been promoted by the National Governor's Association in recent reports on the status of education reform (David et. al., 1990; National Governors Association, 1990). This interest stems from a growing belief that "market-based" programs offer an alternative to the regulatory approaches implied in mandates and sanctions designed to ensure local responsiveness to state reform goals. There is also a growing sense that it is more appropriate for the state merely to monitor district performance in meeting established goals while leaving specific program decisions to the local officials who are most familiar with the realities of their situation.

Proponents of incentives argue that incentives are a morally superior way to garner voluntary compliance with policy goals and that they minimize the need for "coercion as a means of organizing society" (Schultze, 1977). The current political movement to reduce the size of government generally has made this argument popular. By shifting decision-making authority from the state to local school districts, incentive proponents can claim that spending increases are a result of locally established priorities, and not part of a growing and bloated bureaucracy. Some, however, dispute the voluntary aspects of incentive plans because the withdrawal of previously awarded incentives looks like punishment. Supporters of incentives also claim that incentives are more effective in attaining the ends of public policy than are regulation and mandates. Unfortunately, there have been few empirical studies of this claim—in or out of education (Church and Heumann, 1989).

The most recent education incentive programs began with merit pay and career ladder programs. The intention was to reward individuals in the education system who were doing an especially good job. Merit pay and career ladder programs have been studied extensively, and their problems documented in studies by Richards (1985), Murnane and Cohen (1986), and Johnson (1986). Other studies have proposed new approaches for paying teachers for productivity (Lawler, 1990; Blinder, 1990; Odden and Conley, forthcoming). Teacher compensation need not be the only domain of incentive programs, however. Other incentive strategies include (1) the use of intergovernmental grant theory to build incentives directly into the education finance formula; (2) school-based performance incentives; and (3) budget incentives built into site-based management programs. Each of these areas is described in this chapter.

SCHOOL FINANCE FORMULA INCENTIVES

The fiscal federalism structure used in Chapter 4 to analyze school district response to general, categorical, and matching grants can be applied to the analysis of school finance formula–based incentives. Chapter 4 shows that districts receiving grants generally use only a portion of that grant to increase educational expenditures and use the balance to reduce local tax effort. The simulation model in the Appendix to this text assumes, for example, that as much as half of all new state aid received by a school district is returned to the taxpayers in the form of lower property taxes. To limit this behavior on the part of school districts, states and the federal government have enacted categorical grant programs designed to ensure that fund recipients spend all the money they receive on the grant program. Although these grants have been more successful in getting school districts to spend the money they receive for the intended purpose, Chapter 4 shows that even with categorical grants some of the funds are often returned to local taxpayers.

One way to avoid developing more stringent regulations to ensure that all categorical dollars are spent on the targeted purpose is to provide funds to districts only if certain performance expectations are met. For example, if an incentive grant were offered to a local school district with the condition that certain service levels be achieved and maintained, it would be reasonable for the state to ignore variations across districts in the use of the incentive grants and focus attention on maintaining service levels. Decisions on how incentive funds would be spent are left to the recipient district, as long as the service requirements of the grant are achieved.

The advantage of an incentive grant is that it allows the recipient district considerable latitude in determining how to provide the new level of service. On the other hand, since local districts are not required to accept the incentive funds, 100 percent compliance with legislative goals is unlikely. Assuming incentive grants are available to all districts that elect to comply with the incentive, or who are already in compliance, the following effects of an incentive grant can be identified:

I. The district currently operates the program.
  A. The district is in compliance with the requirements of the incentive. It takes the money and uses it as a general grant. The state has spent money and not accomplished anything.
  B. The district is not in compliance with the requirements.
    1. The cost of compliance is less than the amount of the grant. The district complies, takes the grant, and uses the excess as a general grant. The state has accomplished compliance, but the cost has been greater than mandating it and paying the full costs of the mandate.
    2. The cost to the district is greater than the amount of the grant.
      a. The district complies and accepts the grant. Extra district money is used to comply. The grant therefore has a multiplier effect; that is, it stimulates spending of more on the program than the grant itself provides.
      b. The district does not comply and does not take the grant. The state has failed in getting the district to accept the requirements, but there has been no cost to the state.
II. The district does not currently operate the program.
  A. The cost of compliance is less than the amount of the grant. The district complies, takes the grant, and uses the excess as a general grant. The state has accomplished compliance, but the cost has been greater than mandating it and paying the full costs of the mandate.
  B. The cost to the district is greater than the amount of the grant.
    1. The district complies and accepts the grant. Extra district money is used to comply. The grant has had a multiplier effect.
    2. The district does not comply and does not take the grant. The state has failed in getting the district to accept the requirements, but there has been no cost to the state.

Because finance formula incentives are a relatively new school finance concept, little empirical research on their effectiveness is available. In one California study, Picus (1988) analyzed the effect of formula-based incentives for a longer school year and longer school day in that state's 1983 education reform act and found the incentives had a stimulative impact on district spending for instructional programs.

Under Senate Bill (SB) 813, California school districts were eligible for incentive payments of $35 per student in 1984–85 if they increased the length of the school year to 180 days. Districts that already had 180-day school years also received these incentive payments. In addition, districts that increased the length of the school day to a state-established minimum received incentive payments of $20 per pupil in grades K–8 and $40 per pupil in grades 9–12 for each of three years beginning in 1984–85. Almost all districts in the state took advantage of these incentives.

An important component of the incentive program was that once a district met the time requirements and received the incentive payments, future payments were rolled into the district's revenue limit. Including the payment as part of a district's (block grant) revenue limit ensured continued funding for the program. To keep local districts that were receiving the funds and the related increase in their future revenue limit from reverting back to old schedules that did not meet the incentive program's minimum requirements, the legislature enacted a penalty provision that reduces a district's state aid by an amount greater than what it received through the incentive program. As a result, districts that elected to extend their school days and years to receive the incentive funds have not shortened school time "after the fact."

Picus (1988) pointed out that the legislature expected districts to use the incentive funds to increase spending on direct instructional programs. Figure 11.1 shows Picus' estimates of changes in spending by program area that resulted from a one-dollar increase in incentive revenue for California unified districts. What this figure indicates is that for every incentive dollar a district received, it increased spending on instruction by over $2.00. Figure 11.1 shows other changes in district spending patterns as a result of the incentive program. For example, a one-dollar increase in incentive funds led to an increase of approximately 78 cents in spending on administration, and a smaller increase in spending on maintenance and operations. On the other hand, spending for instructional support, transportation, auxiliary, and student services declined in response to the incentive funding.

Picus concluded that experience in California following passage of SB 813 showed incentive programs were effective in getting school districts to implement legislatively established goals. By offering funding incentives to increase the length of the school day and school year, and to increase beginning teacher salaries, the legislature got local districts to increase the share of total expenditures devoted to instructional programs. Although California did not guarantee that student performance would improve, or dropout rates decline, interviews with state legislators and other participants in the education policy

FIGURE 11.1 Estimated Impact of a Dollar Increase in Incentive Revenue on School District Spending by Expediture Category: California Unified School Districts, 1984–85 to 1985–86

Expenditure Classification	Incentive Revenue
Instruction	2.05
Administration	0.78
Auxiliary	−0.36
Instructional support	−1.18
Maintenance and operations	0.24
Transportation	−1.09
Pupil services	−0.04

Source: Lawrence O. Picus, *The Effect of State Grant-in-Aid Policies on Local Government Decision Making: The Case of California School Finance*, Santa Monica, CA: The RAND Corporation.

arena indicated the level of spending on instruction was viewed as one measure of the success of the reform components of SB 813. It must be pointed out that Picus' analysis also found that by the end of the six-year period studied, as the level of new incentive funds declined, district spending patterns began to return to the pattern observed prior to enactment of the incentive program.

Picus also found that SB 813's incentive grants were more successful in directing expenditures toward instruction than other grant instruments that have typically been used. School districts responded to the incentive grants by increasing the percentage of total expenditure devoted to instruction, whereas the response to general, categorical, and federal grants resulted in smaller spending increases in instruction and relatively larger increases in other program areas. It is possible that state categorical programs designed to increase instructional spending might have been equally successful, but data on that type of revenue instrument were not available because the California Legislature elected to use incentives rather than categorical grants. Picus' findings have implications for both school finance policy and state-local intergovernmental fiscal relations in general.

His finding that formula-based incentive programs are more effective than other grant mechanisms in getting school districts to implement legislative goals has important implications for the use of intergovernmental grants generally. Incentives are a powerful tool for gaining local acceptance of state-established goals. Incentives do not carry the negative connotations associated with mandates, and their voluntary nature makes it possible for school districts or local governments to opt out of programs they dislike. On the other hand, carefully designed incentives make substantial compliance with legislative goals a real possibility.

There are a number of factors that must be considered if formula-based incentives are to be successful. Incentive programs are most effective when the funding represents a small portion of a school district's budget. If incentives represent a substantial share of district budgets, they have the effect of mandates since districts will have to meet the incentive requirements to balance their budgets.

Incentives can be expected to achieve higher participation rates in times of fiscal constraint. School districts facing revenue shortfalls will be more willing to accept funds, even if they come with strings attached, than will local governments with adequate fiscal resources.

Incentive programs may only be successful in the short run, particularly if the funds are rolled into general assistance programs in future years. School districts will modify their spending patterns to qualify for the grant, but over time can be expected to return to previous patterns. Even when incentive programs require maintaining service levels, it may be possible for districts to use some of the funds in other program areas once those service levels are implemented.

Finally, incentives may be successful only under limited conditions and for limited time periods. The harder it is for school districts to retreat from the grant requirements, the greater the long-term success of the incentive program. The ability of a school district to retreat from the grant requirements depends on how difficult and costly it is to do so. Incentives that require major reorganizations, although they may be less successful in gaining compliance, are more likely to have a lasting impact on school districts. On the other hand, incentives that are easily implemented, and at relatively low cost, may gain greater compliance, but maintaining that compliance may be more difficult.

Picus found that legislatures can influence school district spending decisions through the use of formula-based fiscal incentives. However, there is some slippage between legislative goals and local response. He argued that state policymakers should remember there will be many individual interpretations of the state's policy goals. Allowing local governments the flexibility to implement state policies in a manner consistent with their view of local needs will make them more responsive to the varying needs of their constituents, but it also means that legislators will not find implementation of their policies to be as neat as they would like. In some instances, legislative goals will not be attained, whereas in others they will be exceeded. Meeting the challenge of providing quality public services requires the continued interest, support, and patience of the state's policymakers as locals strive to implement legislatively established goals.

School-Based Fiscal Incentives

School-based fiscal incentives pose a host of different issues. Though somewhat of a novelty in education today, they are increasingly being used in the private sector and in some other public sectors. The approach taken more and more often is to provide incentives for operational units (production divisions or departments—the analogue in education would be schools or university academic departments) rather than for individuals. In the private sector, incentives are linked not to the productivity of an entire firm, but to individual units, which are rewarded on the basis of performance over a multiple-year time period (Stansberry, 1985; Swinford, 1987; Goggin, 1986; and Blinder, 1990). Moreover, in both the private sector and schools, there is increasing recognition that individual performance incentives can work at cross-purposes to the kind of team efforts required to develop and sustain a productive organizational climate (Swinehart, 1986; Conley and Bacharach, in press; Rosenholtz, 1989).

One of the reasons school-based incentive programs have not received much attention until recently is the old dilemma about whether performance-based incentives make sense in education. Rewarding schools that perform well places extra resources where things are going well but denies them to schools most in need of assistance. Second, incentives rewarding school or district performance may not put money in the pockets of the individuals whose efforts make the district look good in the first place; thus there is only a weak incentive to perform.

However, the reform movement of the 1980s may make these issues of less concern in the design of performance-based incentives for schools. Barro (1989) argues that these reforms have eliminated some of the earlier restrictions on how states distribute funds to schools. As states become more involved in defining minimum requirements and course curricula and ensuring services are provided to at-risk students, it is possible to establish mechanisms that allow states to reward individual or group performance and at the same time provide extra resources to areas doing poorly.

In designing a school-based incentive program, policymakers need to consider four general areas: (1) eligibility requirements, (2) the size of the incentive program, (3) the distribution mechanics, and (4) how the incentive funds can be used by recipients.

First, policymakers need to determine the eligibility requirements for the program. Among the issues that must be addressed are the level for measuring performance, the period of performance, the standard for which an incentive award is received, and the performance measure that will be used.

Many incentives are aimed at the school level. For example, the U. S. Department of Education's outstanding school awards are based on the performance of school sites, as are many state award programs. However, incentives can also be focused more broadly at school districts, or more narrowly by grade, department, or even classroom. The period of performance is also a critical policy variable in the design of incentive programs. Will schools (or other units) be rewarded for performance on an annual basis, or for their performance over a period of time, say two or three years. As the discussion in Chapter 10 shows, single-year gains are often achieved at the expense of future performance. Thus, using a two- or three-year average might encourage long-term development of successful educational practices rather than implementation of quick fixes designed to improve test scores quickly.

Another allocation issue has to do with establishing a performance standard. Richards and Shujaa (1989) describe two such standards: fixed and competitive. A fixed performance standard provides incentive awards to all schools that meet some predetermined criteria for receiving an award, and a competitive standard indicates that schools must compete with other schools to receive the award. Theoretically, all schools in a state could receive incentive awards under the fixed standard method. On the other hand, only a certain percentage of the schools in a state could receive an incentive reward based on a competitive performance standard.

Finally, a performance measure must be established. The most common measure of performance is student achievement, as measured through some kind of achievement test. Incentives can then be based either on a school's overall achievement level or, more often, on some measure of improvement.[1] Other testing issues must be resolved, including which test to use and what score to consider. For example, do you compare the scores at some percentile across schools, or compare the average for each school in determining which site is eligible for the incentive? Also, since there is evidence that students will produce more learning gains if they spend time with high-achieving students than they will if they are grouped with low-achieving students, it may be desirable to weight the scores in favor of the bottom percentile schools.

In addition to test scores, other measures that have been used in school-based incentives include enrollment measurements such as the number of students in advanced placement courses or the number in core academic programs. Teacher and student attendance rates are also used as a basis for incentive programs in some states. The description of South Carolina's incentive program below shows how one state has combined achievement test data with teacher and student attendance rates in structuring an incentive program. Finally, other measures could be used, including lowering the dropout rate, improving postsecondary enrollments, and measuring community satisfaction.

The second issue policymakers must consider is the size of the program in comparison to the state's overall school finance system. If the award is too small, schools may choose not to compete for the incentives, yet if it is too large, other components of the finance formula may suffer. South Carolina provides approximately $30 per pupil in incentive funds. This amounts to a relatively small portion of the total state funding for education, but the award level is large enough to generate high interest among schools.

Most school-based incentive programs are distributed through separate categorical programs. The issues surrounding the distribution of incentive funds

---

[1] There are a number of important issues surrounding the use of achievement tests to measure school performance. These are addressed in Chapter 3's discussion of equity frameworks.

through the state aid formula are discussed above. In general, incentives for performance appear to be better distributed through separate programs, whereas incentives designed to encourage districts to enact certain types of programs may be better distributed through the general aid formula. The discussion at the end of this section on using the general aid program to distribute incentive funds covers the effects of these grants on the equalization functions of general aid programs. At present, most incentive programs are small enough that they don't pose a significant threat to the equalization component of state school finance structures.

Finally, the range of allowable uses of incentive funds distributed to the schools is an important policy issue. For example, can the funds be used to give teachers bonus payments? If so, must all teachers share equally in those payments? How are teachers to be evaluated if incentive bonuses are not distributed equally to teachers? In California's Cash for CAP program (described below), schools were not allowed to use the funds they receive for payments to teachers. Instead, the funds had to be used for instructional materials and supplies. Another question is whether the funds can be used to reward the students in some way, for example, to pay for a field trip or finance a special event on campus.

A number of states have experimented with a variety of site-based incentive programs. Some have enjoyed greater success than others. Two examples of school-based incentive programs are described below.

South Carolina's School Incentive Reward Program

The School Incentive Reward Program is one part of what Peterson (1988) refers to as South Carolina's "carrot and stick" approach to school accountability. The program provides approximately $4 million a year to roughly 250 schools making the largest achievement gains compared to similar schools. In addition, bonuses are available for high student and teacher attendance. If a school meets all three outcome standards, it can receive about $30 per student. A school must meet the comparative achievement standard to qualify for any award. Eighty percent of the annual per-pupil award is based on the achievement standard. The attendance incentives are based on fixed standards, and schools can get an additional 10 percent of the per-pupil award for each of the two standards it meets. In addition to the financial rewards, schools receive flags and certificates signifying their performance. Honorable mention awards are presented to schools whose performance approaches but does not meet the standards required for a monetary reward.

Cibulka (1989) states that the program has proven to be a source of motivation to school and teachers. He indicates that there is a great deal of support for the program among educators, and that the greatest support has been found among schools with fewer resources and historically lower achievement gains. Because of the program's success, legislation was introduced to release schools that win awards two years in a row from state regulations. Richards and Shujaa (1989) point out that this will complicate analysis of the South Carolina program's success because the most successful schools will be able to escape requirements that limit their performance. If deregulation really does promote higher levels of performance, then repeat winners will have an advantage over other schools for future incentive payments.

South Carolina also has a school district intervention program to help poorly performing schools and districts—the "stick." South Carolina schools that have low performance levels on achievement tests, poor student or teacher attendance, and/or high dropout rates, or do not meet accreditation standards, are declared to be an "impaired district" (Peterson, 1988). Impaired districts are then visited by a team of educators, who issue recommendations that, once approved by the State Board of Education, must be implemented by the local school district. Districts failing to comply with the recommendations face withholding of funds or removal of the district superintendent. State technical assistance is also provided to impaired schools. By 1988 only nine districts in the state had been identified as impaired.

Intervention programs such as South Carolina's can be thought of as "negative" incentive programs. They encourage districts to perform well to avoid some negative consequence such as a state intervention or, as can happen in New Jersey, a state takeover of district operations. Although most incentive programs are thought of as rewarding good performance (however defined), there is no reason to assume programs that punish poor performance are less successful in improving school performance. Moreover, such negative incentives solve the problem of allocating resources to districts least in need of additional assistance at the expense of those needing the most assistance. These programs target resources at the schools and school districts that have been identified as doing the worst job in a state.

California's Cash for CAP

Although South Carolina's school-based incentive program appears to be a great success, not all states have been as fortunate. In addition to the formula-based incentives described above, California's SB 813 included a program to provide schools with cash awards for high performance on the California Assessment Program (CAP) test. Specifically, high schools received awards on the basis of increases in the standardized achievement test scores obtained on the twelfth-grade CAP test.

The legislature appropriated over $14 million for this program in both 1984–85 and 1985–86. The program was eliminated the following year. In the first year of operation, approximately 49 percent of the state's high schools received awards ranging from $5 to $192,000 and averaging $26,047. In the second year, 48 percent of the state's high schools received awards. Awards were discretionary and could be used in any manner, as determined by the school—except to increase salaries.

The program appeared to be successful, in that senior test scores improved and the number of seniors taking the test increased. However, there were a number of serious implementation problems. Some schools managed to artificially lower the CAP scores in the base year in order to maximize their improvement during the award years. Other schools tried to change the definition of a senior so that those most likely to do poorly on the test would not have to take it, thus raising the gain score above what it would otherwise have been. There is also anecdotal evidence of high school seniors threatening to do poorly on the test unless administrators agreed to spend the award funds in a manner designated by the students. There also appear to be cases where students intentionally failed the test to lower their school's gain score.

Implications for School Finance

An important question not yet answered is whether school- or district-based incentives will have an impact on state equalization programs. Since funds are usually distributed to schools on the basis of performance, regardless of wealth or expenditure level, it is entirely possible that an incentive program would have a disequalizing impact on the state financing structure. Among the programs implemented to date, this seems to be a minor concern because the incentives have generally amounted to less than $50 per pupil. Another reason this may not be a major concern is that a ceiling effect on most achievement tests used as an outcome measure in incentive programs results in low-performing schools showing larger average gains than high-performing schools. If low-performing schools receive a larger than average proportion of the incentive funds, and if high performance is indeed correlated with wealth, there may even be an equalizing effect. Richards and Shujaa (1989) point out that in South Carolina the distribution of incentive grants has been proportionately greater in low-wealth schools. Thus, even though state education policymakers need to be aware of incentive programs' potential to interact negatively with equalization programs, it appears that this is a problem that does not materialize unless incentive programs grow to represent a major share of state funds.

BUDGET INCENTIVES

Over the past 20 years, there has been a trend in general management practice to give local managers more financial discretion and, in exchange, to require more explicit accountability for outcomes (see, for example, Arrow, 1971; Jensen and Meckling, 1976). A similar trend is evident in the current reforms being proposed for education. Current calls for restructuring schools argue that rather than telling local managers how to spend money, revenue providers should instead try to create incentives for local managers to use their knowledge to achieve desired goals. If properly structured, the incentives will cause the local managers to act as if they have the same goals as the revenue providers.

This represents a significant change from the way most school districts allocate funds to the schools within their jurisdiction. Today, most revenue providers maximize their preferences by establishing distribution rules to allocate resources to local school sites. Under a budget incentive system, however, a lump sum budget is provided and desired outcomes are specified. Local officials are then empowered to make decisions on the deployment of those resources with the understanding that they are better able to maximize the efficient allocation of resources to meet the desired outcomes. In exchange for "giving up" direct control over the specifics of how dollars are used locally, revenue providers are more than compensated by improved local decision making and, presumably, higher levels of goal attainment.

These budget incentives have led to the growing popularity of site-based management programs in school districts. Site-based management, or decentralized decision making as it is frequently called, places more decision-making authority at the school level. In exchange for this increased control over local or site matters, the school agrees to be held accountable for some agreed-upon level of performance or achievement. Because of the importance of site-based management, this topic is discussed in depth in Chapter 12.

SUMMARY

The school finance reform movement of the 1980s has generated considerable interest in the use of fiscal incentives to improve school performance. This chapter has identified three types of incentives that have been used: (1) the use of intergovernmental grant theory to build incentives directly into the education finance formula, (2) school-based performance incentives, and (3) budget incentives built into site-based management programs.

Placing incentives in a state's school finance formula is an alternative that has been tried on a limited basis, but with apparent success. In California, incentives for extending the length of the school day and school year resulted in a considerable increase in spending on direct instruction. However, as the incentive funds were rolled into the general aid grant portion of the formula, districts seemed to return to the spending habits exhibited prior to enactment of the incentives. Thus, incentives included in the finance formula may be successful, but their use must be monitored closely.

A number of states, particularly South Carolina, have had substantial success with school-based performance incentives, although other states have had less success. In order for performance incentives to succeed, states must establish reasonable performance measures, decide whether incentives should be based on a comparative or fixed standard, and choose acceptable student achievement measurement instruments. To date, most performance incentives have primarily been based on improvements on student achievement tests, but other factors such as attendance, reduced dropout rates, and increased enrollments in advanced classes have also been used.

Finally, much attention has been devoted recently to site-based budget incentives. Rather than telling local school administrators how to operate programs for their students, funding providers use these incentives, which offer a lump sum payment in exchange for meeting certain performance standards. Increasingly popular in private industry, holding local managers accountable for outcomes without specifying production techniques is becoming more popular in education as well. The issues surrounding this decentralization, or site-based management, are discussed in depth in Chapter 12.

Site-Based Management and School-Based Decision Making

Chapter 11 began the discussion of one of the most important educational reforms to emerge during the 1980s, school- or site-based management. School-based management involves fundamental changes in the way authority and resources are allocated between a school district and its school sites. This issue is different from that of the allocation of funds from the state to school districts, which is the primary focus of this book. However, site-based management's emergence as a major component of school reform, and its possible impact on state allocation systems, requires special treatment in a book on school finance.

This chapter starts by defining what is meant by site-based management. After a general model of site-based management has been established, the second section discusses how this differs from current models of school management. The third section outlines the kinds of structural changes school districts need to consider as they seek to implement a site-based management system. Continuing with the theme of authority relationships, the fourth section outlines the role of school-site councils in the management of local schools under various manifestations of site-based management. The fifth section discusses the ways site-based management may help improve school accountability, productivity, and flexibility. The sixth section contains a discussion of how the trend toward site-based management might affect the allocation and distribution of state funds to school districts.

SITE-BASED MANAGEMENT—A DEFINITION

There is general agreement about the definition of site-based management. Brown (1990), for example, states that school-based management "means simply that schools within a district are allotted money to purchase supplies, equipment, personnel, utilities, maintenance, and perhaps other services according to their own assessment of what is appropriate." Clune and White (1988) offer a similar definition, stating that "school-based management is a system designed to improve education by increasing the authority of actors at the school site." They argue that the rationale behind site-based management is a belief that the more closely a decision is made to a student, the better that decision is likely to serve the student. Although the concept of site-based management is not new—Clune and White (1988) found one district that has been using site-based management for over 34 years—it has become more prominent in the last ten years for three reasons:

1. The importance of site-based management in the effective schools literature (see, for example, Purkey and Smith, 1985)
2. The importance ascribed to decentralization in the so-called second wave of educational reform (see, for example, Carnegie Forum on Education and the Economy, 1986)
3. The availability of inexpensive, yet powerful, computing and networking tools that make it possible to transfer budget and other management information between school sites and central offices in a timely fashion

Because site-based management places greater authority in the hands of school-site personnel, it is not surprising to find wide variety in the way site-based management plans have been developed and implemented. In its various forms, site-based management provides greater school-site autonomy over some combination of budget, personnel, and program decisions (Malen, Ogawa, and Kranz, 1990). Most site-based management plans also include a formal governance structure at the school site to involve local parents and teachers in the decision-making process. The actual role and authority of these site councils varies widely, from an advisory role in many districts to authority to hire and fire the school's principal under Chicago's school-based management program begun in 1989.

The literature on site-based management is dominated by project descriptions, status reports, and position pieces, with few systematic, empirical examinations of the topic (Malen, Ogawa, and Kranz, 1990). In fact, most of the literature describes exemplary programs giving little insight into the impact they might have on school-district, district-state, or school-state relationships. Perhaps this is a result of the recent attention site-based management has received, and over time more systematic examinations of the subject will be undertaken.

In order to fully understand how site-based management models change existing authority relationships within a school district, an analysis of common practice prior to instigation of site-based programs is important. Although site-based reforms typically involve one or more of budgeting, personnel decisions, and program matters, this discussion begins with budgeting and its role in site-based management. The next section summarizes typical budgeting systems in school districts. That is followed by a discussion of the kinds of changes that are necessary to implement site-based management.

SCHOOL DISTRICT BUDGETING PROCEDURES

Budgeting, or the allocation of resources to achieve institutional or organizational goals, is one of the most important functions of school district management. In most school districts in the United States, this function is carried out centrally, with limited input from individual school sites. Discussions of budget theory are filled with high expectations. Hartman (1988) states that the school district budget "is an important tool for school administrators to understand and utilize in achieving their basic mission—educating children in the most effective and cost-efficient manner." Unfortunately, as Hentschke (1988) argues, "actual budgeting practices fall far short of these high aspirations."

Typically, a district's budget is a process of balancing expenditures with revenues. After estimating revenues for the next year, budget officials ascertain the costs of providing the existing program in the following year. After providing for current programs, if additional funds are available, new programs may be funded. On the other hand, if resources are not adequate to fully fund the current program, reductions are required. As a result, school district budgets are typically incremental in nature. That is, changes in spending patterns, if they are made at all, occur at the margins, with little change in the year-to-year allocation of resources among schools and between the central office and school sites (for a discussion of incrementalism, see Wildavsky, 1975; 1988).

To allocate funds across sites and programs, districts typically use a set of allocation rules (Hentschke, 1986). These allocation rules focus on three components: (1) formulaic ratios, (2) centrally controlled budget categories, and (3) pay scales (Guthrie, 1988). Enrollment projections are crucial to the allocation of funds since they drive both the revenue received from the state and the allocation of resources to school sites. Kirst (1988) notes that districts usually use two allocation formulas: (1) a staffing formula and (2) a funding formula for supplies, materials, and textbooks.

Staffing formulas for teachers are usually established on the basis of a predetermined average class size. For example, a district may provide one teacher for every 23 elementary school students or one teacher for every 18 high school students. Administrative staff are often assigned on the basis of school size. Almost all schools have a principal.[1] Larger schools may require additional administrative staff, and a district may have a policy of providing an assistant principal for any school over a certain size. Counselors and guidance personnel are typically provided on a ratio basis, such as one counselor for every 350 or 400 students. Clerical positions are filled on the basis of school enrollment or number of teaching positions. Other classified staff such as custodians, gardeners, and maintenance personnel are frequently assigned on the basis of the same factor such as building square footage, number of classrooms, or site acreage. It should be remembered that these allocation rules are determined by individual districts and may vary considerably across districts.

Funding formulas for supplies, materials, and textbooks are typically based on enrollments or staff positions as well. Some districts have very detailed allocation procedures, providing separate formulas for each item or group of items, whereas other districts provide a lump sum payment, usually based on enrollment, for schools to purchase these items as they see fit. Central control over supplies, materials, and textbooks often extends beyond these allocation formulas, with schools being required to purchase items through a central purchasing system.

These allocation rules assume that there is a single best production process for instruction, and that that process is imbedded in those rules. Moreover, these allocation rules greatly simplify the work of the central administration. In addition to providing a measure for distribution of resources, they are politically useful because they are objective and treat schools in an equal manner (Hentschke, 1988).

Hentschke concludes that current budgeting practice "rules out all but the most marginal decisions about improved instructional programming" (1988: 312). He points out that two proposed reforms of the 1960s and 1970—Planning, Programming, Budgeting Systems (PPBS) and Zero Based Budgeting (ZBB)—did little to change school district budgeting practice. Hentschke suggests that the initial popularity of PPBS and ZBB was based on the assumption that improved budgeting technology would lead to better decisions about the allocation of school resources.

---

[1] In one-school districts, the principal may serve in the dual role of superintendent/principal, or the school may be managed by a head teacher/principal. In addition, districts with very small schools may assign one principal to two schools. But, in general, most schools in the United States have a full-time principal.

PPBS is a top-down budgeting system that requires agreement on the goals of the institution and an analysis of those programs that will best achieve those goals. Alternatives are analyzed, and those found to be most cost-effective are implemented. Enactment of a full PPBS system in any jurisdiction requires considerable change in the structure of the budget process, and in many cases requires evaluations of alternatives that are difficult to make since it is hard to measure the output of educational processes.

ZBB, on the other hand, is a bottom-up process that requires production units (for example, schools) to develop and project the cost of a set of decision packages. These packages are ranked, then funded on the basis of the rankings until available resources are consumed.

Neither of these reforms has had much impact on school budget processes. Brackett, Chambers, and Parrish (1983) provide an excellent summary of these budgetary reforms and the reasons they were not successful in educational institutions. Hentschke (1988) adds an additional reason for the failure of these budgetary reforms in schools, arguing they did not change the authority relationships over the distribution of resources within a school district. He argues that to implement a school-based management system, certain changes in these authority relationships are essential.

AUTHORITY CHANGES FOR SITE-BASED MANAGEMENT

Because site-based management can take a number of forms, it is difficult to ascertain which provisions of a site-based management plan actually alter decision-making arrangements in schools and school districts (Malen, Ogawa, and Kranz, 1990). Yet it is not surprising to expect that decentralization of school systems results in some kinds of changes in authority relationships between schools and school districts. Hentschke (1988) argues that before site-based management can be successfully implemented, changes in the formal authority relationships between central district offices and school sites must occur. Six changes are discussed below.

Authority over Utilities and Substitute Teachers

Substitute teachers and utilities are two examples of school resources that are typically allocated centrally. Expenditures for these items are controlled through the central office and budgeted on the basis of past experience. Local school sites have no incentive to minimize expenditures on these items because any savings that accrue are realized by the central office and not by the school site.

Hentschke (1988) argues for providing each school with the resources for these items. If utilization levels were less than budgeted, the school could then share in the savings, using the funds for resources that work more directly to achieve educational goals. Moreover, the central office would not be able to penalize school site savings by budgeting less in future years. To make this system work, however, the school site would also have to share in at least part of the risk of overexpenditures.

Authority over Staff Development, Curriculum Development, and Other Central Office Support

Staff development, curriculum development, and other central office support functions are typically provided to schools by the central office. Often the support service needs of the schools are determined centrally, with little or no consultation with the school sites. Expenditures for these services are made, and the school site's option is to take advantage of what is offered or do without.

Hentschke (1988) proposes making these support functions accountable to the school sites by turning them from "cost centers" to "revenue centers." In other words, Hentschke suggests that building-level staff be given the authority to decide what level of central office support they want to purchase. Sites would not only choose how much of each support service to purchase, but also whether to purchase the service from the central office or from an outside source. By deciding what services it deemed important and allocating its resources accordingly, the school could be held accountable for educational outcomes while the central office would be held accountable for providing the services requested at the school sites.

Authority over the Mix of Professionals

As described above, school districts typically establish allocation formulas for personnel. Under Hentschke's proposed changes in authority relationships, schools would be granted something on the order of personnel units, which could be used for a variety of positions. For example, one school might choose to eliminate an assistant principal position in favor of an additional teacher to reduce class size, whereas another school might choose slightly larger classes but provide a part-time aide in each classroom in the school, and a third might trade a teaching position for a counselor to deal with problem or at-risk students. Providing this type of staffing flexibility would allow school sites to develop educational programs that more closely meet their ideals.

Authority over the Source of Supply

Most districts operate central purchasing programs to minimize the costs of materials and supplies. However, such centralization typically comes with limits on the variety of items that a school site can purchase. Hentschke (1988) proposes that these restrictions need to be eliminated if site-based management is to be implemented. He argues that schools should be able to purchase resources from district or nondistrict suppliers as they see fit. He even extends this to the provision of instructional services, using as an example a school in Dade County, Florida, that used Berlitz to teach Spanish to its students because the school's administrators thought it was a more cost-effective way to provide this foreign language instruction.

Authority to Carry Over Resources to the Next Fiscal Year

Under most school district budgeting systems, departments and school sites have an incentive to spend all of their appropriations before the end of the fiscal year because failure to do so usually means that the resources will be lost. Hentschke suggests that more efficient spending decisions would be possible if school sites were able to carry over the unexpended funds to the next fiscal year without penalty. This would allow them to consider larger equipment purchases, such as computer systems, which would not be possible under a system that takes back any unspent balance in an appropriation account.

Relief from Regulation

Although not mentioned by Hentschke, a common approach to site-based management is to release schools from certain requirements of school district policy or from certain portions of employee contracts. Often, district policy and employee contracts restrict the actions of a school. A number of recent site-based management programs have provided for relaxation of these restrictions in schools that develop their own educational plan. For example, once a school develops its own plan, the school board will provide exemptions to district policies that would prevent some of the actions desired on the part of the school. Schools seeking to undertake actions prevented by the district contract with the teachers must also receive approval from the bargaining representatives. Generally, programs that release a school from district or contractual rules require the submission and approval of a school plan prior to allowing the relaxation of the standards.

Establishment of Site Authority

There is one other authority issue that must be considered in looking at site-based management programs. That is the determination of who will be responsible for local or site decision making. Is the principal responsible for making all site decisions? What role do teachers and parents play in the management of a local school? And how are the sometimes conflicting interests of these parties resolved? This important issue is the topic of the next section of this chapter.

THE ROLE OF SCHOOL SITE COUNCILS

Although school districts are managed by a professional staff headed by a superintendent of schools, final authority over district operations lies with the Board of Education. As more authority is vested at the school site, it seems logical that interested parties should have a voice in determining both the goals and objectives of the school's educational program and the methods used to meet those goals and objectives. Consequently, virtually all site-based management programs include provisions for school site councils. The role and function of those councils is often a matter of considerable debate and acrimony. This section considers three issues regarding the composition and operation of school site councils: (1) how is membership on the site council determined? (2) what matters should the site council consider? and (3) who has formal decision-making authority, the principal or the council? These matters have been resolved differently in different locations. Although local variation in the role of the site council is to be expected, it is important that site councils function cooperatively if the goals of site-based management are to succeed.

Council Membership

School site councils are not a new phenomenon at local schools. Many federal and state categorical programs have for years required the establishment of a site advisory council. For example, schools receiving Chapter 1 funds or bilingual money from the federal government are required to establish parent advisory councils to provide input into the operation of the program. In California, the School Improvement Program requires that schools receiving funds establish an advisory council to provide guidance to the principal in the development and implementation of improvement plans. In addition, many states and local districts have their own requirements for parent advisory councils at school sites, regardless of the acceptance of categorical program funds.

Consequently, most schools, and their principals, have had some experience working with advisory councils. Two of the major differences between those and most school site councils established under site-based management programs are (1) the role of teachers on the site council, and (2) the level of decision-making authority.

Because the mission of most school site councils, regardless of their final decision-making authority, includes the overall operation of their school, as opposed to advising school staff on one individual program, the potential power of the council is considerable. As a result, teachers have demanded that they play an important role on the site council. In fact, many teacher organizations argue that teachers should constitute a majority of the council's membership. In most cases, the argument boils down to whether the teacher representatives should constitute one-half of the site council or a majority of the council.

Each district has resolved this issue itself. Typical models include a council with 50 percent public members and 50 percent teachers, with the principal representing the tiebreaker, but others provide a one-member majority for either the public or the teachers. Of course, a simple majority in no way guarantees control of the council, because teachers may have disagreements over the school's goals and because not all community members will be automatically opposed to everything the teachers think is important.

Another issue that must be resolved is the make-up of the public membership. Should site council members be required to have children attending the school, or is it beneficial to allow nonparents to participate in school decisions? Moreover, how should public membership be established—through a community election, as in Chicago, through appointment by the principal, or by some combination of the two? Similarly, who appoints the teacher representatives, the school's union representative, and the bargaining unit, or should the teachers at each school hold an election to determine membership?

Finally, once a site council has been selected, what rules guide its decision making? Many attempt to operate through consensus. If a consensus can't be reached, majority voting policies seem like a logical alternative for formulating council policies and goals. However, this makes the problem of membership and representation of different groups on the council even more important. One option might be to give each group one vote and require that they reach consensus among themselves first. For example, regardless of the council membership, the teachers would have one vote, the public one vote, and the principal one vote. This alternative might reduce some of the difficulties associated with determining the membership composition of the site council.

School Site Council Authority

Once matters of membership and organization have been decided, it is still critical to determine what issues the council can consider. Is the council's role one of fundraising and "cheerleading," or will it be expected to play a substantive role in the educational program of the school? In a true site-based management program, one would expect the council to be able to consider whatever matters it deemed important. However, many districts, either through policy or as a result of the terms of the collective bargaining agreement with the teachers, have limited the authority of the site council. Assuming that the council is charged with establishing the educational goals of a school, what role should the site council play in determining how progress toward meeting the goals should be measured, how instruction should take place, and what materials should be used? Beyond these issues, what role should the site council play in hiring teachers and other staff, in determining teaching assignments, in establishing discipline policy, and in allocating school resources across program areas?

These are important considerations if the council is to operate successfully. Moreover, they are closely related to the final issue to be considered here, the relative authority of the council and the school principal.

Location of Formal
Decision-Making Authority

Perhaps the most controversial issue of all is the formal decision-making responsibility vested in the site council. What is the role of the principal in relation to the site council? Who has final authority and thus responsibility for major policy decisions and for day-to-day operations of the school? How these issues are resolved plays a crucial role in the way the site council operates. For example, does the principal have the authority to override a decision of the site council, or must he or she carry out the decisions of that council? Who has authority to hire and fire school principals—the district's central administration or the site council?

For the most part, site council powers seem to be limited to an advisory role, with the principal having final authority over most matters. This is not universally the case, however. In Chicago, the recent school-based management reforms have placed final authority for the operation of a school in the hands of the locally elected site-based council. That council has the authority to employ the principal, and by the end of the 1990–91 academic year, all of the site-based councils in the district will have made a decision as to whether or not to renew their principals' contracts. Half of the site councils made that decision during the 1989–90 school year. Although most chose to renew their principal's contract, 49 of 272 school councils did not do so (Wohlstetter and McCurdy, in press). In some instances, the sitting principal was allowed to reapply for his or her position, although no guarantees were provided.[2]

The relative authority of the site council and the school principal will have a strong influence on the motivation of teachers and community members to serve on the site council. Principals and administrator organizations are universally opposed to placing final decision-making authority in the hands of the site council, arguing that it is hard to hold a committee accountable and that it is unreasonable to hold the principal accountable for actions he or she is required to carry out by order of a site council. Since this is a relatively new issue, there is little empirical evidence about the success of different authority structures. Over time, as more districts struggle with this issue and make decisions regarding the role of the site council, more evidence on the merits of various options will emerge.

The remaining question then is, of what benefit is site-based management, and how can it help improve schools? The next section of this chapter describes how site-based management may help improve school accountability, productivity, and flexibility.

---

[2] At the time of publication, the Illinois Supreme Court had ruled that the Chicago reform was unconstitutional. Although the court's decision was based on a technicality in the way the law was passed, the future of the program was unclear in early 1991.

SITE-BASED MANAGEMENT AS A TOOL FOR IMPROVING SCHOOL ACCOUNTABILITY, PRODUCTIVITY, AND FLEXIBILITY

Brown (1990) says that the chief outcomes of site-based management or organizational decentralization include more accountability for schools, increased
productivity, and flexibility of decision making.

Accountability

One of the most important tenets of the school reform movement of the 1980s
has been the desire to hold schools accountable for the educational outcomes
of their students. Site-based management does not improve accountability per
se, but it does provide two ways to make schools more accountable for their
performance: (1) by making the community part of the management process
and (2) by making school officials more accountable to the community.

An important role for any site council is to help establish the educational
goals of the school it represents. In addition to establishing goals, it must decide upon measurement standards for judging how well the school is performing
in relation to its stated goals. By participating in this process, the site council becomes part of the accountability process. If the school is successful, the
members of the council can share in that success. If the school fails to meet its
established goals, the public can look to both the professionals in the school
and the site council for explanations and improvements. Instead of simply crit-
icizing the school, community members will be challenged to help resolve the
problems that keep the local school from achieving its goals.

The school becomes progressively more accountable to the community as
the site council becomes involved in the school's operation. Parents, through
their involvement, will gain more confidence in school budgeting and financial
practices. Moreover, by reporting to the parents, school officials will be more
aware of community concerns and thus more responsive to issues of public
concern.

Productivity

Although scant, the literature on site-based management indicates three areas
where productivity might be enhanced: (1) increased services or reduced costs,
(2) increases in student access, and (3) lower costs of administering decentralized schools. Brown (1990) indicates that studies of decentralized schools have
revealed greater variation in the ways schools spend funds for supplies. He suggests that if one assumes local personnel know best how much should be spent
on supplies relative to other educational priorities, then spending, at least for
supplies, in decentralized school districts would be more efficient.

Brown also suggests that site-based management could improve equality of educational opportunity since the site could tailor programs to meet

the needs of the students enrolled at that particular school. He argues that one way to achieve greater equality among students, particularly disadvantaged students, is to give school personnel the discretion to use resources for students as they see fit, rather than based on a set of requirements handed down from the state or federal government or from the district's central office.

Finally, Brown quotes a study that estimates that site-based management will result in additional administrative tasks at the school site, something that might require additional resources. His analysis, however, does not consider the impact of decentralization on the central office. If central office positions can be eliminated, then economies in the cost of administration may be available, further enhancing the productivity of site-based management. Moreover, the advent of relatively inexpensive microcomputers and networks makes it possible to develop management systems that minimize the additional workload at the school site and provide better information for making critical decisions. These factors, which may come with initial investment costs, appear to have long-term potential for reducing the costs of administration in school systems.

Flexibility

Although it seems obvious that increasing local authority would result in increased flexibility for schools that benefit from this increased authority, such may not be the case. Even under site-based management, many schools must still meet certain district and state requirements. For example, California has strict pupil-teacher ratios that must be adhered to by grade level. These restrictions could eliminate a certain amount of flexibility within a school. Similarly, resource constraints, a common problem for school districts, could limit the flexibility a local site has to establish an educational program.

To the extent that site-based management programs allow waivers from state or district requirements, flexibility is enhanced. Obviously, such waivers and decentralization do not have to go hand-in-hand, but to the extent that the two are related in state or district policy, the greater potential flexibility schools will have as they initiate their own educational programs.

IMPLICATIONS FOR STATE SCHOOL FINANCE SYSTEMS

The question remaining is what impact site-based management programs will have on the way states choose to provide funds to local school districts. There is no simple or direct answer to this question. The problem is that state finance systems are designed to provide revenue to school districts, with the allocation of funds within a district left to local decision makers. As a result, it is possible for a district to establish a site-based management program without affecting the way state funds are allocated to that district. This is the case wherever state funds still come to school districts through unrestricted grant mechanisms.

States that wish to encourage site-based management programs could provide incentives to districts implementing these programs. The incentives could take the form of additional funds allocated to districts that establish site-based management programs, or it could take the form of reduced state regulation for those districts that elected to decentralize their operations. Since site-based management requires local participation, it seems unlikely that state mandating of decentralized management of schools would meet with much success. Schools that did not want to establish site management would find many creative ways to resist the mandate.

Some finance structures seem more supportive of site-based management programs than others. For example, state systems that fund classroom units, and then provide for the teacher's salary as part of the unit funding, appear to offer less flexibility to local school sites than do state programs that provide block grant funding on an enrollment basis. In any case, the success of site-based management programs seems dependent more on the willingness of the school district's central administration to give up some of its authority and resources to the school sites than on the way states elect to distribute funds to local districts. Malen, Ogawa, and Kranz (1990) argue that more research on site-based management is needed. Their analysis of the existing literature on site-based management found that to date there is little evidence that programs to decentralize school district decision making succeed in altering authority relationships or developing the qualities associated with academically effective schools.

SUMMARY

Site-based management is a procedure whereby some portion of a district's management authority is transferred to the school site. The rationale for doing this stems from the assumption that it is the individuals at the local school who best understand the needs of the children enrolled in the school and what programs will best serve them.

A number of authors have argued that for site-based management programs to succeed, authority relationships between the school site and the central office need to change. Specifically, these authors suggest that local schools be given more discretion in deciding what central office services they wish to use and which services they purchase from some other source. They further argue that school sites should have more autonomy in allocating budget resources and should be given the ability to carry over unspent funds whether they accrue through skillful management of resources (such as substitute teachers or energy conservation) or through savings programs designed to allow the purchase of major items that can't be financed with one year's funding allocation.

One of the major issues in site-based management is the establishment of a school-site council. Many issues regarding the membership, voting procedures, and authority of the council need to be established if site-based programs are to be successful. Site-based management also appears to offer several potential advantages in terms of school accountability, productivity, and flexibility, although the literature on these subjects to date is rather limited.

Finally, if states wish to encourage school district decentralization, they can either offer incentives for site-based management programs or at least provide large portions of state aid in the form of general Grants that won't unduly restrict school districts from implementing these programs.

—*Appendix* ———————————————————

Using the School Finance Simulation

The school finance simulation was designed as an integral component of this book. This appendix describes how to install and use the simulation on your computer. Two versions of the simulation are available, one for Macintosh computers and another for IBM PC or compatible computers. The simulation was designed using common spreadsheet programs—Excel for the Macintosh and Excel with Windows for IBM and compatibles—and requires access to these programs to run. Both are commonly available in university microcomputer laboratories. Although the simulation relies on a spreadsheet program, it has been designed so that students with little or no knowledge of Excel can use the programs immediately. Once it has been installed, operation of the simulation is identical on both systems.

For each computing system, the simulation has two components: (1) a 10-district sample, and (2) a shell to use for analysis of a 100-district sample from your individual state. The 10-district sample analyzes the impact of school finance formulas on a data set created for this book. All the examples in the text use these 10 sample districts to compare the equity effects of school finance formula alternatives.

The 100-district shell will perform the same calculations as the 10-district sample. We have included data for 100 sample districts with the shell, but we recommend that you replace this data with information from your own state.

Once these data have been entered into the system, you will be able to use the simulation to estimate the effects of different school finance options on the various equity measures described in this book, and the effect of these options on state and local spending for education.

Both the 10-district sample and the 100-district shell provide the capability to print the results of each simulation option you choose. In addition, the simulation allows you to graph district revenue against property wealth per pupil. Copies of these graphs can also be directed to your printer.

Specific directions for installing and using the simulation on both types of computers are described below.

MACINTOSH SYSTEMS

System Requirements

The simulation for Macintosh computers was designed using Microsoft Excel Version 2.2. To operate the 10-district simulation, you will need a Macintosh Plus, Classic, SE, SE/30, LC, II, IIc, IIcx, IIsi, IIci, or IIfx computer with at least one megabyte of random access memory (RAM), and either two 800-kilobyte diskette drives or one 800-kilobyte diskette drive and a hard disk. You will need System Version 6.0.1 or later and Finder version 4.1 or higher, as well as Microsoft Excel version 2.2. The 100-district shell requires more memory to run. Consequently, you cannot use it on a Macintosh Plus or any other Macintosh computer with less than two megabytes of RAM.

If you don't have the correct versions of Excel, the System, or the Finder, consult your university microcomputer laboratory consultant, or if you are operating this on your personal computer, your Apple dealer.

Many features of the simulation take advantage of the Macintosh's color graphics capabilities. However, the system is fully operational with monochrome displays. Because the simulation requires a substantial number of calculations, the 10-district simulation may take as long as 60 seconds to complete some calculations on older (and slower) computers. In early tests, recalculation of a 10-district school finance option took between 10 seconds, on a Mac IIcx, and nearly 60 seconds on a Mac Plus. Both systems utilized a hard disk. Your times will vary, depending on the capabilities and configuration of your system.

It will take substantially longer to run the 100-district model. Because of the large number of calculations required, estimation of the 100-district model takes three to four minutes on a Mac II, and as long as 30 minutes on a Mac SE with two megabytes of RAM and no math coprocessor.

Installation

Making a Backup Copy of the School Finance Simulation   Before beginning installation, you should make a backup copy of the simulation diskette that came with the text book. The directions for making this backup copy are contained at the beginning of the installation instructions for both two-diskette systems and hard disk systems. Once you have made a backup copy, use the backup to conduct the simulations and store the original diskette in a safe place so you can make another copy should something happen to the copy you use every day.

> The simulation diskette is not copy protected. However, we assume that you will adhere to all copyright laws that apply to the use of computer software.

Two-diskette drive systems   The first step in installing the simulation on a two-diskette drive system is to make a backup copy of the disk that came with your textbook. To do this, put the simulation diskette in one of the drives and a blank, formatted diskette in the other drive.

> If you don't have a formatted diskette, place an unformatted diskette in the drive and follow the prompts that appear on the screen. For more information on formatting diskettes, refer to the manuals that came with your Macintosh computer.

Move the arrow over the icon for the simulation diskette and open the icon by clicking on it, and then *pulling down* the **file** menu, *dragging* the mouse until the **open** option is highlighted, and releasing the mouse button. Alternatively, you can *double click* on the icon. For more information about *double clicking*, refer to your Macintosh manuals.

> If you are unfamiliar with the terms *mouse, pointing, clicking,* and *dragging,* refer to the manuals that came with your Macintosh computer.

You will see one folder named "simulation" on the diskette. To copy the contents of the simulation diskette to your backup diskette, *click* and *drag* the folder icon from the installation diskette to the icon representing the backup diskette.

Now put the original simulation diskette away in a safe storage place so that you can use it to make another backup copy in the event something happens to the backup copy you just made. Then use the backup diskette to run the school finance simulations described in the text.

No further installation is required. Simply put your Excel diskette into one of the drives (this should be a start-up diskette) and the simulation diskette into the other drive. *Double click* on the simulation diskette icon, *double click* on the folder labeled "simulation," and finally *double click* again on the folder labeled "ten district."

You are now ready to begin using the simulation. To continue, refer to the "Operation" section below.

Hard Drive Systems   If your Macintosh has a hard disk drive, you should copy the contents of the simulation folder from the simulation diskette to a folder on your hard disk using the following steps:

1. Create a new folder on your hard disk. You do this by **opening** the icon for your hard disk, *pulling down* the **file** menu, *dragging* the mouse down until **new folder** is highlighted, and releasing the mouse button. A new folder, with the title "Empty Folder," will appear. Since "Empty Folder" is highlighted, any name you type *before* pressing the carriage return or enter key will become the new name for the folder you just created. You may use any name you wish. For the purposes of this example, we will name the folder "School Finance Simulation." To do this, type "School Finance Simulation" and press the carriage return key.

2. **Open** the simulation diskette icon. You do this by placing the arrow on the icon and *clicking* once, then *pulling down* the **file** menu from the menu bar across the top of the screen, *dragging* the mouse until the **open** option is highlighted, and *releasing* the mouse. Alternatively, you can *double click* on the diskette's icon.

> Note: If you are unfamiliar with the terms *mouse, pointing, clicking,* and *dragging,* refer to the manuals that came with your Macintosh computer.

3. Copy the simulation folder from the simulation diskette to the folder you just created. To copy the contents of the simulation diskette to the folder on your hard disk, *click* and *drag* the simulation folder icon from the installation diskette to the icon representing the folder you just created. Now put the original simulation diskette away in a safe storage place so that you can use it to make another backup copy in the event something happens to the backup copy you just made, and use the files on your hard disk to run the school finance simulations described in the text.

4. *Double click* on the folder labeled "simulation" and again use the folder labeled "ten district." You are now ready to begin operating the simulation. For further instructions in the operation of the simulation, refer to the next section, "Operation."
5. Install Excel version 2.2 if it is not already installed on your system. Refer to the manuals that come with Excel for installation instructions.

Starting the Simulation

To begin operating the school finance simulation, make sure that no software programs are operating. If other programs are operating, exit from them now. It is important that Excel *not* be running when you start the simulation. The Macintosh Finder and System will start Excel when you open the simulation file. If Excel is already running, you will get a system-error prompt on your screen. If this happens, make sure you have exited from Excel and any other programs before beginning again.

Open the icons and folders necessary until you have opened the folder labeled "ten district." One of the files in this folder is called "Ten District Example." This is an Excel file. Opening this file will launch Excel and begin operation of the simulation.

IBM OR COMPATIBLE SYSTEMS

System Requirements

The simulation runs under Microsoft Excel 3.0 with Windows. Therefore, you must have an IBM or compatible computer with Excel 3.0 and Windows 3.0. Operation of this software requires a hard disk. You will also need approximately one megabyte of storage space. The 10-district sample will run under any configuration that will accept versions 3.0 of Windows and Excel. It is recommended that your computer have a least two megabytes of RAM if you want to run the 100-district simulation.

Installation

The files for the simulation are contained in two directories on the installation disk. Before installing the simulation, you need to determine where you want the files ro reside on your hard disk. It is recommended that you establish a directory call "Sim" to hold these files. The following directions assume that when you turn on your computer, the active drive is C and that you want to create a directory called "Sim" to store the simulation files. You can install the files anywhere on your hard drive or drives by replacing the C:> with the name of another drive (e.g., A, B) and "Sim" with any other legal directory name.

To install the simulation of an IBM or compatible computer, follow these steps:

1. Start your computer. If Windows automatically begins operation when you start your computer, exit from Windows by *double clicking* on the DOS icon.
2. Create a directory named "Sim." At the C:> prompt type
   C:>**md Sim [CR]**
3. Make "Sim" the active directory. At the C:> prompt type
   C:>**cd Sim [CR]**
   (Your prompt should now read **c:\SIM:>**. If your system does not show the active directory at the prompt, you can check to make sure you are in the correct directory by typing **cd [CR]** at the C:> prompt. The computer will respond with the path describing the active directory.)
4. Place the Installation Disk in drive A or B as appropriate.
5. Begin the install program by typing one of the following, depending on which drive your simulation diskette is in:
   C:\SIM:>**A:Installa [CR]**
   C:\SIM:>**B:Installb [CR]**
   The install program will create two new subdirectories: TENDIST and 100DIST. TENDIST contains the files for the 10-district simulation and 100DIST the files for the 100-district simulation.
6. When the files have been copied, you will see a message on your screen indicating that the installation is complete and telling you how to start the program.

Starting the Simulation

Once the simulation is installed, you are ready to start using it. To start the simulation, follow these steps:

1. Start Windows. Return to the root directory and type C:>**win [CR]**.
2. Start the File Manager. *Double click* on the File Manager icon.
3. Using the File Manager's features, *double click* on drive names, directory names and subdirectory names until you see the files in either the TENDIST or 100DIST subdirectory.
4. If you want to run the 10-district simulation, from inside the TENDIST directory, *double click* on the file TENDIST.XLW. Excel will start, and the simulation will load itself.
5. If you want to run the 100-district simulation, from inside the 100DIST directory, *double click* on the file 100DIST.XLW. Excel will start, and the simulation will load itself.

Once the simulation has started, its operation is identical to the operation of the Macintosh version of the simulation. Specific directions for using the simulation follow.

Operation of the simulation is identical for both Macintosh and IBM or compatible computer systems. As described above, once the simulation has been installed, simply *double click* on the icon representing the file you want to open, either "Ten District Example" or "100 District Sample" on a Macintosh, or "TENDIST.XLW" or "100DIST.XLW" on PC compatibles. This will launch Excel, loading the files needed to run the simulation. This process could take as long as two minutes on some computers, so please be patient.

You will see a Welcome screen appear briefly; then a number of other screens will appear one after another. After a brief period of time, the Welcome screen will reappear. When the program is fully loaded and ready for use, the computer will *beep* at you.

Another way to know when the program is fully loaded and ready for use is to look at the mouse arrow. If the arrow has turned into a "watch" or "hourglass" icon, the program is still loading. If the arrow has returned, or if it has become a large plus (+) sign, the program is fully loaded. The plus sign is the cursor indicator used by Excel.

The simulation has been designed so that users do not need to have any knowledge of Excel. In fact, *users familiar with Excel's operation should refrain from using any of Excel's capabilities and features and follow the instructions below to ensure that the files are not damaged.*

If the window containing the simulation does not fill the entire screen of your computer, you can enlarge the display by *clicking* on the box on the right-hand side of the Excel title bar. *Clicking* on this box once will expand the window to fill the screen. *Clicking* on the box again will return the window to its original size.

Running a Simulation

This section will walk you through the steps needed to run a simple simulation, view and print the output, and graph expenditures against wealth per pupil.

Look at the top of the Excel screen. The only menu option available to you is called **Model**. This is the only menu item you will need to use to operate the school finance simulation.

If you just started the simulation, you should have the Welcome screen displayed on your monitor. If you don't, either start the simulation using the directions above, or if you have started the simulation, use the arrow bars on the side and bottom of the window to move the location boxes to the left (bottom bar) and top (side bar). This will put you in cell A1, and the welcome screen should be visible.

Now, *pull down* the **Model** menu. You will see the following options:

Pupil Weights
View Base Data
Simulation Option
   No State Aid
   Flat Grant
   Foundation
   GTB
   Combination Foundation/GTB
Print Results
   Base Data
   No State Aid
   Flat Grant
   Foundation
   GTB
   Combination
Graph of Revenue v. Wealth
   Base Data
   No State Aid
   Flat Grant
   Foundation
   GTB
   Combination
Exit From Simulation

> If you do not see all of these options on your screen, there will be a small arrow at the bottom of the last visible option. To view and access additional options, *drag* the mouse down past the last visible option. Additional options will scroll into view. Continue *dragging* the mouse until the last option, **Exit from Simulation**, is visible. To access an option that is now above your field of view, drag the mouse back up toward the **Model** menu option.

To choose an option, *drag* the mouse until the option you want is highlighted and release the mouse button. You will use these options to run the entire school finance simulation. Each of the options is described in the "Reference" section below. First, this section walks you through a simple simulation.

To begin the simulation, *pull down* the **Model** menu. Since we want to start by running a simulation, highlight one of the options in the section of the menu titled **Simulation Option**. For this example, highlight the option titled **Foundation** and release the mouse button. This will simulate a Foundation program on the sample of 10 school districts.[1] A dialog box will appear in the center of your screen.

The dialog box is the way you will tell the simulation program what parameters you want to simulate. As you can see, there is a data entry box titled **Foundation Level**. The number in that data entry box is highlighted. If the number in that box is different from the one you want to simulate, all you have to do is type the desired number. In this case, let's try a foundation level of $1,600 per pupil. To do this, just type the number 1600. Do not include a dollar sign or a comma. Text in the dialog box reminds you to type only the numbers. You will see that the number that had previously been in the **Foundation Level** box has been replaced by 1600. *Do not* type an **enter** or **carriage return** at this point.

> This highlights one of the most powerful features of Macintosh computers. Anytime you use the mouse to highlight a portion of text, anything you type once that text has been highlighted will replace the highlighted text.

Now use the mouse to move the cursor to the **Required Tax Rate** data entry box. Alternatively, pressing the **Tab** key will move the cursor to this data entry box. Notice that, as you move the arrow around in the dialog box with the mouse, the arrow turns into an "I" bar when it enters a data entry box. Place this "I" bar on the left-hand side of the entry in the data box, then *click* and *drag* with the mouse until the entire contents of the box are highlighted. Now you can type in a new required tax rate. In this case, enter a tax rate of 16.

Once you have entered all the parameters in the dialog box, move the arrow to the **enter** box and *click* the mouse once. At this point, the computer will begin simulating the options you suggested. A screen will tell you that the computer is calculating the results. These calculations will take between 10 and 60 seconds, depending on the configuration of your computer.

When the calculations are complete, the computer will beep at you, and the display will show a portion of the data displayed in Figure A.1. The portion of this figure visible on the screen will depend on the size of your monitor. You can view other portions of the data for the foundation program by using the mouse to scroll around the worksheet.

Now, assuming you want a permanent record of your simulation, you can print out the results. *Pull down* the **Model** menu. Under the section titled **Print Results**, highlight the **Foundation** option and release the mouse button.

---

[1] A discussion of Foundation programs is contained in Chapter 7.

FIGURE A.1 Ten-District Sample: Foundation Program (foundation level: $1,600; required tax rate (mills): 16)

Pupil weights		
Regular	1.00	Comp. 1.00
Handicapped	1.00	LEP 1.00

District	Pupils	Property Value per Pupil ($)	Old Property Tax Rate (mills)	New Property Tax Rate (mills)	Old Local Revenue per Pupil ($)	New Local Revenue per Pupil ($)	New State Revenue per Pupil ($)	Change in State Revenue per Pupil ($)	Total Revenue per Pupil ($)	Total Gain (Loss) per Pupil ($)
A	10,040	36,670	30.43	29.95	1,116	1,098	1,013	35	2,112	18
B	7,028	46,845	28.33	16.00	1,327	750	850	(38)	1,600	(615)
C	7,985	55,203	26.86	16.00	1,483	883	717	(77)	1,600	(677)
D	4,152	64,875	25.61	16.00	1,661	1,038	562	(58)	1,600	(681)
E	5,148	71,762	24.39	16.00	1,750	1,148	452	(120)	1,600	(722)
F	6,216	81,913	23.54	16.00	1,928	1,311	289	(188)	1,600	(805)
G	3,666	92,949	23.28	16.00	2,164	1,487	113	(324)	1,600	(1,001)
H	2,961	106,195	21.72	25.59	2,307	2,718	0	(411)	2,718	0
I	3,472	135,496	19.52	22.38	2,645	3,033	0	(388)	3,033	0
J	848	306,766	10.52	11.71	3,227	3,593	0	(366)	3,593	0
Weighted average		71,277	25.69	19.63	1,688	1,335	558	(128)	1,893	(481)
Standard deviation		40,819	3.73	5.75	484	700	352	143	490	361
Median		64,875	25.61		1,661				1,600	

	Totals	Change
Pupils	51,516	
Local revenue	$68,789,859	($18,156,941)
State revenue	$28,745,545	($ 5,271,698)
Total revenue	$97,535,404	($23,428,639)

State aid

Number of winners 1
Number of losers 9

Equity Measures

Horizontal equity
Range	$1,993
Range ratio	.896
Coef. of variation	.259
McLoone index	1.000
Gini coefficient	.117

Fiscal neutrality
Correlation	.706
Elasticity	.285

321

A copy of the results will be directed to your printer. If you used the options suggested above, your printout should be nearly identical to Figure A.1.

Look briefly at Figure A.1 (or your own printout if you made one). As you can see, Figure A.1 shows a foundation level of $1,600 and a required tax rate of 16 mills.

To the right of this information is a box indicating the pupil weights you have chosen.[2] Since you did not choose to use pupil weights, all of the weights are shown as 1.0. The default is to not use pupil weights. If you want to simulate a weighted pupil model, you must choose the **Pupil Weights** option from the **Model** menu. This is described in detail in the "Reference" section below.

Below this information is a district-by-district printout of relevant characteristics. Make sure you understand what each of these columns represents. If you don't, refer to Chapter 7.

Below the district detail is summary information including weighted averages,[3] standard deviations, and medians. In addition, the total number of pupils, the total local and state revenue, and the change in local and state revenue from the base case are displayed. Finally, the printout displays a number of equity measures and shows how many districts gained state aid and how many lost state aid.

For each simulation you run, all of these statistics are calculated and displayed on the screen. Moreover, every time you choose the **print** option from the **Model** menu, the results of the most recent simulation will be printed.

Another feature of the simulation is its ability to provide you with a graph of district revenue against property wealth per pupil. To view the graph of revenue versus property wealth per pupil, *pull down* the **Model** menu, highlight the **Foundation** option under the **Graph of Revenue v. Wealth** section of the menu, and release the mouse button.

A graph of revenues against property wealth per pupil will appear on your screen. The significance of this graph is discussed in Chapter 7. The graph title indicates which model you simulated, and the parameters you chose are displayed in the lower right-hand corner of the graph. Notice that the **Model** menu is still available. *Pull down* the **Model** menu and you will see that there are only two options: (1) **Return to Ten District Sample**; and (2) **Print Graph.** Try printing the graph, and then return to the **Ten District Sample.** A printout of this graph is included as Figure A.2 for your reference.

Before going on, try some additional simulations on your own. Choose one of the other options, answer the questions in the dialog box, and view the results, both on the screen and (if possible) as a printout. Don't worry yet about what the numbers mean. Just get comfortable with simulation so that when you are asked to answer problems, or conduct analyses for class, you will be comfortable accessing and using the school finance simulation.

---

[2] For a description of pupil weights see Chapter 8.

[3] The weighted averages are calculated on the basis of pupils, not districts. Thus, the $71,277 figure for Property Value Per Pupil is not the average of the ten values listed in the detail above, but an average of those ten values weighted by the number of students in each district. See Unit of Analysis in Chapter 3.

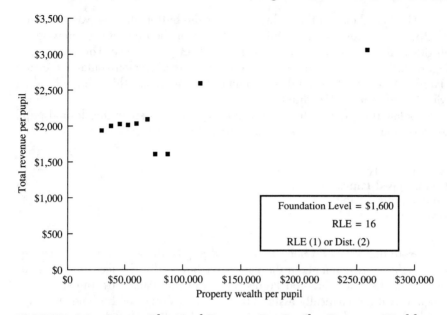

FIGURE A.2   Scatter Plot Total Revenue Per Pupil v. Property Wealth Per Pupil Foundation Program

When you are finished running simulations, exit from the simulation by choosing the **Exit from Simulation** option under the **Model** menu. This will close all the open files and get you out of the Excel application. Remember that if the **Exit from Simulation** menu item is not visible on your screen, all you have to do is scroll down the menu until it becomes visible.

> Do not use any other Excel commands to exit from the simulation; doing so will damage the simulation program files.

REFERENCE

TEN-DISTRICT SAMPLE

This section serves as a reference to the use of the simulation. It describes each of the options on the **Model** menu in more detail. They are discussed in the order in which they appear in the menu.

Pupil Weights

This menu option produces a dialog box that allows the user to control whether or not you will simulate a weighted pupil program, and to choose what those weights will be for regular, compensatory, handicapped, and LEP children.

The first choice in the dialog box is a radio button allowing you to choose whether or not you will use pupil weights. If you choose to use pupil weights, all titles in the data tables will change to reflect your choice. For example, in Figure A.1, the second column in the district detail section contains the title "Pupils." If you elect to simulate a weighted pupil option, this column heading will change to read "Weighted Pupils."

Below the radio buttons are data entry boxes to enter the desired pupil weights. You will see that the default entries are as follows:

Regular Pupils	1.0
Handicapped Pupils	2.0
Compensatory Pupils	1.3
LEP pupils	1.3

Note that if you do not use weighted pupils, there is no need to change the weighting assignments in the data entry boxes. If you select the "no" radio button for the **Use Weighted Pupils** section of the dialog box, the simulation program will automatically assign all students a weight of 1.0, and the pupil weight box on each of your data printouts will indicate weights of 1.0. If you select the "yes" button, the weights you enter in the data entry boxes will be used in the simulation and will appear in that box on each printout.

The number of pupils in each of the weighting categories by district has been predetermined and cannot be changed in the simulation. Figure A.3 shows the number of pupils by special need category for all of the 10 sample districts.

View Base Data

An important component of any simulation consists of the base data to which alternatives are compared. These data are contained in the Excel spreadsheet and can be viewed by choosing the **View Base Data** option from the **Model** menu. Note that you can get a printout of this data, along with the summary and equity statistics, by choosing the **Base Data** option under the **Print Results** option. You can also graph revenue against wealth per pupil for this data by using the **Base Data** option in the **Graph Revenue v. Wealth** section of the menu.

Simulation Option

This section of the **Model** menu is the heart of the simulation program. By choosing one of five options, the user can simulate a variety of state finance programs. The options available include:

- No State Aid
- Flat Grant
- Foundation Program
- Guaranteed Tax Base (GTB)
- Combination Foundation/GTB

FIGURE A.3 Pupils in Special Needs Categories: 10 Sample Districts

District	Total Unweighted Pupils	Total Weighted Pupils	Regular		Handicapped		Compensatory		LEP	
			Unweighted	Weighted	Unweighted	Weighted	Unweighted	Weighted	Unweighted	Weighted
A	10,040	12,277	5,462	5,462	1,234	2,468	2,298	2,987	1,046	1,360
B	7,028	8,583	3,939	3,939	898	1,796	1,550	2,015	641	833
C	7,985	9,555	4,870	4,870	908	1,816	1,489	1,936	718	933
D	4,152	5,059	2,312	2,312	507	1,014	989	1,286	344	447
E	5,148	6,171	3,134	3,134	598	1,196	1,004	1,305	412	536
F	6,216	7,295	4,071	4,071	622	1,244	1,045	1,359	478	621
G	3,666	4,451	2,371	2,371	567	1,134	697	906	31	40
H	2,961	3,580	1,783	1,783	379	758	598	777	201	261
I	3,472	4,054	2,388	2,388	367	734	516	671	201	261
J	848	996	596	596	103	206	98	127	51	66
Total	51,516	62,021	30,926	30,926	6,183	12,366	10,284	13,369	4,123	5,360

With the exception of the **No State Aid** option, all the options produce a dialog box allowing the user to select the parameters of the simulation.[4] All these options work with and without pupil weights. The summary data at the top of each printout and on each graph indicate which parameters have been selected to help the user identify alternatives later.

Print Results

This section of the **Model** menu is used to print the results of each simulation. When users highlight an option, Excel highlights the relevant area for printing and sends the necessary signals to the printer. It is assumed that the user's computer is attached to a printer, and that the printer has been selected through the chooser. Output should print to any Macintosh or compatible printer.

The **Model** menu in the graph mode also contains a printout option. It works exactly as described above, sending a printout of the graph being viewed to the printer.

Graph of Revenue vs. Wealth

As described in Chapter 7, an analysis of alternative school finance formulas is incomplete without consideration of the correlation between revenue and property wealth per pupil. This relationship is often easier to understand if presented graphically. Consequently, the simulation allows the user to view a graph of these two variables at any time. Selection of any of the graph options will produce a graphic screen plotting the most recent data for the simulation option being plotted. As described under **Print Results** above, a printout can be obtained by choosing that option from the **Model** menu appearing at the top of the graph screen.

Exit from Simulation

To quit working with the simulation program, choose this option. *Do not exit Excel in any other way, as doing so may result in damage to the simulation files.* When you choose this option, the program will save the most recent versions of each simulation and exit from Excel. Again, depending on the capability and configuration of your computer, this may take a few minutes.

THE 100-DISTRICT SHELL

The 100-district shell operates almost exactly the same way as the 10-district example. The **Model** menu has been modified slightly, and the program includes procedures for adding your own state data to the simulation.

---

[4] There is no need for a dialog box for the **No State Aid** option since it is really a flat grant program with a grant of zero. Beyond that, no choices need be made by the user.

The procedure for starting the 100-district shell is similar to the procedure for starting the 10-district example. Open the folder titled **100 district** and *double click* on the file named **100 district sample**. Once the program is loaded, you will see the welcome screen. As with the 10-district example, the only menu available to you is the **Model** menu.

Pull down the **Model** menu. You will notice that it is somewhat different from the **Model** menu for the 10-district sample. The following items are contained in the **Model** menu for the 100-district sample:

> Model
> Enter or Edit Data
>   Enter Sample Data
>   End Data Entry
> View Base Data
> Run Simulations
> View Graphs
>   Base Data
>   Simulated Data
> Print Results
>   Base Data
>   Simulated Data
> Exit from Simulation

Enter or Edit Data

One of the most important features of the 100-district sample is that it allows you to enter data from a sample of 100 districts in your own state. Unfortunately, it is not possible to design a simulation like this to accommodate the variation of school finance formulas found in each of the 50 states. Consequently, you will have to modify individual district data to fit into the simulation. Specifically, the simulation will only accept the following information:

> Pupils
> Total property value
> Tax rate in mills[5]
> Total local revenue
> Total state revenue, or state general aid revenue

Once you have collected this information for 100 districts in your state, you are ready to enter it into the simulation. To do this, pull down the **Model** menu and choose **Enter Sample Data**.

A new screen will appear. You will see headings corresponding to the five categories of information you need to enter, along with a column numbered

---

[5] A table showing how different tax rates can be converted to mills is contained in Chapter 7.

from 1 to 100. The number of rows displayed will depend on the size of your Macintosh display.

> Note that all Excel menus are available during the data entry process. This will make it possible for you to use the powerful **Copy** and **Paste** functions of the Macintosh as well as any other Excel features you may be familiar with. If you have not used Excel before, it is still possible to enter all of your data without using any menu except the **Model** menu.

You will also see the data that were provided with the 100-district simulation. As you enter your own data, it will replace the information that came with the simulation. To begin entering data, simply move the cursor to cell AB30 and type in the number of pupils in the first district of your sample data. Press the right arrow key, and then enter the total property value for that district. Continue across the screen until you have filled in all of the information for the first district. To enter data for the second district, move the cursor to cell AB31 and repeat the process just described. Continue until the data for all 100 districts have been entered.

> If you are an experienced Excel user, you will note that you can create a separate spreadsheet with the data for your 100 districts and use the Macintosh's **Copy** and **Paste** functions to enter the data in the simulation.

Once you have entered all of the data for the 100 districts, *pull down* the **Model** menu and choose the **End Data Entry option.** Note that the **Model** menu is located on the right-hand side of the menu bar at this time. The simulation will enter the data and calculate the summary and equity statistics for you. This may take several minutes.

Running a Simulation

To run a simulation, pull down the **Model** menu and choose the **Run Simulations** option. You will see a dialog box asking you to choose a simulation option. *Click* on one of the radio buttons, and the dialog box for the simulation you selected will appear. The simulation dialog boxes are identical to the simulation dialog boxes for the 10-district example. After choosing the parameters you wish to model, *click* on the **Enter** button. As with the 10-district model, when the calculations are complete, the screen will display the summary and equity statistics for your model.

The major difference between the display for the 100-district sample and that of the 10-district sample is the fact that for the 100-district sample data have been summarized by pupil deciles. The pupil deciles are ranked by per-pupil expenditures. The Gini coefficient is not included in the 100-district sample because a substantial increase in calculation time and disk storage space would have been required.

To view a graph of the simulated data, *pull down* the **Model** menu and select the **Simulated Data** option under **View Graphs**. The **Model** menu on the graph gives you the option of printing the graph or returning to the 100-district sample.

To print the summary data for your simulation, pull down the **Model** menu and select the **Simulate Data** option under **Print Results**.

If you want to print or graph your base data, use the **Base Data** options under the **Simulate Data** or **Print Results** sections of the **Model** menu.

Exit from Simulation

To quit working with the simulation program, choose this option. *Do not exit Excel in any other way, as doing so may result in damage to the simulation files.* When you choose this option, the program will save the most recent versions of each simulation and exit from Excel. Again, depending on the capability and configuration of your computer, this may take a few minutes.

Glossary

This glossary contains a number of tax, education, and statistical terms that are used in school finance research and policy analysis. In order to make comparisons of tax and expenditure data among school districts, adjustments must be made in many measures. The purpose of these adjustments is to create a set of comparable numbers and a set of common terms. Standard procedures are used to make these adjustments, and this glossary indicates how some of the adjustments are made.

ADA, ADM   ADA is an abbreviation for student average daily attendance, and ADM is an abbreviation for student average daily membership. ADA and ADM are the official measures that most states use to represent the number of students in a school district for the purpose of calculating state aid. ADA is always less than ADM.

assessment ratios   The assessed valuation of property in most states is usually less than the market value of the property. In other words, owners are able to sell property for a price higher than the assessed valuation of that property. Although most states have a legal standard at which all property should be assessed, assessed valuations are usually below even the legal level and may vary widely among jurisdictions in a state. The assessment ratio, or actual assessment level, is determined by comparing actual assessed valuations to market values.

assessed valuation   The assessed valuation is the total value of property subject to the property tax in a school district. It is usually established by a local government officer and is only a percentage of the market value of the property.

assessed valuation, adjusted   Because local assessing jurisdictions in a state usually have different actual assessment ratios, the reported assessed valuations need to be adjusted in order to compare them among school districts. The best way to make such adjustments is to convert the assessed valuations to what they would be if all counties assessed at 100 percent of market value and then adjust them to the legal standard, for example, $33\frac{1}{3}$ percent. The mathematical way to make the adjustment is to divide the assessed valuation by the assessment ratio and multiply the result by the legal standard. The result is called the adjusted assessed valuation. For example, consider two school districts, A and B. District A has an assessed valuation of $200,000, and District B has an assessed valuation of $250,000. If we focus just on assessed valuations, District A would appear to be poorer in property wealth than District B. However, assume that the actual assessment ratio in District A is 20 percent and 25 percent in District B. If the legal ratio is $33\frac{1}{3}$ percent, the computation of the adjusted assessed valuation for District A is as follows:

$$\text{Adjusted assessed valuation} = \frac{\$200,000}{0.20} \times 0.333 = \$333,333$$

The computation of the adjusted assessed valuation for District B is

$$\text{Adjusted assessed valuation} = \frac{\$250,000}{0.25} \times 0.333 = \$333,333$$

Both school districts have the same adjusted assessed valuation. That is, both school districts effectively have the same total tax base, despite the differences in the reported assessed valuation. Adjusted assessed valuations must be used to compare property wealth among school districts and should be the basis on which state equalization aid is calculated.

assessed valuation per pupil, adjusted The adjusted assessed valuation per pupil is the adjusted assessed valuation for a school district divided by the district's total ADA or ADM.

categorical programs This term refers to state aid that is designated for specific programs. Examples would be transportation aid, special education aid, and aid for vocational education. Equalization formula aid is not an example of categorical aid. Formula funds provide general aid that can be used for any purpose.

correlation Correlation is a statistical term indicating the relationship between two variables. When two variables are said to be positively correlated, one variable tends to increase as the other variable increases. When two variables are said to be negatively correlated, one variable tends to increase as the other decreases.

correlation coefficient The correlation coefficient is a number indicating the degree of correlation between two variables. Because of the way a correlation coefficient is calculated, it always will have a value between -1.0 and $+1.0$. When the correlation coefficient is around $+0.5$ to $+1.0$, the two variables have a *positive relationship* or are *positively correlated*—when one variable gets larger, the other tends to get larger. When the correlation coefficient is around zero, the two variables do not appear to have any relationship. When the correlation coefficient is between -0.5 and -1.0, the variables have a *negative relationship* or are *negatively correlated*—as one gets larger, the other tends to get smaller.

current operating expenditures Current operating expenditures are those for the daily operation of the school program, such as expenditures for administration, instruction, attendance and health services, transportation, operation and maintenance of plant, and fixed charges.

district power equalization District power equalization (DPE) refers to a state aid program that "equalizes" the ability of each school district to raise dollars for education. In a pure DPE program, the state guarantees to both property-poor and property-rich school districts the same dollar yield for the same property tax rate. In short, equal tax rates produce equal per-pupil expenditures. In the property-poor school districts, the state makes up the difference between what is raised locally and what the state guarantees. In property-rich school districts, excess funds may or may not be "recaptured" by the state and distributed to the property-poor districts. Most DPE state laws do not include recapture provisions. However, Montana and Utah have recapture mechanisms in their new school finance laws. DPE programs are given different names in many states, including guaranteed tax base programs (GTBs), guaranteed yield programs, and percentage equalizing programs. DPE programs focus on the ability to support education and thus enhance the local fiscal role in education decision making. DPE would satisfy the "fiscal neutrality" standard without achieving "uniformity" of expenditures among school districts.

elasticity of tax revenues This term refers to the responsiveness of the revenues from a tax to changes in various economic factors in the state or nation. In particular, policymakers may want to know whether tax revenues will increase more rapidly, as rapidly, or less rapidly than changes in personal income. The revenues from an elastic tax will increase by more than 1 percent for each 1 percent change in personal income. Income taxes are usually elastic tax sources. In general, elastic tax sources have progressive patterns of incidence, and inelastic tax sources have regressive patterns of incidence. Expenditure elasticity may be defined similarly.

equalization formula aid Equalization formula aid is financial assistance given by a higher-level government—the state—to a lower-level government—school districts—to equalize the fiscal situation of the lower-level government. Because school districts vary in their abilities to raise property tax dollars, equalization formula aid is allocated to make the ability to raise such local funds more nearly equal. In general, equalization formula aid increases as the per-pupil property wealth of a school district decreases.

expenditure uniformity Expenditure uniformity is part of the horizontal equity standard in school finance requiring equal expenditures per pupil or per weighted pupil for all students in the state. (See ***fiscal neutrality***.)

fiscal capacity Fiscal capacity is the ability of a local governmental entity, such as a school district, to raise tax revenues. It is usually measured by the size of the local tax base, usually property wealth per pupil in education.

fiscal neutrality Fiscal neutrality is a court-defined equity standard in school finance. It is a negative standard, stating that current operating expenditures per pupil, or some resource, cannot be related to a school district's adjusted assessed valuation per pupil or some fiscal capacity measure. It simply means that differences in expenditures per pupil cannot be related to local school district wealth. (See ***expenditure uniformity***.)

flat grant programs   A flat grant program simply allocates an equal sum of dollars to each public school pupil in the state. A flat grant is not an equalization aid program because it allocates the same dollars per pupil regardless of the property or income wealth of the local school districts. If *no local* dollars are raised for education and all school dollars come from the state, a flat-grant program becomes equivalent to full state assumption.

foundation program   A foundation program is a state equalization aid program that typically guarantees a certain foundation level of expenditure for each student, together with a minimum tax rate that each school district must levy for education purposes. The difference between what a local school district raises at the minimum tax rate and the foundation expenditure is made up in state aid. In the past, foundation programs were referred to as *minimum foundation programs,* and the foundation level of expenditure was quite low. Today, most newly enacted foundation programs usually require an expenditure per pupil at or above the previous year's state average. Foundation programs focus on the per-pupil expenditure level and thus enhance the state government's fiscal role in education.

full state assumption   Full state assumption (FSA) is a school finance program in which the state pays for all education costs and sets equal per-pupil expenditures in all school districts. FSA would satisfy the expenditure per pupil "uniformity" standard of equity. Only in Hawaii has the state government fully assumed most of the costs of public education.

guaranteed tax base program (GTB)   See *district power equalization.*

guaranteed yield program   See *district power equalization.*

median family income   Median family income usually is that reported in the decennial U.S. census. It reflects income for the year before the census was taken, i.e., 1989 income for the 1990 census. If the income of all families in a school district were rank-ordered, the median income would be the income of the family midway between the lowest- and the highest-income families.

municipal overburden   Municipal overburden is an argument that refers to the fiscal position of large cities. Municipal overburden includes the large burden of noneducation services that central cities must provide and that most other jurisdictions do not have to provide, or at least do not have to provide in the same quantity. These noneducation services may include above-average welfare, health and hospitalization, public housing, and police, fire, and sanitation services. These high noneducation fiscal burdens mean that education must compete with many other functional areas for each local tax dollar raised, thus reducing the ability of large city school districts to raise education dollars. The fiscal squeeze caused by the service overburden, together with the concentration of the educationally disadvantaged and children in need of special education services in city schools, puts central city school districts at a fiscal disadvantage in supporting school services.

percentage equalizing programs   See *district power equalization.*

progressive tax   A progressive tax is one that increases proportionately more than income as the income level of the taxpayer increases. Under a progressive tax, a high-income taxpayer will pay a larger percentage of income than a low-income taxpayer.

property tax circuit breaker program   This is a tax relief program, usually financed by the state, that focuses property tax relief on particular households presumed to be overburdened by property taxes. That is, it is intended to reduce presumed regressivity of the property tax. A typical circuit breaker attempts to limit the property tax burden to a percentage of household income and applies only to residential property taxes. The percentage usually rises as income rises, so that the overall burden is progressive. Most states enacted circuit breaker programs initially just for senior citizens, but a few states have extended circuit breaker benefits to all low-income households, regardless of the age of the head of the household. The circuit breaker is based on actual or estimated taxes paid on residential property and generally takes the form of a credit on state income taxes.

property tax incidence or burden—traditional and new views   The traditional view of property tax incidence divided the tax into two components: that which fell on land and that which fell on improvements, i.e., structures. Property taxes on land were assumed to fall on landowners. The part on improvements was assumed to fall on homeowners in the case of owned homes, to be shifted forward to tenants in the case of rented residences and to be shifted forward to consumers in the case of taxes on business property. Nearly all empirical studies based on the traditional view found the incidence pattern to result in a regressive burden distribution, markedly regressive in lower income ranges. The new view of property tax incidence considers the tax to be an essentially uniform tax on all property in the country. Such a tax is borne by owners of capital, and thus the burden distribution pattern is progressive. Although the new view allows for modifications caused by admitted tax rate differentials across the country, adherents of the new view hold that even with the modifications the tax would exhibit a progressive pattern of incidence over much of the range of family incomes.

proportional tax   A proportional tax is a tax that consumes the same percentage of family income at all income levels.

pupil-weighted system or weighted-pupil programs   A pupil-weighted system is a state aid system in which pupils are given different weights based on the estimated or assumed costs of their education program; aid is allocated on the basis of the total number of weighted students. Usually, the cost of the education program for grades 4–6 is considered the standard program and weighted 1.0. For states such as Florida that choose to invest more dollars in the early school years, pupils in grades K–3 are given a weight greater than 1.0, typically around 1.3. In other states, high school students are weighted about 1.25, although these secondary weightings are slowly being eliminated. The two major programmatic areas where numerous weightings have been used are special and vocational education. Weighted-pupil programs, therefore, recognize that it costs more to provide an education program for some students than for others, and they include the extra costs via a higher weighting. State aid is then calculated and distributed on the basis of the total number of weighted students in each school district. Determining the appropriate weight is, however, a difficult matter.

regressive tax   A regressive tax is one that increases proportionately less than income as the income level of the taxpayer increases. Under a regressive tax a low-income taxpayer will pay a larger percentage of income than a high-income taxpayer.

revenue gap   A revenue gap exists when projected expenditures exceed projected tax revenues. Although revenue gaps usually are not allowed to exist in fact for current fiscal years, the projected values are important. If revenue gaps are projected, tax rate increases or expenditure cuts, both politically difficult, will be required. Revenue gaps usually occur when the elasticity of expenditures exceeds the elasticity of revenues. This often happens at the state and local level because state and local taxes are, in most instances, less elastic than expenditures. If states want to eliminate the occurrence of revenue gaps and the constant need to increase tax rates or decrease projected expenditure levels, attention must be given to ways to increase the elasticity of state tax systems, usually by increasing reliance on income taxes. (See *elasticity of tax revenues*).

school district tax rate   School district tax rate is the term states use to indicate the local school property tax rate. The tax rate often is stated as the amount of property tax dollars to be paid for each $100 of assessed valuation or, if given in mills, the rate indicates how much is raised for each $1,000 of assessed valuation. For example, a tax rate of $1.60 per hundred dollars of assessed valuation means that a taxpayer pays $1.60 for each $100 of his total assessed valuation; a tax rate of 16 mills indicates that $16 must be paid for each $1,000 of assessed valuation.

state aid for current operating expense   State aid for current operating expense is the sum of the equalization formula aid and categorical aid for vocational education, special education, bilingual education, transportation, and other categorical aid programs. (See *catergorical programs.*)

tax burden (or sometimes *tax incidence*)   Tax burden typically refers to the percentage of an individual's or family's income that is consumed by a tax or by a tax system. Usually, one wants to know whether a tax or tax system's burden is distributed in a progressive, proportional, or regressive manner. In the United States, a tax system that is progressive overall seems to be the most acceptable to a majority of people. Tax burden analysis takes into account the extent of tax shifting.

tax incidence   See *tax shifitng* and *tax burden.*

tax price   The tax price is generally the tax rate a district must levy to purchase a given level and quality of school services. Poor districts generally have to levy a higher tax rate, and thus pay a higher tax price, to purchase a given bundle of school services than a wealthy district because, at a given tax rate, the poor district would raise fewer dollars per pupil than the wealthy district.

tax shifting (or *tax incidence*)   Tax shifting refers to the phenomenon wherein the party that must legally pay a tax, for example, a store owner, does not in fact bear the burden of the tax but shifts the tax to another party, for example, the consumer of what is sold in the store. Taxes can be shifted either forward or backward. For example, a landlord might be able to shift his property taxes forward to tenants in the form of higher rents, and a business might be able to shift property or corporate income taxes backward to employees in the form of lower salaries. The ability to shift taxes depends on a variety of economic factors, and there is great debate among economists over the extent to which some taxes are shifted. It is usually agreed, however, that individual income taxes are not shifted and rest on the individual taxpayer. It is also generally agreed that sales taxes are shifted to the consumer. There is argument over the extent to which corporate income taxes are shifted to consumers in the form of higher prices or to employees in the form of lower wages versus falling on the stockholders in the form of lower dividends. There is also debate about who effectively pays the property tax. *Tax incidence analysis* examines how various taxes may or may not be shifted.

References

Aaron, Henry J. (1975). *Who Pays the Property Tax? A New View*. Washington, DC: The Brookings Institution.

Adams, E. Kathleen. (December 1980). *Fiscal Response and School Finance Simulations: A Policy Perspective*. Denver, CO: Education Commission of the States, Report No. F80-3.

Adams, E. Kathleen, and Allan Odden. (1981). "Alternative Wealth Measures." In K. Forbis Jordan and Nelda H. Cambron-McCabe, eds., *Perspectives in State School Support Programs*. Cambridge, MA: Ballinger, pp. 143–165.

Advisory Commission on Intergovernmental Relations. (1984). *Significant Features of Fiscal Federalism: 1982–83 Edition*. Washington, DC: U.S. GPO.

Advisory Commission on Intergovernmental Relations. (1989a). *Local Property Taxes Called Worst Tax*. News release of 18th annual ACIR poll. Washington, DC: Author

Advisory Commission on Intergovernmental Relations.(1989b). *Significant Features of Fiscal Federalism, 1989 Edition*, vol. 1. Washington, DC: Author, Report M-163.

Alexander, Arthur J. (1974). *Teachers, Salaries and School District Expenditures*. Santa Monica, CA: The RAND Corporation.

Alexander, Kern. (1982). "Concepts of Equity." In Walter McMahon and Terry Geske, eds., *Financing Education*. Urbana, IL: University of Illinois Press.

Arrow, Kenneth J., ed. (1971). *Control in Large Organizations: Essays in the Theory of Risk-Bearing*. Chicago: Markham Publishing Company.

Augenblick, John, and E. Kathleen Adams. (1979). *An Analysis of the Impact of Changes in the Funding of Elementary/Secondary Education in Texas: 1974/75 to 1977/78*. Denver, CO: Education Commission of the States.

Bahl, Roy W. (1990). "States and the Financial Condition of Cities." *Proceedings of the Eighty-Second Annual Conference, 1989*. Columbus, OH: National Tax Association–Tax Institute of America, pp. 81–85.

Bailey, Stephen, Robert T. Frost, Paul E. Marsh, and Robert C. Wood. (1962). *Schoolmen and Politics: A Study of State Aid to Education in the Northeast.* Syracuse, NY: Syracuse University Research Corporation.

Bailey, Stephen, and Edith Mosher. (1968). *ESEA—The Office of Education Administers a Law.* Syracuse, NY: Syracuse University Press.

Baratz-Snowden, Joan. (1990). "The NBPTS Begins Its Research and Development Program." *Educational Researcher,* 19(6),19–24.

Barnett, Steven. (1985). "Benefit-Cost Analysis of the Perry Preschool Program and Its Policy Implications." *Educational Evaluation and Policy Analysis,* 7(4), 333–342.

Barro, Stephen M. (1972). *Theoretical Models of School District Expenditure Determination and the Impact of Grants-In-Aid.* Santa Monica, CA: The RAND Corporation.

Barro, Stephen M. (1989). "Fund Distribution Issues in School Finance: Priorities for the Next Round of Research," Educational Evaluation and Policy Analysis, 11(1), 17–30.

Barro, Stephen M., and Stephen J. Carroll. (1975). *Budget Allocation by School Districts: An Analysis of Spending for Teachers and Other Resources.* Santa Monica, CA: The RAND Corporation.

Bell, Michael E., and John H. Bowman. (1986). "Direct Property Tax Relief." In *Final Report of the Minnesota Tax Study Commission,* vol. 1. St. Paul and Boston: Butterworth's, pp. 291–326.

Berke, Joel. (1974). *Answers to Inequity: An Analysis of the New School Finance.* New York: Russell Sage Foundation.

Berke, Joel S., and John J. Callahan. (1972). "*Serrano v. Priest*: Milestone or Millstone for School Finance?" *Journal of Public Law,* 21(1), 23–70.

Berke, Joel, Maragaret E. Goertz, and Richard J. Coley. (1984). *Politicians, Judges and City Schools.* New York: Russell Sage Foundation.

Berne, Robert. (1988). "Equity Issues in School Finance." *Journal of Education Finance,* 14(2), 159–180.

Berne, Robert, and Leanna Stiefel. (1979). "Taxpayer Equity in School Finance Reform: The School Finance and Public Finance Perspective." *Journal of Education Finance,* 5 (1), 36–54.

Berne, Robert, and Leanna Stiefel. (1984). *The Measurement of Equity in School Finance.* Baltimore, MD: Johns Hopkins University Press.

Berne, Robert, and Leanna Stiefel. (1990). "Measuring School Finance Equity in the 1990s: Old Dogs or New Tricks?" Paper presented at the Annual Research Conference of the Association for Public Policy Analysis and Management, San Francisco.

Bernstein, Charles D., William T. Hartman, and Rudolph S. Marshall. (1976). "Major Policy Issues in Financing Special Education." *Journal of Education Finance,* 1(3), 299–317.

Berrueta-Clement, J. R., Lawrence Schweinhart, Steve Barnett, A. Epstein, and David Weikart. (1984). *Changed Lives: The Effects of the Perry Pre-School Program on Youths Through Age 19.* Ypsilanti, MI: High Scope.

Black, D. E., K. A. Lewis, and C. K. Link. (1979). "Wealth Neutrality and the Demand for Education." *National Tax Journal,* 32 (2), 157–164.

Blinder, Alan. (1990). *Paying for Productivity.* Washington, DC: The Brookings Institution.

Bobbitt, Sharon A., and Marilyn Miles McMillen. (1990). "Teacher Training, Certification and Assignment." Paper presented to the annual meeting of the American Educational Research Association, Boston.

Borg, Walter. (1980). "Time and School Learning." In Carolyn Denham and Ann Lieberman, eds., *Time to Learn*. Washington, DC: The National Institute of Education.

Bowman, John H. (1974). "Tax Exportability, Intergovernmental Aid, and School Finance Reform." *National Tax Journal*, 27(2), 163–173.

Brackett, J., Jay Chambers, and Tom Parrish, (1983). *The Legacy of Rational Budgeting Models in Education*. Stanford, CA: Institute for Education Finance and Governance, Project Report 83-A21.

Brazer, Harvey E. (1974). "Adjusting for Differences Among School Districts in the Costs of Educational Inputs: A Feasibility Report." In Ester Tron, ed., *Selected Papers in School Finance: 1974*. Washington, DC: U.S. Office of Education.

Brazer, Harvey E., and Therese A. McCarty. (1987). "Interaction Between Demand for Education and for Municipal Services." *National Tax Journal*, 60 (4), 555–566.

Break, George F. (1980). *Financing Government in a Federal System*. Washington, DC: The Brookings Institution.

Brown, Byron, and Daniel Saks. (1980). "Production Technologies and Resource Allocations Within Classrooms and Schools: Theory and Measurement." In Robert Dreeben and J. Alan Thomas, eds., *The Analysis of Educational Productivity, Volume I: Issues in Microanalysis*. Cambridge, MA: Ballinger, pp. 53–117.

Brown, Byron, and Daniel Saks. (1987). "The Microeconomics of the Allocation of Teachers' Time and Student Learning." *Economics of Education Review*, 6(4), 319–332.

Brown, Daniel J. (1990). *Decentralization and School-Based Management*. London: The Falmer Press.

Brown, Lawrence L., et al. (1977). *School Finance Reform in the Seventies: Achievements and Failures*. Washington, DC: U.S. Department of Health, Education and Welfare, Office of the Assistant Secretary for Planning and Evaluation and Killalea Associates, Incorporated.

Brown, Patricia, and Richard Elmore. (1982). "Analyzing the Impact of School Finance Reform." In Nelda Cambron-McCabe and Allan Odden, eds., *The Changing Politics of School Finance*. Cambridge, MA: Ballinger, pp. 107–138.

Brownlee, O. H. (1960). *Estimated Distribution of Minnesota Taxes and Public Expenditure Benefits*. Minneapolis: University of Minnesota Press.

Callahan, John, and William Wilken. (1976). *A Legislator's Guide to School Finance*. Washington, DC: National Conference of State Legislatures.

Cardenas, Jose, J. J. Bernal, and N. Kean. (1976). *Bilingual Education Cost Analysis: Texas*. San Antonio, TX: Intercultural Development Research Association.

Carnegie Forum on Education and the Economy. (1986). *A Nation Prepared: Teachers for the 21st Century*. New York: Carnegie Corporation.

Carpenter-Huffman, P., and S. M. Samulon. (1981). *Case Studies of Delivery and Cost of Bilingual Education Programs*. Santa Monica, CA: The RAND Corporation.

Carroll, Stephen J., and Rolla Edward Park. (1983). *The Search for Equity in School Finance.* Cambridge, MA: Ballinger.

Catterall, James. (1989). "Resources and Commitment." In Richard Shavelson, Lorraine McDonnell, and Jeannie Oakes, eds., *Indicators for Monitoring Mathematics and Science Education.* Santa Monica, CA: The RAND Corporation, pp. 25–39.

Chambers, Jay G. (1978). *Educational Cost Differentials Across School Districts in California.* Denver, CO: Education Commission of the States.

Chambers, Jay G. (1980). *The Development of a Cost of Education Index for the State of California.* Final reports, Parts 1 and 2, prepared for the California State Department of Education.

Chambers, Jay G. (1981). "Cost and Price Level Adjustments to State Aid for Education: A Theoretical and Empirical View." In K. Forbis Jordan and Nelda Cambron-McCabe, eds., *Perspectives in State School Support Programs.* Cambridge, MA: Ballinger, pp. 39–85.

Chambers, Jay and William T. Hartman., eds. (1983). *Special Education Policies: Their History, Implementation and Finance.* Philadelphia: Temple University Press.

Chambers, Jay G., Allan Odden, and Phillip E. Vincent. (1976). *Cost of Education Indices Among School Districts.* Denver, CO: Education Commission of the States.

Chambers, Jay and Thomas Parrish. (1983). *The Development of a Resource Cost Model Funding Base for Education Finance in Illinois.* Stanford, CA: Associates for Education Finance and Planning.

Childs, T. Stephen, and Charol Shakeshaft. (1986). "A Meta-Analysis of Research on the Relationship Between Educational Expenditures and Student Achievement." *Journal of Education Finance,* 12(2), 249–263.

Choy, Ronald H., and Bernard R. Gifford. (1980). "Resource Allocation in a Segregated School System: The Case of Los Angeles." *Journal of Education Finance,* 6 (1), 34–50.

Church, T. W., and M. Heumann. (1989). "The Underexamined Assumptions of the Invisible Hand: Monetary Incentives as Policy Instruments." *Journal of Policy Analysis and Management,* 8 (4), 641–657.

Cibulka, James G. (1989). "State Performance Incentives for Restructuring: Can They Work?" *Education and Urban Society,* 21(4), 417–435.

Cline, Robert. (1986). "Personal Income Tax." In Steven D. Gold, ed., *Reforming State Tax Systems.* Denver: National Conference of State Legislatures, pp. 185-210.

Clotfelter, Charles T., and Phillip J. Cook. (1989). *Selling Hope: State Lotteries in America.* Cambridge: Harvard University Press.

Clune, William, and Paula White. (1988). *School-Based Management: Institutional Variation, Implementation and Issues for Further Research.* New Brunswick, NJ: Rutgers University, Center for Policy Research in Education.

Cobb, Roger W., and Charles D. Elder. (1982). "Issue Creation and Agenda Building." In James E. Anderson, ed., *Cases in Public Policy-Making.* New York: Holt, Rinehart and Winston, pp. 3–11.

Cohn, Elchanan. (1974). *Economics of State Aid to Education.* Lexington, MA: Heath Lexington Books.

Cohn, Elchanan. (1979). *The Economics of Education*, Cambridge, MA: Ballinger.

Cohn, Elchanan, and Terry G. Geske. (1990). *The Economics of Education*, 3rd edition. Oxford: Pergamon Press.

Committee for Economic Development. (1985). *Investing in Our Children: Business and the Public Schools*. New York: Committee for Economic Development.

Committee for Economic Development. (1987). *Children In Need*. New York: Committee for Economic Develoment.

Conley, Sharon E., and Samuel Bacharach. (1990). "Performance Appraisal in Education: A Strategic Consideration." *Journal of Personnel Evaluation in Education, 3, 309–319.*

Coons, John, William Clune, and Stephen D. Sugarman. (1970). *Private Wealth and Public Education*. Cambridge, MA: Belknap Press of Harvard University Press.

Council of Chief State School Officers. (1990). *State Education Indicators: 1990*. Washington, DC: Author.

Cubberly, Elwood Patterson. (1905). *School Funds and Their Apportionment*. New York: Teachers College Press.

Cubberly, E. P. (1906). *School Funds and Their Apportionment*. New York: Teachers College Press.

Cummins, James. (1980). "The Exit and Entry Fallacy in Bilingual Education," *NABE Journal, 4, 25–60.*

Cummins, James. (1986). "Empowering Minority Students: A Framework for Intervention." *Harvard Educational Review, 56 (1), 16–36.*

Darling-Hammond, Linda, and Barnett Berry. (1988). *The Evolution of Teacher Policy*. Santa Monica, CA: The RAND Corporation.

David, Jane L., Michael Cohen, Dean Honetschlager, and Susan Traiman. (1990). *State Actions to Restructure Schools: First Steps*, Washington DC: National Governors' Association.

DeLeeuw, Frank, and Nkanta Ekanem. (1971). "The Supply of Rental Housing." *American Economic Review, 62, 806–817.*

Denham, Carolyn, and Ann Lieberman, eds. (1980). *Time to Learn*. Washington, DC: The National Institute of Education.

Doyle, Denis, and Terry Hartle. (1985). *Excellence in Education: The States Take Charge*. Washington, DC: American Enterprise Institute.

Ebel, Robert D., and James Ortbal. (1989). "Direct Residential Property Tax Relief." *Intergovernmental Perspective, 16, 9–14.*

Education Commission of the States. (1984). *Action in the States*. Denver, CO: Author.

Elmore, Richard, and Susan Fuhrman. (1990a). "Governors and Education Policy in the 1990s." Paper presented at the 1990 meeting of the Association of Public Policy Analysis and Management, San Francisco.

Elmore, Richard, and Susan Fuhrman. (1990b). *Legislatures and Education Policy*. New Brunswick, NJ: Eagleton Institute of Politics, Center for Policy Research in Education.

Feldstein, Martin S. (1975). "Wealth Neutrality and Local Choice in Public Education." *American Economic Review, 64, 75–89.*

Finn, Chester. (1991). *We Must Take Charge: Our Schools and Our Future.* New York: The Free Press.

Folger, John. (1990a). "The Cost-Effectiveness of Adding Aides or Reducing Class Size." Paper presented at the annual meeting of the American Educational Research Association, Boston.

Forgione, Pascal, chair. (1990). *A Guide to Improving the National Education Data System: An Agenda of the National Forum on Educational Statistics.* Washington, DC: National Center for Educational Statistics.

Fox, James. (1987). "An Analysis of Classroom Spending." *Planning and Changing,* 18(3), 154–162.

Fox, William F. (1981). "Reviewing Economies of Size in Education." *Journal of Education Finance,* 6(3), 273–296.

Fox, William F., and Matthew Murray. (1988, March). "Economic Aspects of Taxing Services." *National Tax Journal,* 41(1), 19–36.

Fuhrman, Susan. (1978). "The Politics and Process of School Finance Reform." *Journal of Education Finance,* 4 (3), 158–178.

Fuhrman, Susan. (1982). "State Level Politics and School Financing." In Nelda Cambron-McCabe and Allan Odden, eds., *The Changing Politics of School Financing.* Cambridge, MA: Ballinger, pp. 53–70.

Fuhrman, Susan H. and Richard F. Elmore. (1990). "Understanding Local Control in the Wake of State Education Reform." *Educational Evaluation and Policy Analysis,* 12 (1), 82–96.

Garcia, O. (1977). "Analyzing Bilingual Education Costs." In G. Banco, et al., eds., *Bilingual Education: Current Perspectives.* Arlington, VA: Education Center for Applied Linguistics.

Garms, Walter I. (1979). "Measuring the Equity of School Finance Systems." *Journal of Education Finance,* 4 (4), 415–435.

Gaughan, James M., and Glasheen, Richard J. (1979). *Interim Report: Study on Special Pupil Needs.* New York State Special Task Force on Equity and Excellence in Education.

General Accounting Office. (1988). *Lesiglative Mandates: State Experiences Offer Insights for Federal Action.* Washington, DC: Author.

Ginsberg, Alan, Jay H. Moskowitz, and Alvin S. Rosenthal. (1981). "A School Based Analysis of Inter- and Intradistrict Resource Allocation." *Journal of Education Finance,* 6(4), 440–455.

Glass, Eugene, and Mary Lee Smith. (1979). "Meta-Analysis of Research on Class Size and Achievement." *Educational Evaluation and Policy Analysis,* 1(1), 2–16.

Goertz, Margaret. (1983). "School Finance in New Jersey: A Decade After *Robinson v. Cahill.*" *Journal of Education Finance,* 8(4), 475–489.

Goertz, Margaret. (1988). *School Districts' Allocation of Chapter 1 Resources.* Princeton, NJ: Educational Testing Service.

Goggin, Z. (1986). "Two Sides of Gain Sharing." *Management Accounting,* 68, 47–51.

Gold, Steven D. (1979). *Property Tax Relief.* Lexington, MA: D.C. Heath and Company.

Gold, Steven D. (1983). *State and Local Fiscal Relations in the Early 1980s.* Washington, DC: The Urban Institute.

Gold, Steven D. (1984). "State Tax Increases of 1983: Prelude to Another Tax Revolt?" *National Tax Journal,* 37 (1), 9–22.

Gold, Steven D. (1986a). "State Tax Policy: Recent Trends and Future Directions." In Steven D. Gold, ed., *Reforming State Tax Systems.* Denver, CO: National Conference of State Legislatures, pp. 11–30.

Gold, Steven D., ed. (1986b). *Reforming State Tax Systems.* Denver, CO: National Conference of State Legislatures.

Gold, Steven D. (1988). "A Review of Recent State Tax Reform Activity." In Steven D. Gold, ed., *The Unfinished Agenda for State Tax Reform.* Denver, CO: National Conference on State Legislatures, pp. 11–30.

Gold, Steven D. (1990). "The Effect of Earmarked Revenue on School Spending." Paper presented at the 1990 meeting of the American Education Finance Association, Las Vegas, NV.

Grieson, Ronald. (1973). "The Supply of Rental Housing: Comment." *American Economic Review,* 63, 303–307.

Grubb, W. Norton, and J. Osman. (1977). "The Causes of School Finance Inequalities: Serrano and the Case of California." *Public Finance Quarterly,* 5 (3), 373–392.

Grubb, W. Norton, and Stephan Michelson. (1974). *States and Schools: The Political Economy of Public School Finance.* Lexington, MA: Lexington Books.

Guss-Zamora, M., R. Zarate, M. Robledo, and Jose Cardenas. (1979). *Bilingual Education Cost Analysis: Utah.* San Antonio, TX: Intercultural Development Research Association.

Guthrie, James W. (1979). "Organizational Scale and School Success." *Educational Evaluation and Policy Analysis,* 1(1), 17–27.

Guthrie, James. (1988). *Understanding School Budgets.* Washington DC: U.S. Department of Education.

Guthrie, James W., Michael W. Kirst, and Allan R. Odden. (1990). *Conditions of Education in California, 1989.* Berkeley, CA: University of California, School of Education, Policy Analysis for California Education.

Haller, Emil, David H. Monk, Alyce Spotted Bear, Julie Griffith, and Pamela Moss. (1990). "School Size and Program Comprehensiveness: Evidence from *High School and Beyond.*" *Educational Evaluation and Policy Analysis,* 12 (2), 109–120.

Hamilton, Stephen F. (1983). "The Social Side of Schooling: Ecological Studies of Classrooms and Schools." *Elementary School Journal,* 83, 313–334.

Hanushek, Eric. (1979). "Conceptual and Empirical Issues in the Estimation of Educational Production Functions." *Journal of Human Resources,* 14 (3), 351–388.

Hanushek, Eric. (1981). "Throwing Money at Schools." *Journal of Policy Analysis and Management,* 1 (1), 19–41.

Hanushek, Eric. (1986). "The Economics of Schooling: Production and Efficiency in Public Schools." *Journal of Economic Literature,* 24 (3), 1141–1177.

Hanushek, Eric. (1989). "The Impact of Differential Expenditures on Student Performance." *Educational Researcher,* 18 (4), 45–52.

Hargrove, Erwin. (1983). "The Search for Implementation Theory." In Richard J. Zeckhauser and Derek Leebaert, eds., *What Role for Government?* Durham, NC: Duke University Press, pp. 280–294.

Harris, Russell. (1978). "Reforming School Finance in Pennsylvania." *Journal of Education Finance,* 3(4), 487–501.

Hartman, William T. (1980). "Policy Effects of Special Education Funding Formulas." *Journal of Education Finance,* 6 (2), 135–139.

Hartman, William T. (1988a). *School District Budgeting.* Englewood Cliffs, NJ: Prentice Hall.

Hartman, William T. (1988b). "District Spending: What Do the Dollars Buy?" *Journal of Education Finance,* 13(4), 436–459.

Hawkins, Evelyn K. (1989). "The Effect of the Reform Movement on Levels of Elementary and Secondary Public School Expenditure in the 1980s." Paper presented at the annual meeting of the American Educational Research Association, San Francisco.

Hayward, Gerald C. (1988). *The Two Million Dollar School.* Berkeley, CA: University of California, School of Education, Policy Analysis for California Education.

Heclo, Hugh. (1978). "Issue Networks and the Executive Establishment." In Anthony King, ed., *The New American Political System.* Washington, DC: American Enterprise Institute, pp. 87–124.

Hentschke, Guilbert C. (1986). *School Business Administration: A Comparative Perspective.* Berkeley, CA: McCutchan.

Hentschke, Guilbert C. (1988). "Budgetary Theory and Reality: A Microview." In David H. Monk and Julie Underwood, eds., *Microlevel School Finance: Issues and Implications for Policy.* Cambridge, MA: Ballinger, pp. 311–336.

Hickrod, G. Alan, Ramesh B. Chaudhari, and Ben C. Hubbard. (1981). *Reformation and Counter-Reformation in Illinois School Finance: 1973–1981.* Normal, IL: Center for the Study of Education Finance.

Hodge, Michael. (1981). "Improving Finance and Governance of Education for Special Populations." In K. Forbis Jordan and Nelda Cambron-McCabe, eds., *Perspectives in State School Support Programs.* Cambridge, MA: Ballinger, pp. 3–38.

Hybels, Judith H. (1979). "The Impact of Legalization on Illegal Gambling Participation." *Journal of Social Issues,* 35.

Hyman, D., and E. Pasour. (1973). "Property Tax Differentials and Residential Rents in North Carolina." *National Tax Journal,* 26, 303–307.

Jensen, Michael C., and William H. Meckling. (1976). "Theory of the Firm: Managerial Behavior, Agency Costs and Ownership Structure." *Journal of Financial Economics,* 3 (October), 305–360.

Johns, Roe, Kern Alexander, and K. Forbis Jordan, eds. (1971). *Planning to Finance Education, vol. 3.* Gainesville, FL: National Education Finance Project.

Johnson, Susan Moore. (1986). "Incentives for Teachers: What Motivates, What Matters." *Educational Administration Quarterly,* 22 (3), 54–79.

Jordan, K. Forbis, and Mary McKeown. (1990). "State Fiscal Policy and Education Reform." In Joseph Murphy, ed., *The Educational Reform Movement of the 1980s: Perspectives and Cases.* Berkeley, CA: McCutchan, pp. 97–120.

Jung, Richard, and Michael Kirst. (1986). "Beyond Mutual Adaptation, into the Bully Pulpit: Recent Research on the Federal Role in Education." *Educational Administration Quarterly,* 22 (3), 80–109.

Kakalik, James. (1979). "Issues in the Cost and Finance of Special Education." In *Review of Educational Research, vol. 7.* Washington, DC: American Educational Research Association, pp. 195–222.

Kakalik, James, W. S. Furry, M. A. Thomas, and M. F. Carney. (1981). *The Cost of Special Education.* Santa Monica, CA: The RAND Corporation.

Kearney, Phillip, Li-Ju Chen, and Marjorie Checkoway. (1988). *Measuring Equity in Michigan School Finance: A Further Look.* Ann Arbor, MI: University of Michigan, School of Education.

Kenny, L., D. Denslow, and Irving Goffman. (1975). "Determination of Teacher Cost Differentials Among School Districts in the State of Florida." In Ester Tron, ed., *Selected Papers in School Finance.* Washington, DC: U.S. Office of Education, pp. 153–221.

King, Richard A. (1985). "Resource Allocation: From Macro- to Micro-Level Analyses." *Planning and Changing,* pp. 226–233.

Kirlin, John, and Donald Winkler. (1985, 1986, 1987, 1988). *California Policy Choices, vols. 1–4.* Los Angeles: University of Southern California, School of Public Administration.

Kirst, Michael. (1977). "What Happens at the Local Level After School Finance Reform?" *Policy Analysis,* 3 (1), 302–324.

Kirst, Michael. (1978). "Coalition Building for School Finance Reform: The Case of California." *Journal of Education Finance,* 4 (2), 29–45.

Kirst, Michael. (1988). "The Internal Allocation of Resources within U.S. School Districts: Implications for Policymakers and Practitioners." In David Monk and Julie Underwood, eds., *Microlevel School Finance.* Cambridge, MA: Ballinger, pp. 365–389.

Kirst, Michael, Gail Meister, and Stephen Rowley. (1984). "Policy Issue Networks: Their Influence on State Policymaking." *Policy Studies Journal,* 13 (2), 247–263.

Knickman, James, and Andrew Reschovsky. (1981). "Municipal Overburden: Its Measurement and Role in School Finance Reform." In Ester Tron, ed., *Papers in School Finance.* Washington, DC: U.S. Department of Education, pp. 445–471.

Krashen, Steve, and Douglas Biber. (1988). *On Course: Bilingual Education's Success in California.* Sacramento: California Association for Bilingual Education.

Ladd, Helen F. (1975, June). "Local Education Expenditures, Fiscal Capacity, and the Composition of the Property Tax Base." *National Tax Journal,* 28 (2), 145–158.

Ladd, Helen, and John Yinger. (1989). *America's Ailing Cities: Fiscal Health and the Design of Urban Policy.* Baltimore: Johns Hopkins University Press.

Ladd, Helen, and John Yinger. (1990). "Recent Trends in City Fiscal Health." In *Proceedings of the Eighty-Second Annual Conference, 1989.* Columbus, OH: National Tax Association–Tax Institute of America, pp. 72–80.

LaMorte, Michael. (1989). "Courts Continue to Address the Wealth Disparity Issue." *Educational Evaluation and Policy Analysis,* 11(1), 3–16.

Lawler, Edward, III. (1990). *Strategic Pay.* San Francisco: Jossey-Bass.

Leppert, Jack, and Dorothy Routh. (1979). *A Policy Guide to Weighted Pupil Education Finance Systems: Some Emerging Practical Advice.* Washington, DC: National Institute of Education.

Levin, Betsy. (1977). "New Legal Challenges in Educational Finance." *Journal of Education Finance,* 3(1), 54–69.

Levin, Betsy, Thomas Muller, and Corazon Sandoval. (1973). *The High Cost of Education in Cities.* Washington, DC: The Urban Institute.

Levin, Henry. (1989). "Financing the Education of At-Risk Students." *Educational Evaluation and Policy Analysis,* 11(1), 47–60.

Levin, Henry, Gene Glass, and Gail Meister. (1987). "Cost-Effectiveness of Computer Assisted Instruction." *Evaluation Review,* 11(1), 50–72.

Lieberman, Ann, ed. (1988). *Building a Professional Culture in Schools.* New York: Teachers College Press.

Long, James E. (1988). "Taxation and IRA Participation: Re-examination and Confirmation." *National Tax Journal,* 61(4), 585–589.

MacPhail-Wilcox, Bettye, and Richard A. King. (1986a). "Resource Allocation Studies: Implications for School Improvement and School Finance Research." *Journal of Education Finance,* 11(4), 416–432.

MacPhail-Wilcox, Bettye, and Richard A. King. (1986b). "Production Functions Revisited in the Context of Educational Reform." *Journal of Education Finance,* 12(2), 191–222.

Malen, Betty, Rodney T. Ogawa, and Jennifer Kranz. (1990). "What Do We Know About School Based Management? A Case Study of the Literature — A Call for Research." In William H. Clune and John F. Witte, eds., *Choice and Control in American Education,* volume 2, *The Practice of Choice, Decentralization and School Restructuring.* Bristol, PA: The Falmer Press, pp. 289–342.

Massel, Diane, and Michael Kirst. (1986). "State Policymaking for Education Excellence: School Reform in California." In Van Mueller and Mary McKeown, eds., *The Fiscal, Legal and Political Aspects of State Reform of Elementary and Secondary Education.* Cambridge, MA: Ballinger, pp. 121–144.

McClure, William. (1976). "Pupil Weightings." *Journal of Education Finance,* 2 (1), 72–82.

McDonnell, Lorraine, Leigh Burstein, Tor Ormseth, James Catterall, and David Moody. (1990). *Discovering What Schools Really Teach: Designing Improved Coursework Indicators.* Santa Monica, CA: The RAND Corporation.

McDonnell, Lorraine, and Susan Fuhrman. (1986). "The Political Context of Reform." In Van Mueller and Mary McKeown, eds., *The Fiscal, Legal and Political Aspects of State Reform of Elementary and Secondary Education.* Cambridge, MA: Ballinger, pp. 43–64.

McGuire, C. Kent. (1982). *State and Federal Programs for Special Student Populations.* Denver, CO: Education Commission of the States.

McKnight, C. C., F. J. Crosswhite, J. A. Dossey, E. Kifer, S. O. Swafford, K. J. Travers, and T. J. Cooney. (1987). *The Underachieving Curriculum: Assessing U.S. Mathematics from an International Perspective.* Champaign, IL: Stipes Publishing.

McLaughlin, Milbrey W., and Sylvia Yee. (1988). "School as a Place to Have a Career." In Ann Lieberman, ed., *Building a Professional Culture in Schools.* New York: Teachers College Press, pp. 23–44.

Meno, Lionel. (1984). "Sources of Alternative Revenues." In L. Dean Webb and Van D. Mueller, eds., *Managing Limited Revenues.* Cambridge, MA: Ballinger, pp, 129–146.

Mieszkowski, Peter. (1972). "The Property Tax: An Excise Tax or Profits Tax?" *Journal of Public Economics*, 1, 73–96.

Mikesell, John L. (1986). "General Sales Tax." In Steven D. Gold, ed., *Reforming State Tax Systems*. Denver, CO: National Conference of State Legislatures, pp. 211–230.

Mikesell, John L. and C. Kurt Zorn. (1986). "State Lotteries as Fiscal Savior or Fiscal Fraud: A Look at the Evidence." *Public Administration Review*, pp. 311–319.

Miner, Jerry. (1963). *Social and Economic Factors in Spending for Public Education*. Syracuse, NY: Syracuse University Press.

Miner, Jerry, and Seymour Sacks. (1980). *A Study of Adjustments of New York State School Aid Formula to Take Account of Municipal Overburden*. Report prepared for the New York State Task Force on Equity and Excellence in Education.

Monk, David H. (1981). "Toward a Multilevel Perspective on the Allocation of Educational Resources." *Review of Educational Research*, 51(2), 215–236.

Monk, David. (1987). "Secondary School Size and Curriculum Comprehensiveness." *Economics of Education Review*, 6(2), 137–150.

Monk, David. (1989). "The Education Production Function: Its Evolving Role in Policy Analysis." *Educational Evaluation and Policy Analysis*, 11(1), 31–46.

Monk, David. (1990). *Educational Finance: An Economic Approach*. New York: McGraw-Hill.

Monk, David, and Emil Haller. (1990). "High School Size and Course Offerings: Evidence from High School and Beyond." Paper presented at the annual meeting of the American Educational Research Association, Boston, MA.

Moore, Mary T., E. William Strang, Myron Schwartz, and Mark Braddock. (1988). *Patterns in Special Education Service Delivery and Cost*. Washington, DC: Decision Resources Corporation.

Moore, Mary, Lisa Walker, and Richard P. Holland. (1982). *Finetuning Special Education Finance: A Guide for Policymakers*. Princeton, NJ: Educational Testing Service.

Moynihan, Daniel. (1972). "Equalizing Education: In Whose Benefit?" *The Public Interest*, Fall.

Mueller, Van, and Mary McKeown, eds. (1986). *The Fiscal, Legal and Political Aspects of State Reform of Elementary and Secondary Education*. Cambridge, MA: Ballinger.

Mullis, Ina V. S., Eugene H. Owen and Gary W. Phillips. (1990). *Accelerating Academic Achievement: A Summary of Findings from 20 Years of NAEP*. Princeton, NJ.: Educational Testing Service.

Murnane, Richard. (1983). "Quantitative Studies of Effective Schools: What Have We Learned?" In Allan Odden and L. Dean Webb, eds., *School Finance and School Improvement: Linkages for the 1980s*. Cambridge, MA: Ballinger, pp. 193–209.

Murnane, Richard, and David Cohen. (1986). "Merit Pay and the Evaluation Problem: Why Some Merit Pay Plans Fail and a Few Survive." *Harvard Educational Review*, 56 (1), 1–17.

Murphy, Joseph. (1990). *The Educational Reform Movement of the 1980s: Perspectives and Cases*. Berkeley, CA: McCutchan.

Murphy, Joseph, and Phillip Hallinger. (1987). "Instructional Leadership in the School Context." In William Greenfield, ed., *Instructional Leadership.* Boston: Allyn and Bacon, pp. 179–203.

Murphy, Kevin, and Finis Welch. (1989). "Wage Premiums for College Graduates: Recent Growth and Possible Explanations." *Educational Researcher,* 18 (4), 17–26.

Musgrave, Richard, and Darwin Daicoff. (1958). "Who Pays the Michigan Taxes?" *Michigan Tax Study Papers.* Lansing: Michigan Tax Study Committee.

Musgrave, Richard and Peggy Musgrave. (1989). *Public Finance in Theory and Practice.* New York: McGraw-Hill.

National Center for Education Statistics. (1980). *Financial Accounting for Local and State School Systems.* Washington, DC: U.S. GPO.

National Center for Education Statistics. (1989). *Digest of Educational Statistics, 1989.* Washington, DC: National Center for Education Statistics.

National Commission on Excellence in Education. (1983). *A Nation at Risk: The Imperative of Educational Reform.* Washington, DC: U.S. Department of Education.

National Governors Association. (1986). *Time for Results.* Washington, DC: Author.

National Governors Association. (1990). *Educating America: State Strategies for Achieving the National Educational Goals,* Washington, DC: Author.

Nelson, F. Howard. (1984). "Factors Contributing to the Cost of Programs for Limited English Proficient Students." *Journal of Education Finance,* 10, 1–21.

Netzer, Dick. (1966). *Economics of the Property Tax.* Washington, DC: The Brookings Institution.

Netzer, Dick. (1974). "State Education Aid and School Tax Efforts in Large Cities." In Ester Tron, ed., *Selected Papers in School Finance.* Washington, DC: U.S. Department of Health, Education and Welfare, U.S. Office of Education.

Oakes, Jeannie. (1989). "What Educational Indicators? The Case for Assessing the School Context." *Educational Evaluation and Policy Analysis,* 11 (2), 181–199.

Oakes, Jeannie. (1990). *Lost Talent: The Underparticipation of Women, Minorities and Disabled Persons in Science.* Santa Monica, CA: The RAND Corporation.

Oates, Wallace E. (1972). *Fiscal Federalism.* New York: Harcourt, Brace, Jovanovich.

Odden, Allan. (1975). "The Incidence of the Property Tax Under Alternative Assumptions: The Case in Minnesota, 1971." Unpublished paper. Denver, CO: Education Commission of the States.

Odden, Allan. (1978). "Missouri's New School Finance Structure." *Journal of Education Finance,* 3 (3), 465–475.

Odden, Allan. (1979). "Simulation Results: Third Round." Prepared for the New York State Task Force on Equity and Excellence in Education. Denver, CO: Education Commission of the States.

Odden, Allan. (1980). "Simulation Results: Fourth Round." Prepared for the New York State Task Force on Equity and Excellence in Education. Denver, CO: Education Commission of the States.

Odden, Allan. (1982). "School Finance Reform: Redistributive Policy at the State Level." In Joel Sherman, Mark Kutner, and Kimberly Small, eds., *New Dimensions of the State-Federal Partnership in Education*, Washington, DC: The Institute for Educational Leadership.

Odden, Allan. (1986). "The School Finance Context of State Policies Designed to Enhance the Teaching Profession." *Elementary School Journal*, 86 (4), 369–388.

Odden, Allan. (1987). "The Economics of Financing Education Excellence." Paper presented at the annual meeting of the American Educational Research Association, Washington, DC.

Odden, Allan. (1988). "How Fiscal Accountability and Program Quality Can Be Insured for Chapter I." In Denis Doyle and Bruce Cooper, eds., *Federal Aid to the Disadvantaged: What Future for Chapter I?* New York: Falmer Press, pp. 181–202.

Odden, Allan. (1990a). "School Funding Changes in the 1980s." *Educational Policy*, 4 (1), 33–47.

Odden, Allan. (1990b). *A New School Finance for Public School Choice*. Los Angeles: University of Southern California, Center for Research in Educational Finance.

Odden, Allan. (1990c). "Educational Indicators in the United States: The Need for Analysis." *Educational Researcher*, 19 (4), 24–29.

Odden, Allan. (1990d). "Class Size and Student Achievement: Research-Based Policy Alternatives." *Educational Evaluation and Policy Analysis*, 12 (2), 213–227.

Odden, Allan. (1990e). "The Changing Contours of School Finance." Paper prepared for the Far West Regional Educational Laboratory.

Odden, Allan, ed. (1991). *Education Policy Implementation*. Albany: State University of New York Press.

Odden, Allan, and John Augenblick. (1981). *School Finance Reform in the States: 1981*. Denver, CO: Education Commission of the States.

Odden, Allan, Robert Berne, and Leanna Stiefel. (1979). *Equity in School Finance*. Denver, CO: Education Commission of the States.

Odden, Allan, and Sharon Conley. (1991). *Restructuring Teacher Compensation Systems to Foster Collegiality and Help Accomplish National Education Goals*. Los Angeles: University of Southern California, Center for Research in Educational Finance.

Odden, Allan, and Van Dougherty. (1984). *Education Finance in the States, 1984*. Denver, CO: Education Commission of the States.

Odden, Allan, C. Kent McGuire, and Grace Belsches-Simmons. (1983). *School Finance Reform in the States: 1984*. Denver, CO: Education Commission of the States.

Odden, Allan, Robert Palaich, and John Augenblick. (1979). *Analysis of the New York State School Finance System, 1977–78*. Denver, CO: Education Commission of the States.

Odden, Allan, and Phillip E. Vincent. (1976). *The Regressivity of the Property Tax*. Denver, CO: Education Commission of the States, Report No. F76-4.

Office of Bilingual Education, California State Department of Education. (1984). *Schooling and Language for Minority Students: A Theoretical Frame-*

work. Los Angeles: Evaluation, Dissemination and Assessment Center, California State University, Los Angeles.

Orland, Martin E. (1988). "Relating School District Resource Needs and Capacities to Chapter 1 Allocations: Implications for More Effective Service Targeting." *Educational Evaluation and Policy Analysis*, 10 (1), 23–36.

Orland, Martin E. and Richard Apling. (1986). "The Impact of Federal Compensatory Education Budget Changes on the Intensity of Services Provided." *Journal of Education Finance*, 12 (Summer), 122–139.

Orr, Larry. (1968). "The Incidence of Differential Property Taxes on Urban Housing." *National Tax Journal*, 12, 253–262.

Pallas, Aaron, Gary Natriello, and Edward McDill. "The Changing Nature of the Disadvantaged Population: Current Dimensions and Future Trends." *Educational Researcher*, 18 (5): 16–22.

Park, Rolla Edward, and Stephen J. Carroll. (1979). *The Search for Equity in School Finance: Michigan School District Response to a Guaranteed Tax Base*. Santa Monica, CA: The RAND Corporation, R-2393-NIE/HEW.

Pechman, Joseph A. (1985). *Who Paid the Taxes, 1966–85*. Washington, DC: The Brookings Institution.

Pechman, Joseph A. (1986). *Who Paid the Taxes, 1966–85, Revised Tables*. Washington, DC: The Brookings Institution.

Pechman, Joseph A., and Benjamin A. Okner. (1974). *Who Bears the Tax Burden?* Washington, DC: The Brookings Institution.

Peterson, Terry. (1988). *New Education Accountability Measures Focusing on Results: School Incentives, District Intervention and State Oversight of Reforms*. Prepared for the Texas Governor's Select Committee on Education, Austin.

Phares, Donald. (1980). *Who Pays State and Local Taxes?* Cambridge, MA: Oelgeschlager, Gunn and Hain.

Phillips, Robyn. (1988). "Restoring Property Tax Equity." In *California Policy Choices*, vol. 4. Los Angeles: University of Southern California, School of Public Administration, pp. 143–169.

Picus, Lawrence O. (1988). *The Effect of State Grant-In-Aid Policies on Local Government Decision Making: The Case of California School Finance*. Santa Monica, CA: The RAND Corporation.

Porter, Andrew O. (Forthcoming). "Creating a System of School Process Indicators." *Educational Evaluation and Policy Analysis*.

Porter, Andrew, and Jere Brophy. (1988). "Good Teaching: Insights from the Work of the Institute for Research on Teaching." *Educational Leadership*, 45(8), 75–84.

Puelo, V. T. (1988). "A Review and Critique of Research on Full-Day Kindergarten." *Elementary School Journal*, 88, 425–439.

Pulliam, John D. (1987). *History of Education in America*, 4th ed. Columbus, OH: Merrill.

Purkey, S. C., and Smith, M. S. (1985). "The District Policy Implications of the Effective Schools Literature." *Elementary School Journal*, 85, 353–389.

Quick, Perry D., and Michael J. McKee. (1988, September). "Sales Tax on Services: Revenue or Reform?" *National Tax Journal*, 41(3), 395–410.

Ravitch, Diane. (1983). *The Troubled Crusade*. New York: Basic Books.

Richards, Craig. (1985). "The Economics of Merit Pay: A Special Case of Utility Maximization." *Journal of Education Finance,* 11(2), 176–189.

Richards, Craig, and Mwalimu Shujaa. (1989). *State-Sponsored School Performance Incentive Plans: A Policy Review.* New Brunswick, NJ.: Rutgers University, Center for Policy Research in Education.

Riew, John. (1986). "Scale Economies, Capacity Utilization and School Costs: A Comparative Analysis of Secondary and Elementary Schools." *Journal of Education Finance,* 11(4), 433–446.

Robledo, M., M. Zarate, M. Guss-Zamora, and Jose Cardenas. (1978). *Bilingual Education Cost Analysis: Colorado.* San Antonio, TX: Intercultural Development Research Association.

Rosenholtz, Susan. (1989). *Teachers' Workplace: The Social Organization of Schools.* New York: Longman.

Rosenshine, Barak, and Robert Stevens. (1986). "Teaching Functions." In Merlin Wittrock, ed., *Handbook of Research on Teaching.* New York: Macmillan, pp. 376–391.

Rossmiller, Richard. (1983). "Resource Allocation and Achievement: A Classroom Analysis." In Allan Odden and L. Dean Webb, eds., *School Finance and School Improvement: Linkages for the 1980s.* Cambridge, MA: Ballinger.

Rossmiller, Richard, et al. (1970). *Educational Programs for Exceptional Children: Resource Configurations and Costs.* Madison: Department of Educational Administration, University of Wisconsin.

Rossmiller, Richard, and Lloyd E. Frohreich. (1979). *Expenditures and Funding Patterns in Idaho's Programs for Exceptional Children.* Madison: University of Wisconsin Press.

Sacks, Seymour. (1974). *The Municipal Overburden.* Syracuse, NY: Syracuse University Research Corporation.

Salmon, Richard, Christina Dawson, Steven Lawton, and Thomas Johns. (1988). *Public School Finance Programs of the United States and Canada: 1986–87.* Blackburg, VA: Virginia Polytechnic Institute and State University and American Education Finance Association.

Sarrel, Robert, and Bruce S. Cooper. (Forthcoming). "Managing for School Efficiency and Effectiveness: It Can Even Be Done in New York City." *Administrator's Notebook.*

Schultze, Charles. (1977). *The Public Use of Private Interest.* Washington DC: The Brookings Institution.

Schwartz, Myron, and Jay Moskowitz. (1988). *Fiscal Equity in the United States: 1984–85.* Washington, DC: Decision Resources Corporation.

Schwille, J., Andrew Porter, G. Belli, R. Floden, D. Freeman, L. Knappen, T. Kuhs, and W. Schmidt. (1982). "Teachers as Policy Brokers in the Content of Elementary School Mathematics." In Lee Shulman and Gary Sykes, eds. *Handbook of Teaching and Policy.* New York: Longman, pp. 370–391.

Sexton, Patricia C. (1961). *Education and Income.* New York: Viking Press.

Shavelson, Richard, Lorraine McDonnell, and Jeannie Oakes. (1989). *Indicators for Monitoring Mathematics and Science Education.* Santa Monica, CA: The RAND Corporation.

Sher, Jonathan, and Rachel B. Tompkins. (1977). "Economy, Efficiency and Equality: The Myths of Rural School and District Consolidation." In Jonathan P. Sher, ed., *Education in Rural America. Boulder,* CO: Westview Press, pp. 43–77.

Sjogren, Jane. (1981). "Municipal Overburden and State Aid for Education." In K. Forbis Jordan and Nelda Cambron, eds., *Perspectives in State School Support Programs.* Cambridge, MA: Ballinger, pp. 87–111.

Slavin, Robert. (1984). "Meta-Analysis in Education: How Has it Been Used?" *Educational Researcher,* 13 (8), 24–27.

Slavin, Robert. (1989a). "Achievement Effects of Substantial Reductions in Class Size." In Robert E. Slavin, ed., *School and Classroom Organization.* Hillsdale, NJ: Erlbaum, pp. 247–257.

Slavin, Robert, ed. (1989b). *School and Classroom Organization.* Hillsdale, NJ: Erlbaum.

Slavin, Robert, Nancy Karweit, and Nancy Madden., eds. (1989). *Effective Programs for Students at Risk.* Boston: Allyn and Bacon.

Smith, Marshall. (1988). "Educational Indicators." *Phi Delta Kappan,* 69 (7), 487–491.

Solorzano, L. (1987). "Beating Back the Education 'Blob.'" *U. S. News and World Report.* April 27, p. 39.

Sparkman, William E. (1990). "School Finance Challenges in the Courts." In Julie K. Underwood and Deborah A. Verstegen, eds., *The Impacts of Litigation and Legislation in Public School Finance.* New York: Harper & Row, pp. 193–224.

Stansberry, J. W. (1985). "New Productivity Incentives for Defense Contractors." *Harvard Business Review,* 85 (1), 156–160.

Stern, David. (1973). "Effects of Alternative State Aid Formulas on the Distribution of Public School Expenditures in Massachusetts." *Review of Economics and Statistics,* 55, 91–97.

Stern, David, Charles Dayton, Il-Woo Paik, and Alan Weisberg. (1989). "Benefits and Costs of Dropout Prevention in a High School Program Combining Academic and Vocational Education: Third-Year Results from Replications of the California Peninsula Academies." *Educational Evaluation and Policy Analysis.* 11 (4), 405–416.

Strayer, George, and Robert Haig. (1923). *Financing of Education in the State of New York.* New York: MacMillan.

Strike, Kenneth. (1988). "The Ethics of Resource Allocation in Education: Questions of Democracy and Justice." In David H. Monk and Julie Underwood, eds., *Microlevel School Finance.* Cambridge, MA: Ballinger, pp. 143–180.

Struyk, Raymond J. (1970). "Effects of State Grants-In-Aid on Local Provision of Education and Welfare Services in New Jersey." *Journal of Regional Science,* 10 (2), 225–235.

Summers, Anita A. and Barbara L. Wolfe. (1977). "Do Schools Make a Difference?" *The American Economic Review,* 67(4), 639–652.

Swinehart, D. P. (1986). "Compensation: A Guide to More Productive Team Incentive Programs." *Personnel Journal,* 65(7), 112–117.

Swinford, D. (1987). "Unbundling Divisional Management Incentives." *Management Review,* 76, 35–38.

Task Force on Education and Economic Growth. (1983). *Action for Excellence.* Denver, CO: Education Commission of the States.

Texas State Board of Education. (1986). *1985–86 Accountable Cost Study.* Austin, TX: Texas Education Agency.

Thomas, J. Alan. (1980). "Resource Allocation in School Districts and Classrooms." *Journal of Education Finance,* 5 (3), 246–261.

Thomas, Stephen B., and L. Dean Webb. (1984). "The Use and Abuse of Lotteries as a Revenue Source." *Journal of Education Finance,* 9, 289–311.

Tiebout, Charles M. (1956). "A Pure Theory of Local Expenditures." *Journal of Political Economy,* 54, 416–424.

Tomlinson, Tommy M. (1989). "Class Size and Public Policy: Politics and Panaceas." *Educational Policy,* 3 (3), 261–273.

Tsang, Mun C., and Henry R. Levin. (1983). "The Impacts of Intergovernmental Grants on Education Spending." *Review of Educational Research,* 53 (3), 329–367.

Tyack, David, and Elizabeth Hansot. (1982). *Managers of Virtue.* New York: Basic Books.

U.S. Bureau of the Census. (1988). *Government Finances in 1986–87.* Washington, DC: U.S. GPO.

Usdan, Michael, and Jacqueline P. Danzberger. (1986). *School Boards.* Washington, DC: Institute for Educational Leadership.

Verstegen, Deborah. (1988). *School Finance at a Glance.* Denver, CO: Education Commission of the States.

Verstegen, Deborah. (1988–89). "Assessment and Reform: District Response to Mandated Change." *National Forum of Educational Administration and Supervision Journal,* 5 (3), 78–105.

Vincent, Phillip E., and Kathleen Adams. (1978). *Fiscal Response of School Districts: A Study of Two States—Colorado and Minnesota.* Denver, CO: Education Finance Center, Education Commission of the States, Report No. F78-3.

Wendling, Wayne. (1981a). "Capitalization: Considerations for School Finance." *Educational Evaluation and Policy Analysis,* 3 (2), 57–66.

Wendling, Wayne. (1981b). "The Cost of Education Index: Measurement of Price Differences of Education Personnel Among New York State School Districts." *Journal of Education Finance,* 6 (4), 485–504.

Wendling, Wayne, and Judith Cohen. (1981). "Education Resources and Student Achievement: Good News for Schools." *Journal of Education Finance,* 7(1), 44–63.

The White House. (1990). "National Education Goals." Paper developed at the February meeting of the National Governors Association.

Wildavsky, Aaron. (1975). *Budgeting: A Comparative Theory of Budgetary Processes.* Boston, MA: Little, Brown.

Wildavsky, Aaron. (1988). *The New Politics of the Budgetary Process.* Glenview, IL: Scott, Foresman.

Wilde, James A. (1968). "The Expenditure Effect of Grant-In-Aid Programs." *National Tax Journal,* 21 (3), 340–361.

Wilde, James A. (1971). "The Analytics of Grant Design and Response." *National Tax Journal*, 24 (2), 143–155.

Wilken, William, and David Porter. *State Aid for Special Education: Who Benefits?* Washington, DC: National Foundation for the Improvement of Education, 1977.

Wise, Arthur. (1969). *Rich Schools–Poor Schools: A Study of Equal Educational Opportunity.* Chicago: University of Chicago Press.

Wise, Arthur. (1983). "Educational Adequacy: A Concept in Search of Meaning." *Journal of Education Finance*, 8 (3), 300–315.

Wittrock, Merlin, ed. (1986). *Handbook of Research on Teaching.* New York: Macmillan.

Wohlstetter, Priscilla, and Karen McCurdy. (1991). "The Link Between School Decentralization and School Politics." *Urban Education*, 25 (4), 391–414.

Wycoff, James. (Forthcoming). "The Intrastate Equality of Public Elementary and Scondary Education Resources in the U.S., 1980–87." *Economics of Education Review.*

INDEX

Aaron, Henry, 145, 148
Accountability, 308
Achievement:
  authentic assessment, 59
  criterion referenced, 59
  measures, 59
  norm-referenced measures, 58
  student, 277–281
  variables, 58
Adams, E. Kathleen, 74, 85, 89, 91, 240
Adjustments:
  allocation rules, 225
  appropriate services, 219
  compensatory education, 210, 224
  costs of, 220
  different pupil needs, prices, 209
  educational placement, 220
  excess cost reimbursement, 222
  flat grant, 221
  formulas and, 221
  forward funding, 221
  grade levels, 234
  limited English proficient (LEP), 209
  price, 239
  pupil weighting, 222
  School Finance Computer Simulation
    and, 231
  School Finance Computer Simulation
    and pupil weights, 232

School Finance Computer
    Simulation, pupil weights
    equity, 232
  size, 234
  special needs, 219
  state approaches to, 221
  student eligibility, 219
Advisory Commission on
    Intergovernmental Relations
    (ACIR), 79, 80, 131, 151
Aid:
  block grant, 167
  categorical grants, 86, 87
  matching grants, 86
  restructured general, 247
  unrestricted, 84
  (See also grants)
Aid to Families with Dependent
    Children (AFDC), 219
Alexander, Arthur, 269
Alexander, Kern, 50
Allocation:
  attendance rates, 293
  performance measures, 292
  performance standards, 292
  rules, 300–301
  size of program, 292
Arrow, Kenneth, 295
Assessed valuation, 140

Augenblick, John, 75, 240, 243, 265, 279
Authority, site-based management and, 302–304
Authorized Revenue Base (ARB), 13

Bacharach, Samuel, 291
Bailey, Stephen, 211, 243
Baratz-Snowden, Joan, 56
Barnett, Steven, 234, 282
Barro, Stephen, 63, 269, 291
Bell, Michael, 154
Belli, G., 50
Berke, Joel, 10, 33, 34
Berne, Robert, 46, 50, 52, 53, 58, 60, 63, 65, 67, 69, 74, 75, 239, 248
Berrueta-Clement, J., 234
Berry, Barnett, 53
Berstein, Charles, 224
Biber, Douglas, 215, 227
Bilingual education:
    eligibility, 227
    financing, 226
    major costs, 229
    sheltered English, 228
Black, D., 85
Blinder, Alan, 286, 291
Block grant, 167, 288
Borg, Walter, 50
Bowman, John, 85, 154
Brackett, J., 302
Brazer, Harvey, 34, 239
Break, George, 83
Brophy, Jere, 57
Brown, Byron, 281
Brown, Daniel, 299, 308, 309
Brown, Lawrence, 75
Brown, Patricia, 2, 161
Brownless, O., 147
Budgeting, 300–302
Burnstein, Leigh, 57

California Assessment Program (CAP), 294–295
California Revenue and Taxation Code, 81
Callahan, John, 33, 244
Carnegie Forum on Education and the Economy, 299

Carpenter-Huffman, P., 226
Carroll, Stephen, 55, 85, 248, 270
Categorical grants, 87
Catterall, James, 55, 57
Chambers, Jay, 178, 197, 220, 221, 226, 239, 240, 302
Chapter I, 224, 225, 226
Chaudhari, Ramesh, 50, 75, 248
Checkoway, Marjorie, 50, 75
Chen, Li-Ju, 50, 75
Childs, T. Stephen, 279
Choice, Minnesota and, 47
Church, T., 286
Cibulka, James, 293
Civil Rights Act, 211
Clause:
    state education, 29
    state education and deprivation, 31
Clotfelter, Charles, 134
Clune, William, 10, 25, 32, 56, 184, 192, 299
Cobb, Roger, 242
Coefficient of variation, 66
Cohen, Michael, 280, 281, 286
Cohn, Elchanan, 84, 103, 281
Coley, Richard, 34
Colorado, assessed valuation, 11
Combination foundation and guaranteed tax base:
    fiscal equity, 200
    formula for, 194
    Kentucky and, 193
    Missouri and, 192
    policy issues, 195
    program, 192
    Texas and, 193
    trade-offs, 197
Committee for Economic Development, 251
Compensatory education:
    costs and formulas for, 224
    state approaches, 212
    Texas and, 226
Conley, Sharon, 286, 291
Consumption, 100
Cook, Phillip, 134
Cooney, T., 50
Coons, John, 10, 25, 32, 184, 192
Cooper, Bruce, 256

Correlation coefficient, 69, 74
Council of Chief State School Officers,
    50
Court Cases:
    Abbott v. Burke, 30, 34, 35, 42, 46
    *Alma School District No. 30 v.
        Dupree*, 35
    Blase v. Illinois, 39
    *Board of Education, Cincinnati v.
        Walter*, 43
    Brown v. Board of Education, 24
    Burruss v. Wilkerson, 20, 21, 24, 26,
        31, 39
    Buse v. Smith, 45
    City of Trenton v. New Jersey, 80
    *Council for Better Education v.
        Wilkinson*, 40
    Dansen v. Casey, 43
    *East Jackson Public Schools v. State
        of Michigan*, 41
    Edgewood v. Kirby, 46
    *Fair School Finance Council v.
        Oklahoma*, 43
    *Helena School District #1 et al. v.
        State of Montana*, 41
    *Henrick Hudson Central School Dis-
        trict Board of Education v. Row-
        ley*, 220, 245
    Hobson v. Hansen, 276
    *Hornbeck v. Somerset County Board
        of Education*, 33, 40
    Horton v. Meskill, 38
    Jesseman v. New Hampshire, 41
    Knowles v. Kansas, 40
    Kukor v. Thompson, 45
    Lau v. Nichols, 211, 215
    Levittown v. Nyquist, 33
    Lujan v. Colorado, 31
    McDaniel v. Thomas, 39
    McInnis v. Shapiro, 20, 21, 24, 26,
        31, 39
    Milliken v. Green, 41
    Northshore v. Kinnear, 44
    Olsen v. State, 43
    Oster v. Kneip, 43
    Pauley v. Bailey, 32
    Pauley v. Kelley, 31, 44
    *Pennsylvania Association of Retarded
        Children v. Pennsylvania (PARC)*,
        215

    People v. Adams, 39
    Robinson v. Cahill, 28, 29, 30, 34, 35,
        42
    Rose v. Council for Better Education,
        40
    *San Antonio Independent School
        District v. Rodriguez*, 20, 27,
        28, 36, 44
    *School Board of Palm Beach City v.
        Board of Education*, 39
    Seattle School District v. State, 44
    Serrano v. Priest, 26, 27, 28, 36, 38,
        270
    Shofstall v. Hollins, 38
    Thomas v. Stewart, 39
    Washakie v. Herschler, 32, 45
    Webby v. King, 41
Crosswhite, F., 50
Cubberly, E. P., 20, 78
Curriculum:
    enacted, 56, 57
    intended, 56

Daicoff, Darwin, 147
Danzberger, Jacqueline, 9
Darling-Hammond, Linda, 53
Data:
    edit, 327–328
    enter, 327–328
    100-district sample, 312, 326, 327
    10-district sample, 162, 312, 313,
        323, 326, 327
David, Jane, 285
Dawson, Christina, 193, 237
Decentralization, 78
Deleeuw, Frank, 147
Denham, Carolyn, 277
Denslow, D., 240
Dillon, John, 80
Dossey, J., 50
Dougherty, Van, 17, 35, 249, 252,
    253
Doyle, Denis, 9

Ebel, Robert, 151
Education Commission of the States,
    251
Education Consolidation and
    Improvement Act (ECIA), 210

Education Finance and Productivity
    Center, 64
Education for All Handicapped
    Children Act, P.L. 94–142,
    215
Efficiency, of service production, 78
Ekanem, Nkanta, 147
Elasticity, 69, 74, 101
Elder, Charles, 242
Elementary and Secondary Education
    Act (ESEA), 81, 210, 211
Elmore, Richard, 1, 2, 161, 249, 250
English as a second language (ESL),
    211
Epstein, A., 234
Equality:
    Equal programs and services, 32, 295
    Equal protection, 21
    Fourteenth Amendment, 22
    fundamental rights, 23, 25
    Kentucky and, 46
    minimal judicial scrutiny, 22
    special education, 215
    strict judicial scrutiny, 23, 27
    suspect classification, 23, 25
Equity:
    children, 53
    children's principles, 60
    effectiveness, 63, 74
    fiscal neutrality, 25, 63, 69
    horizontal, 59, 60, 112
        and taxes, 65
        and weighted pupils, 62
    horizontal assessment of, 61
    measures of, 64
    service distribution, 78
    tax, 102, 103, 112, 120, 127, 133, 145
    unit of analysis, 65
    vertical, 61, 112
    vertical assessment of, 62
ESEA, 211, 215, 224
ESL, 227, 229
Exit, from simulation, 326, 329
Expenditures:
    analysis of, 54
    content area, 257, 258, 277
    defined, 54
    educational, 6, 7
    employee benefit, 266
    equal, 32

functional, 272
New York and, 265, 266
Pennsylvania and, 267, 268
program, 257, 272
special needs, 266
student, 275
total, 258

Factors, income, 92
Fee-for-service, 66
Feldstein, Martin, 91
Finance, school:
    computer simulation, 161, 203, 312
    equity, 161
    formulas, 160, 296
    general aid programs, 166
    measures of, 64
    policy goals, 161
    politics of, 243–248
    problems in, 203–206
Financing, federal advantages of, 77
Finn, Chester, 9
Fiscal capacity:
    alternative measures, 90
    equalization, 77
    school district and, 90
Fiscal federalism:
    decentralization, 79
    efficiency in service production, 78
    equity in service distribution, 78
    fiscal capacity equalization, 77
    intergovernmental grants, 76, 79,
        81, 86
    mandates, 76, 79
    relationships, 285
Fiscal neutrality, 25, 63, 69
Flat grant:
    fiscal equity, 170
    formula for, 168
    programs, 10, 167
    special education, 216
Flexibility, 309
Floden, R., 50
Folger, John, 234, 278
Forgione, Pascal, 50, 55
Foundation:
    equity impacts, 180
    expenditure levels, 178
    formula for, 174

Foundation (*cont.*)
  policy issues, 174, 178
  programs, 10, 173
  shortcomings, 175
  zero-aid district, 179
Fox, William, 126, 130, 238, 274
Framework, equity, 50, 51, 70, 74
Freeman, D., 50
Frost, Robert, 338
Fuhrman, Susan, 1, 243, 245, 246, 247,
    249, 250
Full state funding, 202
  defined, 203
  and Florida, 203

Garcia, O., 229
Garms, Walter, 50
Gaughan, James, 225
Geske, Terry, 103, 281
Gini coefficient, 67
Ginsberg, Alan, 276
Glasheen, Richard, 225
Glass, Gene, 283
Goals:
  local control and, 47
  national educational, 20, 46, 59, 250,
      277, 280
  state, 47
Goertz, Margaret, 34, 50, 75, 224, 225
Goffman, Irving, 240
Goggin, Z., 291
Gold, Steve, 97, 98, 110, 120, 131, 151,
    156, 165, 252, 255
Grants:
  block, 167
  categorical, 86, 87
  flat, 10, 167, 168, 170, 216
  general matching, 86
  intergovernmental, 87
  matching, 86
  unrestricted general, 84
Grieson, Ronald, 147
Griffith, Julie, 238
Grubb, Norton, 85, 88
Guaranteed tax base (GTB):
  fiscal equity impacts, 188
  fiscal neutrality, 190
  formula for, 184
  horizontal equity, 187

local control and, 186, 192
policy issues, 186, 192
program, 86, 87, 182, 240
secondary policy issues, 188
Guthrie, James, 237, 273, 300

Haig, Robert, 85
Haller, Emil, 237
Hallinger, Phillip, 277
Hamilton, Stephen, 238
Hansot, Elizabeth, 9
Hanushek, Eric, 271, 279, 281
Hargrove, Erwin, 244
Harris, Russell, 91
Hartle, Terry, 9
Hartman, William, 224, 265, 300
Hawkins, Evelyn, 253
Hayward, Gerald, 274
Heclo, Hugh, 245
Hentschke, Guilbert, 300, 301,
    302, 303
Heumann, M., 286
Hickrod, G. Alan, 50, 75, 248
Holland, Richard, 219, 220,
    230, 231
Hubbard, Ben, 50, 75, 248
Hybels, Judith, 132
Hyman, D., 147

IBM, 312, 316
Incentives:
  effects of incentive grants, 287
  formula-based, 289
  negative, 294
  outstanding school awards and, 291
  and performance expectations, 288
  performance standards, 292
  school-based fiscal, 290, 291, 292
  size and, 292
  South Carolina and, 293–4, 295, 296
Income:
  as a base, 99
  factors, 92
  tax, 108–118
  transfers, 104
Inputs:
  fiscal, 54
  physical, 54

Intervention:
  cooperative learning, 282, 283
  drop-out prevention, 282
  extended day kindergarten, 282
  and negative incentives, 294
  peer tutoring, 282
Installing the simulation, 313–317
Intergovernmental grants:
  design, 81
  theory, 83, 86, 286

Jensen, Michael, 295
Johns, Thomas, 193, 237
Johnson, Susan, 286
Jordan, K. Forbis, 253, 271
Jung, Richard, 250

Kakalik, James, 230, 231
Karweit, Nancy, 278, 282, 283
Kearney, Phillip, 50, 75
Kenny, L., 240
Kentucky, education reform and, 37,
  250
Kifer, E., 50
King, Richard, 279, 283
Kirst, Michael, 243, 245, 246, 250, 252,
  257, 270, 273, 301
Knappen, L., 50
Knickman, James, 34
Kranz, Jennifer, 299, 300, 302, 310
Krashen, Steve, 215, 227
Kuhs, T., 50

Ladd, Helen, 34, 74, 85, 89, 91
LaMorte, Michael, 37
Lawler, Edward, 286
Lawton, Steven, 193, 237
Leppert, Jack, 231
Levin, Betsy, 21
Levin, Henry, 83, 85, 89, 282, 283
Lewis, K., 85
Lieberman, Ann, 56, 277
Limited-English proficient, state
  approaches to, 217
Link, C., 85
Long, James, 113
Lotteries:
  administration, 133
  basis, 132
  equity, 133
  general, 131
  inefficient revenue and, 254
  yield, 132

Macintosh, 312, 313–316, 318–329
Macphail-Wilcox, Bettye, 279, 283
Madden, Nancy, 278, 282, 283
Malen, Betty, 299, 300, 302, 310
Mandates:
  arguments against, 80
  arguments for, 80
Marsh, Paul, 338
Marshall, Rudolph, 224
Massel, Diane, 252
McCarty, Therese, 34
McClure, William, 231
McCurdy, Karen, 307
McDill, Edward, 219
McDonnell, Lorraine, 50, 54, 57, 249
McGuire, C. Kent, 211, 249
McKee, Michael, 127, 130
McKeown, Mary, 250, 253, 271
McKnight, C., 50
McLaughlin, Milbrey, 239
McLoone, Eugene, 68
McLoone Index, 68, 69, 165, 172, 190
Meckling, William, 295
Meister, Gail, 245, 283
Meno, Lionel, 254
Merit pay, 286
Michelson, Stephan, 84, 85, 88
Mikesell, John, 123, 125, 133, 254
Miner, Jerry 84, 85
Monk, David, 78, 89, 238, 279, 280,
  283
Moody, David, 57
Moore, Mary, 219, 220, 230, 231
Mosher, Edith, 211
Moskowitz, Jay, 71
Moss, Pamela, 238
Moynihan, Daniel, 268
Mueller, Van, 250
Muller, Thomas, 34
Municipal overburden, 33
Murnane, Richard, 279, 286
Murphy, Joseph, 252, 263, 277
Murphy, Kevin, 282
Murry, Matthew, 126, 130
Musgrave, Penny, 77, 83, 98, 148, 156
Musgrave, Richard, 77, 83, 98, 148, 156

National Assessment of Education Progress (NAEP), 60

National Center for Education Statistics (NCES), 75, 257, 259, 260, 261, 264, 265, 272

National Commission on Excellence in Education, 35, 118

National Governors Association, 47, 250, 285

Nation at Risk, 35, 118, 250, 263, 264

Natriello, Gary, 219

NEFP, 230

Nelson, F. Howard, 227

Netzer, Dick, 34, 147

New York State Special Task Force on Equity and Excellence in Education, 225

Oakes, Jeannie, 50, 54, 83, 277, 283

Oates, Wallace, 83

Odden, Allan, 20, 35, 47, 50, 52, 74, 75, 91, 148, 210, 234, 240, 243, 247, 248, 249, 250, 252, 253, 265, 268, 270, 271, 273, 279, 286

Office of Bilingual Education, 227

Ogawa, Rodney, 299, 300, 302, 310

Okner, Benjamin, 148

Orland, Martin, 226

Orr, Larry, 147

Ortbal, James, 151

Osman, J., 85, 88

Palaich, Robert, 265, 279

Pallas, Aaron, 219

Park, Rolla, 55, 85, 248

Parrish, Thomas, 178, 220, 221, 226, 302

Pasour, E., 147

Pechman, Joseph, 105, 113, 122, 148, 149

Percentage equalizing programs, formula for, 183

Peterson, Terry, 293, 294

Phares, Donald, 113, 123

Phillips, Robyn, 156, 157

Picus, Lawrence, 253, 270, 288, 289, 290

P.L. 94–142, 220, 222

Planning, Programming, Budgeting Systems (PPBS), 301, 302

Politics, school finance reform:
available revenue, 245
blue ribbon commissions, 246
coalition building, 246
courts, 244
legislation and, 247
political leadership, 245
property tax relief, 244
technical expertise, 245

Porter, Andrew, 56, 57, 283

Price indexes, 240

Production function, 280

Productivity, 308

Property tax:
administration, 151
basis, 136
circuit breaker programs, 154
classification of tax base, 154
compliance, 151
deferrals, 155
economic effects, 150
elasticity of, 143
equity, 145
incidence, 146
low income and, 151
Proposition 13 and, 156
rates, 143
regressivity, 149
social effects, 150
yield, 142

Proposition 13:
basis, 157
equity, 157
overall assessment, 159
yield, 158

Proposition 98, 254

Puelo, V., 234, 282

Purkey, S., 299

Quick, Perry, 127

Range:
defined, 65
federal ratio, 66
restricted, 66

Ravitch, Diane, 211

Regular education initiative, 216

Required levy effort (RLE), 204

Reschovsky, Andrew, 34
Revenue limit, California, 203
Richards, Craig, 253, 286, 292, 294, 295
Riew, John, 237
Rosenshine, Barak, 57
Rossmiller, Richard, 279
Routh, Dorothy, 231
Rowley, Stephen, 220, 245
Rules, allocation, 300

Sacks, Seymour, 33, 34
Saks, Daniel, 281
Sales tax, 118–131
Salmon, Richard, 193, 237
Samulon, S., 226
Sandoval, Corazon, 34
Sarrel, Robert, 256
School Improvement Program, 305
School and staffing survey (SASS), 264
School site councils:
    authority, 306
    Chicago and, 299, 306, 307
    decision making, 307
    membership, 305, 306
Schultze, Charles, 286
Schweinhart, Lawrence, 234
Schwille, J., 50
Senate Bill (SB) 813, 288, 294
Sexton, Patricia, 276
Shakeshaft, Carol, 279
Shavelson, Richard, 50
Sher, Jonathon, 237
Shujaa, Mwalimu, 253, 292, 294, 295
Site-based management:
    accountability and, 308
    authority changes, 302–304
    defined, 299
    flexibility, 309
    productivity, 308
Sjogren, Jane, 34
Slavin, Robert, 234, 278, 282, 283
Smith, Marshall, 50
Smith, Mary Lee, 278
Smith, S., 299
Special education:
    Florida and, 230
    key issues, 230
    program costs, 231
    student identification, 216

Spotted Bear, Alyce, 238
Staffing, 258, 262, 264, 301
Stansberry, J., 291
Stern, David, 85, 282
Stevens, Robert, 57
Stiefel, Leanna, 46, 50, 52, 53, 58, 60,
        63, 65, 67, 69, 74, 75, 239, 248
Strayer, George, 85
Struyk, Raymond, 85
Sugarman, Stephen, 10, 25, 32, 56, 184,
        192
Summers, Anita, 280
Swinehart, D., 291
Swinford, D., 291

Tax:
    administration, 107, 116, 126, 130,
        133
    basis, 98, 108, 119, 126, 132
    comparative assessment, 135
    compliance, 107, 116, 126, 132
    consumption, 100
    economic effects of, 107, 113, 125,
        130
    equity, 102, 112, 120, 127, 133
    exemptions, 109, 124
    incidence, 104
    income, 108–118
    income transfers and, 104
    lotteries, 131–133
    overview, 94, 95
    privilege, 100
    progressivity, 103, 112, 127
    property, 136–159
    proportional, 103
    Proposition 13 and, 97
    regressivity, 103, 112, 127
    sales, 118–131
    spending limits, 249
    yield, 101, 110, 119, 126, 132
Taxpayer revolt, 97
Teachers:
    motivation and, 293
    substitutes, 302
Texas, reform, 35, 37, 270
Thomas, Stephen, 131
Title I, 210, 211
Title VI, 211
Tomlinson, Tommy, 278

Tompkins, Rachel, 237
Tsang, Mun, 83, 85, 89

Unit of analysis, 65
U.S. Department of Education, 291

Value:
   assessed, 140
   market, 138
   true, 138
Verstegen, Deborah, 6, 270
Vincent, Phillip, 89, 91, 148, 240

Walker, Lisa, 219, 220, 230, 231
Wealth, 137
Webb, L. Dean, 131
Weinkart, David, 234
Welch, Finis, 282

Wendling, Wayne, 150, 198, 240, 279, 280
White, Paula, 56, 299
White House, 20, 37, 250
Wildavsky, Aaron, 300
Wilde, James, 83
Wilken, William, 244
Wise, Arthur, 25, 31, 49
Wittock, Merlin, 281
Wohlstetter, Priscilla, 307
Wolfe, Barbara, 280
Wood, Robert, 338
Wycoff, James, 75

Yee, Sylvia, 239
Yinger, John, 34

Zero-based budgeting (ZBB), 301, 302
Zorn, C. Kent, 133, 254